The Samuel and Mary (Myers) Burris Family

Jesse Stallings Burris
Author

Mamie (Burris) Simmons
Co-author

Flora Mae Burris
Co-author

The Samuel and Mary (Myers) Burris Family

by

Jesse Stallings Burris, M.A., Author
Superintendent, Concordia Parish (Louisiana) Schools.

(Lineage: Son of Byron Benton Burris; Byron Benton Burris—son of William Addison Burris; William Addison Burris—son of William Burris; William Burris —son of Samuel Burris.)

and

Flora Mae Burris, B.A., Co-Author
Teacher-Librarian, Franklinton (Louisiana) Elementary School.

(Lineage: Daughter of Robert Lee Burris; Robert Lee Burris—son of William Addison Burris; William Addison Burris—son of William Burris; William Burris —son of Samuel Burris.)

and

Mamie Lettie Burris-Simmons, Co-Author
Businesswoman, Magnolia, Miss.

(Lineage: Daughter of Enos Pinkney Burris; Enos Pinkney Burris—son of Hampton Burris; Hampton Burris—son of Samuel Burris.)

A FIREBIRD PRESS BOOK

PELICAN PUBLISHING COMPANY
Gretna 1998

Manufactured in the United States of America

Published by Pelican Publishing Company, Inc.
1000 Burmaster Street, Gretna, Louisiana 70053

Dedication

To the memory of Samuel and Mary (Myers) Burris, for their lofty ideals and noble traits, which are being perpetuated by their large and ever-increasing number of offspring, this book is affectionately dedicated.

Table of Contents

List of Illustrations

FOREWORD

Out of a desire to learn something about his Burris ancestors, whom he greatly admired and whom he considered unusual, if not exceptional; also, out of a desire to furnish present generations with this information, and, at the same time, preserve it for future generations, the author began this history about the year 1926.

It was a long and an arduous task—one that involved much work, perseverance and expense. Because of poor response from descendants, and a seeming lack of interest by them, the author discontinued work on it two or three times. But not long after each discontinuance, he would hear from some member of the family, or he would get new leads and data, which inspired him to a resumption of the work. Finally, at the Samuel and Mary (Myers) Burris Family Re-union in Smithdale, Miss., in 1948, a history committee, composed of Jesse Stallings Burris, Mrs. Mamie Burris-Simmons and Miss Flora Mae Burris, was appointed. After the appointment of this committee, work on the history was begun in earnest and the progress was rapid, which was due mainly to the splendid work of Mrs. Mamie Burris Simmons and Miss Flora Mae Burris, co-authors of this history.

Because of scanty records and the small number of living members of the early generations of this family, data on this family was difficult to secure. But the search proceeded, even though it was in piecemeal fashion, at times.

Most of the data in this book is authentic. It was secured from various records and other reliable sources. However, some of it is traditional and some of it was written from oral accounts of descendants and other individuals, who drew upon their memories for the information. But, whatever the source, the data contained in this history is considered reliable and trustworthy.

Doubtless the names of many descendants of, and much data on, this family have been left out of this book. Perhaps some of these descendants and some of this data could have been secured had the publishing of the history been postponed. But, since the period of preparation of it was so long; also, because of the exhaustion of practically all sources of information, and the means of securing it, it was decided to publish it without further delay.

The descendants are not listed in age order; and, in view of the

vii

fact that the write-up of this book was begun several years ago, the ages, indicated herein of some of them, are several years younger than their ages are today.

The war-service records of veterans of the various wars were written up according to the statements of the veterans, or members of their families, and not from the official war records.

The author and co-authors wish to acknowledge the assistance given them in securing the data for this history by the following members and friends of the family:

1. Mrs. Olivia Grant (deceased) of Amite, La. Mrs. Grant was a descendant of Mariah Burris-Hamilton (William Burris's widow), by her marriage to William R. Hamilton after William Burris's death. Mrs. Grant supplied the author with data copied from Mariah's Bible, which she had in her possession, and which showed that the original Burris parents, who settled in Amite County, Miss., in 1809, were named Samuel and Mary (Myers) Burris, and not William and Mary (Chandler) Burris, as was first thought. She supplied the author with other valuable data on the William Burris Family, also.

2. Mrs. William Franklin Holmes (nee Catherine Lea "Katie" Jones), of Vicksburg, Miss. It was Mrs. Holmes who first started the work on this history. She had worked on it some time before the author started and had secured considerable data—most all of the data on the George Nelson Burris Family, of which she is a member. Because of poor response and cooperation, she discontinued her work and turned her data over to the author.

3. Mrs. Warner J. Holt (nee Minnie Heathman Smith) of Washington, D. C. Mrs. Holt secured most of the data on the Edmund and Ann (Burris) Smith Family, of which she is a member. She secured data on the descendants of Samuel and Mary (Myers) Burris's other children, also. In addition, she gave valuable advice on the preparation of the history.

4. Miss Josie Jones Burris of Baton Rouge, La. Miss Burris secured most of the data on the Addison Burris Family, of which she is a member.

5. Bryant Eugene Burris of Liberty, Miss. Mr. Burris secured the names of most of the descendants of Hampton Burris who served in wars. Mr. Burris is a member of the Hampton Burris Family.

6. Mrs. Simon Peter Stubblefield (nee Mary Augusta Smith). Mrs. Stubblefield secured data on the Edmund and Ann (Burris)

Smith Family, of which she is a member. In addition, Mrs. Stubblefield checked and corrected data on this family.

7. Miss Helen Eloise Raborn of Baton Rouge, La. Miss Raborn secured data on the Samuel Burris, Jr., Family, of which she is a member.

8. Mr. Henry Lucas of Whatley, Ala. Mr. Lucas secured data on the Charles F. and Sarah Ann (Burris) Lucas Family, of which family he is a member. Sarah Ann Burris-Lucas was the daughter of William Burris, Samuel and Mary (Myers) Burris's son.

9. Mr. Rudolph Marks of Jackson, Ala. Mr. Marks secured data on the Fleming R. and Elizabeth Mariah (Burris) Marks Family, of which he is a member. Elizabeth Mariah Burris-Marks was the daughter of William Burris, Samuel and Mary (Myers) Burris's son.

10. Mr. William (Billy) Pigott of Greensburg, La. Mr. Pigott secured data on the Samuel Burris, Jr., Family. Mr. Pigott is a friend of the Burrises and a cousin of the author on his mother's side.

11. Mr. Charles R. Strickland (deceased) of Greensburg, La. Mr. Strickland furnished data, which he had previously secured, on the Samuel James and Elizabeth (Burris) Denman Family, of which he is a member. Elizabeth Burris-Denman was Samuel and Mary (Myers) Burris's daughter.

12. Miss Nora Inez Calloway of Vidalia, La. Miss Calloway secured data on the Addison Burris Family, of which she is a member.

13. Mr. John H. Parker of Liberty, Miss., Chancery Clerk of Amite County. Mr. Parker gave much assistance to the authors when they reviewed the records of his office. In addition, he secured valuable data on members of the family.

14. Mr. S. E. Babington, president of the Magnolia Bank, Magnolia, Miss. Mr. Babington secured data, transmitted messages from one author to another, and in various other ways assisted in the preparation of this history.

15. Mr. William Otto Burris (deceased) of Franklinton, La., late assessor of Washington Parish, La. Mr. Burris secured data and assisted in various other ways with this history. He was a devoted and loyal member of the Samuel and Mary (Myers) Burris Family and was one of the most enthusiastic promoters of this undertaking. He was a member of the William Burris branch.

16. Mr. and Mrs. Richard Alton Burris of Smithdale, Miss.

They secured data and assisted in various other ways with this history. They are devoted members of the Samuel and Mary (Myers) Burris Family and were most enthusiastic promoters of this undertaking. Richard Alton Burris is a member of the Hampton Burris branch.

17. Mrs. Merritt G. Allen (nee Ida Roberta Strickland) of Greensburg, La. Mrs. Allen secured data on the descendants of the Elizabeth Burris-Denman Family, of which family she is a descendant.

18. Mr. Alton Graves Burris of Smithdale, Miss. Mr. Burris helped secure funds with which to pay the cost of publishing this history and assisted in other ways with this undertaking. He is Hampton Burris's grandson.

19. Mrs. Nannie Belle Simmons-Webb of Swiftown, Miss. Mrs. Webb secured data on the descendants of James Smith Simmons, who was Harriett Almira Burris-Simmons's son. Mrs. Webb is a member of the Harriett Almira Burris branch.

J. S. B.

PART I

OUTLINE OF THE SAMUEL AND MARY (MYERS) BURRIS FAMILY

AA. Samuel Burris (Wife: Mary Myers). Children:

    I. William Burris (Wife: Mariah Theresa Andrews). Children:

        A. Mary Burris

        B. Louisa Burris

        C. Lucy Burris (Husband: Phillip Kirchbain). Children:

            1. Emma Kirchbain (Husband: .... Borho)

            2. Phillip Kirchbain, Jr.

        D. Martha Lucretia Burris

        E. James Madison Burris (First Wife: Rebecca (Becky) Magee)

        James Madison Burris (Second Wife: Sarah Ellis). Children:

            1. Mary Mariah Burris (Husband: O. P. Morris). Children:

                a. James Edward Morris

                b. Sally Morris (Husband: .... Holland). Children:

                    (1). Roxie Mae Holland

            2. James Madison Burris, Jr. (Wife: Mary Gabe Magee). Children:

                a. William James Burris (Wife: Nina Hood). Children:

                    (1). Josephine Burris (Husband: Donald White). Children:

                        (a). Joan White

                        (b). Larry White

                    (2). James Madison Burris III (First Wife: June Sweeney). Children:

                      (a). Ginger Burris

                    James Madison Burris III (Second Wife: Frances Rieley). Children:

                      (b). Jill Burris

                    James Madison Burris III (Third Wife: Glyndora Schilling). Children:

                      (c). James Madison Burris IV

(3). William Hood Burris (Wife: Ruth Crisler).
Children:
    (a). William James Burris II

b. Allie Sarah Burris (Husband: Hammon E. Richardson). Children:

    (1). Mary Verne Richardson (Husband: Abner Poole Wood). Children:
        (a). Mary Jeanette Wood

    (2). Gladys Lynette Richardson (Husband: Emile E. McMillan). Children:
        (a). Mary Linda McMillan
        (b). Gladys Susan McMillan

    (3). Donna Lee Richardson (Husband: Monroe O. Webb). Children:
        (a). Patricia Fay Webb
        (b). Monroe Oliver Webb, Jr.

c. Wiley Stephen Burris (Wife: Nelie K. Dobson). Children:

    (1). Wiley Stephen Burris, Jr.

    (2). Katherine Ursula Burris (Husband: William Towle). Children:
        (a). Patricia Towle
        (b). Rickey Towle

d. Bessie Lenora Burris (Husband: Arthur E. Hood). Children:

    (1). Arthur E. Hood, Jr. (Wife: Sue Field). Children:
        (a). Bonnie Sue Hood
        (b). Arthur Preston Hood

    (2). Thomas Jefferson Hood (Wife: Marie Kent). Children:
        (a). Lindy Lou Hood
        (b). Thomas Hood, Jr.

e. Vanda Victoria Burris (Husband: Hyman Ottis Simmons). Children:

    (1). Hyman Ottis Simmons, Jr. (Wife: Katherine Joan Richardson). Children:
        (a). Michael Ottis Simmons

    (2). Ronald Burris Simmons

f. E. John Burris

g. Hampton M. Burris

h. Howard L. Burris
i. Nelie Kathryn Burris (Husband: Lex V. Stringer).
Children:
(1). Jimmy Dudley Stringer
j. Marah Lee Burris (Husband: George Moore). Children:
(1). George Duke Moore
(2). Mary Janice Moore
3. Amanda Burris (Husband: Marcus F. Magee).
4. Ella Lucy Burris (Husband: Willie E. Bickham). Children:
a. Mamie Belle Bickham (First Husband: Bose Brock)
Mamie Belle Bickham (Second Husband: Judge Ellis Ott). Children:
(1). W. C. Ott
b. Lillie Bickham (Husband: James H. Dickinson). Children:
(1). Nella Dickinson (Husband: Edmund Henry Gabriel). Children:
(a). Edmund Dickinson Gabriel
(b). James Harry Gabriel
(2). James Harold Dickinson (Wife: Mildred Lockhart Rankin).
c. Benton Edgar Bickham (Wife: Carrie Holmes). Children:
(1). Margie Ann Bickham (First Husband: Rodney Williams). Children:
(a). Armethia Ann Williams
Margie Ann Bickham (Second Husband: William Addison Burris)*
(2). Benton Edgar Bickham, Jr. (Wife: Walterine Hunter). Children:
(a). Benton Bradley Bickham
(b). Carrie Jane Bickham
d. Rosa Bickham (Husband: Percy Ott). Children:
(1). Mary Ellen Ott (Husband: .... Evans)
(2). James Bickham Ott
(3). Carolyn Rose Ott
e. Stella Bickham (First Husband: John W. Warner). Children:

---

*An interfamily marriage. Children listed under husband.

(1). John W. Warner, Jr.

Stella Bickham (Second Husband: .... Cole)

Stella Bickham (Third Husand: Geo. B. Campbell)

f. Addison Bickham

g. Ethel Bickham

h. Viola Bickham (Husband: Floyd Frank). Children:

(1). Marilyn Sue Frank

5. John A. Burris (Wife: Laura Burkhalter). Children:

a. Robert Edward Burris (Wife: Mabel Cantrelle). Children:

(1). Lura Burris

(2). Charles Edward Burris

(3). Joyce Mae Burris (Husband: .....Sudderth). Children:

(a). Ted David Sudderth

b. William A. Burris (First Wife: Iris Alexander). Children:

(1). Willie Katherine Burris

William A. Burris (Second Wife: June Pierce). Children:

(2). William Dale Burris

c. Maude Ellis Burris (Husband: Robert Charles Riley). Children:

(1). Elizabeth D'Autrey Riley

(2). Eloise Riley (Husband:.........McClendon). Children:

(a). Robert Pierce McClendon

(b). Jean Ellis McClendon

d. John A. Burris, Jr. (Wife: Audis Stafford). Children:

(1). John Allan Burris

6. Wesley Burris

7. Lillie M. Burris

8. Steve Hampton Burris (Wife: Alma Varnado). Children:

a. Jeni Burris (Husband: Murphy J. Sylvest). Children:

(1). ....(adopted)

b. Newton Alexander Burris

c. James Oscar Burris

d. Steve Hampton Burris, Jr.

4

e. Ora Burris (Husband: R. B. Stinespring)
f. Lura Burris (Husband: W. M. McLain). Children:
   (1). Ora Marie McLain (Husband: Clyde Fussell). Children:
      (a). Beverly Marie Fussell
      (b). Benjamin Ray Fussell
   (2). Lorelle McLain (Husband: William Addison Wood). Children:
      (a). William Addison Wood, Jr.
   (3). Alton McLain
g. Cecil Addison Burris (Wife: Mary Leggette). Children:
   (1). Steve Hampton Burris II
   (2). Mary Jane Burris
   (3). Leggette Burris
   (4). Cecil Addison Burris, Jr.
h. Alma Burris (Husband: Aubrey Wilkins). Children:
   (1). Carolyn Wilkins
i. Myra Burris (Husband: C. Emery Lane). Children:
   (1). C. Emery Lane, Jr.
9. Philip F. Burris
10. Sarah Jane Burris (Husband: Hamp Magee)
11. William E. Burris

F. Sarah Ann Burris (Husband: Charles F. Lucas). Children:
1. Benjamin F. Lucas
2. Charles F. Lucas, Jr.
3. Richard Dyke Lucas
4. Mariah B. Lucas (Husband: H. S. Burkhalter)
5. Susan A. Lucas (Husband: H. S. Burkhalter)
6. William Tate Lucas (Wife: Martha D. Spinks). Children:
  a. Charles E. Lucas (Wife: Viola Whatley). Children:
    (1). Vivian Lucas (Wife: Mary E. Lowery). Children:
       (a). Betty V. Lucas
       (b). Mary Jo Lucas
    (2). Clarence Lucas
    (3). Edward Lucas (Wife: Kathleen Blount). Children:

(a). Edward Kathryn Blount

(b). Mary Martha Blount

b. William Burris Lucas

c. Henry Lucas

d. Enoch B. Lucas

e. Lula A. Lucas (Husband: Shellie A. Wilson). Children:

(1). Viola Wilson (Husband: Rex Cooper). Children:

(a). Ralph Cooper

f. Mary Ellen Lucas (Husband: Joseph Henry Hendrix). Children:

(1). Mary Ellen Hendrix (Husband: Marvin Hicks)

(2). Arnold Hendrix

(3). Billie Hendrix

g. Nina Pilley Lucas

h. John Frazier Lucas (Wife: Mary V. Elmer). Children:

(1). John F. Lucas, Jr.

(2). Mary Martha Lucas (Husband: Anthony C. Spano). Children:

(a). Anthony John Spano

(b). Christopher Frank Spano

7. Bettie Lucas (Husband: Mose Hendrix). Children:

a. Charlie Hendrix

b. Edna Hendrix

c. Margaret Hendrix

d. Will Hendrix

e. Henry Hendrix

f. Wheeler Hendrix

g. Alfred Hendrix

h. Aaron Hendrix

i. Lizzie Hendrix

j. Joseph Hendrix (Wife: Mary Ellen Lucas)*

G. Elizabeth Mariah Burris (Husband: Fleming R. Marks). Children:

1. William Buster Marks

2. Ginnella Inez Marks (Husband: William Byron Wilson). Children:

---

*Children listed under wife's name, an inter-family marriage.

a. Walter Lee Wilson (Wife: Lillian May Burge). Children:
   (1). Mamie Lee Wilson (Husband: Henry Andrew Bailey)
   (2). Walter Byron Wilson
b. William Fleming Wilson
c. Mamie Elizabeth Wilson (Husband: Nat Hood, Jr.). Children:
   (1). Walter Nathaniel Hood
3. Fleming Richard Marks, Jr. (Wife: Lola Anderson). Children:
   (a). Mamie Inez Marks (Husband: Willard E. Hudson). Children:
   (1). Mary Alice Hudson
4. Rebecca Marks (Husband: Tim Wilson). Children:
a. John Fleming Wilson
b. Thomas Jewett Wilson
c. Albert Wilson
5. Robert Lee Marks (Wife: Callie Gordon). Children:
a. Rudolph R. Marks (Wife: Mary Lee Thompson). Children:
   (1). Nettie Lee Marks (Husband: Saint Elmo McLendon)
   (2). Robert Warren Marks
   (3). Roy Flinn Marks
   (4). Fred Vinson Marks
   (5). Myrtle Lorraine Marks
   (6). Alfred Rudolph Marks
   (7). Ethel Mae Marks
b. Bessie Marks (Husband: Edward Few, Sr.). Children:
   (1). Edward Few, Jr.
   (2). Earl Frederick Few
   (3). Jerry Donald Few
   (4). Thomas Jesse Few
   (5). Howard David Few
   (6). Flora Mae Few
c. Bertha Marks (Husband: Estell Griffen)
d. Gordon Marks (Wife: Josephine Cornley). Children:
   (1). Callie Marie Marks

6. Mary Marks (Husband: Dr. Frederick Meeker). Children:

    a. Henry Frederick Meeker

H. William Addison Burris (Wife: Flora Lavonia Magee). Children:

    1. James William Burris (Wife: Mary M. Bickham). Children:

        a. Anna Sarah Burris (Husband: Fletcher D. Cooper). Children:
            (1). Sadye Lenora Cooper (Husband: Henry Ephraim Rester)
            (2). Mary Ruth Cooper (Husband: T. J. Hosey). Children:
                (a). Suzanne Hosey (adopted)
            (3). James Ray Cooper (Wife: Bernice Stone). Children:
                (a). James Ray Cooper, Jr.
            (4). Martha Christine Cooper (Husband: Paul Harris Murdoch). Children:
                (a). Deborah Murdoch
                (b). Paul Harris Murdoch, Jr.
                (c). Scott Alan Murdoch
            (5). Elizabeth Jane Cooper
            (6). Marjorie Elaine Cooper

        b. William Otto Burris (Wife: Eunice Foil). Children:
            (1). Wilda Estelle Burris (Husband: Hal Kilbourne). Children:
                (a). Don Burris Kilbourne
            (2). William Shelby Burris (Wife: Sarah Mabel Anglin). Children:
                (a). Ann Burris
            (3). Joseph Harold Burris (Wife: Gwendolyn Sylvest). Children:
                (a). Sylvia Lynn Burris
                (b). William Joseph Burris

        c. Wincie Ora Burris (Husband: William Andrew Page). Children:
            (1). Virginia Ann Page (adopted)

        d. Walter Addison Burris (Wife: Electa Sylvest). Children:
            (1). Kenneth James Burris (Wife: Jeanne Knight)

(2). Karl Hampton Burris (Wife: Versie Viola Hodges

(3). Mary Lenore Burris (Husband: Lavell Crain). Children:

    (a). Dennis Lavell Crain

(4). Walter Allen Burris

e. Benton Blocker Burris (Wife: Myrtle Pettitt). Children:

  (1). Benny B. Burris (adopted).

f. Hampton Burris

2. Byron Benton Burris (Wife: Lenora Graves). Children:

a. Ralph Louie Burris

b. Ollie Burris (Husband: Otis B. Bradley). Children:

  (1). Otis B. Bradley, Jr. (Wife: Wilda McAnulty). Children:

    (a) Wilda Ann Bradley

  (2). Milton Bradley (Wife: Dorothy Lee Show)

  (3). Mildred Bradley (Husband: Otho Bunyan Stansell). Children:

    (a). Linda Lou Stansell

    (b). Otho Bunyan Stansell, Jr.

  (4). Jesse Allen Bradley

c. Nellie Burris (Husband: Paul E. Greenlaw). Children:

  (1). Dorothy Alice Greenlaw (Husband: Harold O'Neil Marquart). Children:

    (a). Paul Emerson Marquart

    (b). Dianne Runnells Marquart (Husband: James Clayton Moore)

    (c). Sidney Suzanne Marquart

    (d). Harold O'Neil Marquart, Jr.

    (e). Michael Vincent Marquart

  (2). Katherine Russell Greenlaw (Husband: Coleman Simmons). Children:

    (a). Sara Michael Simmons

  (3). Eleanor Ruth Greenlaw (Husband: George Lewis Brown). Children:

    (a). George Lewis Brown, Jr.

  (4). Lawrence Dade Greenlaw

d. William Nathaniel Burris (Wife: Bessie Hale)

e. Jesse Stallings Burris (Wife: Addie Bruce Campbell)
f. Inez Burris
g. Belma Pearl Burris
h. Harvey Ellis Burris (Wife: Marguerite Forrester)

3. Edmund Andrews Burris (Wife: Ruth Bateman). Children:
   a. Hugh Addison Burris
   b. .... (Infant son)
   c. Flora Elma Burris
   d. Robert Hampton Burris (Wife: Ophelia Pope). Children:
      (1). Dorothy Louise Burris (Warren W. Seal). Children:
         (a). Judith Lennon Seal
         (b). Rebecca Ann Seal
         (c). Robert Warren Seal
      (2). Elaine Burris (Husband: Gradon Eldred Mongar). Children:
         (a). Carol Ann Mongar
   e. Beatrice Olivia Burris (Husband: Joseph Newton Magee). Children:
      (1). Patricia Ruth Magee
      (2). Joseph Edmund Magee

4. Sarah (Sallie) Burris (Husband: Daniel McSween Wadsworth). Children:
   a. Lucy Lavonia Wadsworth
   b. John Addison Wadsworth (Wife: Emily Bateman). Children:
      (1). Sarah Elizabeth Wadsworth
      (2). James Addison Wadsworth
   c. Winnie Davis Wadsworth (Husband: H. E. Rester). Children:
      (1). Ruth Rester
      (2). Henrietta Rester (Husband: John Gates Seaman). Children:
         (a). John Gates Seaman, Jr.
      (3). Winnie Marie Rester (Husband: Wilbur Eugene Lyon). Children:
         (a). Linda Gene Lyon
         (b). Ann Marie Lyon

(c). John Alan Lyon
d. Iddo Franklin Wadsworth (Wife: Ruby Moak)
e. William Hamilton Wadsworth
f. Sarah Margaret Wadsworth
g. Daniel McSween Wadsworth, Jr. (Wife: Eileen Coakley)
h. Flora Wadsworth
i. Jane Wadsworth
5. Robert Lee Burris (Wife: Martha Clotilde Wood). Children:
(a). Nathan Benton Burris (Wife: Gladys Bateman). Children:
(1). Robert Nathan Burris (Wife: Keitha Cassonova)
b. Hugh Preston Burris (Wife: Velma Bateman). Children:
(1). Harvey Hugh Burris (Wife: Agnes Aylene Wood)
(2). Olive Velma Burris
c. Jesse Daniel Burris
d. Flora Mae Burris
e. Emma Gay Burris
f. Alma Ernestine Burris (Husband: Lamar Merriot Richardson). Children:
(1). Lamar Merriot Richardson II
g. James Wilson Burris (Wife: Mary Margaret Watts). Children:
(1). James Wilson (Jimmy) Burris, Jr.
(2). Jesse Daniel Burris
h. William Addison Burris (Wife: Margie Ann Bickham). Children:
(1). William Addison Burris II
i. Roy Lee Burris (Wife: Wilda Eugene Breland). Children:
(1). Martha Jean Burris
(2) Roy Lee Burris, Jr.
j. Roberta (Bobbie) Burris (Husband: Andrew Griffith Johnson). Children:
(1). Andrew Griffith Johnson, Jr.
I. Amanda Caroline Burris (Husband: George Magee). Children:

1. John William Magee (Wife: Ellen Rebecca Daniels)
2. Dora Magee (Husband: W. J. Brumfield). Children:
    a. George Brumfield (First Wife: Una Mizell). Children:
        (1). Ollie Brumfield (Husband: Robert W. Prescott). Children:
            (a). Edrie LaUna Prescott (Husband: Thomas Wilkins)
            (b). Evelyn Dora Prescott (Husband: Cliff Lawrence)
            (c). Robert W. Prescott, Jr. (Wife: Laura Marie . . . .)
            (d). George O. Prescott
        George Brumfield (Second Wife: Tella Sylvest). Children:
        (2). Max Oliver Brumfield (Wife: Matalee Phares). Children:
            (a). Max Oliver Brumfield, Jr.
            (b). Martha Ann Brumfield
        (3). Bert Brumfield (Wife: Mildred Foy). Children:
            (a). Lenora Sue Brumfield
            (b). Bert Brumfield, Jr.
    b. William Brumfield (First Wife: Corinne Brumfield). Children:
        (1). William Brumfield, Jr.
        (2). Clyde Brumfield
        (3). Helen Brumfield
        William Brumfield (Second Wife: Lillian . . . .)
    c. Fleet Brumfield
    d. Hampton Addison Brumfield (Wife: Mattie Simmons). Children:
        (1). Virgie Brumfield (Husband: Charles Blount). Children:
            (a). Charles Edward Blount
            (b). Mattie Sandra Blount
            (c). Golda Rae Blount
            (d). Lucy Dora Blount
            (e). Danny Craig Blount
        (2). Hampton Addison Brumfield, Jr.

> (3). Maudene Brumfield (Husband: Louis Leland Bush)

> e. Anna Brumfield (Husband: Jim Buntin)

> f. .... (A son; died in infancy)

3. Ollie Magee
4. Earnest Magee
5. Sidney Magee (Wife: Amanda May). Children:
   a. George Magee
   b. Clayton Magee
   c. Albert William Magee (Wife: Jemima Roberts). Children:
      (1). Albert William Magee, Jr.
      (2). Patricia Ann Magee
   d. Mary Magee
   e. Mamie Magee

II. Harriett Almira Burris (Husband: Samuel B. Simmons). Children:
   A. Amanda Melvina Simmons (First Husband: William Frith). Children:
      1. Charles Henderson Frith (Wife: Martha C. Turnipseed). Children:
         a. George Dardon Frith (Wife: Rosalie Woodall)
         b. Will H. Frith
         c. Susie Frith (Husband: Will Simmons)*. Children:
            (1). Carl Simmons
            (2). Earl Simmons (Wife: Vera Hughey). Children:
               (a). Catherine Simmons (Husband: Murray Seal). Children:
                  i. Eddie Seal
                  ii. Catherine Jean Seal
            (3). Mattie Simmons
            (4). Katie Simmons
         d. John Turnipseed Frith
         e. Lida Frith (Husband: Frank Spurlock). Children:
            (1). Annie Spurlock (Husband: ....). Children:
               (a). ....
               (b). ....
            (2). Hazel Spurlock (Husband: ....).

---

*An interfamily marriage.

13

(3). Mildred Spurlock (Husband: Ed Newlin). Children:
    (a). Geraldine Newlin
    (b). Edwin Newlin
    (c). Shirley Jean Newlin
(4). Carroll Spurlock
(5). Edwin Spurlock
f. Charles Henderson Frith, Jr. (Wife: Allie Denman). Children:
    (1). Herbert Denman Frith (Wife: Nell Hall). Children:
        (a). Herbert Edward (Eddie) Frith
        (b). Ronald Kent (Ronnie) Frith
    (2). William T. Frith
    (3). Aline Gwendoline Frith (Husband: Lonnie N. Smith, Jr.). Children:
        (a). Richard Grant Smith
        (b). Louis Terrill Smith
        (c). Stephen Alan Smith
    (4). Gerald Howard Frith
    (5). Bobby Ray Frith
    (6). Faye Elizabeth Frith
2. Victoria Adeline Frith (Husband: James F. Anderson).
Amanda Melvina Simmons-Frith (Second Husband: Wm. S. Smith)
B. Mary Simmons (Husband: Thos. E. McKnight). Children:
1. Leonard McKnight (Wife: Blanche Moore). Children:
a. W. Bryant McKnight (Wife: Allie Marsalis). Children:
    (1). J. B. McKnight (Wife: Bertha Garley). Children:
        (a). Julia Ann McKnight
        (b). Linda Darline McKnight
        (c). John Wayne McKnight
b. Lois McKnight (Husband: Leslie Bates). Children:
    (1). Elldred Bates
c. Annie McKnight (Husband: Joe Denman). Children:
    (1). Annie Ray Denman
    (2). Eloise Denman (Husband: Fred McDaniel). Children:

(a). ....

(3). W. B. Denman

d. Leonard McKnight, Jr. (Wife: Mattie McCann).
Children:

(1). Yvonne McKnight

(2). Dorsie McKnight

(3). Jim McKnight

e. Ray McKnight (Wife: Bernice Marsalis). Children:

(1). Evie Lee Felder-McKnight (adopted) (Husband: Winton Burris)*

f. Hosea B. McKnight (Wife: Inez Quin). Children:

(1). James Leonard McKnight (Wife: ....).

(2). Billy McKnight

(3). H. B. McKnight

2. Thomas J. McKnight (Wife: Rebecca Cain). Children:

a. Charlie McKnight

b. Katie McKnight (Husband: Eddie Campbell)

3. James McKnight

4. Robert McKnight

5. Harriet A. McKnight (Husband: Henry Bates). Children:

a. Harriet (Shug) Bates (Husband: Maurice Allen Brashear). Children:

(1). Mary Etha Brashear

(2). Samuel Vernon Brashear

(3). Wiley Eddie Brashear (Wife: Stella Iris Ditto). Children:

(a). Ellis Allen Brashear (Wife: Mae Tolar). Children:

i. Amanda Lynn Brashear

(b). George Miller Brashear (Wife: Nolene Brady). Children:

i. George Miller Brashear, Jr.

ii. Harriett Ann Brashear

iii. Edna Nolene Brashear

(c). Lester Merrill Brashear (Wife: Georgene Mobley)

(4). Dollie Elzine Brashear

(5). Catherine Vella Brashear

(6). Henry Maurice Brashear

---

*Interfamily marriage—children listed under husband.

(7). Bessie Louise Brashear (Husband: Davis Lee Berryhill)

6. Mary G. (Katherine) McKnight (Husband: James E. Bates). Children:
   a. James E. Bates, Jr. (First Wife: Mattie Robinson). Children:
      (1). ....
      James E. Bates, Jr. (Second Wife: Betty Graves). Children:
      (1). Beulah Bates
   b. Lee Bates (Wife: Lillie ....). Children:
      (1). Raymond Bates (Wife: ....). Children:
         (a). ....
         (b). ....
      (2). Robert Lee Bates
      (3). Carl Bates
   c. Mary Beulah Bates (Husband: Pleasant Culpepper Webb, Jr.). Children:
      (1). Carl Vernon Webb (Wife: Myrtis Simmons). Children:
         (a). Elsie Webb (First Husband: J. D. Brabham). Children:
            i. James Vernon Brabham
            Elsie Webb (Second Husband: Maurice Catha). Children:
            ii. Maureen Catha
            iii. George Russell Catha
         (b). Edward Collinsworth Webb (Wife: Pauline ....)
         (c). Mary Adelia Webb (Husband: Otis Varnado). Children:
            i. Mary Margaret Varnado
      (2). Winchester Merrill (Chess) Webb (Wife: Frances Smith). Children:
         (a). Beulah Cornelia Webb (Husband: J. O. Lanier). Children:
            i. John Merrill Lanier
            ii. Frank Webb Lanier
            iii. William Lanier

(b). James Buford Webb (Wife: Wilda Stokes). Children:
    i. Jimmy Dale Webb
    ii. Joseph Hilton Webb
(3). James Leroy Webb (Wife: Ouida Mae Taylor). Children:
    (a). John Culpepper Webb (Wife: Lillian Young)
    (b). James Leroy Webb, Jr.
    (c). Taylor Webb
    (d). Bae Webb (Husband: Joseph P. Brent). Children:
        i. James Preston Brent
(4). Alma Lee Webb (Husband: Julian Purser Noland)
(5). Charles Carey Webb (Wife: Reine Georges). Children:
    (a). James Merrill Webb (Wife: Patricia ....). Children:
        i. Victoria Rene Webb
    (b). Eugenia Alma Webb (Husband: C. L. Klotz). Children:
        i. Carey Klotz
        ii. Eugene Klotz
        iii. Clifton Klotz
    (c). Charles Firmin Webb (Wife: Katherine Rowe). Children:
        i. Robert Charles Webb
        ii. Leslie Webb
    (d). Claudette Reine Webb
(6). Katie Lou Webb
(7). Edgar Culpepper Webb (Wife: Myrtle Bloodsworth)
d. Hattie Bates (Husband: Sidney McElveen). Children:
    (1). Grace McElveen (Husband: James Q. Cain). Children:
        (a). Jimmie Lou Cain (Husband: E. H. Hurst). Children:
            i. Sidney Jean Hurst
            ii. Margaret Ann Hurst

            iii. E. H. Hurst, Jr.
            iv. Martha Jane Hurst
            v. Billy Joe Hurst
       (b). Irma Cain (First Husband: Henry Burns). Children:
            i. Henry Lou Burns
           Irma Cain (Second Husband: Laverne Dixon)
       (c). Elois Cain (Husband: Carl Helm). Children:
            i. Carlene Helm
            ii. George Helm
    (2). Herbert McElveen (Wife: Edna Wilkinson). Children:
       (a). Frances McElveen (Husband: Buddy Ford). Children:
            i. Christy Ford
    (3). Beulah McElveen (Husband: Hallie Barron)
    (4). Edna McElveen (First Husand: Lee Mayers). Children:
       (a). Raymond Mayers
       (b). Marlene Mayers
       Edna McElveen (Second Husband: Edgar Whittington)
    (5). Winnie McElveen (Husband: Herman Wilson). Children:
       (a). Dorothy Ann Wilson

7. Margaret Alma (Maggie) McKnight (Husband: Dr. Christopher Harbert Bates). Children:
  a. Maude Alma Bates
  b. Dr. William Harbert Bates (Wife: Laura Miller). Children:
    (1). Margaret E. Bates (Husband: William Horace Jervis). Children:
       (a). John Vincent Jervis
       (b). William Horace Jervis, Jr.
    (2). William Harbert Bates, Jr. (Wife: Grace Martin). Children:
       (a). William Harbert Bates III
       (b). Christopher Martin Bates

(3). Martha Miller Bates (Husband: Xavia Milton Holt). Children:
    (a). Xavia Milton Holt, Jr.
c. Allie Ann Bates
d. Christopher Ellison Bates
e. Margaret Eloise Bates (Husband: D. Eugene Newman). Children:
    (1). Christine Newman (Husband: Mort Ray). Children:
        (a). Derrell Walter Ray
        (b). Roland Everett Ray
f. Randolph Bates
8. Adelia McKnight (Husband: Scott Cockerham). Children:
  a. Myrtis Cockerham (Husand: Will Wilson). Children:
    (1). Matha Wilson (Husband: Bernard H. Burris)*
    (2). Leo Wilson (Wife: Eva Robinson). Children:
        (a). Vernon Wilson (Wife: Freddie Garner)
        (b). Clayton Wilson
    (3). Herman Wilson (Wife: Winnie McElveen)†
    (4). Charles Wilson (Wife: Ann Darwin)
  b. Claude Lafayette Cockerham (Wife: Winnie Anders). Children:
    (1). Scott Ross Cockerham (Wife: Christine Coleman). Children:
        (a). Jerry Ross Cockerham
        (b). John Cresley Cockerham
    (2). George Lane Cockerham (Wife: Elsie Eugenia Sharp). Children:
        (a). Linda Lane Cockerham
        (b). Wilda Dean Cockerham
    (3). Claude Lafayette Cockerham, Jr. (Wife: Katharine Brown). Children:
        (a). Claude Layafette Cockerham III
        (b). Katharine Cecelia Cockerham
    (4). Lewyl Cockerham (Wife: Anna Katharine Lutz). Children:
        (a). Lewyl Glenn Cockerham

---

*Interfamily marriage. Children listed under husband.
†Interfamily marriage. Children listed under wife.

(5). Winnie B. Cockerham (Husband: Rufus Houston Hagan). Children:
- (a). Richard Nores Hagan
- (b). Sharon Wynn Hagan
- (c). Janis Lou Hagan

c. Epho Cockerham (Husband: John J. Newman). Children:
- (1). John J. Newman, Jr. (Wife: Mary Lee Cooper)
- (2). Marjorie Newman (Husband: John A. Gerard, Jr.). Children:
  - (a). Jeanne Gerard (Husband: Lester L. Scarborough). Children:
    - i. Lester L. Scarborough, Jr.
  - (b). Carol Ann Gerard
  - (c). Jere Gerard
- (3). Harold R. Newman (Wife: Mildred Laird). Children:
  - (a). Linda Kay Newman
  - (b). Harold R. Newman, Jr.
- (4). Warren H. Newman
- (5). Eloyse Newman (Husband: John Glenn Hollingsworth). Children:
  - (a). John Glenn Hollingsworth, Jr.

d. Robert Cockerham (Wife: Alice Nunnery). Children:
- (1). Robbie Cockerham (First Husband: Cecil Hyer). Children:
  - (a). Virginia Hyer
  Robbie Cockerham (Second Husband: Pollard Hayes)
- (2). Pascal Cockerham (Wife: Marjorie Leddy)
- (3). Geraldine Cockerham (Husband: . . . . Magee).

e. Zula Cockerham (First Husband: Kirk Turner). Children:
- (1). Kirk Hilton Turner
Zula Cockerham (Second Husband: Gaines Bates)

f. Tommye Cockerham (Husband: Proby Cloy). Children:
- (1). James Alfred Cloy

g. Vola Cockerham (First Husband: Elliot Bates). Children:
  (1). Frances Bates (First Husband: Merkel Brady). Children:
    (a). Kathryn Brady
    Frances Bates (Second Husband: W. S. McDaniel)
  Vola Cockerham (Second Husband: Boyd Williams). Children:
  (2). A. Boyd Williams (Wife: Ora Lee Graves). Children:
    (a). Sandra Gene Williams
    (b). Quin Dale Williams
    (c). Ronnie Williams
9. Nathan McKnight (Wife: Fannie Cockerham). Children:
  a. Sidney McKnight (First Wife: Cora Barron). Children:
    (1). Henry Nathan McKnight (Wife: Jewel Moak). Children:
      (a). Imagene McKnight
    Sidney McKnight (Second Wife: Maud Barron). Children:
    (2). Carrie Lee McKnight (Husband: Elbert Kirby)
    (3). Robert McKnight
    (4). Annie Belle McKnight (Husband: J. P. Davis). Children:
      (a). Sidney Lee Davis
      (b). Jerry Alton Davis
      (c). Sandra Faye Davis
    (5). Earl McKnight (Wife: Johnnie Mozelle Anderson)*
    (6). Jewell V. McKnight (Husband: Onzell B. Ford)
  b. Ansel McKnight
  c. Eva McKnight (First Husband: John Rutland). Children:
    (1). Monroe Roosevelt Rutland (Wife: Annie Reid). Children:
      (a). Horace Rutland
      (b). Melvin Rutland

---

*Interfamily marriage.   Children listed under wife.

  (c). James Rutland

  (d). Geraldine Rutland

 Eva McKnight (Second Husband: Armiston Reid)

d. Naomi McKnight (Husband: Ivy Blue). Children:

 (1). Houston Blue (Wife: Louella Fletcher). Children:

  (a). Carloss Blue

  (b). Fletcher Blue

e. Ira McKnight

f. Chris McKnight

g. Lucy McKnight (First Husband: Houston Terrell). Children:

 (1). Gladys Terrell (Husband: Elvin Marsdale). Children:

  (a). Joyce Marsdale (Husband: Eddie Rainey). Children:

   i. Samuel Rainey

  (b). Samuel Alton Marsdale

 Lucy McKnight (Second Husband: James Carroll). Children:

 (2). Leroy Carroll (Wife: Avvie Michon). Children:

  (a). Garry Lee Carroll

 Lucy McKnight (Third Husband: Grover Oliphant)

 (3). Robert Oliphant

 (4). Nathan Oliphant (Wife: Nelda Davis)

 (5). E. L. Oliphant

 (6). Leroy Oliphant

10. .... (A boy)

11. .... (A girl)

C. Almina Simmons (Husband: John E. Frith)

D. Ann Eliza Simmons (Husband: William Blake). Children:

1. Jim Ella Blake (Husband: James Theodore Hammond)

E. Samuel Eccles Simmons

F. Catherine Elizabeth Simmons

G. Martha Jane Simmons (Husband: .... Mock)

H. James Smith Simmons (Wife: Augusta Skidmore). Children:

1. Crosby Skidmore Simmons (First Wife: Julia Vinson). Children:

a. Nola Augusta Simmons (Husband: Joshua Killebrew Toler). Children:
  (1). Julia Gaynelle Toler (Husband: Richard Lister). Children:
    (a). Richard Toler Lister (Wife: Lila Mae Brannon). Children:
      i. Lillian Jane Lister
      ii. Richard Toler Lister, Jr.
  (2). Paul Toler (Wife: Laura Lee Hollingsworth)
b. Ernie Estelle Simmons
Crosby Skidmore Simmons (Second Wife: Mary Gassaway). Children:
c. Nannie Belle Simmons (Husband: Bias Wells Webb). Children:
  (1). Crosby Steve Webb (Wife: Margaret Case). Children:
    (a). Virginia Dianne Webb
d. Crosby Samuel Simmons (Wife: Lena Wixon). Children:
  (1). Lena Louise Simmons (Husband: Charles Edward Rode). Children:
    (a). Sandra Ilene Rode
  (2). Lois Juanita Simmons (Husband: William Alsie Jones). Children:
    (a). William Crosby Jones
    (b). Duke Wixon Jones
  (3). Katherine Samuel Simmons (Husband: Edward McWilliams Jones). Children:
    (a). Rose Mary Jones
  (4). Crosby Samuel Simmons, Jr. (Wife: Martha Turner). Children:
    (a). Martha Lynn Simmons
e. Birdie Mae Simmons (Husband: Paul Krivos)
f. James Echols Simmons (Wife: Anna Laura Brown). Children:
  (1). James Robert Simmons (Wife: Livie Posey Steinreide). Children:
    (a). James Robert Simmons, Jr.
    (b). William Mark Simmons
  (2). Wiley Hardy Simmons
  (3). Marion Lamar Simmons

g. Roy Skidmore Simmons (Wife: Emma Mason). Children:
   (1). Mary Hunt Simmons
h. Thomas Mark Simmons (Wife: Nona Nell Ingold). Children:
   (1). Thomas Mark Simmons, Jr.
i. Mary Louise Simmons (Husband: James Willie Gammons). Children:
   (1). Billie Marie Gammons
   (2). Dwayne Simmons Gammons
   (3). Thomas Roy Gammons

2. Daniel Jett Simmons (Wife: Mary Lillian Huffstickler). Children:
   a. Esma Simmons
   b. Samuel Skidmore Simmons (Wife: Katherine Bartling). Children:
      (1). Katherine Sue Simmons (Husband: J. W. Roberts).
      (2). Mavis Simmons
      (3). Samuel Skidmore Simmons, Jr.
      (4). Harry Daniel Simmons
   c. Johnie Erin Simmons (Husband: Robert Corden McKewen). Children:
      (1). Robert Corden (Red) McKewen, Jr. (Wife: Mary Lynn Ricketts). Children:
         (a). Robert Michael McKewen
   d. Anna Augusta Simmons (Husband: William Arnold Switzer). Children:
      (1). Frances Switzer (Husband: George Henry Shuey, Jr.). Children:
         (a). George Henry Shuey III
         (b). Anna Karen Shuey
      (2). William Arnold Switzer, Jr. (Wife: Mervin Crawford). Children:
         (a). Dennis Ray Switzer
         (b). Lynn Switzer
   e. Daniel Jett Simmons, Jr. (Wife: Rena Martin)
   f. William Jennings Bryan Simmons
   g. Isaac Herbert Simmons (Wife: Doris Inez Calhoun). Children:
      (1). Lucille Elizabeth Simmons

(2). Herbert Aaron Simmons (Wife: Dorothy Irene McKie). Children:
  (a). Marijett Simmons
  (b). Herbert Aaron Simmons, Jr.
(3). Lillie Erin Simmons (Husband: Harold James Blessitt). Children:
  (a). Gwendolyn Murray Blessitt
  (b). Harold James Blessitt II
(4). Inez LaRue Simmons (Husband: Jesse Floyd Brown, Jr.)
(5). Sammie Kathryn Simmons (Husband: Willie Clyde Alford). Children:
  (a). Terry Linn Alford
  (b). Harry Glynn Alford
(6). William Duncan Simmons
(7). Augusta Frances Simmons
(8). Sylvia Maude Simmons

h. Ivor Simmons (First Husband: O. McDaniel). Children:
  (1). Mavis Ray McDaniel (Husband: Joe McBride). Children:
    (a). Percy Haynes McBride
    (b). Joe McBride, Jr.
Ivor Simmons (Second Husband: Percy Haynes)

i. Beatrice Simmons (Husband: Eston Switzer). Children:
  (1). Eston Linwood Switzer
  (2). Dannie Hall Switzer

j. Eston Simmons (Wife: Artie Brazwell). Children:
  (1). Nettie Helen Simmons (Husband: .... McClure)
  (2). Elizabeth Ann Simmons

  3. James Echols Simmons
  4. C. Augustus Simmons
 I. John Simmons
 J. Harriett Adeline Simmons
 K. Margaret Simmons (Husband: .... Doyle)

III. John Burris
IV. Elizabeth (Betsy) Burris (First Husband: James Wilson). Children:
 A. Bruce Myers Wilson (Wife: Saline Andrews). Children:

1. Rose Wilson (Husband: Lawrence Robinson). Children:
   a. Eugene Robinson
   b. Maude Robinson (Husband: H. P. Mosely). Children:
      (1). H. P. Mosely, Jr. (Wife: Cenie Hargrove)
   c. Alma Robinson
   d. Helen Robinson (Husband: Jerry Walker). Children:
      (1). Rosalyn Walker
      (2). Wiley Walker
   e. Maggie Robinson (Husband: A. Storm). Children:
      (1). Jane Storm
   f. Laurence Robinson (a girl) (Husband: B. T. Walker). Children:
      (1). Bill Walker (Wife: Gussie Reid). Children:
         (a). Oma Belle Walker
         (b). Betsy Walker
      (2). Jerry T. Walker
2. Malena Wilson (Husband: Marshall Enos Burris)*
3. Mattie Wilson (Husband: John Robinson). Children:
   a. Rose Ella Robinson (Husband: Ira Wyatt). Children:
      (1). Eddie Lee Wyatt (Wife: Willie Carr). Children:
         (a). Barbara Jean Wyatt
      (2). Eugene Wyatt (Wife: Hilda Beaner). Children:
         (a). Robert Eugene Wyatt
         (b). William Lee Wyatt
   b. Emma Robinson (First Husband: Walter Brumfield). Children:
      (1). Etta Mae Brumfield (Husband: Bennett Butler)
      (2). Lucille Brumfield (Husband: Dr. D. T. Brock)
      (3). Hilda Brumfield (Husband: Jack H. Ewing). Children:
         (a). Lucy Claire Ewing
         (b). Jack Hilton Ewing
      Emma Robinson (Second Husband: J. W. Butler)
   c. John Robinson, Jr. (Wife: Kate Holmes). Children:

---

*Interfamily marriage. Children listed under husband.

(1). Atwood Robinson (Wife: Loucerna Williams)

(2). Marguerite Robinson (Husband: Stanton Key Calhoun). Children:

    (a). Stanton Key Calhoun, Jr.

(3). Juanita Robinson

(4). Seth Eugene Robinson (Wife: Edith Pope). Children:

    (a). Gloria Jean Robinson

    (b). Dean Carlton Robinson

(5). Dean Carlton Robinson

d. Thomas J. Robinson (Wife: Bessie Elizabeth Turnipseed). Children:

  (1). Carl Robinson (Wife: Ira Belle Caraway). Children:

    (a). Betty Jean Robinson

    (b). Peggy Lanelle Robinson

    (c). Carl Douglas Robinson

  (2). Jerry Robinson (Wife: Ella Lee Touchstone). Children:

    (a). Jerry Wyatt Robinson

    (b). Cynthia Kay Robinson

    (c). Cheryl Fay Robinson

    (d). John Harry Robinson

  (3). Laurence Robinson (Wife: Essie Ray Pray). Children:

    (a). Thomas Ray Robinson

    (b). Elizabeth Ann Robinson

    (c). Jimmie Louis Robinson

  (4). Hugh Marvin Robinson (Wife: Daisy Christine Raley). Children:

    (a). Hugh Robinson

  (5). Ira Lee Robinson (Wife: Hazel Touchstone). Children:

    (a). Anna Margaret Robinson

e. Ammie Robinson (Husband: Harry Butler). Children:

  (1). Caro Lee Butler (Husband: Oscar Lee Wells). Children:

    (a). Martha Ann Wells (Husband: Merwin Burris)*

---

*An interfamily marriage.

        (b). Rita Rose Wells

        (c). Harry Butler Wells

    (2). Marjorie Butler (Husband: L. E. Wolfe, Jr.). Children:

        (a). Carolyn Wolfe

    (3). Grace Butler (Husband: Earl Gillis). Children:

        (a). Cary Wayne Gillis

f. Eddie Robinson (Wife: Eva Louise Hinton). Children:

    (1). Edith Frances Robinson (Husband: Harold Lane Sisson). Children:

        (a). Nelda Carolyn Sisson

        (b). Michael Lane Sisson

    (2). Evelyn Lorraine Robinson (Husband: Dr. James A. Avant). Children:

        (a). Lorraine Adair Avant

        (b). Ruth Victoria Avant

        (c). Frances Evelyn Avant

g. Charlie Robinson (Wife: Ruth Darville). Children:

    (1). Charles Ray Robinson (Wife: Mary Alice Stockman). Children:

        (a). Charla Mary Robinson

        (b). Charles Ray Robinson, Jr.

        (c). Mary Elizabeth Robinson

Elizabeth (Betsy) Burris (Second Husband: James Denman). Children:

B. Martha Ann Denman (Husband: Dr. Jacob Burton Strickland). Children:

1. Cade Drew (Dick) Strickland (First Wife: Lucinda Wright). Children:

a. Delila Strickland (Husband: John Coleman). Children:

    (1). Jesse Coleman (Wife: Adie Perchard). Children:

        (a). Octavia Coleman (Husband: Other Taylor). Children:

            i. Leon Taylor

            ii. Wilbur Taylor

            iii. Francis Taylor

        (b). Arthur Coleman

(c). Grace Coleman (Husband: Buster Cooper). Children:
    i. Margaret Cooper
(d). Loyd Coleman
(2). Ted Coleman (Wife: Mary Smith). Children:
    (a). Airlea Coleman (Husband: U. V. Taylor). Children:
        i. Charles Taylor
    (b). Mildred Coleman (Husband: C. B. Kirl). Children:
        i. Runia Kirl
    (c). Catherine Coleman
    (d). Donald Coleman
(3). Roy Coleman
(4). Lou Coleman (Husband: Putman Thomas)
(5). Mamie Coleman (Husband: Jesse Neal). Children:
    (a). Jewel Neal (Husband: Elmo Eubanks). Children:
        i. David Eubanks
        ii. Glinda Sue Eubanks
    (b). Daisy Neal
    (c). Velma Neal
    (d). Betty Lou Neal
    (e). Robert Neal

Cade Drew (Dick) Strickland (Second Wife: Ary Poole). Children:

b. Ruth Strickland (Husband: Henry Butler Smith). Children:
(1). Cade Smith (Wife: Mary Smith). Children:
    (a). Lucy Smith
    (b). Allen Cade Smith
(2). James (Jimbo) Smith (Wife: Sallie Love)
(3). Lena May Smith
(4). Mary Smith (Husband: Ted Coleman)*

c. Lucy Strickland (Husband: Charles Smith). Children:
(1). Jettie Smith (Wife: Eula Neal). Children:
    (a). Adrian (A. D.) Smith

---

*Interfamily marriage. Children listed under husband.

  (b). Maurice (girl) Smith (Husband: Otis
    Decker). Children:
     i. Adrian Decker
     ii. Linda Dianne Decker
 d. Lena Strickland
 e. Nita Strickland
 f. Jacob (Jake) Strickland
2. John Spencer Strickland (Wife: Emma C. Powell).
 Children:
 a. Martha Ann Strickland (First Husband: T o m
  Beatty). Children:
  (1). Richard Beatty
  (2). Cordia Beatty
  (3). Hugh Beatty
  (4). Anna Beatty
  Martha Ann Strickland (Second Husband: ....
  McElveen)
 b. Elizabeth Strickland (Husband: ....
  Williams)*
 c. Mildred Strickland (Husband: John T. Newman).
  Children:
  (1). Blanche Newman
  (2). Hazel Newman
  (3). Mildred Newman
 d. Annie Strickland (Husband: John T. Newman).
  Children:
  (1). Leon Thomas Newman
  (2). John Strickland Newman (Wife: Martha Ida
    Wall). Children:
    (a). Mary Annie Newman
    (b). Martha Emma Newman
    (c). Marie Alice Newman
    (d). Henry Earl Newman
    (e). Dudley John Newman
  (3). Joseph C. Newman (Wife: Jacqueline Arp).
    Children:
    (a). Joseph C. Newman, Jr.
  (4). Annie Laura Newman (Husband: August
    Mikkola). Children:

---

*Thought to be Alex Wattley Williams and an interfamily marriage. Children listed under husband.

        (a). Arthur Mikkola
    (5). Robert Reed Newman
    (6). Carl Kennon Newman
  e. Velma Pinkie Strickland (Husband: Judson Emmett Martin)*
  f. Dewitt Strickland
  g. John Spencer Strickland, Jr.
  h. Cade Drew Strickland (Wife: Elizabeth Phillips). Children:
    (1). Bruce Strickland
    (2). Cade Drew Strickland, Jr.
    (3). Fay Strickland
    (4). Thelma Strickland
    (5). Betty Strickland
3. Jane Elizabeth Strickland (Husband: Hardy S. Bridges). Children:
  a. Jackson J. Bridges (Wife: Martha (Sis) Grice). Children:
    (1). Zellie Bridges
    (2). Geneva Bridges
    (3). Harry Bridges
    (4). Kelly Bridges
    (5). Willard Bridges
    (6). Kitty Bridges
  b. Jimmie Bridges (Husband: Dave White)
  c. Martha Bridges (First Husband: Bud Womack). Children:
    (1). Janie Womack (Husband: Charlie Harrell). Children:
      (a). Troy Harrell
    (2). Nettie Womack (Husband: Albert Harrell). Children:
      (a.) Eudora Harrell
      (b). Hazel Harrell
      (c). Jessie Mae Harrell
      (d). Victor Harrell
      (e). Phillip Harrell
    (3). Abner Womack
    (4). Euna Cook Womack
    Martha Bridges (Second Husband: Hanse Simmons)

*Interfamily marriage. Children listed under husband.

31

d. Bessie Bridges (Husband: Tom Burch). Children:
   (1). Clyde Burch
   (2). Read Burch
   (3). O. W. Burch
e. Henry Bridges (Wife: Daisy Sandifer). Children:
   (1). Hosey Bridges
   (2). Jewell Bridges
   (3). Alvin Bridges
   (4). Claud Bridges
   (5). Valley Bridges
   (6). Ruby Bridges
f. Hardy S. Bridges, Jr. (Wife: Jessie Bridges). Children:
   (1). Launa Pearl Bridges
   (2). Otis Virgil Bridges
4. Ruth Victoria Strickland (Husband: Peter F. Hutchinson). Children:
   a. Sallie Hutchinson (Husband: Boykin Bridges)
   b. Mary Hutchinson (Husband: Willie Guy). Children:
      (1). Ruth Elizabeth Guy (Husband: Willie T. Allen)
   c. Martha Hutchinson (Husband: Josh Guy). Children:
      (1). Ola Guy
      (2). Sallie Guy
      (3). Lora Guy (Husband: Clyde Dayton Strickland)*
      (4). Georgia Guy
   d. Merritt Hutchinson (Wife: Aryie Newman). Children:
      (1). Sitman Hutchinson
      (2). Grace Hutchinson
      (3). Daisy Hutchinson
      (4). Helen Hutchinson
      (5). L. T. Hutchinson
      (6). Carrie Hutchinson
   e. Jake Hutchinson (Wife: Rosa Branch). Children:
      (1).Preston Hutchinson
      (2). Jake Henry Hutchinson
      (3). Tisha Mae Hutchinson

---

*Interfamily marriage. Children listed under husband.

5. Jeptha Joe Strickland (Wife: Ida Elizabeth Taylor). Children:
   a. Charles Richmond Strickland (Wife: Cassie C. Wales). Children:
      (1). Clayton Clifton Strickland (Wife: Grace Hurst). Children:
         (a). Clovis Strickland
         (b). C. Grace Strickland
         (c). Robert C. Strickland
      (2). Clyde Dayton Strickland (Wife: Lora Guy). Children:
         (a). Bettie Lee Strickland
   b. John Taylor Strickland (Wife: Mary E. Blades). Children:
      (1). Herbert Burton Strickland (Wife: Janie Webb). Children:
         (a). John Strickland
         (b). Mary L. Strickland
         (c). Burton Strickland
      (2). Glynn E. Strickland (Wife: Lucille Furrow). Children:
         (a). Carol Ann Strickland
         (b). Rosie Myre Strickland
         (c). Joe G. Strickland
         (d). Helen Anita Strickland
      (3). Clyde C. Strickland (Wife: Erna Voss). Children:
         (a). Roy Clifton Strickland
         (b). Elizabeth Ann Strickland
   c. Joseph Quincy Strickland (Wife: Etta Smith). Children:
      (1). Lehman Erwin Strickland (Wife: Margie Bennett)
   d. Ida Roberta Strickland (Husband: Merritt G. Allen). Children:
      (1). Hulon Merritt Allen (Wife: Anna Belle Landry). Children:
         (a). Shirley Ann Allen
         (b). Hulon David Allen
         (c). Frances Fay Allen

(2). Thomas Gaylon Allen (Wife: Rainer Estelle Cox). Children:
    (a). Raymond Gaylon Allen
(3). Vera Mae Allen (Husband: Johnny Lee Hodges). Children:
    (a). Dennis Ralph Hodges
    (b). Daryll Allen Hodges
(4). Evelyn Geraldine Allen (Husband: Clifford N. Battles). Children:
    (a). Judith Kay Battles
    (b). June Lynette Battles
(5). Gladys Leona Allen (Husband: Lea Toler Hanks). Children:
    (a). Connie Lea Hanks
(6). Hubert Price Allen
(7). Ernie Joe Allen (Husband: Alvin Clifton Thompson)
  e. James Wirt Strickland (Wife: Janie Venable). Children:
    (1). Wilbur Burke Strickland
    (2). Aline Elizabeth Strickland
    (3). Vernon Leroy Strickland
    (4). Edith Marion Strickland
6. Henry Willis Strickland
7. James Denman Strickland
C. Samuel James Denman
V. James Burris
VI. Samuel Burris, Jr. (Wife: Julia Ann Everett). Children:
  A. John Burris (Wife: Nancy Anglin)
  B. Mary Burris (Husband: Lafayette Swearingen). Children:
    1. George Washington Swearingen (Wife: Mary Jane (Mollie) Wall). Children:
      a. Octavia Swearingen (Husband: Tom Redmond). Children:
        (1). Ada Lou Redmond (Husband: George Tidwell). Children:
          (a). Lillie Mae Tidwell
          (b). Norma Tidwell (Husband: Bob Christopher). Children:
            i. Bob Christopher, Jr.

  ii. Perry Christopher

 (c). Evonne Tidwell

b. Ida Swearingen

c. Ella Swearingen (Husband: Fred Varnado). Children:

 (1). R. F. Varnado (Wife: Thelma Geraldine Williams). Children:

  (a). Laura Ella Varnado

 (2). Helen Marie Varnado (Husband: Cecil Paul Young). Children:

  (a). Jerry Dianne Young

 (3). Willie Ray Varnado

 (4). Mary Frances Varnado

 (5). Alton Lamar Varnado

 (6). Ella Grace Varnado

d. George Monroe Swearingen (Wife: Ada Florine Jordan). Children:

 (1). Constance Gene Swearingen (Husband: John William Casey III)

 (2). George Monroe Swearingen, Jr.

e. Lafayette Swearingen (Wife: Vesta Alford). Children:

 (1). Velo B. Swearingen (Wife: Tincie Strickland). Children:

  (a). Jerry Swearingen

  (b). Norman Swearingen

 (2). Benamay Swearingen (Husband: Iley Simmons). Children:

  (a). I. W. Simmons

  (b). Bennie Gaylan Simmons

 (3). Leveta Swearingen (Husband: Downey Miller). Children:

  (a). Dennis Wayne Miller

  (b). Carolyn Ann Miller

 (4). Marie Swearingen (Husband: Leslie Roberts). Children:

  (a). Donald Roberts

 (5). Quentin Swearingen (Wife: Della Gohram). Children:

  (a). Beverly Jean Swearingen

  (b). Connie Sue Swearingen

(6). Loudean Swearingen (Husband: Jewel Simpson). Children:
  (a). Glynn Elbert Simpson
  (b). Sandra Simpson
  (c). Kenneth Wayne Simpson
f. Willie Swearingen (Wife: Lucille Sumerall). Children:
  (1). Evelyn Swearingen
  (2). Inez Swearingen (Husband: ....)
  (3). Nolan Swearingen
  (4). Clayton Swearingen
  (5). Richie Swearingen
g. Benjamin Everett Swearingen (Wife: Mollie Darden Bell). Children:
  (1). Lillie Opal Swearingen (Husband: David Pinkney Edwards)
  (2). Iola Bell Swearingen (Husband: Albert Lewis Moeschle)
  (3). Benjamin Everett Swearingen, Jr. (Wife: Mary Hellen Smith). Children:
    (a). Benjamin Everett Swearingen III
  (4). Acey Avolea Swearingen (Wife: Emma Jeane Greenwood)
  (5). Michael Darden Swearingen (Wife: Eunice Loyce Whitted). Children:
    (a). Michael Darden Swearingen, Jr.
    (b). Molly Inez Swearingen
    (c). Patricia Loyce Swearingen
  (6). Arra Marie Swearingen (Husband: Harry Edwin Overlock). Children:
    (a). Harry Edwin Overlock, Jr.
    (b). Mary Ann Overlock
    (c). Timothy Lee Overlock
  (7). Iris Ella Swearingen (First Husband: Cortney C. Morrison). Children:
    (a). Penelope Marie Morrison
    (b). Phoebe Jean Morrison
    Iris Ella Swearingen (Second Husband: Ollie (Jack) Strickland). Children:
    (c). Idona Iris Strickland

h. Seborn Elbert Swearingen (Wife: Eva Hodges). Children:

    (1). Geraldine Swearingen (Husband: Charles Wells). Children:

        (a). Charles Seborn Wells

        (b). Beverly Jean Wells

    (2). Glenn Elbert Swearingen

2. Dora Swearingen (Husband: Theodore Brabham). Children:

  a. Lafayette Brabham (First Wife: Flora McDonald). Children:

    (1). Dora Brabham (Husband: Reuben Matthews). Children:

        (a). R. L. Matthews (Wife: ....). Children:

           i. Harold Matthews

           ii. Murel Matthews

        (b). Ethel Linda Matthews (Husband: James Lea). Children:

           i. Jamie Lea

           ii. ....

        (c). Donald Matthews (Wife: ....).

        (d). Mavis Matthews (Husband: ....). Children:

           i. ....

           ii. ....

        (e). Larry Matthews

        (f). Hattie Pearl Matthews

        (g). Elena Matthews

    (2). Ludie Brabham (Husband: Elliott Bates). Children:

        (a). Richard Bates

        (b). Milford Bates

        (c). Dewitt Bates

        (d). Murray Bates

        (e). E. C. Bates (Wife: .... Burnett). Children:

           i. Bernice Bates

        (f). Marjorie Bates

        (g). Beatrice Bates (Husband: T. F. Randall). Children:

   i. T. F. Randall, Jr.
   ii. Evonne Randall
   iii. Gary Randall
  (h). Henry Marshall Bates (Wife: ....).
   Children:
   i. Buddy Bates
   ii. Pat Bates
  (i). Theodore Bates
(3). Gladys Brabham (Husband: Earl Bryant).
  Children:
  (a). Roy Bryant
  (b). Alton Bryant (Wife: ....).
   Children:
   i. Buddy Bryant
   ii. ....
(4). Eula Brabham (First Husband: John Earl
  Blalock). Children:
  (a). Florine Earline Blalock (Husband: Willie
   Lea Newcomb). Children:
   i. Guindal Lee Newcomb
   ii. Ester Gale Newcomb
   iii. Ivey Earline Newcomb
   iv. Avery Louise Newcomb
  (b). Kathryn Irene Blalock (Husband: Floyd
   L. Tarver). Children:
   i. Floyd Earl Tarver
  (c). Henry Earl Blalock
  (d). William Kenneth Blalock
  (e). Paul Julius Blalock
  (f). Ivey Bell Blalock
  (g). Avery Nell Blalock
  (h). John Hilton Blalock
  Eula Brabham (Second Husband: Marvin
   Beasley). Children:
  (i). Linda Faye Beasley
(5). Mabel Brabham (Husband: Reuben Kirkland).
  Children:
  (a). William Kirkland (Wife: Marie Granger). Children:
   i. Sue Kirkland
   ii. Billie Kirkland

      (b). Juanita Kirkland (Husband: Robert Earl Ogle)

      (c). Reuben Kirkland, Jr.

      (d). Julius Kirkland

      (e). Janie Mae Kirkland

   (6). Julius Brabham (Wife: Bertha Ellen Hodges). Children:

      (a). Arie Jean Brabham

      (b). Herbert Brabham

      (c). Quin Brabham

      (d). Dewitt Brabham

      (e). Oliver Brabham

      (f). Alexzene Brabham

   (7). Dewitt Brabham (Wife: Mabell . . . .). Children:

      (a). Betty Brabham (adopted)

Lafayette Brabham (Second Wife: Kate Bellue)

b. Eugene (Bud) Brabham (Wife: Minnie Hurst). Children:

   (1). Lorena Brabham (Husband: . . . .)

c. Charlie Brabham (Wife: Mim Jones). Children:

   (1). C. M. Brabham

   (2). Dale Brabham

   (3). Hugh Brabham

   (4). Eunice Brabham

   (5). Ethel Brabham

   (6). Inez Brabham

   (7). Mim Brabham

   (8). Bonnie Brabham

d. T. M. (Mack) Brabham (Wife: Betty Powell). Children:

   (1). Grace Brabham (Husband: Guy Rosary Serio). Children:

      (a). Grace Louise Serio

      (b). Guy Rosary Serio, Jr.

      (c). Betty Lynn Serio

      (d). Margie Joyce Serio

   (2). Alawee Brabham (Husband: Howard Melton). Children:

      (a). Howard Melton, Jr.

      (b). Frances Melton

(3). Theodore Brabham (Wife: Evelyn Day). Children:
  (a). Mack Brabham
  (b). Joe Brabham
  (c). Jack Brabham
(4). Marjorie Brabham (Husband: J. T. Walsh). Children:
  (a). Tommy Jean Walsh
  (b). Ronnie Walsh

e. Emmett Brabham (Wife: Gertrude Schilling). Children:
(1). Dudley Brabham
(2). Sam Brabham
(3). Mary Brabham
(4). Maudie Brabham

f. Mary (Sis) Brabham (First Husband: Kim Brame). Children:
(1). Murel Brame (Husband: Fleet Williams)
Mary (Sis) Brabham (Second Husband: Eugene Dickey). Children:
(2). Bonnie B. Dickey (Husband: Edwin Simmons). Children:
  (a). Dorothy Simmons
(3). Minnie Mae Dickey (Husband: Curtis Raborn)
(4). T. C. Dickey (Wife: Mary Cutrer). Children:
  (a). Tom Dickey
  (b). Mary Ann Dickey

g. Estelle Brabham (Husband: Alva R. Hughes). Children:
(1). Merble Hughes (Husband: Hollis Jones). Children:
  (a). Dorothy Dell Jones (Husband: John D. Sudduth). Children:
    i. Nena Grace Sudduth
(2). James Floyd Hughes (Wife: Grace Cook)
(3). Edyce Hughes (Husband: James Little). Children:
  (a). Ary Jean Little (Husband: Ralph Helton)
(4). Charlie Hughes (Wife: Eulalie Schneider). Children:
  (a). Barbara Jo Hughes

(b). Noel Hughes
(5). Minnie Hughes (Husband: Julius Little). Children:
    (a). Freddie LaNell Little (Husband: Paul Campbell). Children:
        i. Beverly Jean Campbell
    (b). Kenneth Little
(6). Hettie Hughes (Husband: Aubrey LeGette). Children:
    (a). Mary Ellen LeGette
    (b). Alvanell LeGette
    (c). John Carl LeGette
(7). Blanche Hughes (Husband: Elmer Minks). Children:
    (a). Jimmy Minks
    (b). Roy Hughes Minks
    (c). Sharon Sue Minks
(8). A. R. Hughes (Wife: Claudine Conerly). Children:
    (a). Renny Hughes (adopted)
(9). Ray Hughes (Wife: Burkett Burnyce Wall). Children:
    (a). Hugh Ray Hughes
    (b). H. A. Hughes
    (c). Frances Jane Hughes
    (d). James Floyd Hughes
(10). Roy Hughes
(11). Hilda Estelle Hughes (Husband: Charles Womack). Children:
    (a). Michael Womack
    (b). Darryl Womack
    (c). Robin Faye Womack

h. Anna Brabham (Husband: Robert Wall). Children:
    (1). Velma Wall
    (2). Evelyn Wall
    (3). Clytie Wall
    (4). Merle Wall
    (5). R. J. Wall
    (6). Morris Wall

i. Pearl Brabham (Husband: Johnnie Bean). Children:
    (1). Lillie Opal Bean

      (2). Oville Bean
  j. Minnie Brabham (Husband: Buck Simmons). **Children:**
      (1). Audrey Simmons
      (2). Joyce Ann Simmons
  k. Ola Brabham (Husband: Frank Allison)
  l. Irene Brabham (Husband: Robert Lindsey). **Children:**
      (1). T. W. Lindsey
      (2). Lamar Lindsey
      (3). James Lindsey
      (4). Hughey Lindsey
      (5). Shirley Joyce Lindsey
      (6). Betty Jo Lindsey

3. Joseph Lafayette Swearingen (First Wife: **Dora Jones**). Children:
  a. Everett Swearingen (Wife: Lottie Lee Wilkinson)
  b. Iris Swearingen (Husband: Carl Lea). Children:
      (1). Helen Lea (Husband: T. J. Pluscett)
      (2). Hilda Jean Lea (Husband: Dr. J. L. Custer)
  c. Myrtis Swearingen
  d. Jewel Swearingen (Wife: Tracey Rice). Children:
      (1). Joe Ann Swearingen
  e. Thelma Swearingen (Husband: Frank Batterford). Children:
      (1). Frankie Batterford
  f. Clifton Swearingen (Wife: Janette Keith). Children:
      (1). Malcolm Swearingen
      (2). Rachel Swearingen
      (3). Dora Joe Swearingen
  g. Nolan Swearingen (Wife: Vera Rapp Green)
  Joseph Lafayette Swearingen (Second Wife: Auline Tucker Coney)

4. Hattie Swearingen (Husband: J. S. Simmons)

5. Piney Jane Swearingen (First Husband: Dan Westbrook). Children:
  a. Elbert Westbrook (Wife: Martha Davidson)
  b. Irma Westbrook
  c. Joe Westbrook

Piney Jane Swearingen (Second Husband: Will Lambert)
6. Mattie Swearingen
7. Rosalie Swearingen
8. Mary Swearingen (Husband: Winfield White). Children:
    a. Ellis White (First Wife: Annie Kirkland). Children:
        (1). Clyde White
        (2). Hewitt White
        (3). Annie Mae White
        (4). Walton Ellis White
        Ellis White (Second Wife: Mrs. Maud White)
9. J. Monroe Swearingen (Wife: Mary E. Newman). Children:
    a. John Neafus Swearingen (First Wife: Carrie Epperson). Children:
        (1). May Irene Swearingen
        John Neafus Swearingen (Second Wife: Lizzie Maud Devereux). Children:
        (2). John Neafus Swearingen, Jr.
    b. Bessie L. Swearingen (Husband: Lyman Oscar Casebier)
    c. George Washington Swearingen (Wife: Parthenia Ophelia Van)
    d. David L. Swearingen (Wife: Emily Josephine Wall). Children:
        (1). Mary D. Swearingen (Husband: Melvin A. Figeroid). Children:
            (a). Nancy Jo Figeroid
    e. Lea Bridewell Swearingen
    f. May Irene Swearingen
    g. Albert Jesse Swearingen (First Wife: ....).
        Albert Jesse Swearingen (Second Wife: ....)
    h. Doyle Denver Swearingen
    i. Ellis Arville Swearingen (Wife: Marie Stahl). Children:
        (1). Cheryl Ann Swearingen
        (2). James Ellis Swearingen
C. Harriett Burris (Husband: Harvey D. Martin). Children:
1. Eugene Martin (Wife: Nina Marsalis). Children:

a. Guidry Martin
b. Delsie Martin
2. Melissa (Mickie) Martin (Husband: J. C. Stuart)
3. Judson Emmett Martin (Wife: Velma Pinkie Strickland). Children:
   a. Emma Martin
   b. June Martin
   c. Ada Martin
4. Mary Julia (Mollie) Martin (Husband: Chas. Wall). Children:
   a. Eula Wall (Husband: Lawrence Jones)
   b. Earnest Wall (adopted)
5. Della Martin (Husband: August Sturkins)
6. Oceola (Babe) Martin (Husband: Willie Thomas Bridges). Children:
   a. Gracie Bridges (Husband: Pierce Phillips). Children:
      (1). Christina Phillips
      (2). Willie Pierce Phillips
      (3). Joe Phillips
      (4). Wilda Phillips
   b. Nellie Bridges (Husband: Lawrence Jones). Children:
      (1). Quinn Jones
      (2). Denzel Jones
      (3). Newt Jones
      (4). Wilva Nell Jones
   c. Lena Bridges (First Husband: Charlie Phillips). Children:
      (1). Percy Phillips
      (2). Charles Phillips, Jr.
      Lena Bridges (Second Husband: Setman Sims)
   d. William V. Bridges
   e. Thomas E. Bridges (Wife: Nathalie Ryan). Children:
      (1). Donald Bridges (adopted)
   f. Minnie Lou Bridges (Husband: B. T. Young). Children:
      (1). Geraldine Young
      (2). Evelyn Young
      (3). Burgess Young, Jr.

44

(4). Adrienne Young

    g. Ruby Bridges (First Husband: George Kippers). Children:

    (1). George Kippers, Jr.

    Ruby Bridges (Second Husband: Amos Taushey)

    h. Lucy Bridges (Husband: Arthur Guerra). Children:

    (1). Arthur Guerra, Jr.

    i. Wilma Bridges (Husband: Tom Blackwell)

    j. Virginia Bridges (Husband: William W. McGinity). Children:

    (1). William W. McGinity, Jr.

D. Victoria Burris (Husband: William Lee). Children:

  1. Regina Lee (Husband: J. G. DeArmond). Children:

    a. Velfort Judson DeArmond (Wife: Madge M. Brown). Children:

    (1). V. J. DeArmond, Jr.

    (2). Dorothy Marie DeArmond

    (3). Alfred Josh DeArmond

    (4). Barbara Ann DeArmond

    b. Maple Joshua DeArmond

    c. Virgil Lee DeArmond (Wife: Eunice Daigle). Children:

    (1). Lance DeArmond

    (2). Donald DeArmond

    (3). Dane DeArmond

    d. Lorena Bell DeArmond

    e. Willie Donald DeArmond (Wife: Shirley Lunsford). Children:

    (1). Arthur DeArmond

    f. Maurice Lewis DeArmond (Wife: Virginia Jackson). Children:

    (1). Wayne DeArmond (adopted)

    g. Stanley Adrian DeArmond

    h. Reymond Houston DeArmond

E. Ellen Elizabeth Burris (Husband: Leroy Bellue). Children:

  1. William Howard Bellue

  2. Samuel Wayne Bellue (Wife: Phoebie Starch Fluker). Children:

a. Percy I. Bellue (Wife: Mabel Beatrice Stewart). Children:
  (1). James Derrell Bellue (Wife: Madge Elizabeth Causey). Children:
    (a). Eula Elizabeth (Beckie) Bellue
  (2). Julia Laverne Bellue (Husband: Cleon Earl Allen). Children:
    (a). Merwin Earl Allen
    (b). Beverly Diane Allen
  (3). Mavourleen Bellue (Husband: Sheldon Derwood Bean). Children:
    (a). Richard Lane Bean
    (b). Constance Marie Bean
    (c). Robert Irwin Bean
  (4). Willie Mae Bellue
  (5). Charles Irwin Bellue
  (6). Phebia Lanell Bellue
  (7). Peggy Ruth Bellue
b. Carl Bellue (Wife: Maggie Lee Frazier). Children:
  (1). Carline Bellue (Husband: Rudolph Jenkins). Children:
    (a). Carl Wayne Jenkins
    (b). .... (a boy)
  (2). Betty Jean Bellue
  (3). Bennie Belton Bellue
  (4). Naomi Dell Bellue
  (5). Donald Bellue
  (6). Patricia Ann Bellue
c. Woodrow Bellue (Wife: Mary Idelle Lea). Children:
  (1). Helen Willena Bellue
  (2). Edna Ruth Bellue
  (3). Bennie Ray Bellue
  (4). Samuel Wayne Bellue
  (5). Wm. Howard Bellue
d. James Bellue
e. Webb Bellue (Wife: Eunice Watson)
f. Effie Rae Bellue (Husband: Joe C. Allen). Children:
  (1). Ellzey Allen
  (2). Morris Allen
g. Addie Bellue

h. Maydelle Bellue (Husband: Jack Asbeck). Children:
   (1). Eddie Wayne Asbeck
   (2). ....
i. Julius Bellue
3. Emma Bellue (Husband: Adolphus Frazier). Children:
   a. Vernon Frazier (Wife: .... Davis). Children:
      (1). ....
   b. Gladys Frazier (Husband: .... Bernard). Children:
      (1). Alfred Bernard
   c. Tollie Frazier (Wife: Doris Brabham). Children:
      (1). Evelyn Frazier (Husband: ...... Whitehead)
      (2). Estelle Frazier
      (3). Roy Frazier
   d. Claude Frazier (First Wife: Mollie Davidson)
      Claude Frazier (Second Wife: Irma Lee Goldman). Children:
      (1). Hulon Frazier
      (2). Margaret Ellen Frazier
      (3). James Adolphus Frazier
      (4). Emma Mae Frazier
      (5). Roy Douglas Frazier
      (6). Thelma Lea Frazier
      (7). Vernon Allen Frazier
      (8). Clifton Lamar Frazier
   e. Clifton Frazier (Wife: Maggie Lee). Children:
      (1). Jeanette Frazier
      (2). Jackie Frazier
      (3). Charles Frazier
4. Mollie Bellue (Husband: James Osburn Lee). Children:
   a. Minnie Irene Lee (Husband: Atkerson Frazier). Children:
      (1). Prentiss E. Frazier (Wife: Annette McDaniel). Children:
         (a). Judy Gayle Frazier
         (b). Janice Ann Frazier
         (c). Prentiss E. Frazier, Jr.
         (d). Ronnie Keith Frazier
      (2). Grace Frazier
      (3). Elbert Frazier

(4). Reed Frazier

   b. Hollis Lee (Wife: Velma Lee Frazier). Children:

     (1). Leopold Lee

     (2). Yvonne Lee (Husband: Alex Sibley)

     (3). Eudora Lee

     (4). Herbert Lee

   c. Homer Lee

   d. Howard Lee

 5. Lee Bellue (Wife: Effie Smiley). Children:

   a. Zack Bellue

   b. Howard Bellue

   c. .... (a boy)

   d. Hughey Bellue

   e. Everett Bellue

   f. Margaret Ellen Bellue

   g. Sybil Bellue

   h. Willie Bellue (a girl)

   i. Starr Bellue (a girl)

   j. Stone Bellue (a boy)

 6. Pinkie Bellue

 7. Maude Bellue

F. Julia Burris (Husband: Nathaniel (Nat) Dykes). Children:

 1. Napoleon Dykes (Wife: Fannie Marshall)

 2. Estelle Dykes (Husband: Dr. A. G. Root). Children:

   a. A. G. Root, Jr. (Wife: Gladys Travis). Children:

     (1). A. G. Root, III

     (2). Barrett Root

 3. Fred N. Dykes (Wife: Iona Tillery). Children:

   a. Fred N. Dykes, Jr. (Wife: Alice Mary Clark). Children:

     (1). Frederick James Dykes

     (2). Michael Clark Dykes

G. Judson Burris (Wife: Sarah (Sallie) Rand). Children:

 1. Charles Levy Burris

 2. .... (a daughter)

 3. .... (a daughter)

H. Amanda Burris

I. Alice Burris (Husband: Hardy Dekalk Travis). Children:

 1. Lelia Travis (Husband: John Seaborn (Bruce) Brabham). Children:

a. Jewel Travis Brabham (Husband: Charles George Dupree). Children:
   (1). L. D. Dupree
   (2). Charles George Dupree, Jr.
b. John Hardy Brabham (Wife: Joyce ....). Children:
   (1). Judy Kay Brabham
   (2). Vickie Cheryl Brabham
   (3). John Neil Brabham
c. Alice Lanelle Brabham (Husband: J. E. McIntyre)
2. Lance Travis
3. Myrtis Udora Travis (Husband: Enos James Newman). Children:
   a. Ella Mae Newman (Husband: Herman Newman). Children:
      (1). Louise Lurline Newman
      (2). Christine Sue Newman
   b. Louise Newman (Husband: Earl Williams)
   c. William Lee Newman (Wife: Dicy Neva Smith). Children:
      (1). Myrtis Lou Newman
      (2). William Lee Newman, Jr.
   d. Fred Firman Newman (Wife: Pearl Blades). Children:
      (1). Fred Firman Newman, Jr.
   e. Albert Dekalk Newman (Wife: Maydell Frazier). Children:
      (1). Albert Dekalk Newman, Jr.
      (2). Carolyn Warnell Newman
   f. Leonard Enos Newman (Wife: Faye Goings). Children:
      (1). Leonard James Newman
   g. Enos James Newman, Jr.
4. Herman Hardy Travis (Wife: Ethel Brabham). Children:
   a. Hardy Virgil Travis (Wife: Ethel Marie Rutland). Children:
      (1). Gary Virgil Travis
      (2). Gilbert Hardy Travis
   b. Herman Hardy Travis, Jr.

c. Ethel Velma Travis (Husband: Vernell Leon Hendry). Children:

(1). Richard Vernell Hendry

d. Irma Estelle Travis

e. Maye Aline Travis (Husband: James Marion Norsworthy II). Children:

(1). Vivian Elizabeth Norsworthy

(2). James Marion Norsworthy III

f. Richard Everett Travis

g. Willie Reid Travis (Wife: Marguerite Wilkinson). Children:

(1). Arthur Reid Travis

(2). Douglas Travis

(3). Marilyn Travis

h. Vivian Travis

5. Richard Everett Travis

6. William Lee Travis (Wife: Eula Eugenia Powell). Children:

a. William Lee Travis II

b. Eugenia Powell Travis (Husband: Donald Arthur Bousquet)

J. Alma Burris

K. Adeline Burris (Husband: Thomas Melton). Children:

1. Benton Burris Melton

2. Ada Melton (Husband: Adolphus Frazier)

3. Fleta Melton

4. Serena Melton

5. Effie Marian Melton (Husband: Albert Bunyan Raborn). Children:

a. Percy Melton Raborn (Wife: Lucille Denham)

b. Helen Eloise Raborn

c. Addie Mae Raborn (Husband: Clifton D. Turner). Children:

(1). Elbert Ray Turner

(2). Beverly Turner

(3). Glynn Turner

(4). Harold Turner

(5). Christine Turner

(6). Gloria Mae Turner

(7). Catherine Turner

(8). Janelle Turner

d. Thomas Bunyan Raborn (Wife: Verna Achord).
Children:
  (1). Thomas Ronald Raborn
  (2). Kenneth Dale Raborn
  (3). Nelda Sue Raborn
e. Fleta Estelle Raborn (Husband: Francis I. Whiting)

VII. Ann Burris (First Husband: Phillip Raiford). Children:

A. Phillip Raiford, Jr.

Ann Burris (Second Husband: Edmund Smith). Children:

B. William Burris Smith (First Wife: Peninna Gillespie).
Children:
  1. Georgia Ann Smith (Husband: Dr. William Benjamin Martin). Children:
    a. Nina Martin (Husband: Dr. Cecil Dickerson). Children:
      (1). Dr. Cecil Dickerson, Jr.
      (2). Dr. Martin Dickerson
    b. Monroe Martin
  2. Eugenia Smith (Husband: Robert Moore)
  William Burris Smith (Second Wife: Hattie Ingraham Boyer). Children:
  3. William Burris Smith, Jr. (First Wife: Ione (Onie) Stubblefield). Children:
    a. William Burris Smith III
    b. Robert Stubblefield Smith
    William Burris Smith, Jr. (Second Wife: Elvira ....). Children:
    c. Francis Smith
    d. James P. Smith
    e. Paul F. Smith
    f. David M. Smith
    g. Marvin M. Smith
    h. ....
    i. ....
    j. ....
  4. Samuel Pinkney Smith
  5. Homer Smith

C. James Harley Smith (Wife: Frances Ann Stubblefield).
Children:
  1. Edmund Harley Smith (Wife: Mabel Barker). Children:

a. Julia Smith (Husband: Pembroke Stubblefield)

2. James David Smith (Wife: Mabelle Moseley). Children:
   a. Mabelle Moseley Smith (Husband: William Garrard). Children:
      (1). William Garrard, Jr.
      (2). James Garrard
      (3). Mabelle Garrard
      (4). Robert Garrard
      (5). Mary Jane Garrard
   b. George Kinnebrew Smith (Wife: Ella Faison). Children:
      (1). Elinor Smith
      (2). Mabelle Smith
      (3). George Smith
      (4). Richard Smith
      (5). Jack Smith
      (6). Garrard Smith
   c. Rebecca Smith (Husband: James Moseley Hairston). Children:
      (1). Katherine Hairston
      (2). James Moseley Hairston, Jr.
   d. Ann Smith (Husband: Earnest H. Tanner)
   e. Marion Smith (Husband: Dr. James Rives). Children:
      (1). ....
3. Addison Burris Smith (First Wife: Beatrice Holt). Children:
   a. Mary Augusta Smith (Husband: Simon Peter Stubblefield). Children:
      (1). Mary Elizabeth Stubblefield
      (2). Gloria Stubblefield
      (3). Ann Augusta Stubblefield
   b. Cromwell Orrick Smith (Wife: Edith Scott). Children:
      (1). Cromwell Orrick Smith, Jr.
      (2). Cromwell Scott Smith
      (3). Addison Burris Smith III
   Addison Burris Smith (Second Wife: Ada Love.) Children:
   e. DeWitt Love Smith

Addison Burris Smith (Third Wife: Mamie Pollock). Children:

d. Addison Burris Smith, Jr.

e. Frances Pollock Smith (Husband: Jeff Collins). Children:
   (1). Frances Ann Collins
   (2). Jeff Collins, Jr.

f. Allen Harley Smith (Wife: Mary Elizabeth Mitchell). Children:
   (1). Harley Smith
   (2). Ann Smith
   (3). Petrie Smith

4. Mary Elizabeth Smith
5. Raiford Smith

D. George Kinnebrew Smith (Wife: Augusta Heathman). Children:

1. Minnie Heathman Smith (Husband: Warner J. Holt). Children:
   a. Addison Heathman Holt
   b. Warner J. Holt, Jr. (Wife: Vivian Settlemyre). Children:
      (1). Richard Wayne Holt
      (2). Dianne Julene Holt

2. Faison Heathman Smith (Wife: Jessye Gooch). Children:
   a. George Kinnebrew Smith (Wife: Clendenning Baird). Children:
      (1). Catchings Baird Smith
      (2). George Smith
      (3). Richard Smith
   b. Faison Heathman Smith, Jr. (Wife: Elizabeth McKnight). Children:
      (1). Faison Heathman Smith III
      (2). Robin Smith
   c. Jessye Smith (Husband: Gordon Grantham). Children:
      (1). Jessye Grantham
      (2). . . . . (a daughter)
      (3). . . . . (a daughter)

3. James Martin Smith (Wife: Anne Gourley Lombard-Fowlkes). Children:

a. Amy Smith (Husband: Jerry Porter, Jr.). Children:
(1). ....
(2). ....
b. Martin Robert Smith (Wife: Mary Glenn Yeager)
c. Edmund Smith

4. Mabelle Augusta Smith (Husband: Herman Glenn). Children:

a. Lillian Glenn (Husband: Robert Payne). Children:
(1). Robert Glenn Payne
b. Mary Elizabeth Glenn (Husband: William C. Cox). Children:
(1). Glenn Cox

5. Edmund Burrage Smith (Wife: Winnie Vance). Children:

a. Martha Vance Smith (Husband: Capt. Richard Denman Crow)

E. Samuel Pinkney Smith
F. Seaborn Smith
G. Ann Smith (First Husband: John Waites)

Ann Smith (Second Husband: George W. Faison). Children:

1. Walter Faison
2. Edmund Faison (Wife: Gertrude Hardy). Children:

a. Ann Elizabeth Faison (Husband: Jack Gordon). Children:

(1). Faison Gordon (a girl)
b. Edmund Gertrude Faison

3. James Faison
4. Adelaide Faison (Husband: .... McMahon). Children:
a. Edward McMahon

5. William Murff Faison (Wife: Janie Birdsong). Children:
a. William Faison
b. Janie Faison (Husband: Clayton Tolar)

VIII. George Nelson Burris (Wife: Elizabeth Thompson). Children:

A. Mary Ann Catherine Burris (Husband: Dr. William Jones). Children:
1. Alice Elizabeth Jones

2. Seaborn Tecumseh Jones (Wife: Nancy Josephine Lea). Children:
   a. Catherine Lea (Katie) Jones (Husband: William Franklin Holmes). Children:
      (1). Katie Nell Holmes (adopted) (Husband: T. J. Ogletree). Children:
         (a). William Clay Ogletree
         (b). Linda Ogletree
         (c). Brenda Ogletree
   b. Alice Gertrude Jones (Husband: Henry Clay Fuller). Children:
      (1). Deyette Fuller
      (2). Bryan Fuller
      (3). Brand Fuller
      (4). Henry Clay Fuller, Jr.
      (5.) Seaborn Fuller
      (6). Townsend Fuller
      (7). Katie Lea Fuller
   c. Emily Ella (Nell) Jones (Husband: Thomas J. Donahue). Children:
      (1). Catherine Donahue (Husband: Dewitt Estess). Children:
         (a). Emily Estess
         (b). Dewitta Estess
         (c). Nell Estess
         (d). .... (daughter)
      (2). Thomas J. Donahue, Jr.
   d. Leonidas Ludwell Jones (Wife: Hattie Nix). Children:
      (1). Harry Jones
      (2). Leonidas Ludwell Jones, Jr.
   e. Harry Aldrich Jones (Wife: Annie Nix). Children:
      (1). Louise Jones
      (2). Harry Aldrich Jones, Jr.
   f. James Monroe Jones (Wife: Bertha Rosa Ott)*
   g. Josephine Viola Jones (First Husband: Clyde Wesley Brumfield)
      Josephine Viola Jones (Second Husband: David White). Children:
      (1). .... (an adopted daughter)

---

*Interfamily marriage. Children listed under wife.

h. William Reed Jones

3. Mary Emily Jones (Husband: Thomas Charles Ott). Children:

    a. Charles Monroe Ott (Wife: Gertrude McMillan). Children:

        (1). Ronald Howard Ott (Wife: Irene Hunt). Children:

            (a). William Ott

            (b). James Ott

            (c). Peggy Sue Ott

        (2). Mildred Bertha Ott (Husband: William W. Brown). Children:

            (a). Mildred Louise Brown

            (b). William W. Brown, Jr.

        (3). Clifford Davis Ott (Wife: Hortense Harrell). Children:

            (a). Carol Jean Ott

            (b). William Ott

            (c). Clifford Davis Ott, Jr.

            (d). Wendell H. Ott

            (e). Steve Edward Ott

            (f). Charles Philip Ott

            (g). Linda Ann Ott

    b. Thomas Edward Ott (Wife: Ella Shattuck). Children:

        (1). Clara Belle Ott (Husband: Paul Zeigler). Children:

            (a). Eleanor Zeigler

            (b). Paul Zeigler, Jr.

            (c). Edward Zeigler

        (2). Paul Shattuck Ott

    c. William Jones Ott (Wife: Margaret Ott). Children:

        (1). Marguerite Ott (Husband: Wallace Forshag)

        (2). Dr. Azel Justin Ott (Wife: Frances Phipps). Children:

            (a). Helen Judith Ott

            (b). Mary Frances Ott

        (3). Dr. William Jones Ott, Jr. (Wife: Mary Carlton). Children:

            (a). Carol Ott (adopted)

(4). Ruby Mae Ott (Husband: Joe Stubbs). Children:
- (a). Susan Little Stubbs
- (b). A. J. Stubbs, Jr.

(5). Thomas Truett Ott (Wife: Anita Williamson). Children:
- (a). Sandra Ott
- (b). Thomas Truett Ott, Jr.

d. Annie Eleanor Ott (Husband: J. L. Slay). Children:

(1). Mary Catherine Slay (Husband: C. S. Sykes). Children:
- (a). Margaret Ann Sykes
- (b). John Ott Sykes

e. Carrie Pearl Ott

f. Bertha Rosa Ott (Husband: James Monroe Jones). Children:

(1). Hettie Ott Jones (Husband: Marvin Zipp). Children:
- (a). Eric Stoll Zipp

(2). Landon Lea Jones (Wife: Mary Edna Jones). Children:
- (a). Landon Booth Jones

(3). William Jones (Wife: Alice Graham)

g. Seaborn Grover Ott

h. Harry Leon Ott (Wife: Mabel DeBruhl). Children:
(1). Polly Ott (Husband: Sam Magee)

(2). Pearl Ernestine Ott (Husband: Robert Raborn). Children:
- (a). Robert Raborn, Jr.
- (b). Gene Ott Raborn

(3). Harry Leon Ott, Jr.

(4). Mary Thomas Ott

B. Salina Jane Burris (Husband: Thad Gray). Children:
1. Mary Elizabeth Gray (Husband: Daniel W. Dooley). Children:
- a. Elizabeth Dooley (Husband: J. N. Butler)
- b. John Dooley
- c. Daniel Dooley
- d. Annie Dooley

2. Sherrod Nelson Gray

3. Mijamon Lafayette (Max) Gray (Wife: ....
White)
4. Lelia Salina Gray (Husband: Frank Cook)
5. Minnie Gray (Husband: John Price)
6. Thomas Gray (Wife: Anna Smith)
7. Ary Gray (Husband: Robert Harper)
8. Burris Gray (Wife: Laura Hobbs)

C. Marshall Enos Burris (Wife: Malena Wilson). Children:
1. Minnie Burris (Husband: Rev. Wm. K. Anderson). Children:
   a. Lucy Anderson
2. Lucy Ora Burris (Husband: Thos. M. Honea). Children:
   a. Pearla Lutishia Honea (Husband: Frank E. Stocklin)
   b. Enos Honea (Wife: Myrtis McDaniel). Children:
      (1). Morris E. Honea (Wife: Mary Cutrer). Children:
         (a). James Shelton Honea
         (b). Thomas Edward Honea
         (c). Harold Clifton Honea
         (d). Morris E. Honea, Jr.
         (e). George Randolph Honea
         (f). Michael McDaniel Honea
         (g). Jack Hughes Honea
      (2). Wilma Honea (Husband: Frank Martin). Children:
         (a). Frank Martin, Jr.
         (b). Wilma Louise Martin
      (3). James Honea (Wife: Marie Schwing). Children:
         (a). Patty Lou Honea
      (4). Ernestine Honea (Husband: Hollis Griffin). Children:
         (a). Jerry Wayne Griffin
         (b). Donald George Griffin
      (5). Paul Honea
   c. Monette Minnie Honea (Husband: Jewell Anderson). Children:
      (1). Jewell Anderson, Jr. (Wife: Louise Brumfield)

58

(2). Mamie Anderson (Husband: Henry L. Ross). Children:

(a). John Lamar Ross

(b). Jimmie Ross

(3). Thomas H. Anderson

(4). Virginia Anderson (Husband: James Cook)

(5). Wilma Frank Anderson (Husband: Earl Scott). Children:

(a). Sandra K. Scott

(6). Betty Jean Anderson (Husband: Bernard Cook). Children:

(a). A. Darrel Cook

d. Lelia Honea (Husband: Lonnie Anderson). Children:

(1). Johnnie Mozelle Anderson (Husband: Earl McKnight). Children:

(a). Beverly Lou McKnight

(b). Dicky Lynn McKnight

(2). Pearl Louise Anderson

(3). George Leon Anderson (Wife: Elaine Powell). Children:

(a). George Wesley Anderson

(b). Gary Winston Anderson

(c). Charlotte Anderson

(d). James Oliver Anderson

(4). W. L. Anderson, Jr. (Wife: Laverne Thomas). Children:

(a). Billy Joe Anderson

(b). Martha Lynn Anderson

(5). .... (a son)

(6). Geraldine Anderson (Husband: Sidney Blailock). Children:

(a). Michael Blailock

(b). Teresa Blailock

e. Marshall Leslie Honea (Wife: Elma Barron). Children:

(1). Leroy Honea

(2). Leslie Moore Honea

f. Ruth Honea (Husband: Wiley Williams). Children:

(1). Floyd Williams (Wife: Teresa Brown). Children:

        (a). Ava Lou Williams

        (b). Jettie Ruth Williams

        (c). Mary Ann Williams

        (d). Floyd Lamar Williams

        (e). Martha Sue Williams

    (2). Julia Mae Williams

    (3). Laurence Williams (Wife: Margie Westbrook)

    (4). Lynelle Williams (Husband: Maurice McDaniel)

    (5). Charles Williams

g. Thomas Leon Honea (Wife: Lillian Smith). Children:

    (1). Ruby Mae Honea (Husband: Hamp Lee). Children:

        (a). Patricia Lee

    (2). John Norman Honea

    (3). Phyllis Honea

3. Pearla Nelson Burris (Husband: John Wolf). Children:

a. Madeline Wolf (Husband: Kirby Payne). Children:

    (1). Joe Frank Payne

    (2). John Nelson Payne

    (3). Bee Payne

    (4). Mary Ellen Payne

    (5). Henry Payne (a girl)

    (6). Hilda Mae Payne

    (7). Eva Payne

    (8). Jeanette Payne

b. Grace Wolf

c. Minnie Wolf

d. Hilton Wolf

e. Pearla Mae Wolf

4. George Enos Burris (Wife: Hattie Barron). Children:

a. Velma A. Burris (Husband: Vernon Y. Felder, Sr.)

b. Mable L. Burris (Husband: Roy Newman). Children:

    (1). Flora Nell Newman (Husband: Kenneth Gordon)

    (2). Ruby Joyce Newman (Husband: John Davis Tynes). Children:

        (a). Johnie Lee Tynes

        (b). David Michael Tynes

     (3). Paul Newman

  c. Omer E. Burris (Wife: Hilda Bostick). Children:

     (1). Edwin E. Burris (Wife: Johanna McDaniel)

     (2). Barbara Burris (Husband: Wyman Raborn). Children:

        (a). Sylvia Dianne Raborn

        (b). Mary Camille Raborn

  d. Etta Mae Burris

  e. Agnes R. Burris (Husband: M. T. Causey)

  f. Georgie P. Burris (Husband: Louis Wells). Children:

     (1). Janice Wells

     (2). Raymond Wells

  g. Marshall Randolph Burris (Wife: Myrtis Velma Wall). Children:

     (1). Thomas Burris

  h. Juanita Burris (Husband: Dallas Stevenson). Children:

     (1). James Stevenson

  i. Raiford G. Burris (Wife: Wanza Rimes). Children:

     (1). Raiford G. Burris, Jr.

     (2). George Arthur Burris

5. Ada Burris (Husband: Thos. Pray)

D. Harriett Malinda (Minnie) Burris

E. Thomas J. Burris

F. William Alexander Burris (Wife: Nora Marsalis)

G. Ivy J. L. Burris

H. Amanda Eunice Burris (Husband: J. Merritt Taylor). Children:

1. Cassie Lou Taylor

2. Louie Taylor

I. Jaheel Jasper (Dock) Burris (Wife: Julia Marsalis). Children:

1. Stella Burris

2. Nora Burris

3. Bessie Burris

4. Virgie Burris

5. Claude Burris

6. George Burris

J. Emily A. Burris (Husband: William J. (Bill) Taylor). Children:

    1. Adella May Taylor (Husband: Dave T. Smith). Children:

        a. Mamie Smith

        b. Thomas Lee Smith

    2. Lyda Lou Taylor

K. Almine Rosetta Burris (Abbie) (Husband: Rev. Wilborn Monroe Thompson). Children:

    1. Winchester Monroe Thompson

    2. Leslie Lea Thompson (Wife: Lucy D. Creighton). Children:

        a. Wilborn Monroe Thompson

        b. Ida Pearl Thompson (Husband: . . . .)

    3. Ivy Finch Thompson

    4. Minnie Eudora Thompson

    5. Bessie Ida Thompson (Husband: George Ashford)

    6. Augustus Allen Thompson

L. Nancy L. Burris

M. George Nelson Burris, Jr.

IX. Enos Burris

X. Hampton Burris (First Wife: Mary (Polly) Magee). Children:

A. Mary Elizabeth Burris (Husband: John Gatlin). Children:

    1. Mary Elizabeth Gatlin (Husband: W. F. Ellzey). Children:

        a. Myrtis Ellzey (Husband: Willie J. F. Fortenberry). Children:

           (1). Eric Fortenberry (Wife: Leone Bardwell). Children:

               (a). Jimmie Fortenberry

               (b). Jerry Fortenberry

               (c). Glyn Fortenberry

               (d). Betty Sue Fortenberry

               (e). Charles Fortenberry

           (2). Lucille Fortenberry

           (3). Jackson V. Fortenberry (Husband: Clarence Bennett). Children:

               (a). Anita Bennett

           (4). Mildred Fortenberry (Husband: Johnnie Brumfield). Children:

(a). Harold Edwin Brumfield

(5). William Harold Fortenberry (Wife: Selma Bennett). Children:

(a). Joe Kenneth Fortenberry

b. Edgar John Ellzey (First Wife: Bertha Tullos). Children:

(1). Evelyn Devoyx Ellzey

(2). La Verne Ellzey (Wife: Belle Milner). Children:

(a). Barbara Ellzey

(b). John Ellzey

Edgar John Ellzey (Second Wife: Lorene Tullos). Children:

(3). Audimese Ellzey

(4). Betty Gene Ellzey

c. Eric Wyatt Ellzey

d. Rodger T. Ellzey (First Wife: Lottie Brumfield). Children:

(1). Bertile Ellzey (Husband: Earl Fortenberry). Children:

(a). Glynn Fortenberry

(b). Bobby Earl Fortenberry

(2). Rodger T. Ellzey, Jr. (Wife: Edith Breland). Children:

(a). Patricia Ann Ellzey

(b). Betty Lou Ellzey

(c). Nancy Ellzey

(3). Wayland Ellzey (Wife: Gwin Brumfield). Children:

(a). Susan Ellzey

(b). Wayland Alan Ellzey

(4). Cecil Ellzey (Wife: Margie Nell Brumfield)

(5). Gertrude Ellzey (Husband: Ford McKenny). Children:

(a). Billy McKenny

(b). Barbara Ellen McKenny

(c). Bobby Bert McKenny

(6). Mary Ellen Ellzey (Husband: James Carlise). Children:

(a). ....

(7). Thomas Ellzey

(8). Charles Lindy Ellzey

Rodger T. Ellzey (Second Wife: Monie Branch)

e. Grady Ellzey (Wife: Bertha Fortenberry). Children:

  (1). Wesley Ellzey (Wife: Elaine Johnson). Children:
    (a). Michael Wesley Ellzey
    (b). Randall Clyde Ellzey
  (2). Odean Ellzey (Husband: Lamar Simmons). Children:
    (a). Gayle Dean Simmons
    (b). Jimmie Lamar Simmons
  (3). Carroll Ellzey (Husband: June Prescott). Children:
    (a). Sherra Ann Ellzey
    (b). Daniel James Ellzey
  (4). Ellen Ellzey (Husband: James McDaniel). Children:
    (a). James Conred McDaniel

f. Smithy Vernon Ellzey (First Wife: Rose Wooster). Children:

  (1). Vernon Ellzey
  (2). Evelyn Sue Ellzey

Smithy Vernon Ellzey (Second Wife: Margeria Ferris). Children:

  (3). Yvonne Ellzey
  (4). Nancy Lee Ellzey
  (5). Margeria Ann Ellzey

g. Lois Ellzey (Husband: Laney L. Pope). Children:

  (1). Mary Eleanor Pope (Husband: Brown Simmons). Children:
    (a). Sherra Simmons
    (b). Joyce Simmons
    (c). Bill Simmons
    (d). Mavis Simmons
  (2). Zelma Pope (Husband: Lloyd Roberts). Children:
    (a). Tilford Lane Roberts
    (b). Jimmie Roberts
    (c). John Roberts

(3). Nelson Winston Pope (Wife: Sybil McElveen).
Children:
   (a). . . . . (a daughter)
   (b). Sammy Nelson Pope
(4). Hansford Pope (Wife: Sadie Rose Robinson).
Children:
   (a). Sylvia Jo Pope
(5). Everett Pope
(6). Wilda Pope (Husband: Eugene Rhodes). Children:
   (a). Michael Eugene Rhodes
(7). Clayton Pope
(8). Maxine Pope
  h. Mamie Eudine Ellzey (Husband: Joe Minton).
Children:
(1). Joseph Eugene Minton (Wife: Lucille Bruner).
Children:
   (a). Jimmie Minton
   (b). Edwin Minton
(2). Bernell Minton (Husband: Ralph Conerly).
Children:
   (a). Mary Elizabeth Conerly
   (b). Ralph Conerly, Jr.
(3). Charles Minton
(4). Marlan Clyde Minton
  i. William Clyde Ellzey (Wife: Ruth Miller). Children:
(1). Marilyn Ellzey
(2). Carol Lee Ellzey
(3). Sandra Ellzey
2. Charles (Sonny) Gatlin
B. John Addison Burris (Wife: Laura Toler). Children:
1. Lois Saton Burris
2. Mary Blanche Burris
3. Willie Burris (Wife: Hattie Hewitt). Children:
  a. Lillie Belle Burris
  b. Ollie Burris (Husband: Vertram C. Westbrook).
Children:
(1). Lillie Belle Westbrook (Husband: George Temple). Children:
   (a). Mary Olive Temple

(2). Olga Addie Westbrook (Husband: Roy Temple). Children:
    (a). L. D. Temple
    (b). Annie Lethia Temple
    (c). Addie Laura Temple
    (d). Mavis Temple
    (e). Grace Temple
(3). Rema Westbrook
(4). Vertram C. Westbrook, Jr. (Wife: **Eurlene Steele**). Children:
    (a). Dianne Westbrook
(5). Orien Westbrook
(6). Eunice Westbrook
(7). R. E. Westbrook
(8). Nellie Rae Westbrook (Husband: James Trueman Hodge). Children:
    (a). Alice Dell Hodge
(9). Hattie Anita Westbrook (Husband: Fosby Laird). Children:
    (a). Glynn Laird
    (b). Willie V. Laird
    (c). Phillip W. Laird
    (d). Hilda Anita Laird
    (e). Joe Estess Laird

c. Thelma Burris (Husband: Corbet Edward Ratcliff). Children:
(1). Emily Ratcliff (Husband: J. C. Kersten). Children:
    (a). Jimmy Kersten
(2). William Benjamin Ratcliff (Wife: Zella Smith). Children:
    (a). Peggy Ratcliff
    (b). William Edward Ratcliff
(3). Ned Ratcliff (Wife: Neva Stockhouse). Children:
    (a). James Arthur Ratcliff
(4). Corbet Edward Ratcliff, Jr.
(5). Joseph Ratcliff
(6). Paul Clyde Ratcliff

d. Maureen Burris
e. Annie Hewitt Burris

4. Lucius Toler Burris (Wife: Willie Hudson Gunby). Children:
   a. Jeannette Laura Burris (Husband: John Buren Nobles). Children:
      (1). Wilhelmina Rebecca Nobles
   b. Hubert Marvin Burris (Wife: Eleanor James). Children:
      (1). Marvin Eugene Burris
      (2). Lilliace Ann Burris
   c. Eileen Errol Burris (Husband: Leland Lyle Stokes). Children:
      (1). Leland Lyle Stokes, Jr.
      (2). James Lucius Stokes
      (3). Richard Wayne Stokes
   d. Lucius Harold Burris (Wife: Adelyn Lavender). Children:
      (1). Betty Ann Burris
      (2). Gloria Burris
      (3). Lucius Harold Burris, Jr.
   e. Dorothy Pearl Burris (Husband: Fred Dixon Robertson). Children:
      (1). Fred Dixon Robertson, Jr.
      (2). William Lucius Robertson
      (3). James Lee Burris
   f. Lionel Toler Burris (Wife: Lillian Hendrix). Children:
      (1). Sherry Lynn Burris (adopted)
5. Lillie Mae Burris (Husband: William Benjamin Dickerson). Children:
   a. Hilton Burris Dickerson (Wife: Margaret Law). Children:
      (1). Beverly Jean Dickerson
      (2). Hilton Burris Dickerson, Jr.
   b. Henry Addison Dickerson (Wife: Margaret Blanche Leap). Children:
      (1). Margaret Scott Dickerson
      (2). Jane Addison Dickerson
   c. Willie Mae Dickerson (Husband: Fant Ewing Hulsey). Children:
      (1). Mikell Patricia Hulsey
      (2). Fant Ewing Hulsey, Jr.

d. Benjamin Howard Dickerson (Wife: Elizabeth Hassett). Children:
  (1). Jeffrey Hilton Dickerson
  (2). Janet Susan Dickerson
e. Frank C. Dickerson (Wife: Doris Roberts). Children:
  (1). Judith Lynn Dickerson
6. Jacob Oscar Burris (First Wife: Stella Patterson). Children:
  a. .... (a son)
  b. Annie Idelle Burris (Husband: E. M. Newman). Children:
    (1). James Newman (Wife: Sammie Harris). Children:
      (a). Terry Lee Newman
    (2). Tommie Newman
  c. James Oscar Burris (Wife: Anne Ruth King). Children:
    (1). Louise Ann Burris
    (2). James Oscar Burris, Jr.
  d. Fay Avanelle Burris (Husband: Burton Coulter). Children:
    (1). Frances Ann Coulter
  e. Hugh Benton Burris (Wife: Margaret Catherine Mulcay). Children:
    (1). Marsha Lynn Burris
    (2). Hugh Benton Burris, Jr.
    (3). Sue Ellen Burris
  f. Thomas Donald Burris (Wife: Miriam Ott)
  Jacob Oscar Burris (Second Wife: Ethel Wilkinson-Burris)
7. Joe A. Burris (Wife: Madge Hall). Children:
  a. Burmah Burris
  b. Barbara Burris (Husband: Jack Ritchey). Children:
    (1). Jackie Ritchey, Jr.
    (2). Joe Ritchey
    (3). Jimmie Ritchey
    (4). Jerry Ritchey
  c. Joe A. Burris, Jr. (Wife: Katherine Rogers). Children:
    (1). Martha Madge Burris

d. Malcolm Burris (Wife: Sarah Prichard)

e. Mary Burris (Husband: Albert Green). Children:

(1). Albert Green, Jr.

(2). Burmah Kay Green

8. Hugh Chilson Burris (Wife: Edna Earle Gordon). Children:

a. Gordon Douglas Burris (Wife: Mary Scavelli). Children:

(1). Gordon John Burris

b. Anna Loyd Burris (Husband: Floyd C. Watts). Children:

(1). Anna Llewelynn Watts

c. Betty Claire Burris (Husband: Daniel Orthillo Lewman)

9. Bryant Eugene Burris (First Wife: Retha Branch). Children:

a. Wilda Burris

b. Hilda Burris (Husband: Alfred Bogen, Jr.). Children:

(1). Alfred Bogen, III

(2). Vesta Ann Bogen

Bryant Eugene Burris (Second Wife: Eva Tynes)

10. Laura Estella Burris (Husband: Fenton Lee Kenna). Children:

a. William Burris Kenna (Wife: Joyce Terrell)

b. Miriam Evelyn Kenna (Husband: Gordon Covington, Jr.)

c. Fenton Lee Kenna, Jr.

11. Gertrude Burris (Husband: Willie J. Branch)

12. John Hampton Burris (Wife: Fannie Alford). Children:

a. Hazel Juanita Burris (Husband: George M. Cain). Children:

(1). Patricia Kirk Cain

(2). George Douglas Cain

b. Julius Addison Burris

c. Wilton Enoch Burris

13. James M. Burris

C. William Louis Burris

D. Jacob Fleet Burris (First Wife: Luretta Swearingen)

Jacob Fleet Burris (Second Wife: Amazon Cain). Children:

1. Mollie E. Burris (Husband: Cero Jones). Children:
   a. Eslie Jones
   b. Lillian Lozaine Jones (Husband: Dewitt Talmadge Foster). Children:
      (1). Ray Louie Foster (Wife: Gladys Lucille Myers). Children:
         (a). Edwin Earl Foster
         (b). Charles Ray Foster
         (c). Nelda Kay Foster
      (2). William Grady Foster (Wife: Lois Thelma Boyd)
      (3). Lucy Mae Foster
      (4). John Talmadge Foster (Wife: Ellen Erwin). Children:
         (a). John Talmadge Foster, Jr.
         (b). Jerry Lynden Foster
      (5). Lillian Emily Foster
      (6). Clifton Cero Foster (Wife: Margaret Fern Gunby). Children:
         (a). Larry Dana Foster
      (7). Marion Dewitt Foster
      (8). Lois Frances Foster
   c. Emma Julia Jones (Husband: Frank A. Williams). Children:
      (1). Albert Luther Williams (First Wife: Anna Mae Starr). Children:
         (a). Linda Yvonne Williams
         (b). .... (a son)
         Albert Luther Williams (Second Wife: Elizabeth Ruth Grigsby). Children:
         (c). Jack Melvin Williams
      (2). Frank Eslie Williams (Wife: Edna Leoda Roth). Children:
         (a). Frank Eslie Williams, Jr.
         (b). Albert Louis Williams
         (c). Ronald Charles Williams
         (d). Richard Earl Williams
      (3). Fannie Lee Williams

(4). Bryant Jefferson Williams (Wife: Alma Bell George). Children:

    (a). John Dempsey Williams

    (b). Bryant Jefferson Williams, Jr.

(5). Mary Emily Williams (Husband: Louis D. Cunningham).

(6). Frances Ann Williams

(7). Linda Sue Williams

d. John Jones

2. Hardy H. Burris

3. Frank Horace Burris (Wife: Inez Jones). Children:

    a. Velma Lucille Burris (Husband: Clarence Arnold)

    b. Frank Rupert Burris (Wife: Fay Brandon). Children:

        (1). Paul Brandon Burris

    c. Mabel Ivenora Burris

    d. Eugene Quitman Burris (Wife: Lola Jordan). Children:

        (1). Eugene Quitman Burris, Jr.

        (2). Mary Fay Burris

        (3). Lola Annette Burris

    e. Jacob Hampton Burris (Wife: Jimmie Orenne Mathews). Children:

        (1). Russell Winford Burris

        (2). Relda Ann Burris

4. Sarah Alice Burris (Husband: Virgil Chisholm). Children:

    a. William Jewel Chisholm

5. Luretta E. Burris

6. Amazon Rebecca Burris (First Husband: Gus Cotton). Children:

    a. Jacob Cotton

    b. Asa Cotton

    c. Rayford Cotton

Amazon Rebecca Burris (Second Husband: .... Poole)

7. William A. Burris (Wife: Lillie Cotton). Children:

    a. Hardy Burris (Wife: Nova Smith). Children:

        (1). Nelda Jean Burris

        (2). Toba Faye Burris

    b. Claude Burris (Wife: Pauline McManus). Children:

      (1). Aaron James Burris

  c. Lizzie Burris (Husband: C. C. Martin). Children:

      (1). Leroy Martin (Wife: Helen Cupit)

      (2). Earl Martin

  d. Leon Burris (Wife: Gladys Arnold). Children:

      (1). Bobbie Nell Burris

      (2). Carolyn Joyce Burris

      (3). Robert Leon Burris

  e. Ammie Lottie Burris (Husband: Thomas Eli Cupit). Children:

      (1). Claudell Cupit

      (2). Clayton Eli Cupit

      (3). Doris Glen Cupit

      (4). W. L. Cupit

      (5). Nina Dale Cupit

  f. Jim Burris (Wife: Louise McGehee). Children:

      (1). Jimmie Burris

  g. Laura Alyce Burris (Husband: Warren Aaron Porter). Children:

      (1). Jo Nita Porter

      (2). Tama Rea Porter

      (3). Rodney Earl Porter

      (4). LaVelle Porter

      (5). Patsy Ella Porter

      (6). Warren Aaron Porter, Jr.

  h. Nolan Burris (Wife: DeLores Pevey). Children:

      (1). Nolan Dee Burris

      (2). Kenney Bee Burris

      (3). Bruce Darryl Burris

  i. John Burris (Wife: Golda Mae Smith). Children:

      (1). Linda Sue Burris

8. Laura Lenorah Burris (Husband: Clem Mullins). Children:

  a. William Prentiss Mullins (Wife: Pearl Nesbit). Children:

      (1). Carolyn E. Mullins

      (2). William Prentiss Mullins, Jr.

  b. Eddie Fleet Mullins (First Wife: Ruby Laird). Children:

      (1). Analo Mullins (Husband: Merle Scott). Children:

(a). Merle Scott, Jr.

(b). Sue Scott

(2). Gus Mullins

Eddie Fleet Mullins (Second Wife: Retha Ann Freeman). Children:

(3). La Nell Mullins

(4). Eddie Glenn Mullins

c. Ray Mullins (Wife: Adee Almeda Lewis). Children:

(1). Billie Ray Mullins

d. Carroll Mullins

e. Lola Lenorah Mullins (Husband: Claude Quitman Bowlin). Children:

(1). Barbara Ann Bowlin

(2). Claude Quitman Bowlin, Jr.

(3). Clement Wiley Bowlin

f. Clement Leroy Mullins (Wife: Willie Mae Wallace). Children:

(1). Clement Leroy Mullins, Jr.

(2). Danny Wallace Mullins

(3). Harry Miller Mullens

g. Percy Hubert Mullins

h. Rita Victoria Mullins (Husband: Raleigh Henley). Children:

(1). Raleigh Henley, Jr.

(2). Richard Paul Henley

9. Dempsey Eddie Burris (Wife: Louvinia Elizabeth Coward). Children:

a. Hazel Edith Burris

b. William Linton Burris (Wife: Josie Mae Henderson). Children:

(1). William Dempsey Burris

(2). Mary Frances Burris

(3). Joy Charldene Burris

c. Jacob Fleet Burris III

d. John Dempsey Burris (Wife: Fern Lewis). Children:

(1). Louvinia Odessa Burris

(2). Jacqueline Burris

e. James Ford Burris (Wife: Mary Ileen Wells). Children:

(1). Juanita Faye Burris

(2). Pollard Ford Burris

   f. Aaron Henderson Burris (Wife: Maidee Dillon). Children:

(1). Linda Dianne Burris

   g. Hugh Vance Burris (Wife: Flora Mae Hambright). Children:

(1). Dew Wayne Burris

10. Luna Hall Burris (Husband: Holmes Smith). Children:

   a. Joseph Glen Smith (Wife: Margaret Baudauf). Children:

(1). Glenda Kay Smith

   b. Lennie Lenora Smith (Husband: Paul J. Freeman)

   c. Sarah Dixie Smith (Husband: Guy Richard Lovely). Children:

(1). Guy Richard Lovely, Jr.

   d. Ruby Lorelle Smith (Husband: Robert Rodney LeBlanc). Children:

(1). Peggy Lynn LeBlanc

11. Lula Ball Burris (Husband: G. W. Lewis)

12. Jacob Fleet Burris, Jr. (Wife: Lizzie Ratcliff). Children:

   a. Rettie Burris (Husband: Willie Watson)

   b. Nellie Burris (Husband: Meredith Corban). Children:

(1). Mary Elizabeth Corban

   c. Addison Burris

   d. Albia Burris (Wife: Monte Allred). Children:

(1). William Earl Burris

(2). Margie Louine Burris

(3). James Randel Burris

   e. Andrew Burris (Wife: Merilee Crumbly). Children:

(1). Andrew David Burris

13. Ruby Ray Burris (Husband: William Henderson Coward). Children:

   a. . . . .

   b. Laurine Elmo Coward (Husband: Elmo McGehee). Children:

(1). Relda Joyce McGehee

(2). Wilda McGehee

(3). Margie Ray McGehee

(4). Ward Lynn McGehee

c. Willie Ray Coward (Wife: Edna Smith). Children:
   (1). William Henderson Coward II
   (2). Pollard Ray Coward
   (3). Oscar Coward
   (4). Ellouise Coward
d. Lula Ellen Coward
e. Mavis Burris Coward (Husband: L. G. Young)
f. Norma Vernell Coward

E. Erasmus Theodore Burris (First Wife: Martinetta Gardner). Children:
1. Mabel Burris (Husband: Jeffie J. Branch). Children:
   a. Nettie Branch (Husband: Oscar Ellis Young)
   b. Ruby Branch (Husband: Floyd C. Young). Children:
      (1). Fannie Lynn Young
   c. Joe Lawrence Branch (Wife: Georgina McNair). Children:
      (1). Anne Haughton Branch
   d. Birdie Branch (Husband: William Richard Carroll). Children:
      (1). Kathryn Carroll (Husband: Myron G. Grennell)
      (2). William Richard Carroll, Jr.
      (3). Charles Bryson Carroll
   e. Frank Benjamin Branch (Wife: Lennie Barnett). Children:
      (1). Frank Benjamin Branch, Jr.
   f. Louis Branch
   g. Raiford Earl Branch (Wife: Annie Jo Watson). Children:
      (1). Beverly Branch
      (2). Raiford Earl Branch, Jr.
   h. Callie Branch
   i. Ras Marshall Branch (Wife: Nell Yarborough). Children:
      (1). Katherine Branch
      (2). Betty Branch
2. Louis Burris
Erasmus Theodore Burris (Second Wife: Eliza Toler). Children:

3. Thomas Edgar (Eddie) Burris (Wife: Lula Branch). Children:
   a. Ruth Burris (First Husband: Noel Young). Children:
      (1). Juanita Young (Husband: Roy L. Thompson). Children:
         (a). Marilyn Kay Thompson
      Ruth Burris (Second Husband: Jas. E. Weathersby)
   b. Mildred Burris (Husband: Marvin Avara)
   c. Fred Burris (Wife: Geneva Barron). Children:
      (1). Eddie Milton Burris
      (2). Charles Wilton Burris
   d. Elwin Burris (Wife: Beatrice Strickland)
   e. Annie Mae Burris (Husband: Jewel Williams). Children:
      (1). Tommie Williams (adopted)
      (2). Sylvia Williams (adopted)
   f. Hilburn Burris (Wife: Emily Jane Barlow). Children:
      (1). Roxie Ann Burris
   g. Norman Burris (Harvietta Gonzales Verdia). Children:
      (1). Norman Burris, Jr.
      (2). Susan Burris
      (3). Dickie Burris
   h. Mary Burris (Husband: Winnifred Johnston). Children:
      (1). Mary Ann Johnston
      (2). Kenneth Johnston
   i. Joyce Burris (Husband: Corbett Boyd). Children:
      (1). Mike Boyd
      (2). Thomas Boyd
      (3). Corbett Wayne Boyd
      (4). Nita Jayne Boyd
4. J. Curtis Burris (Wife: Fannie Terry). Children:
   a. Pearl Burris (Husband: Loyd C. Williams). Children:
      (1). James Loyd Williams
      (2). Jon Edward Williams
      (3). Janice Pearl Williams
   b. Lena Burris (Husband: Leo McDaniel). Children:

(1). Carolyn Pearl McDaniel (Husband: Larcus McClelland). Children:

    (a). Larcus James McClelland

(2). June Roselyn McDaniel (Husband: Buford Huffman)

c. Richard Alton Burris (Wife: Claudia Moore). Children:

(1). Richard Alton Burris, Jr. (Wife: Sally Kathryn Moore)

(2). Fannie Lexine Burris

d. Mattie Lexine Burris

5. Mattie Lee Burris

6. George Otis Burris (Wife: Gertrude Wilson). Children:

  a. Melba Gertrude Burris

  b. Mattie Lee Burris

  c. Georgia Lynn Burris (Husband: Joe W. Albritton). Children:

(1). Jimmie Glynn Albritton

7. Hampton Burris (Wife: Violet Moore). Children:

  a. Aline Burris (Husband: Earl Wells). Children:

(1). Bobbie Wells

(2). Billie Wells

(3). Gloria Dean Wells

(4). Paulette Wells

  b. Golda Burris

  c. Bennie Loyd Burris

  d. Dorothy Burris (Husband: Billy Whittington). Children:

(1). Donald Glenn Whittington

(2). Kenneth Michael Whittington

  e. Winton Burris (Wife: Evie Lee Felder-McKnight). Children:

(1). Johnnie Ray Burris

  f. Bobbie Glen Burris

8. Frank Burris (Wife: Georgia Gerald). Children:

  a. Virgie Mae Burris (Husband: Jewell D. Norman). Children:

(1). Morris Edwin Norman

(2). Jewell Eugene Norman

  b. Nellie Jean Burris (Husband: John Edward Newman). Children:

(1). Jeffrey Edwin Newman

   c. Emmett F. Burris (Wife: Kathleen Cullom). Children:

      (1). Richard Gerald Burris

   d. Jessie Maude Burris (Husband: Vaught Lenoir). Children:

      (1). Ruth Elise Lenoir

      (2). Lola Jean Lenoir

9. Morris Lane Burris (Wife: Beulah Branch). Children:

   a. Marion Lane Burris

   b. Elsie Lillian Burris (Husband: W. D. Parker)

   c. Morris Grady Burris (Wife: Nellie Rae Wells). Children:

      (1). Randy Morris Burris

      (2). Charles Windell Burris

      (3). James Larry Burris

   d. Mattie Lucille Burris (Husband: Grover Smith). Children:

      (1). Mary Catherine Smith

      (2). Miriam Lanelle Smith

      (3). Grover Elton Smith

   e. Benjamin Ward Burris (Wife: Doris Marie Scott). Children:

      (1). Terry Lane Burris

      (2). Tommy Gene Burris

      (3). Rita Elizabeth Burris

   f. Marshall Audry Burris (Wife: Betty Jean Greenlee). Children:

      (1). Betty Ann Burris

10. Alton Graves Burris (Wife: Alma Garner). Children:

   a. Loraine Burris (Husband: Forrest Edwards). Children:

      (1). Mary Marguerite Edwards

      (2). Joseph Douglas Edwards

      (3). Thomas James Edwards

   b. Merwin Burris (Wife: Martha Ann Wells)*

   c. Ola Marie Burris

11. Alvie Ray Burris (Wife: Alma Roberts). Children:

   a. Raiford Earl Burris (Wife: Ruth Lurlyne Young). Children:

---

*An interfamily marriage.

(1). Beverly Jean Burris
    b. Melba Joy Burris
F. Sarah Jane Burris (Husband: William Ross Walker). Children:
  1. Seth E. Walker (Wife: Lillie Patrick). Children:
    a. Seth E. Walker, Jr.
    b. Laverne Walker (Husband: M. L. Oliveira)
    c. Ruth Walker (Husband: A. F. McWhortar)
  2. Mary Alice Walker
  3. Hampton E. Walker (Wife: Emma Prescott). Children:
    a. Kenneth Walker (Wife: Ida Garner)
  4. W. Alva Walker (Wife: Rosa Belle Coney). Children:
    a. Mildred Walker
    b. Wilma Walker (Husband: Vince Barr). Children:
      (1). V. W. Barr (Wife: Charlene Ivey). Children:
        (a). Wilson Barr
      (2). Wilma Fay Barr (Husband: Bernon Pounds). Children:
        (a). Brenda Fay Pounds
      (3). Richard Wesley Barr (Wife: Martha Lynn . . . .)
      (4). Rodney Barr
      (5). Barbara Ann Barr
    c. Thelma Walker (Husband: O. S. Reeves). Children:
      (1). Henry Alva Reeves (Wife: Emily Claire Havers)
      (2). Russell Reeves
    d. Mabel Walker
    e. W. Alva Walker, Jr. (Wife: Eula Foil). Children:
      (1). W. Alva Walker III
    f. Maude Walker (Husband: Clark Simmons). Children:
      (1). Clark Simmons, Jr.
    g. Joe Walker (Husband: J. P. Creel). Children:
      (1). Rosa Belle Creel
    h. Sarah Loyd Walker (Husband: B. L. Stacks). Children:
      (1). Nancy Walker Stacks
    i. Bonnie Belle Walker (Husband: Roy Sanders). Children:

(1). Linda Joe Sanders

j. Helen Walker

k. Ruth Walker (Husband: James H. Tucker). Children:

(1). James H. Tucker, Jr.

5. Annie R. Walker (Husband: George Raborn). Children:

a. Hollis Raborn (Wife: Lena Foster). Children:

(1). Hollis Raborn, Jr.

b. Lois Raborn (Husband: Claude W. Holmes). Children:

(1). Virginia Ann Holmes (Husband: John P. Reeves). Children:

(a). John P. Reeves, Jr.

c. James Purser Raborn (Wife: Wilmuth Travis). Children:

(1). Lena Wilmuth Raborn

d. Jessie D. Raborn (Husband: Cecil P. Cook). Children:

(1). Ann Dolores Cook

e. George L. Raborn (Wife: Cecile Ghisaborti). Children:

(1). Carol Ann Raborn

(2). George L. Raborn, Jr.

6. M. Emma Walker (Husband: Sidney Allen). Children:

a. Houston Allen (Wife: Lois Sandifer). Children:

(1). Nelda L. Allen (Husband: John Pavlica). Children:

(a). Janice L. Pavlica

(b). J. Dale Pavlica

(2). Betty S. Allen (Husband: Verbon L. Anthony). Children:

(a). Norman L. Anthony

(3). V. Pansy Allen

(4). W. Wayne Allen

(5). Warren S. Allen

7. .... (a son)

G. James Nelson Burris

Hampton Burris (Second Wife: Mary Turner). Children:

H. Thomas Raiford Burris (Wife: Julia Pate). Children:

1. Julius Alva Burris (Wife: Ethel Wilkinson). Children:

a. Floy Delle Burris (First Husband: E. L. Wages)
   Floy Delle Burris (Second Husband: Ralph O. Rodenor)
b. Lillian Camille Burris (First Husband: W. Bruce French)
   Lillian Camille Burris (Second Husband: Herschel H. Davis)
2. Raiford Burris
3. Ross Miller Burris
4. Lessie Lillian Burris (Husband: Lucius Branch)
5. Lawrence Homer Burris (Wife: Ruby Butler). Children:
   a. Leslie Everett Burris
   b. Alice Ruth Burris (adopted) (Husband: Dr. Benton Hewitt)
6. Thomas Roy Burris (Wife: Mavis Burkhalter). Children:
   a. Julie Lu Burris
I. Enos Pinkney Burris (Wife: Lulu Alma Weathersby). Children:
   1. Walter Hampton Burris (Wife: Ida Hilbun). Children:
      a. Alma Evelyn Burris (Husband: Ted E. Varnado). Children:
         (1). Ted E. Varnado, Jr.
      b. Ruby Ava Burris (Husband: Charlie Wall). Children:
         (1). Donald Wall
         (2). Walter Elwin Wall
         (3). Freddie Wall
      c. William James Burris (Wife: Beulah Williams). Children:
         (1). Carol Ann Burris
         (2). William James Burris, Jr.
      d. Ida Murel Burris (Husband: William H. Davis). Children:
         (1). William H. Davis, Jr.
         (2). Cris Davis
      e. Walter Hampton Burris, Jr. (Wife: Anna Fay Davis). Children:
         (1). Walter Hampton Burris III
         (2). Bonnie Louise Burris

2. Mamie Lettie Burris (Husband: John Arnold Simmons). Children:
   a. John Lynn Simmons (Wife: Ruby Pigott). Children:
      (1). John Wayne Simmons
      (2). Mamie Lynette Simmons
3. Nolan Pinkney Burris (First Wife: Murel Willis)
   Nolan Pinkney Burris (Second Wife: Pearl Forshag). Children:
   a. Nolan Pinkney Burris, Jr. (Wife: Zoe Habisreitinger)
   b. John Forshag Burris (Wife: Anne Darwin). Children:
      (1). Carolyn Elise Burris
   c. Beverly Ann Burris (Husband: Carlos Christina)
4. Bernard Hatton Burris (Wife: Matha Wilson).* Children:
   a. Osburn Burris (Wife: Nelda Montgomery)
   b. Donald Burris (Wife: Mildred Roussel). Children:
      (1). Judy Ann Burris
      (2). Donna Susan Burris
   c. Harold L. Burris (Wife: Mary Lou Pearson)
5. Leon Louis Burris (Wife: Clara Burns). Children:
   a. Laura Lavada Burris (Husband: John Smith Allen). Children:
      (1). Robert Earl Allen
      (2). Dora Dean Allen
      (3). Dorothy Ann Allen
      (4). Eva Louise Allen
   b. Lewis Enos Burris (Wife: Catherine Smith)
   c. Mary Etta Burris (Husband: Burnell Morris). Children:
      (1). Brenda Dianne Morris
      (2). Mickey Vernon Morris
      (3). Loretta Gale Morris
   d. Paul Ester Burris (Wife: Mayme Inez Hodge)
   e. Carolyn Burris
6. William Culpepper Burris (First Wife: Lenora Gillelan). Children:
   a. William Cullen (Billy) Burris

---

*An interfamily marriage.

b. Leo Gillelan (Sonny) Burris (Wife: Virginia Alford). Children:

(1). Michael Leo Burris

William Culpepper Burris (Second Wife: Josephine Thornton)

J. George Ernest Burris (First Wife: Cora Prestridge). Children:

1. Bryan Burris (First Wife: Tiche Arnold)

Bryan Burris (Second Wife: Irene May Reddicks). Children:

a. Donald Bryan Burris
b. Cora May Burris

2. Maida Lee Burris (Husband: Marvin Schilling). Children:

a. Faril Marvin Schilling (Wife: Elnora Miller). Children:

(1). Robert Harry Schilling

b. Ruby Laverne Schilling (Husband: J. B. Lane). Children:

(1). Sylvia Laverne Lane

c. Bobby Schilling (Wife: Nedri Mae Morris)
d. Hilton J. Schilling

George Ernest Burris (Second Wife: Mary Alice Butler). Children:

3. Mary Elizabeth Burris (Husband: Hubert H. Wright). Children:

a. Rebecca Burris Wright
b. Hubert H. Wright, Jr.
c. Ronald Glen Wright

4. Lawrence Miller Burris (Wife: Linda Forrest). Children:

a. Patsy Lynn Burris

K. Maggie Elizabeth Burris

XI. Addison Burris (First Wife: Sarah Alice Flowers). Children:

A. Sarah Alice Flowers Burris (Husband: Dr. Joel Watley Williams). Children:

1. Cecil Williams (Wife: Harriet Lambert). Children:
a. Nonnie Williams
b. Oma Williams (Husband: Robert Webb). Children:

(1). Maurice Webb (Wife: Bertha Raborn). Children:
  (a). Myrtis Webb
  (b). Willie Mac Webb
  (c). Natalea Webb
  (d). Robert Maurice Webb
  (e). Elaine Webb
  (f). Eva Lois Webb
  (g). Jo Ann Webb
  (h). Dianne Webb
(2). Dewitt Webb (Wife: Annie Rohner). Children:
  (a). Charlie Glenn Webb
(3). Glen Webb
(4). Elzy Dees Webb
(5). Margie Webb (Husband: Mike Drensky). Children:
  (a). Mike Lamar Drensky
(6). Percell Webb
(7). Argie Webb (Husband: Carolton Kemp). Children:
  (a). Bobbye Joyce Kemp
  (b). Johnnie Lois Kemp
(8). Pete Webb (Wife: Olivia Robinson). Children:
  (a). Syvilia Webb
  (b). Patsy Webb
  (c). Robert Wayne Webb
(9). Hollis Webb
(10). Dewey Webb
(11). Percy Webb
(12). T. C. Webb
(13). Ray Cecil Webb
c. Sammie Williams
d. Betrus Williams
e. Maggie Williams (Husband: Amile Bert)
f. Lottie Williams (Husband: Joseph K. Holmes). Children:
  (1). Beulah Lee Holmes (Husband: A. P. Ramsey)
  (2). Odell Holmes
  (3). Johnnie Cecil Holmes
  (4). Zella Holmes (Husband: Wilton B. Oliphant)
  (5). Edson C. Holmes

(6). Gladys Amile Holmes

g. Horace C. Williams (Wife: Betty Bennett). Children:
(1). Luther H. Williams

h. Realus J. Williams (Wife: Addie Bennett). Children:
(1). Fred Williams
(2). Halzie Lea Williams
(3). Morris Williams
(4). Elcee Williams
(5). Realus Williams, Jr.

i. .... (an infant)

j. Alex Wattley Williams (Wife: Elizabeth Jane Strickland). Children:
(1). Myrtis Dean Williams
(2). Lillian Mildred Williams (Husband: Peter Callia). Children:
(a). Peter Callia, Jr.
(b). Ellen Mae Callia
(c). Roger James Callia
(3). Dewitt Ottis Williams (Wife: Louise Loretta Gitz). Children:
(a). Kenneth Blaun Williams
(b). Betty Jean Williams
(c). Mildred Evonne Williams
(4). Janie Elizabeth Williams (Husband: Claude Messersmith)
(5). Johnnie Leuna Williams (Husband: Timothy Di Domenica). Children:
(a). Arnold Ray Di Domenica
(6). James Eward Williams
(7). Donis Williams (Husband: Tracy Brown). Children:
(a). Sigrid Ann Elizabeth Brown
(8). Alta Dale Williams

2. Marshall Eugene Williams (Wife: Missouri Ellen Wall). Children:
a. Addie Williams (Husband: Joel Bridges). Children:
(1). Mynne Bridges
(2). Clytee Bridges
(3). Odessa Bridges

(4). R. D. Bridges
(5). Dalton Bridges
(6). Barney Bridges
(7). Loray Bridges
(8). Dale Bridges
(9). Russell Bridges
(10). Kenneth Bridges

b. Leon Wolf Williams (Wife: Dollie Griffin). Children:

(1). Evelyn Williams (Husband: Peter Grimes)

c. Leonard Eugene Williams (Wife: Lois Stewart). Children:
(1). Stewart Williams
(2). Dorothy Williams

d. Eunyce Williams (Husband: Floyd Harrell). Children:
(1). James Fabat Harrell (Wife: Velma Lawson). Children:
(a). Harlene Harrell
(b). James Wendell Harrell
(2). Eula May Harrell

e. Burnyce Williams
f. Vernon Williams
g. Virgil Reed Williams
h. Daisy May Williams (Husband: Burket Wall). Children:
(1). Hugh V. Wall (Wife: Evie Easley)
(2). Burkett Burnyce Wall (First Husband: Leslie Wall). Children:
(a). Janice Kent Wall
Burkett Burnyce Wall (Second Husband: Ray Hughes)*

3. Alice Williams (Husband: Jake Miller Carter). Children:
a. McKinnis Carter
b. James Carter (Wife: Pearl Anders). Children:
(1). Elaine Carter (Husband: Byron Schilling)
(2). Charles Ray Carter
(3). Kenneth Eugene Carter
c. Mamie Carter (Husband: Nathan Allen). Children:

*Interfamily marriage. Children listed under husband.

(1). J. T. Allen
d. Joel Watt Carter (Wife: Dora Kirkland). Children:
   (1). Audrey Mae Carter
   (2). Joel Watt Carter, Jr.
   (3). Vernon Lee Carter
e. Samantha Carter (Husband: Clarence Lilly). Children:
   (1). Alice Lilly (Husband: William T. Bridges)
   (2). Olivia Lilly (Husband: Arthur Hilbun)
   (3). McKinnis Lilly
f. Bettie Carter
g. Itaska Carter (Husband: Herman Frazier). Children:
   (1). Herman Frazier, Jr.
   (2). Melba Frazier

4. Dewitt Williams (Wife: Bessie Stewart). Children:
a. Allie Williams (Husband: Leon Dudley Williams). Children:
   (1). Leon Dudley Williams, Jr.
   (2). Reginald Roy Williams
   (3). Noraleen Williams
   (4). Donald Beverly Williams
   (5). Billie Stewart Williams
b. Felix Dreyfus Williams (Wife: Claudie Dunn). Children:
   (1). Felix Dreyfus Williams, Jr.
c. Dewitt Colliband Williams
d. Leopold Elliott Williams (First Wife: Jessye Addison). Children:
   (1). Pauline Dare Williams
   (2). Lee Joyce Williams
   (3). Jessie Jacqueline Williams
Leopold Elliott Williams (Second Wife: Norma DeCoux). Children:
   (4). James Elliott Williams
e. Bessie Bell Williams (Husband: Lamar Wilson). Children:
   (1). Wilton Wilson
   (2). Princeton Wilson
   (3). Teddy Emile Wilson
   (4). Jerry Gale Wilson

  (5). Claude Lowrey Wilson

5. Andrew W. (Dick) Williams (Wife: Lela Stewart). Children:
 a. Effie Williams (Husband: Thoburn Welch). Children:
  (1). Thelma Welch
  (2). Erma Lee Welch
  (3). Conway Welch
 b. Otis Williams
 c. Gladys Williams
 d. Birdie Williams (Husband: Reginald White). Children:
  (1). Richard White
  (2). Reginald White, Jr.
 e. Louise O. Williams
 f. Andrew Dewitt (A. D.) Williams (Wife: Geraldine Dyson). Children:
  (1). Dianne Williams

6. Martin E. Williams (Wife: Jessie E. Easley). Children:
 a. Alma Alene Williams
 b. Odie Bernice Williams (Husband: James Marshall Williams)
 c. Myrtle Williams
 d. Edith Vera Williams (Husband: Ansel J. Bean)
 e. Johnnie Ruth Williams (Husband: Thomas Jefferson Rogers)
 f. Marjorie Dene Williams (Husband: Sam Desmond)

7. Sallie Williams (Husband: Jack Cleveland). Children:
 a. Lorena Cleveland (Husband: Arthur Spears). Children:
  (1). Sherra Virginia Spears
  (2). Dudley Kirkland Spears
 b. Ethel Cleveland (Husband: Hollis Wilson). Children:
  (1). Mildred Wilson (Husband: R. D. Barron)
 c. Jack Cleveland, Jr. (Wife: Bonita Hughey). Children:
  (1). Margie Cleveland (Husband: Marshall Bowlin)
  (2). Luther Cleveland
 d. Hilda Cleveland (Husband: Murray Nunnery). Children:

(1). Reginald Nunnery (Wife: Justelia Austin)

    e. Mae D. Cleveland (Husband: Hubert Campbell). Children:

(1). Peggy Dianne Campbell

Addison Burris (Second Wife: Mrs. Becky Williams). Children:

B. James D. Burris

Addison Burris (Third Wife: Rebecca Irion Ogden). Children:

C. Duncan H. Burris

D. Annie Ogden Burris

E. Isabel Ogden Burris

F. Lucy Mary Burris (First Husband: .... Knox)

    Lucy Mary Burris (Second Husband: Everett Gibbens). Children:

    1. Everett Gibbens, Jr. (Wife: Irene McGregor)

    2. William Gibbens (Wife: .... Skelly)

    3. Buffington Gibbens (Wife: Jessie McNamee). Children:

        a. Doris Rae Gibbens

G. Marcy Ann (Mattie) Burris (Husband: Henry Clay Phipps). Children:

    1. Mary Rebecca Phipps (First Husband: Otey H. Phipps). Children:

        a. Thaddeus Freeman Phipps

    Mary Rebecca Phipps (Second Husband: James Washington Biard). Children:

        b. Maude Elizabeth Biard

    2. Maude Elizabeth Phipps (Husband: Charles A. Lightcap). Children:

        a. Elizabeth Phipps Lightcap

    3. Henry Clay Phipps, Jr. (Wife: Nevellene Morton)

    4. Addison Burris Phipps (Wife: Ella Moore)

    5. Frelenghuysen Phipps (Wife: Bess Story). Children:

        a. Betty Jean Phipps (Husband: ....)

    6. Christopher Henderson Phipps (Wife: Mirth Jones). Children:

        a. Mary Elizabeth Phipps (Husband: Irving A. Walrath). Children:

            (1). Barbara Ann Walrath

            (2). Michael Phipps Walrath

            (3). Katherine Walrath

b. Barbara Mirth Phipps (Husband: Clarence T. Sebesta)
7. George Herchener Phipps

H. Enos Hampton Burris (Wife: Clara Smizer-Kitchen). Children:
1. Charles Burris
2. Bessie Rebecca Burris (Husband: B. Hugh Smith). Children:
   a. Irene Virginia Smith (Husband: H. S. Wright). Children:
      (1). Sally Rebecca Wright
   b. Mary Inez Smith
   c. Anne Ione Smith (Husband: E. C. Dunn)

I. Dr. William Addison (Billy) Burris (Wife: Anna Knox). Children:
1. Mabel Burris (Husband: Francis Tharin)
2. William Knox Burris (Wife: Mary Lee Brown)
3. Ellesly Burris (Wife: .... Fox)

J. George Samuel Burris (Wife: Clara Stuart). Children:
1. Stuart Pike Burris
2. William Blake Burris (Wife: Vera Hebert). Children:
   a. Rose Merilyn Burris (Husband: Irving Paul Mac-Taggart). Children:
      (1). Sheila Ann MacTaggart
      (2). Timothy Paul MacTaggart
      (3). Patrick David MacTaggart
      (4). Kelly MacTaggart
      (5). Colleen MacTaggart
   b. William Blake Burris, Jr. (Wife: Audrey Shovan). Children:
      (1). William Blake Burris III
      (2). Norma Kathleen Burris
      (3). Lynda Carol Burris
   c. Stuart Hebert Burris
3. Josie Jones Burris

K. Nora Rebecca Burris (Husband: George S. Sharp). Children:
1. Lucy Sharp
2. Mary Serena Sharp
3. Ogden Sharp (Wife: Edith Kean)
4. William Joseph Sharp (Wife: Ada Trahan). Children:

a. Robert Sharp (Wife: Hilda Mae Whitehead). Children:
  (1). Lynda Ann Sharp
  (2). Kenneth Armand Sharp
  (3). Valiria Sharp
  (4). Sharron Lee Sharp
b. Armand Sharp (Wife: Willie Mae Mixon)
c. William Joseph Sharp, Jr. (Wife: Bertha Jane Hardisty). Children:
  (1). Darwin Cyril Sharp
  (2). Thomas W. Sharp
d. Cyril Ogden Sharp (Wife: Maryland Alanzo)
e. George Trahan Sharp
5. Annie Burris Sharp (Husband: R. C. Calloway). Children:
a. Nora Inez Calloway
b. Ruby Annie Calloway (Husband: Clovis J. Mire). Children:
  (1). Clovis Annie Mire
  (2). Janette Faye Mire
c. Francis William Calloway (Wife: Dorothy Case). Children:
  (1). William Louis Calloway
6. Leodocia Clark Sharp (Husband: C. M. Downs)
7. Samuel Robertson Sharp (Wife: Elaine Cobb)
8. Georgie Lenora Sharp (Husband: Lloyd Triche)
9. Joseph Jones Sharp (Wife: Evelyn Harelson). Children:
a. Jane Ellen Sharp
L. Hattie Henderson Burris (Husband: R. M. Hays). Children:
1. Addison Burris Hays (Wife: Frances Stanley). Children:
a. Frances Ann Hays

PART II

DATA ON THE SAMUEL AND MARY (MYERS) BURRIS FAMILY

AA. SAMUEL AND MARY (MYERS) BURRIS

One of the first families by the name of Burris, and one of the pioneer families to settle in Amite County, Mississippi, was doubtless the Samuel and Mary (Myers) Burris Family. They migrated there from Darlington District, South Carolina, in 1809.

The true reasons for Samuel and Mary (Myers) Burris's migration to Amite County will probably never be known. Since Mississippi Territory (it was still a territory and not a state at the time of their migration) was new, undeveloped, and slightly settled, they may have migrated there because they thought it offered opportunities to improve their economic status. The prior migration to Amite County of close friends may have influenced their migration there. James Chandler, who was from the same section of South Carolina that Samuel and Mary (Myers) Burris migrated from, is known to have been a very close friend of theirs. He appears to have migrated to Amite County in 1807, two years prior to Samuel and Mary (Myers) Burris's migration there. According to American State Papers—Lands II, pp. 243-8—he was granted 320 acres of land on the Amite River in 1807. This place is thought to be on the East Fork of Amite River, about seven miles east of Liberty, Miss., and near the place known as Chandler's Hill, which doubtless got its name from James Chandler. This place is also near the place where Samuel and Mary (Myers) Burris settled. According to a nearby resident of Chandler's Hill, there is an old, broken-up tombstone near an old grave on this hill, which tombstone has James Chandler's name engraved on it, indicating that he was buried there.

Then, they may have migrated to Amite County because relatives had migrated to nearby sections. According to American State Papers—Lands II, pp. 243-8—Arthur Burrows (sometimes spelled *Burris*) was made a grant of 320 acres of land on the Homochitto River in 1807, which is not very far from James Chandler's place. To the south, in the Florida Parishes of Louisiana and to the west in Wilkinson County, Miss., it was noted that there were several Burrusses or Burrowses or Burrises living in these sections along about this time. Whether or not these Burrusses or Burrowses or Burrises were related to Samuel and Mary (Myers) Burris is not known, but it is believed that some of them, at least, were.

These may or may not have been the reasons for Samuel and Mary (Myers) Burris's migration to Amite County, Miss. As stated in the beginning, the true reasons will probably never be known.

Samuel and Mary (Myers) Burris had eleven children. Their names were: William, Harriett Almira, John, Elizabeth, James, Samuel, Jr., Anne, George Nelson, Enos, Hampton, and Addison.

Not much is known of Samuel and Mary (Myers) Burris. They seem to have been typical country people, hardy pioneers, who earned their living by the sweat of their brows. They were not wealthy, nor were they poor—just average people, as people were rated in those days.

Samuel was a farmer, and he seems to have been fairly well fixed financially when he migrated to Amite County. According to his will, which was recorded in the Amite County records at Liberty, Miss., July 10, 1811, two years after his migration there, he had some money, also some property in South Carolina.

Samuel appears to have lived only about three years after settling in Amite County. According to the records in the courthouse in Liberty, Miss., the county seat, his will was probated June 8, 1812, which doubtless occurred shortly after his death.

The following are the tracts that comprised the original Samuel and Mary (Myers) Burris homestead in Amite County: The northwest quarter of section 7, township 3, range 6 east, containing 160 acres; and the northeast quarter of section 12, township 3, range 5 east, containing 160 acres. This land was bought by Mary Burris from the U. S. Government after her husband's death—the patent to the first tract being received July 18, 1817, and to the second Oct. 8, 1820. This land is located on the East Fork of Amite River, the river running through the property, and about halfway between the Thompson Community and East Fork.

Records show that Mary survived her husband, from twelve to fifteen years, it is thought. It is believed that they were buried at East Fork Church or on Chandler's Hill. There are old cemeteries at both of these places with many unmarked graves.

WILL OF SAMUEL BURRIS*

The Last Will and Testament of Samuel Burris as Exhibited by the Executrix, Mary Burris, and James Chandler, Executor

---

*Copied from Amite County, Miss., records.

for Probate Record.

Mississippi Territory ⎱
Amite County ⎰

In the name of God, Amen. I, Samuel Burris, of the Territory and county aforesaid, being weak in body, but of sound mind and memory, blessed be God, do make this my last will and testament, and first give and bequeath to my beloved wife, Mary Burris, all my personal estate, consisting of five Negroes, horses, dogs, cattle, household and kitchen furniture, during her natural life, and, at the same time, what money I have by me and what will arise from the sale of my land in the State of South Carolina, or, at least, as much of it as can be conveniently spared from the necessary support of my family, to be laid out for the lands, at the commencement of the sales of the public lands and the land so bought shall be equally divided amongst my children at the death of their mother, together with all my property, whether real or personal; and, lastly, I do appoint my beloved wife, Mary Burris, Executrix, together with James Chandler, Executor, to this, my last will and testament. I also give and bequeath to my son, John Burris, my shot gun.

In witness whereof I have set my hand and affixed my seal this 10th day of July, in the year of our Lord one thousand eight hundred and eleven, and in the thirty-sixth of the American Independence.

Samuel Burris (L. S.)

John Wilson
Craddock Gober

AN INVENTORY AND APPRAISEMENT OF THE GOODS AND CHATTELS OF SAMUEL BURRIS, LATE OF AMITE COUNTY, DECEASED

(Copied from Amite County, Miss., records)

Negro property—

1 woman named Sely & three children	$ 600
1 boy named Ben	300
1 boy named Peter	200
20 head of cattle	130
40 do of hogs	80
6 do of horses	200
Household furniture	142
Kitchen ditto	20
Plantation tools and utensils	23.50
1500 lbs. clean cotton	50
1 woman's saddle, bridles, etc.	15
Cash, notes and book accts., etc.	1490.54
	$3251.04

Mississippi Territory ⎞
Amite County ⎰

        Came personally before me the undersigned justice of the peace in and for said county, Allen Spurlock and John Wilson, who being duly sworn sayeth that the above inventory is a true statement of the property of Sam'l Burris, as was presented by Mary Burris, Executrix, and James Chandler, Executor.

Allen Spurlock
John Wilson

Before me this 19th
October, 1812,
    William Jones, J. P.

———

Mississippi Territory ⎞
  Amite County ⎰

                Orphans Court—October Term 1812

    Personally appeared in open court James Chandler acting Executor of the last will and testament of Samuel Burris, Dec'd., and being duly sworn saith that the within bill of appraisement contains all the goods, chattels, rights and credits of the deceased which have come to his hands or knowledge or into the hands or possession of any other person or persons for him—

Jas. Chandler

Sworn to in Open Court ⎞
Tho. Batchelor, Regr. ⎰

INVENTORY TAKEN 28TH JUNE 1823 OF THE PERSONAL ESTATE OF SAMUEL BURRIS, DEC'D.

(Copied from Amite County, Miss., records)

As follows to-wit—

    14 Negroes
     1 horse
    32 head of cattle
    35 head of hogs.
household and kitchen furniture, improved
    20 head of sheep
farming utensils, considerably improved
    2 Quarter Sections of land.

I certify that I am fully satisfied with James Chandler for his services as an Executor to the will of my Dec'd. husband, Samuel Burris, which Estate I now hold in my possession according to the tenor of the will of the Dec'd.

Given under my hand 28th June, 1823

Mary Burris

State Of Mississippi ⎱
   Amite County ⎰
                    Personally came and appeared in open court
James Chandler one of the Executors of the Estate of Sam'l Burris,
deceased, and made oath that the within Inventory establishes a true
and correct statement of all the Estate belonging to the said deceased,
which has come into his hands as Executor or into the hands or possession of any other person or persons for him, and that the same has
been handed over by him to the Executrix.

                                           Jas. Chandler

Sworn to in open court
28 June 1823
   W. Phillips, Judge of Probate

THE RELATIONSHIP OF SAMUEL BURRIS AND JAMES CHANDLER

The exact relationship of Samuel Burris and James Chandler, also one of the pioneer settlers of Amite County, Mississippi, from South Carolina, is not known; but a close association of these two men doubtless existed, for it is obvious from the records.

Samuel Burris settled near Chandler's Hill, which place was doubtless named for James Chandler. In his will, Samuel Burris named James Chandler as executor. And, in James Chandler's will, James bequeaths "to the children of my deceased daughter, Martha Burris, the late wife of William Burris* of Darlington District, South Carolina, the number and names of them I do not know, four thousand dollars." Just who this William Burris was, and what kin, if any, to Samuel Burris, is not known. It is thought, though, that he may have been Samuel's brother, or nephew; and that it was for this brother (or nephew) that Samuel named his son, William.

Also, in James Chandler's will, he bequeaths one thousand dollars to his stepson, Sam'l B. Simmons. Samuel Burris's daughter, Harriett Almira, married a man by the same name, and it is thought that he was this stepson of James Chandler's that she married.

Another indication of a close association of Samuel Burris and James Chandler was Samuel's naming of one of his sons, James, which was doubtless after this close associate, James Chandler.

The following document, which was drawn up and executed in Darlington District, S. C., and copied from the Amite County, Miss., records, distinguishes this William Burris of Darlington District, S. C., husband of Martha Chandler, late daughter of James Chandler,

---

*Not to be confused with Samuel Burris's son William.

whom James Chandler mentions in his will, and to whose children he bequeaths some of his estate, from Samuel and Mary (Myers) Burris's William:

State of South Carolina
Darlington District

Personally appeared before me, Hugh E. Cannon, who being first duly sworn, says that he has been acquainted with William Burris and Martha Burris as man and wife since the time that Ira E. Burris was born, who was the second child of said William and Martha—that Benjamin W. Burris was at that time reputed to be the first child of said William and Martha and always contained in the family of said Martha and William as one of their children—further deponent says that the lawful heirs or children of said Martha Burris are eight in number, to-wit: Benjamin W. Burris, Ira E. Burris, William M. Burris, Emily Burris (now Fraser), Samuel N. Burris, Elizabeth Burris, John Burris, and Martha Burris.

Hugh E. Cannon

Sworn to before me this 16th day of
Oct. 1832, Alex D. Sims, J. Q.

(This document is one of several like documents, which were drawn up and executed by these children to establish their identity and to secure their portion of James Chandler's estate).

I. WILLIAM BURRIS.

William Burris was the son of Samuel and Mary (Myers) Burris. It is thought that he was one of the older children of the family, if not the oldest child. He was born in South Carolina May 16, 1791. He married Mariah Theresa Andrews, daughter of Edmund and Lucy (Curry) Andrews, Apr. 3, 1817, and to this union the following children were born: Mary, Louisa, Lucy, Martha Lucretia, James Madison, Sarah Ann, Elizabeth Mariah, William Addison, and Amanda Caroline.

Mariah Theresa Andrews-Burris was born in Amite County, Miss., May 8, 1802. Her mother, Lucy Curry-Andrews, was the daughter of Jacob Curry.

William Burris settled on his mother's, Mary Burris's, homestead, which consisted of the following two tracts of land: The northeast quarter of section 12, township 3, range 5 east, containing 160 acres; and the northeast quarter of section 7, township 3, range 6 east, containing 160 acres. He bought the interest of the other heirs, George Nelson, Enos, Hampton, and Addison Burris, in this place. He paid them something like $800 for their interest. This land is located on the East Fork of Amite River, some of it extending across the river, about two miles south of Thompson.

During the War of 1812, William Burris was drafted Oct. 2, 1814, into the U. S. Army from Amite County, Miss., and served until Mar. 28, 1815, six months, with the rank of corporal. He was ordered to the Creek Indian Nation, and stationed at Fort Claiborne, Alabama. He was a member of Capt. Samuel Gerald's company of the Mississippi militia, which was commanded by Col. Geo. Nixon.

After William Burris's death, and the death of her second husband, William R. Hamilton, Mariah Burris-Hamilton, his widow, secured a pension from the U. S. Government Dec. 7, 1857, on the basis of William Burris's service in the War of 1812. Also, on the basis of this service, she was issued a bounty-land warrant, No. 89904-160-55, Oct. 15, 1859. She did not use the warrant to locate land, but on Nov. 20, 1866, at Washington Parish, Louisiana, she assigned her rights and title in it to Robert Bruce of Ottawa County, Kan. On Apr. 6, 1867, he used the warrant to locate the tract of land described upon the U. S. Official Plats of Survey as the East one-half of the Northwest one-fourth, and the West one-half of the Northeast one-fourth of Section 28, Township 11 South, Range 3 West, 6th Principal Meridian, which lies in what is now Ottawa County, Kan. This location was patented to Robert Bruce by the Federal Government on Mar. 25, 1868.

William Burris died Oct. 24, 1838, at his residence in Amite County, Miss., near East Fork, and is presumed to have been buried nearby.

WILLIAM BURRIS'S OBITUARY*

"Death speeds his shaft and wounds our peace."

Died.—At his residence in this county, on Wednesday, the 24th ult., William Burris, Esq., aged 47 years and 5 months.

Far be it from us to disgust the living and insult the memory of the dead by lavishing (as is usually in obituaries), hightoned, and unmerited panegyric upon the subject of this communication. No, if ever we speak in accents of unvaried truth, it must be in this melancholy hour, when sad desolation sits "o'er hearts divided and o'er hopes destroyed." 'Tis only when the grief-stricken heart seizes upon simple but eternal truth that it can find rest from its troubled emotions. And while we attempt to pay this last tribute to a departed FRIEND, well might we, in

---

*Issue Nov. 3, 1838, of the Piney Woods Planter, a newspaper published in Liberty, Miss., along about this time.

the language of the poet, invoke some angel to guide our pencil while we draw the picture of a good man, which naught but angel can exceed.

Mr. Burris was a native of Darlington District, South Carolina, whence he emigrated to this county at the early age of 18, where he resided until summoned by the cold hand of Death from the scenes of this transitory life to act (as we hope) on a nobler and more exalted theatre. Tho' pinched in early life by penury's chill blast, his sterling integrity, unflinching honesty, and unwearied industry, he surmounted every obstacle in his path, and rose superior to all the ills of adversity, affording in his character a beautiful illustration of the maxim that "an honest man's the noblest work of God"—and in the abundance of this world's goods that he reared around him for the maintenance and comfort of his family, that merit rarely goes unrewarded. As a neighbor, he was kind and obliging, unwilling to reproach others as he was himself to be reproached. Where envy or hatred would extenuate naught, it dare not set down aught in malice against him, but suffered him to go down to his grave without attempting to throw even the dark shadow of suspicion upon his character. His hospitable mansion, from whose door want always went smiling, was alike the retreat of the rich and poor, and long will those of his neighborhood, upon whom fortune has frowned, with a sigh for the heart, and a tear in the eye, bear grateful attestation to the repeated acts of his generosity and benevolence. But while with pleasure we call to mind the remembrance of his virtues, the melancholy thought that he will no more appear in the land of the living, unbidden rushes upon us with dread reality. O! that the tear which flows might blot it out forever!

He has left a large family and numerous relatives and friends to mourn with unavailing regret their great and irreparable loss. Long will his grave be bedewed with the tears of her who now sorrows in pale and sickly melancholy o'er the remembrance of him whose presence was to her the prop and soul of her existence. Bitter are the tears that seven hapless orphans shed for the kindest and fondest of fathers, but more severly yet will they feel the loss of him who was the faithful guiding star of their youthful hopes and aspirations. Poignant too is the grief we feel for a FRIEND, but we mourn not as those that have no hope, shall draw abundant consolation from the contemplation of his virtues, while a cruel fate compels us, unwillingly, to number him among "the lost to sight, to memory dear."—H***

THE LAST WILL AND TESTAMENT OF WILLIAM BURRIS—DEC'D.

(Copied from the Amite County, Mississippi, records—Will Book No. 1)

State of Mississippi ⎱
    Amite County ⎰

                In the name of God, Amen!

I, William Burris, of the State and County aforesaid, do make, ordain, and publish this, my last will and testament, hereby revoking and making void all former wills by me at any time made.

I will and bequeath my soul to God who gave it and my body to the earth from whence it came. And, as to such worldly estate as it hath pleased God to entrust me with I dispose of as follows, viz., - - -

2nd. I direct that all my just debts and funeral expenses be paid as soon after my decease as possible out of the first monies that shall come into the hands of my hereinafter constituted executors from any portion of my estate.

3rd. I will and bequeath unto each of my beloved children one thousand dollars in money or its value in property as soon as they marry or arrive at the age of twenty-one years, to be a part of this legacy, which will be due from my estate, and that portion of my property which may or shall fall due and be received by my several daughters. I will and bequeath it to them and the lawful heirs of their body.

4th. It is my desire that my beloved wife, Mariah Burris (if she should survive me) should keep my property both real and personal altogether, subject to the control of my executors of the above provision, during her natural life, or widowhood, and, if in case she should marry, then it is my desire for my property, both real and personal, saving the right of dower, should be equally divided as soon as it can be done share and share alike amongst my said wife and children. If she should remain single until my youngest child arrives of age, then it is my wish also for my property, both real and personal, be equally distributed between her and my said several children. If I should depart this life before my children receive their education, I do most earnestly entreat my executors to attend the educating of my children and more particularly to the education of my two sons, James and William, Jr. It is my desire for them both to have a good English education, the expense which may accrue in the educating of my children to be paid out of my estate.

I do hereby ordain, constitute and appoint my beloved wife, Mariah Burris, and my brother, George N. Burris, executors of this, my last will and testament. In witness whereof I, William Burris, the testator have to this my will set my hand and seal this 22nd day of October, in the year of our Lord one thousand eight hundred and thirty-eight. Signed and sealed and acknowledged in the presence of us.

William Burris   (Seal)

Peter H. Marsalis

T. I. Spurlock

William Frith

Executorship Documents on the William Burris Estate

NOTICE

(Published in The Piney Woods Planter Apr. 11, 1840)

We will, at the May term of the Probate Court of Amite County, present an account for final settlement and allowance on the Estate of Edmund Andrews, deceased, for William Burris, former Administrator.

Mariah Burris
Geo. N. Burris
Administrators

NOTICE

(Published in The Piney Woods Planter Dec. 1, 1840)

Letters of testamentary having been granted to the undersigned at the November term of the Probate Court of Amite County, on the estate of William Burris, dec'd, notice is hereby given to all persons endebted to said estate to come forward and liquidate their debts, and those holding claims against the same, to present them duly authenticated within the time prescribed by law, or they will be forever barred.

Mariah Burris, Executrix
G. N. Burris, Executor

LOST OR MISLAID

(Published in The Piney Woods Planter Jan. 26, 1840)

A note of hand, executed by H. Stricklin of Louisiana for $300, payable on the 1st of January, 1839, and in favor of William Burris, deceased, of this county. All persons are forewarned from trading for said note.

Mariah Burris, Adm'r'x
G. N. Burris, Executor

Petition on the Estate of William Burris, Dec'd

State of Mississippi ⎫   To the Hon. John Walker, Judge of the
Amite County   ⎰   Probate Court, in and for the County of
Amite and State aforesaid.

The undersigned petitioner would humbly represent with your honor that he, together with one Mariah, wife and select of William Burris, dec'd, appointed to obtain letters of executorship on the estate of said William Burris sometime in the year of 1838 (if time properly recollected). That said Mariah, one of the executors, has pretty much had the sole control and management of said Estate. That a short time since she intermarried with one William Hamilton of the State of Alabama, which state Hamilton, together with his wife, Mariah, are about to remove the goods, chattels, effects, including the slaves of said estate, greatly to the jeopardy and prejudice of your petitioner. Your petitioner further believes and states upon oath that he has just cause to believe and suspect that the removal of the minors of the said William Burris, together with their property, contrary to the statute in such cases made and provided, will seriously jeopardize their interest and property.

Your petitioner would, therefore, pray your honor to grant the issuance of a precept to the officer of this Court, commanding forthwith to seize the estate about to be removed and that your honor may dispossess Wm. Hamilton and his wife, Mariah, and to revoke the letters of executorship of the estate above mentioned, and to commit such executorship to such other person or persons as your honor, in your discretion, may think fit and proper, and your petitioner will ever pray, &c.

This July 26th, 1841.

Sworn to and subscribed before
me this 26th day of Jan., 1841,   G. N. Burris
S. R. Davis, Clk.

Mariah (William Burris's widow) married William R. Hamilton of Alabama Jan. 7, 1841, and sometime during the latter part of that year, 1841, they moved to Alabama, and carried with them all of the children and slaves. After they moved to Alabama it appears, from the documents that follow, that Hamilton replaced G. N. Burris as executor of the William Burris Estate.

LUCY BURRIS ESTATE EXEMPLIFICATION AND GUARDIAN BOND

State of Alabama)   Orphans' Court—holden on the first Mon-
   Clark County)   day in December, it being the sixth day of said Month, in the year of our Lord, one thousand eight hundred forty-one. Present: The Honorable Joseph P. Portis, judge of said Court.

On application of Lucy Burris, a minor heir of William Burris, deceased, who is over the age of fourteen years, to this court praying that William R. Hamilton be appointed her guardian. It is, therefore, ordered by the court that William R. Hamilton be appointed guardian of the person and property of Lucy Burris, a minor heir of William Burris, deceased, and that he give bond and security in the sum of ten thousand dollars. It is ordered by the court that the bond this day given by William R. Hamilton as the guardian of Lucy Burris, minor heir of William Burris, deceased, for the sum of ten thousand dollars, with James Savage and Robert B. Patterson as his securities, be and the same is hereby approved and accepted by the court.

It is ordered by the court that letters of guardianship be issued to William R. Hamilton, and, upon the goods and chattels, rights, and credentials of Lucy Burris, a minor heir of William Burris, deceased.

A similar estate exemplification and guardian bond was executed by William R. Hamilton, stepfather, for the other children, viz., James M. Burris, William Addison Burris, Sarah Ann Burris, Elizabeth Mariah Burris, and Amanda Caroline Burris.

APPRAISEMENT AND DIVISION OF THE SLAVES OF WILLIAM BURRIS (DECEASED) AMONG THE LEGAL DISTRIBUTEES OF SAID DECEASED

(Copied from Amite County, Miss., records)

No. 1	Elizabeth M. Burris,	Thompson	$450.00
	"	Pleasant	650.00
	"	Jackson	600.00
	"	Washington	250.00
	"	Sampson	150.00
No. 2	James M. Burris,	Lydia	250.00
	"	Terry	850.00
	"	Easter	725.00
	"	Harriett	100.00
	"	Hannah	300.00
No. 3	Sara Ann Burris,	James	950.00
	"	Polly	700.00
	"	Joe	150.00
	"	Eliza	250.00
No. 4	William A. Burris,	David	400.00
	"	Rozza	450.00
	"	Violet	750.00
	"	Senna	575.00
No. 5	Amanda C. Burris,	Ferry	950.00
	"	Tempy	600.00
	"	Elick	125.00
	"	Elijah	200.00
	"	Ben	400.00
No. 6	Mariah Hamilton,	Jenter	850.00
	"	Monroe	700.00
	"	Martin	200.00
	"	Abby	250.00
	"	Margaret	162.50
No. 7.	Lucy Burris,	George	950.00
	"	Mary	500.00
	"	Wesley	675.00
	"	Due No. 3 from No. 2	$ 7.16
	"	Also from No. 5	101.76
	"	Due No. 7 from No. 4	16.80
	"	Also from No. 5	14.32
	"	Also from No. 6	3.58

We, the undersigned commissioners appointed by the Probate Court of Amite County to divide the slaves of William Burris, dec'd, among the legal distributees of said dec'd, do certify that the within is a distribution made by us. Each distribution being placed opposite to the name of distributee to whom it belongs.

Given under our hands and seals this 1st day of Jan., 1842,

E. G. Wicker
Wm. Gardner
Wm. C. Butler
A. Spurlock, Jr.

Probate Court, June Term, 1842

Wm. Gardner, Wm. C. Butler, and Allen Spurlock, Jr., three of the commissioners appointed to divide the slaves belonging to the Estate of Wm. Burris, dec'd, among the legatees of the same, says on oath that the preceding is a true division as made by them in connection with same.

E. G. Wicker
Wm. Gardner
Wm. C. Butler
A. Spurlock

Sworn to in open court 27th
June 1842,

S. R. Davis, Clk.

The Administration Account of William R. Hamilton, Administrator, De Bonis Non, With Will Annexed, of the Estate of William Burris, Deceased, Made at the September Term 1842

(Copied from Amite County, Miss., records)

The administrator charges himself as follows, viz.,

To amount of sales of cotton crop for 1840 & 41...$2254.08
"   " rec'd for hire of slaves, Violet & Cyrina. 100.00
"   " cash rec'd from F. Wigley 400.00

The administrator prays allowance as follows, viz.,

1. By amount paid for provisions, bagging, rope, etc., for the estate 270.00
2. By amount paid Clinton McGehee, Tax Collector, Taxes for 1841 .... 42.55
3. By amount paid Levy Dreyfuss as per voucher...... 8.50
4. "   "   " F. H. Dunn "   "   " 24.75
5. "   "   " Donnella Z. Rudd "   " 15.26
6. "   "   " Caffery Z. Pound "   " 8.72
7. "   "   " Geo. F. Webb "   " 40.94
8. "   "   " W. W. White "   " 47.40

9.	"	"	" Edmund Smith " "	400.00
10.	"	"	" Hanwood Buckley " "	45.75
11.	"	"	" G. N. Burris, allowance	242.99
12.	"	"	" Samuel Tillston, as per voucher.....	30.40
13.	"	"	" Martin Faler " " "	44.52
14.	"	"	" F. H. Dunn " " "	11.87
15.	"	"	" E. L. Tarver for taxes, 1840........	38.39
16.	"	"	" Dr. A. R. Dunn, as per voucher......	38.00
17.	"	"	" Wm. Cook, as overseer.............	300.00
18.	"	"	" Hampton Burris, as per 1840........	400.00
19.	"	"	" S. Tillston, as per voucher.........	6.50
20.	"	"	" E. G. Wicker " "	25.00
21.	By amount paid Charles Felder, as per voucher.....			14.00
22.	"	"	" G. W. Murray " " "	7.50
23.	"	"	" S. B. Stutson, jail and other fees for jury	23.87
24.	By amount paid T. W. Hitchcock & Co., as per voucher			10.00
25.	"	"	" P. C. West, as per voucher.........	32.50
26.	"	"	" Geo. F. (N.?) Burris "	114.60
27.	"	"	" Wilson Tarver " "	2.00
28.	"	"	" Dr. J. Wallace " "	30.00
29.	"	"	" for obstetrical fees for slaves of estate	6.00
30.	"	"	" for 7 gallons of whiskey on day of sale	7.00
31.	For boarding Lucy Burris, 12 mo. @ $8.00.........			96.00
32.	"	"	Jas. M. Burris, 12 mo. @ $8.00........	96.00
33.	"	"	Sarah Ann Burris, 12 mo. @ $8.00....	96.00
34.	"	"	Elizabeth Mariah Burris, 12 mo. @ $8.00	96.00
35.	"	"	William Addison Burris, " ".........	50.00
36.	"	"	Amanda Caroline Burris, 12 mo.......	50.00
37.	For clothing for Jas. M. Burris			80.00
38.	"	"	" Sarah Ann Burris	50.00
39.	"	"	" Elizabeth Mariah Burris	50.00
40.	"	"	" William Addison Burris	50.00
41.	"	"	" Amanda Caroline Burris	30.00

Probate Court, September Term, 1842.

Wm. R. Hamilton says on oath that the preceding account is just and true as he verily believes.

Sworn to in open court 27th Sept., 1842,
S. R. Davis, Clk.

Wm. R. Hamilton

Subsequent detailed administration accounts on the William Burris Estate, as recorded in the Amite County, Miss., records, showed a total of $7,481.14 in receipts and sales. The total value of his personal estate was shown to be $27,781.29, which does not include his plantation.

By her marriage to William R. Hamilton, Mariah had one child, a daughter named Martina, who married Judge T. C. W. Ellis of New Orleans and Amite, La.

After living with him five or six years, Mariah deserted Hamilton and returned to Washington Parish, La., where, according to an old citizen of Washington Parish, she settled directly across Bogue Chitto River from Franklinton, La., about six or seven miles from the town, on or near her brother's place. Later, Mariah is reported to have purchased land on the east side of Bogue Chitto River, a few miles north of Franklinton and settled there. The place was known in later years as the Old Jason Bateman Place. Her oldest son, James Madison Burris, is reported to have purchased land on the northern outskirts of Franklinton and settled there. The place was known in later years as the Old Ada Babington Place. Still later, Mariah purchased land two or three miles farther north, on the Franklinton (La.)-Tylertown (Miss.) Highway, and moved there, where she lived until her death in 1877. This place was known in later years as the Old Ferd Magee Place.

Mariah was buried in the Magee Cemetery, which is located on the Clifton, La.-Mt. Hermon, La., Highway, about one mile west of Clifton.

AN OLD DOCUMENT OF MARIAH THERESA BURRIS-HAMILTON

(Copied from Washington Parish, La., records)

State of Louisiana }
Parish of Washington }

Be it known and remembered that, on this sixteenth day of March, in the year of our Lord one thousand eight hundred and fifty, and in the year of the independence of the United States of America, seventy-fourth.

Before me, Sanderlin Walker Bickham, recorder of the Parish of Washington, State of Louisiana, duly authorized by law to exercise the power of notary public therein, personally came and appeared Mistress Mariah T. Hamilton of this parish, she being herein duly authorized by the judge of the Eighth Judicial District Court of the State of Louisiana, by order filed in the clerk's office this day, and being one of the heirs of the Augustus Marion Andrews, deceased, she hereby gives to John Magee, administrator, a full receipt to the extent of her heirship in and said estate, and acknowledges to have received of the said John Magee, administrator, as aforesaid, the following described Negro man, to-wit: John, or better known as John Callahan, about forty years of age, at the price and sum of seven hundred dollars, and the sum of two hundred fifty seven dollars cash, being the aggregate amount of nine hundred and fifty-seven dollars, which sum she acknowledges to have received, and consents to the release of said administrator, having a knowledge of his having filed his account in the court aforesaid, dated 23rd February A. D., 1850, as administrator, and am satisfied therewith and make no opposition thereby and release him from all liabilities therein. Thus done and passed at the residence of John Magee, the Parish of Washington, the day, month and year first above written, in the presence of Benjamin F. Bickham and William D. Bixler, witnesses of lawful age, and domiciled in the Parish, who, have hereunto, signed their names, together with said appearer and me recorder.

Signed,
Mariah T. Hamilton

B. F. Bickham
W. D. Bixler

S. W. Bickham, Recorder.

AN OLD DOCUMENT OF WILLIAM BURRIS

The following document was copied from records in the Register of State Lands office, Baton Rouge, La.:

Application to change entry made at the land office—west of Pearl River. Communicated to the House of Representative Feb. 22, 1830.

Petitioner sets forth that on, or about the year 1819, one Edmund Andrews, as his friend and agent, entered for him the northwest quarter of section 21, township 3, range 6 east, in the district lands west of Pearl River. Not supposing any mistake had happened, he went on to complete payment for the northeast half of said quarter, that when he received his patent he found the lands that he had purchased were worthless, barren and useless; wherefore, he prays that he may be permitted to withdraw his entry and transfer the money to other lands. Edmund Andrews swears that he entered the land described by the petitioner as his friend and agent, that his intention was to have entered the northeast quarter of the said section, instead of the northwest, and he really believes he told the Register of the Land Office so, but he says it now appears that he was mistaken, or misunderstood by the register, for that money appears to have been paid on the northwest quarter instead of the northeast.

Resolved that the petitioner ought not to have relief upon his petition.

A. MARY BURRIS.—Born in Amite County, Miss., Feb. 1, 1818. Never married. Died quite young.

B. LOUISA BURRIS.—Born in Amite County, Miss., Aug. 30, 1821. Never married. Died quite young.

C. LUCY BURRIS.—Born in Amite County, Miss., Jan. 8, 1823. Married Phillip Kirchbain. Children: Emma and Phillip, Jr.

Philip and Lucy (Burris) Kirchbain migrated to Texas shortly after their marriage, and, when last heard from, they were living in Lampasas, Texas. Lucy Burris-Kirchbain died Oct. 6, 1872, after suffering for a year or more with a very painful disease. It is presumed she was buried in Lampasas, Texas.

1. EMMA KIRCHBAIN.—Married .... Borho Nov. 26, 1872. Mr. Borho was a merchant in Lampasas, Texas.

THE COPY OF AN OLD LETTER FROM EMMA KIRCHBAIN TO HER GRANDMOTHER, MARIAH BURRIS-HAMILTON

Lampasas (Texas), Dec. 1st., 1872.

Dear Grandma

Procrastination has existed between us so long that I am at a loss what to write. I will endeavor to break the ice, and sincerely hope that in the future I may hear from you frequently. You will find me a punctual correspondent, and shall spare no pains in making each letter interesting. As this is the only medium left by which we can know each other's trials, why not enjoy it?

Grandma, ere this, I suppose you have heard of the death of our dear beloved mother, who departed this life the 6th of Oct., 11 o'clock p. m., a pure Christian. After suffering for one year the most excruciating pain, no tongue can express the suffering she bore. And so patiently, without a murmur. Job himself could not have borne his afflication more patiently. Her only desire in this world was to meet you once again. She would often say if I could only see mother once again, how happy I would be. We made every effort to carry her to you, but her health would not permit. Oh how lonely this world is without a mother! What is home without a dear, kind mother, who is always ready with a word of consolation or advice? It is God's will, not ours, to which we have to submit. Ma died with dropsy.

Grandma, how is your health? I hope it is continually improving.

Perhaps you will be somewhat surprised if I tell you that, I, like all other girls take a wild notion to change their names. So it is with me. On the 26th of November I was married and changed my name to *Borho,* a merchant of Lampasas, where I am now living, and having a pleasant home and kind husband.

Pa is living with me.

Phillip has charge of large hardware store in Bremond, therefore we will seldom see each other, but can hear each week. He is well, also Pa, except sore eyes which he has been suffering with for several days.

Dear Grandma, write soon. Give my love to all my relatives. Pa wishes to be kindly remembered by all.

With much love, I remain your aff. neice,

Emma Borho.

P. S.: Direct your letters to Lampasas Springs, Texas.

---

2. PHILLIP KIRCHBAIN, JR.—When last heard from, Oct. 8, 1872, he was living in Bremond, Texas, and was in charge of a large hardware store.

THE COPY OF AN OLD LETTER FROM PHILLIP KIRCHBAIN TO HIS UNCLE, JAMES BURRIS

Bremond, Texas, Oct. 8th (1872).

Mr. James Burris (Franklinton, La.)

Dear Uncle: It falls my lot to inform you of the death of my dear mother. After suffering for 18 long months, God has taken her to Himself in Heaven and at peace. She died on the 6th inst., a true Christian.

I can't write more.

Write to me.

Your nephew, Phillip Kirchbain.

D. MARTHA LUCRETIA BURRIS.—Born in Amite County, Miss., Mar. 10, 1833. Never married. Died quite young.

E. JAMES MADISON BURRIS.—Born in Amite County, Miss., Mar. 5, 1826. Married, first, Rebecca (Becky) Magee of Washington Parish, La. No children. Married, second, Sarah Ellis of Washington Parish, La., daughter of Stephen Ellis. Children: Mary Mariah, James Madison, Jr.; Amanda, Ella Lucy, John A., Wesley, Lillie M., Steve Hampton, Phillip F., Sarah Jane, and William E.

Rebecca (Becky) Magee was Mary (Polly) Magee's (Hampton Burris's wife) sister; also George Magee's (Amanda Caroline Burris's, husband) sister. She was Flora Lavonia Magee's (William Addison Burris's, wife) first cousin.

Sarah Ellis-Burris was born May 30, 1836. She died Oct. 17, 1876, and was buried in Franklinton, La.

After returning to Franklinton from Alabama with his mother, when she deserted her second husband, William R. Hamilton, James Madison Burris settled on a farm near what is now known as the Ada Babington Place in Franklinton. He later entered the mercantile business in Franklinton.

James Madison Burris served in the Confederate Army as first lieutenant of Company A, 18th Battalion, Louisiana Cavalry, during the Civil War. He died Nov. 24, 1908, and was buried in Franklinton.

1. MARY MARIAH BURRIS.—Born in Franklinton, La., June 8, 1859. Married O. P. Morris. Children: James Edward, and Sally (married .... Holland and they had a daughter, Roxie Mae).

Mary Mariah Burris-Morris died Oct. 9, 1889, and was buried in Franklinton.

2. JAMES MADISON BURRIS, JR.—Born in Franklinton, La., Nov. 21, 1857. Married Mary Gabe Magee. Children: William James, Allie Sarah, Wiley Stephen, Bessie Lenora, Vanda Victoria, E. John, Hampton M., Howard L., Nelie Kathryn, and Marah Lee.

James Madison Burris, Jr., was one of the leading merchants of Franklinton and Washington Parish, La., where he lived all of his life. He died Mar. 28, 1929, and was buried in Franklinton.

a. WILLIAM JAMES BURRIS.—Born in Franklinton, La., Dec. 8, 1888. Married Nina Hood, daughter of T. J. Hood. Children: Josephine, James Madison III, and William Hood.

William James Burris was a merchant all of his life. He owned and operated Burris Brothers' Store of Franklinton, his father's store, the leading store of town. He was widely known and very popular. He died Nov. 7, 1939, and was buried in Franklinton.

(1). JOSEPHINE BURRIS.—Born in Franklinton, La., Mar. 24, 1914. Married Donald White, son of Harlan B. White. Children: Joan (born Aug. 18, 1934), and Larry (born Jan. 30, 1936).

Donald and Josephine (Burris) White operate a very successful studio in Bogalusa, La.

(2). JAMES MADISON BURRIS III.—Born in Franklinton, La., Jan. 9, 1916. Married, first, June Sweeney. Children: Ginger (born Feb. 12, 1938). Married, second, Frances Rieley. Children: Jill (born May 27, 1944). Married, third, Glyndora Schilling, daughter of Alfred M. and Edna (Miller) Schilling. Children: James Madison, IV (born July 14, 1951).

James Madison Burris III, is principal owner and operator of Burris Brothers' Store of Franklinton, the same store his father and grandfather owned and operated. Like his father and grandfather, he is one of the leading merchants of the town and parish.

(3). WILLIAM HOOD BURRIS.—Born in Franklinton, La., Nov. 16, 1923. Married Ruth Crisler. Children: William James Burris II (born Dec. 31, 1941).

William Hood Burris served in the U. S. Navy as Aviation Ordnance Man Third Class, during World War II. He enlisted Apr. 2, 1944, and was discharged Mar. 1, 1946. He lives in Franklinton, La.

b. ALLIE SARAH BURRIS.—Born in Franklinton, La., May 25, 1886. Married Hammond E. Richardson, son of S. Pink Richardson, Apr. 17, 1907. Children: Mary Verne, Gladys Lynette, and Donna Lee. Hammond E. Richardson was born Jan. 7, 1886, and died Nov. 9, 1940. Allie Sarah Burris-Richardson lives in Franklinton, La.

(1). MARY VERNE RICHARDSON.—Born in Franklinton, La., Aug. 3, 1908. Married Abner Poole Wood, son of Delos Wood. Children: Mary Jeanette (born July 18, 1933).

Mary Verne Richardson-Wood died Aug. 9, 1933, and was buried in Franklinton, La.

(2). GLADYS LYNETTE RICHARDSON.—Born in Franklinton, La., Sept. 6, 1910. Married Emile E. McMillan, son of Lucius McMillan. Children: Mary Linda (born Jan. 7, 1938), and Gladys Susan (born Feb. 25, 1943; died Dec. 13, 1943; buried in Franklinton, La.).

Emile and Gladys Lynette (Richardson) McMillan reside in Franklinton, La., and operate a grocery store.

(3). DONNA LEE RICHARDSON.—Born in Franklinton, La., July 13, 1912. Married Monroe O. Webb. Children: Patricia Fay (born in Natchitoches, La., July 15, 1935), and Monroe Oliver (born in Flora, La., May 5, 1939).

Donna Lee Richardson-Webb is librarian at the Washington Parish Library, Franklinton, La.

c. WILEY STEPHEN BURRIS.—Born in Franklinton, La.,

William Otto Burris
*Outstanding Political Figure
of Washington Parish (La.)*

Thomas Edgar (Eddie) Burris
Prominent Citizen of Smithdale Community (Miss.)

Mariah (Andrews) Burris-Hamilton
Original Burris Parent of Washington Parish (La.)

The Addison Burris Home, East Baton Rouge Parish (La.)
Built before the War Between the States

Mar. 31, 1892. Married Nelie K. Dobson, daughter of Willie J. Dobson, June 19, 1917. Children: Wiley Stephen, Jr., and Katherine Ursula.

Wiley Stephen Burris was a prominent banker. At the time of his death, May 27, 1942, he held a high position with the Washington Bank & Trust Co. of Franklinton, La., with which bank he was connected all of his life. He was a veteran of World War I. He was buried in Franklinton, La.

(1). WILEY STEPHEN BURRIS, JR.—Born in Franklinton, La., Apr. 7, 1920. Wiley Stephen Burris, Jr., was accidentally killed in an automobile wreck on the Franklinton-Bogalusa Highway Aug. 4, 1940. He was buried in Franklinton, La.

(2). KATHERINE URSULA BURRIS.—Born in Franklinton, La., Jan. 31, 1924. Married William Towle. Children: Patricia and Rickey.

William and Katherine Ursula (Burris) Towle live in Meadville, Penn.

d. BESSIE LENORA BURRIS.—Born in Franklinton, La., Sept. 9, 1894. Married Arthur E. Hood, son of T. J. Hood. Children: Arthur E., Jr., and Thomas Jefferson.

Arthur E. and Bessie Lenora (Burris) Hood live in Amite, La., where he operates an automobile agency.

(1). ARTHUR E. HOOD, JR.—Born in Amite, La., July 16, 1920. Married Sue Field, daughter of Preston Field. Children: Bonnie Sue (born Nov. 27, 1942), and Arthur Preston (born Feb. 4, 1943).

(2). THOMAS JEFFERSON HOOD.—Born in Amite, La., Dec. 28, 1921. Married Marie Kent, daughter of Tom Kent. Children: Lindy Lou (born Oct. 24, 1946), and Thomas, Jr. (born June 19, 1948).

e. VANDA VICTORIA BURRIS.—Born in Franklinton, La., Nov. 17, 1900. Married Hyman Ottis Simmons, son of Hyman Hart Simmons, June 12, 1924. Children: Hyman Ottis, Jr., and Ronald Burris.

They live in Franklinton, La., and are engaged in the mercantile business.

(1). HYMAN OTTIS SIMMONS, JR.—Born in Magnolia, Miss., Feb. 3, 1928. Married Katherine Joan Richardson, daughter of John P. Richardson, Dec. 1, 1946. Children: Michael Ottis (born May 27, 1950).

Hyman Ottis Simmons, Jr., served in the 519th Military Police Battalion of the U. S. Army during World War II. He was stationed in Yokahoma, Japan.

(2). RONALD BURRIS SIMMONS.—Born in Magnolia, Miss., May 25, 1931.

Ronald Burris Simmons is attending Southeastern Louisiana College, being a senior this year, 1951-52, in the school of Business Administration. He is treasurer of the Student Government, a member of the Senate and also the Judiciary Board and vice president of the Sigma Tau Gamma Fraternity. During his junior year, he was president of the class and of his fraternity and held a seat in the Senate of the student body. In his sophomore and junior years, he was a member of the Queen's Court at the annual Carnival Ball held on the S. L. C. Campus. The 1951-52 edition of "Who's Who in American Colleges and Universities" contains his name, which is one of the highest honors a college student can receive. The selection was based on the participation and contribution to the college, scholarship, and leadership qualities.

f. E. JOHN BURRIS.—Born in Franklinton, La., Mar. 6, 1897. Died Aug. 18, 1898. Buried in Franklinton.

g. HAMPTON M. BURRIS.—Born in Franklinton, La., Nov. 16, 1902. Died Aug. 29, 1903. Buried in Franklinton.

h. HOWARD L. BURRIS.—Born in Franklinton, La., Oct. 16, 1904. Died June 16, 1907. Buried in Franklinton.

i. NELIE KATHRYN BURRIS.—Born in Franklinton, La., Apr. 5, 1908. Married Lex V. Stringer, son of Dudley Stringer. Children: Jimmy Dudley (born July 29, 1930).

Lex V. Stringer is a prominent banker. He was connected with the Washington Bank and Trust Co. of Franklinton, La., for many years. He is now located in Winona, Miss.

j. MARAH LEE BURRIS.—Born in Franklinton, La., Sept. 12, 1911. Married George Moore, son of Duke Moore. Children: George Duke (born May 12, 1941), and Mary Janice (born Nov. 28, 1947).

They live in Franklinton, La.

3. AMANDA BURRIS.—Born in Franklinton, La., Feb. 8, 1866. Married Marcus F. Magee of Franklinton, La. No children.

Amanda Burris-Magee died Mar. 26, 1889, and was buried in Franklinton.

4. ELLA LUCY BURRIS.—Born in Franklinton, La., Aug. 30, 1867. Married Willie E. Bickham, son of Charley Bickham. Children: Mamie Belle, Lillie, Benton Edgar, Rosa, Stella, Addison, Ethel, and Viola.

Willie E. Bickham was born in Clifton, La., Aug. 18, 1866. He died Mar. 27, 1935, and was buried in Franklinton, La. He was a merchant.

Ella Lucy Burris-Bickham died Mar. 15, 1916, and was buried in Franklinton, La.

a. MAMIE BELLE BICKHAM.—Born near Clifton, La., in 1888. Married, first, Bose Brock. No children. Married, second, Judge Ellis Ott in 1907. Children: W. C. Mamie Belle Bickham-Ott died in 1909.

b. LILLIE BICKHAM.—Born near Clifton, La., Sept. 21, 1890. Married James H. Dickinson, son of James Edmund and Emma J. Dickinson, May 5, 1909. Children: Nella and James Harold.

James H. Dickinson was born in Denmark, Tenn., May 5, 1883. He has been a school teacher, a banker, and is now a traveling salesman. He lives in Fluker, La.

(1). NELLA DICKINSON.—Born in Hackley, La., May 6, 1912. Married Edmund Henry Gabriel May 8, 1936, in Baton Rouge, La. Children: Edmund Dickinson (born May 22, 1940), and James Harry (born Nov. 9, 1948). They live in Baton Rouge, La.

(2). JAMES HAROLD DICKINSON.—Born in Franklinton, La., Mar. 24, 1914. Married Mildred Lockhart Rankin Apr. 16, 1949, in Norfolk, Va. No children.

They live in Norfolk, Va.

c. BENTON EDGAR BICKHAM.—Born near Clifton, La., Sept. 30, 1892. Married Carrie Holmes. Children: Margie Ann, and Benton Edgar, Jr.

Benton Edgar Bickham has been a stock raiser, merchant, and parish representative from Washington Parish, Louisiana, 1936-40. He was maintenance engineer for the Louisiana State Department of Highways 1928-40. He is now commissioner of highways for the Sixth District of Louisiana. He lives in Franklinton, La.

(1). MARGIE ANN BICKHAM.—Born in Franklinton, La.,

Mar. 30, 1922. Married, first, Rodney Williams. Children: Armethia Ann. Married, second, William Addison Burris. Children: (Listed under William Addison Burris—an interfamily marriage).

They live in Franklinton, La.

(2). BENTON EDGAR BICKHAM, JR.—Married Walterine Hunter. Children: Benton Bradley (born June 29, 1946), and Carrie Jane (born Mar. 16, 1948). Benton Edgar Bickham, Jr. operates the Red and White Grocery in Franklinton. He served in World War II as a paratrooper.

They live in Franklinton, La.

d. ROSA BICKHAM.—Born near Clifton, La., Jan. 28, 1895. Married Percy Ott. Children: Mary Ellen (born July 22, 1922; married .... Evans), James Bickham (born Apr. 11, 1925; served in the U. S. Marines during World War II), and Carolyn Rose (born June 25, 1926).

e. STELLA BICKHAM.—Born near Clifton, La., Mar. 3, 1897. Married, first, John W. Warner (died Feb. 8, 1921). Children: John W., Jr. (born Oct. 16, 1919). Married, second, ... Cole. No children. Married, third, Geo. B. Campbell (dead). No children.

f. ADDISON BICKHAM.—Born near Clifton, La., in 1903.

g. ETHEL BICKHAM.—Born near Clifton, La., Sept. 3, 1905. Teaching in one of the University of Alabama demonstration schools.

h. VIOLA BICKHAM.—Born near Clifton, La., Dec. 2, 1909. Married Floyd Frank. Children: Marilyn Sue (born Aug. 30, 1939).

5. JOHN A. BURRIS.—Born in Washington Parish, La., Dec. 5, 1864. Married Laura Burkhalter. Children: Robert Edward, William A., Maude Ellis, and John A., Jr.

John A. Burris, Sr., died Sept. 10, 1907, and was buried in Franklinton, La. He was a merchant.

a. ROBERT EDWARD BURRIS.—Born in Franklinton, La., Dec. 24, 1889. Married Mabel Cantrelle. Children: Lura, Charles Edward, and Joyce Mae. Robert Edward Burris (or Eddie, as he is known to most people in Franklinton) has been a railway employee (depot agent) all of his life.

(1). LURA BURRIS.—Born Dec. 11, 1916.

(2). CHARLES EDWARD BURRIS.—Born Nov. 13, 1924.

(3). JOYCE MAE BURRIS.—Born Feb. 12, 1927. Married .... Sudderth. Children: Ted David (born June 22, 1948).

b. WILLIAM A. BURRIS.—Born in Franklinton, La., Dec. 5, 1892. Married, first, Iris Alexander July 15, 1913. Children: Willie Katherine (born in Tylertown, Miss., Jan. 25, 1915). Married, second, June Pierce, who was born in Sun, La., July 6, 1904. Children: William Dale (born in Covington, La., April 14, 1925).

William A. Burris (or Willie, as he is known to most people in Franklinton) has been a railway employee (depot agent) all of his life.

c. MAUDE ELLIS BURRIS.—Born in Franklinton, La., July 10, 1894. Married Robert Charles Riley Nov. 10, 1917. Children: Elizabeth D'Autrey, and Eloise.

Robert Charles Riley was born in Evergreen, Ala., Apr. 11, 1892.

(1). ELIZABETH D'AUTREY RILEY.—Born in Sylacauga, Ala., Sept. 9, 1922.

(2). ELOISE RILEY.—Born in Franklinton, La., Aug. 20, 1918. Married .... McClendon. Children: Robert Pierce (born Sept. 18, 1942), and Jean Ellis (born June 19, 1947).

d. JOHN A. BURRIS, JR.—Born in Franklinton, La., June 15, 1906. Married Audis Stafford, daughter of Bose Stafford, Oct. 21, 1927. Children: John Allan (born Dec. 16, 1935).

Like his brothers, John A. Burris, Jr., has worked for railway companies most of his life.

6. WESLEY BURRIS.

7. LILLIE M. BURRIS.—Born in Franklinton, La., Aug. 10, 1872. Never married. Died July 29, 1889, and was buried in Franklinton, La.

8. STEVE HAMPTON BURRIS.—Born in Franklinton, La., July 24, 1870. Married Alma Varnado. Children: Jeni, Newton Alexander, James Oscar, Steve Hampton, Jr., Ora, Lura, Cecil Addison, Alma and Myra.

Steve Hampton Burris died May 9, 1914, and was buried in Franklinton, La. He was a merchant.

a. JENI BURRIS.—Born in Franklinton, La., Aug. 13, 1895. Married Murphy J. Sylvest. Children: .... (adopted daughter).

Jeni Burris-Sylvest died Aug. 29, 1940, and was buried in Franklinton, La. She had an outstanding personality and was very popular.

b. NEWTON ALEXANDER BURRIS.—Born in Franklinton, La., Sept. 30, 1893. Never married. Died Dec. 10, 1914, and was buried in Franklinton, La.

Newton Burris and James Oscar Burris were twins. Newton Burris was accidentally shot and killed while hunting. He was an outstanding student and an eloquent public speaker in high school.

c. JAMES OSCAR BURRIS.—Born in Franklinton, La., Sept. 30, 1893. Died when quite young, and was buried in Franklinton, La.

d. STEVE HAMPTON BURRIS, JR.

e. ORA BURRIS.—Born in Franklinton, La., Aug. 8, 1897. Married R. B. Stinespring. No children.

Prior to her marriage, Ora Burris-Stinespring was a registered nurse and held important positions in several hospitals. They live near Paducah, Kentucky.

f. LURA BURRIS.—Born in Franklinton, La., Aug. 7, 1901. Married W. M. McLain, son of Louis McLain. Children: Ora Marie, Lorelle and Alton.

Lura Burris-McLain died Oct. 28, 1945, and was buried in Franklinton, La.

(1). ORA MARIE MCLAIN.—Born in Franklinton, La., Oct. 5, 1925. Married Clyde Fussell. Children: Beverly Marie and Benjamin Ray (twins—born May 25, 1949). Clyde Fussell is cashier of the Washington Bank & Trust Co. of Franklinton, La.

(2). LORELLE MCLAIN.—Born in Franklinton, La., Jan. 15, 1928. Married William Addison Wood, son of Wiley Wood, June 1949. Children: William Addison, Jr. (born Sept. 3, 1951).

(3). ALTON MCLAIN.—Born in Franklinton, La., Feb. 10, 1932.

g. CECIL ADDISON BURRIS.—Born in Franklinton, La., Jan. 2, 1899. Married Mary Leggette. Children: Steve Hampton II (born Sept. 11, 1930), Mary Jane (born Feb. 6, 1932; died Mar. 23, 1932), Leggette (born Apr. 13, 1934), and Cecil Addison, Jr. (born Oct. 26, 1935).

Cecil Addison Burris died May 28, 1944, and was buried in Franklinton, La. He was a veteran of World War I.

h. ALMA BURRIS.—Born in Franklinton, La., Aug. 5, 1904. Married Aubrey Wilkins. Children: Carolyn (born July 2, 1931).

i. MYRA BURRIS.—Born in Franklinton, La., Sept. 22, 1906. Married C. Emery Lane. Children: C. Emery, Jr.

Myra Burris-Lane died Aug. 23, 1927, and was buried in Franklinton, La.

9. PHILLIP F. BURRIS.—Born in Franklinton, La., Apr. 26, 1875. Died May 30, 1876, and was buried in Franklinton.

10. SARAH JANE BURRIS.—Born in Franklinton, La., Nov. 23, 1861. Married Hamp Magee. No children.

Sarah Jane Burris-Magee died Nov. 12, 1914, and was buried in Franklinton.

11. WILLIAM E. BURRIS.—Born in Franklinton, La., Oct. 4, 1854. Died Oct. 7, 1867, and was buried in Franklinton.

F. SARAH ANN BURRIS.—Born in Amite County, Miss., Aug. 16, 1828. Married Charles F. Lucas of Alabama. Children: Benjamin F., Charles F., Jr., Richard Dyke, Mariah B., Susan A., William Tate, and Bettie.

Sarah Ann Burris-Lucas moved with her mother, Mariah Burris-Hamilton, to Clark County, Ala., when her mother married William R. Hamilton. It was while living in Alabama that she met Charles F. Lucas, married him, and settled there.

Sarah Ann Burris-Lucas died July 16, 1866, and was buried in Manila, Ala.

THE COPY OF AN OLD LETTER FROM F. R. MARKS (SARAH ANN BURRIS-LUCAS'S BROTHER-IN-LAW) TO MARIA BURRIS-HAMILTON (SARAH ANN'S MOTHER)

Mobile, July 24th '66.

Dear Mother

It has been a long time since we have heard from any of the family. This leaves what of us is left well with the exception of myself. My health has been bad for a long time, but am now improving some after a protracted illness of some twelve months or more.

Your daughter, Sarah A. Lucas, departed this life on the 16th of this month about 1 o'clock in the evening. Her disease was an affliction of the heart, followed by dropsy. She died quite sudden to what any one expected. She was sensible of her condition long before her death. She leaves a poor, helpless family. We have the children with us. She has been in an almost destitute condition since the Surrender. We have helped her some little since that time but we are in the same condition of most people out here—hardly able to help ourselves. I think myself trouble came as near killing her as disease did.

I wish to hear from the family soon. I want some advice what to do with what little effects there is left. Outside of her place there is about 8 or 10 head of cattle, one year-old colt, some few head of hogs, sheep and goats, besides the household and kitchen furniture. Her indebtedness I know but little about. I don't think he owes anything outside of her doctor bills and funeral expenses. I wish to know whether or not it would actually be necessary to have the estate administered on or not. Of course that would be the proper course to pursue, but the effects are so small to go in a regular detail of law. It would take about all there is to settle up. If there is anything of the kind to be done, some of the rest of the family will have to attend to it. I cannot. Let me hear from some of the family soon.

Betsy and the children join me in love to you all.

Your affectionate son,
F. R. Marks.

P. S.: Direct your letters to Mobile to the care of Julius Hissu & Co. I am near by and will get them.

The following note was written at the top of the above letter by T. C. W. Ellis to George Magee (T. C. W. Ellis married Martina Hamilton, Sarah Ann Lucas's half sister. George Magee married Amanda Caroline Burris, who was Sarah Ann Lucas's sister.) :

Dear George—

By request of Mrs. Hamilton, I re-mail this letter to you. Please let all of the family see it. We are all tolerably well. Hope you are all the same.

Yours as ever,
T. C. W. Ellis.

Amite July 26, 1866.

---

1. BENJAMIN F. LUCAS.—Dead.

2. CHARLES F. LUCAS, JR.—Dead.

3. RICHARD DYKE LUCAS.—Born in Alabama. Never married. Died on his plantation near Manila, Ala., where he lived for many years, and it is thought that he was buried there.

4. MARIAH B. LUCAS.—Born in Alabama in 1850. Married H. S. Burkhalter of Washington Parish, La. No children.

Mariah B. Lucas-Burkhalter married H. S. Burkhalter after the death of his first wife, Susan A. Lucas, her sister. She had been living with her sister and brother-in-law in Washington Parish, La., before her sister died. Mariah B. Lucas-Burkhalter died Oct. 8, 1899, and was buried in Franklinton, La.

5. SUSAN A. LUCAS.—Born in Alabama. Married H. S. Burkhalter. No children. Dead. Was H. S. Burkhalter's first wife.

6. WILLIAM TATE LUCAS.—Born in Suggsville, Ala., Aug. 21, 1857. Married Martha D. Spinks of Whatley, Ala., Jan. 17, 1878. Children: Charles E., William Burris, Henry, Enoch B., Lula A., Mary Ellen, Nina Pilley, and John Frazier.

Martha D. Spinks-Lucas was born in Whatley, Ala., Jan. 17, 1861. She died Oct. 16, 1941, and was buried in Whatley, Ala.

William Tate Lucas died Apr. 18, 1935, and was buried in Whatley.

a. CHARLES E. LUCAS.—Born in Whatley, Ala., Dec. 21, 1878. Married Viola Whatley, daughter of Ben and Beatrice (Coleman) Whatley. Children: Vivian, Clarence, and Edward.

Charles E. Lucas lives in Calvert, Ala.

(1). VIVIAN LUCAS.—Born in Creola, Ala., Sept. 4, 1907. Married Mary E. Lowery, daughter of H. G. Lowery. Children: Betty V., and Mary Jo. Vivian Lucas lives in Hattiesburg, Miss.

(2). CLARENCE LUCAS.—Born in Mt. Vernon, Ala., Oct. 3, 1910. Unmarried. Lives in Calvert, Ala.

(3). EDWARD LUCAS.—Born in Mt. Vernon, Ala., Aug. 19, 1914. Married Kathleen Blount, daughter of Wilson Blount. Children: Edward Kathryn, and Mary Martha.

Edward Lucas lives in Calvert, Ala.

b. WILLIAM BURRIS LUCAS.—Born in Whatley, Ala., Apr. 18, 1880. Never married. Died Apr. 12, 1909, and it is thought that he was buried in Whatley.

c. HENRY LUCAS.—Born in Whatley, Ala., Jan. 6, 1884. Unmarried. Lives in Whatley.

d. ENOCH B. LUCAS.—Born in Whatley, Ala., Mar. 30, 1886. Never married. Died Apr. 9, 1901, and was buried in Whatley, Ala., it is thought.

e. LULA A. LUCAS.—Born in Whatley, Ala., Oct. 16, 1888. Married Shellie A. Wilson, son of Bruce and Jennie (Cammack) Wilson, in 1927. Children: Viola (married Rex Cooper and has a son, named Ralph; divorced now).

Lula A. Lucas-Wilson died Feb. 24, 1935, and was buried in Whatley, Ala.

      f. MARY ELLEN LUCAS.—Born in Whatley, Ala., Apr. 10, 1891. Married Joseph Henry Hendrix (her first cousin), son of Mose and Bettie (Lucas) Hendrix, in 1921. Children: Mary Ellen (born in Whatley, Ala., in 1925; married Marvin Hicks, who was born in Grove Hill, Ala., in 1925; no children), Arnold (born in Whatley, Ala., in 1923), and Billie (born in Prichard, Ala., in 1931; died in 1950, and buried in Mobile, Ala.).

Joseph Henry Hendrix was born in Monroe County, Ala. He lives in Prichard, Ala.

Mary Ellen Lucas-Hendrix died July 13, 1949, and was buried in Whatley, Ala.

      g. NINA PILLEY LUCAS.—Born in Whatley, Ala., Oct. 21, 1893. Died Jan. 4, 1904, and was buried in Whatley, Ala., it is thought.

      h. JOHN FRAZIER LUCAS.—Born in Whatley, Ala., Aug. 17, 1898. Married Mary V. Elmer, daughter of L. Elmer, Apr. 20, 1921, in Mobile, Ala. Children: John F., Jr. and Mary Martha.

Mary V. Elmer-Lucas was born in Meridian, Miss., Mar. 18, 1894. She died Nov. 25, 1951, and was buried in Meridian, Miss.

John Frazier Lucas is a chef at the Jung Hotel, New Orleans, La., and lives at 2119 Palmyra St., New Orleans, La.

      (1). JOHN F. LUCAS, JR.

      (2). MARY MARTHA LUCAS.—Born in Bessemer, Ala., Sept. 14, 1926. Married Anthony C. Spano, son of A. C. Spano, Mar. 15, 1945, in New Orleans, La. Children: Anthony John, and Christopher Frank.

Anthony C. Spano was born in New Orleans, La., Aug. 16, 1925.

They live at 916 Claiborne Drive, Jefferson Parish, La.

      7. BETTIE LUCAS.—Married Mose Hendrix, a Methodist minister. Children: Charlie (dead), Edna (dead), Margaret, Will, Henry, Wheeler, Alfred, Aaron (dead), Lizzie (dead), and Joseph Henry (married Mary Ellen Lucas, his first cousin; children listed under mother's name).

G. ELIZABETH MARIAH BURRIS.—Born in Amite County, Miss., Oct. 25, 1830. Married Fleming R. Marks of Alabama, Nov. 21, 1848. Children: William Buster, Ginnella Inez, Fleming Richard, Jr., Rebecca, Robert Lee, and Mary.

Fleming R. Marks, Sr., was born Apr. 19, 1821. He died Sept. 24, 1866.

Elizabeth Mariah and Fleming R. Marks owned a large plantation near Gainestown, Ala., and worked slaves on the plantation. After Fleming's death Elizabeth Mariah operated the plantation. One day while riding over the plantation, a Negro slave scared her horse and the horse threw her to the ground. Then the Negro hit Elizabeth Mariah over the head with a pine knot and killed her. The people of the community killed the Negro.

Elizabeth Mariah Burris-Marks was buried in Gainestown, Ala., it is thought.

1. WILLIAM BUSTER MARKS.—Born in Gainestown, Ala., June 17, 1856. Never married. Died Jan. 12, 1947, and was buried in Jackson, Ala., it is thought.

For the last nine years of his life, William Buster Marks lived with his nephew, Rudolph R. Marks, at Jackson, Ala.

2. GINNELLA INEZ MARKS.—Born in Suggsville, Ala., June 3, 1860. Married William Byron Wilson of Gainestown, Ala., Apr. 15, 1874. Children: Walter Lee, William Fleming, and Mamie Elizabeth.

William Byron Wilson was born in Gainestown, Ala., Feb. 19, 1841. He died Apr. 24, 1912, and was buried in Dothan, Ala.

Ginnella Inez Marks-Wilson died June 22, 1928, and was buried in Birmingham, Ala.

a. WALTER LEE WILSON.—Born in Gainestown, Ala., Aug. 3, 1880. Married Lillian May Burge. Children: Mamie Lee, and Walter Byron.

Lillian May Burge was born in Grove Hill, Ala., June 10, 1883.

(1). MAMIE LEE WILSON.—Born in Gainestown, Ala., Nov. 26, 1904. Married Henry Andrew Bailey of Birmingham, Ala., Nov. 23, 1927. No children.

(2). WALTER BYRON WILSON.—Born in Birmingham, Ala., May 4, 1914. Unmarried.

b. WILLIAM FLEMING WILSON.—Born in Gainestown, Ala.,

Jan. 27, 1877. Never married. Died Dec. 13, 1901, and was buried in Gainestown, Ala.

c. MAMIE ELIZABETH WILSON.—Born in Gainestown, Ala., Apr. 3, 1875. Married Nat Hood, Jr., June 15, 1898. Children: Walter Nathaniel (born in Mar., 1899; lives in Rome, Ga.).

Mamie Elizabeth Wilson-Hood died Aug., 1899, and was buried in Piedmont, Ala.

3. FLEMING RICHARD MARKS, JR.—Born in Gainestown, Ala., Apr. 24, 1860. Married Lola Anderson Sept. 24, 1892. Children: Mamie Inez.

Lola Anderson-Marks was born in Walker Springs, Ala., Dec. 11, 1872. She is still living.

Fleming Richard Marks, Jr., is dead.

a. MAMIE INEZ MARKS.—Born in Gainestown, Ala., Oct. 11, 1897. Married Willard E. Hudson July 2, 1919. Children: Mary Alice (born in Gainestown, Ala., May 4, 1920).

Willard E. Hudson was born in Gastonberg, Ala., Feb. 10, 1896.

4. REBECCA MARKS.—Born in Walker Springs, Ala., Feb. 25, 1853. Married Tim Wilson in 1872. Children: John Fleming, Thomas Jewett, and Albert.

Tim Wilson was born in Gainestown, Ala. He is dead. He was buried in Gainestown, Ala.

Rebecca Marks-Wilson lives in Walker Springs, Ala.

a. JOHN FLEMING WILSON.—Born in Gainestown, Ala. Lives in New Jersey.

b. THOMAS JEWETT WILSON.—Born in Gainestown, Ala. Lives in Texas.

c. ALBERT WILSON.—Born in Gainestown, Ala. Dead.

5. ROBERT LEE MARKS.—Born in Gainestown, Ala., Feb. 25, 1866. Married Callie Gordon of Walker Springs, Ala., in 1890. Children: Rudolph R., Bessie, Bertha, and Gordon.

Callie Gordon-Marks is dead. She was buried in Walker Springs, Ala.

Robert Lee Marks died in 1930.

a. RUDOLPH R. MARKS.—Born in Walker Springs, Ala., in 1901. Married Mary Lee Thompson, daughter of Joe Thompson, Mar.

3, 1933, in Walker Springs, Ala. Children: Nettie Lee (born Jan. 26, 1934; married Saint Elmo McLendon, son of William Emmett McLendon, June 17, 1951, in Waynesboro, Miss.; lives near Allen, Ala.), Robert Warren (born May 29, 1936), Roy Flinn (born Mar. 30, 1939), Fred Vinson (born June 8, 1942), Myrtle Lorraine (born May 26, 1947), Alfred Rudolph (born Nov. 28, 1948), and Ethel Mae (born Oct. 28, 1950).

Mary Lee Thompson-Marks was born in Vredenburg, Ala., Sept. 15, 1915.

They live near Jackson, Ala.

b. BESSIE MARKS.—Born in Walker Springs, Ala., in 1898. Married Edward Few, son of George Few, Sept. 12, 1917, in Walker Springs, Ala. Children: Edward, Jr., Earl Frederick, Jerry Donald, Thomas Jesse, Howard David, and Flora Mae.

Edward David Few was born in Catherine, Ala., Nov. 12, 1899.

Bessie and Bertha Marks were twins. Edward Few, Jr., served in the armed forces of the U. S. five years during World War II. He served some of this time in Germany and was staff sergeant. Thomas Jessie Few served one year in Japan during World War II.

c. BERTHA MARKS.—Born in Walker Springs, Ala., in 1898. Married Estell Griffen, son of Bill Griffen, in Walker Springs, May 1923. No children.

Bertha Marks-Griffen died in Mar. 1934, and was buried in the Evergreen Church Cemetery.

d. GORDON MARKS.—Born in Walker Springs, Ala., in 1895. Married Josephine Cornley, daughter of Guy Cornley, in Mobile, Ala. Children: Callie Marie.

Gordon Marks died Apr. 11, 1938, and was buried in Leroy, Ala.

6. MARY MARKS.—Born in Gainestown, Ala., July 17, 1863. Married Dr. Frederick Meeker. Children: Henry Frederick (an outstanding civil engineer of New York).

Mary Marks-Meeker is dead. She was buried in Demopolis, Ala.

H. WILLIAM ADDISON BURRIS.—Born in Amite County, Miss., Dec. 14, 1835. Married Flora Lavonia Magee, daughter of William and Harriett Magee, in Franklinton, La. Children: James William, Byron Benton, Edmund Andrews, Sarah (Sallie), and Robert Lee.

Flora Lavonia Magee was a first cousin of Mrs. James Madison

Burris, Mrs. Hampton Burris, and George Magee (Amanda Caroline Burris's husband). She was born in Washington Parish, La. She died Aug. 17, 1924, and was buried in Franklinton, La.

William Addison Burris was first a farmer, and, later, he worked at the courthouse in Franklinton, La., doing abstract work and the like. It was said that he could handle almost any legal matter about as well as a lawyer.

His old farm, on which he settled after marrying Flora Lavonia Magee, is located on the Franklinton-Tylertown (Miss.) Highway, about three and one-half miles north of Franklinton, La. Prior to his living on this place, it is thought he lived with his mother, Mariah Andrews-Burris-Hamilton, when she lived, first, on her farm, which is now known as the Old Jason Bateman Place, and when she lived, second, on her farm, which is now known as the Old Ferd Magee Place.

William Addison Burris served in the Confederate Army during the Civil War. His service record is as follows: Enlisted at Camp Moore, La., July 7, 1861. Age 29. Appointed third sergeant July 7, 1861. Present to Aug., 1861. Roll for Sept. and Oct., 1861—absent. Sent to Richmond, Va., sick. Discharged at Richmond, Va., Oct. 23, 1861. Was sergeant in Company I, 9th Louisiana Infantry, when discharged. Re-enlisted May 14, 1862, at Franklinton, La. Was private in Company C, 3rd. (Wingfield's) Louisiana Cavalry. Roll not dated. Present. (This record copied from Memorial Hall by the War Department in June 1903). William Addison Burris died in 1906, and was buried in Franklinton, La.

1. JAMES WILLIAM BURRIS.—Born in Franklinton, La., Dec. 10, 1855. Married Mary M. Bickham, daughter of Tom (Trigger) and Christine (Lewis) Bickham. Children: Anna Sarah, William Otto, Wincie Ora, Walter Addison, Benton Blocker, and Hampton.

Mary M. Bickham-Burris was born Dec. 18, 1866. She died June 8, 1922, and was buried in Franklinton, La.

James William Burris was a farmer. He lived on his father's old place on Hayes Creek in Washington Parish, La. He was killed enroute to Franklinton on a mule wagon. The mules became frightened and ran away. He fell off the wagon and it ran over him and killed him. He was buried in Franklinton, La.

a. ANNA SARAH BURRIS.—Born in Franklinton, La., Sept. 10, 1888. Married Fletcher D. Cooper Mar. 28, 1911, in Franklinton,

La. Children: Sadye Lenora, Mary Ruth, James Ray, Martha Christine, Elizabeth Jane, and Marjorie Elaine.

Fletcher D. Cooper was born in Bogalusa, La., Apr. 13, 1887. They live in Bogalusa, La.

(1). SADYE LENORA COOPER.—Born in Bogalusa, La., June 1, 1913. Married Henry Ephraim Rester, son of James G. Rester, Dec. 29, 1945, in Bogalusa, La. No children.

Sadye Lenora Cooper-Rester died May 29, 1950, and was buried in McGehee's Cemetery, near Bogalusa, La.

Henry Ephraim Rester was born in Washington Parish, La., July 8, 1889.

(2). MARY RUTH COOPER.—Born in Bogalusa, La., Dec. 11, 1915. Married T. J. Hosey, son of T. J. and Mary E. (Murphy) Hosey, Oct. 16, 1938, in Poplarville, Miss. Children: Suzanne (adopted; born in Laurel, Miss., Dec. 22, 1951).

T. J. Hosey was born in Laurel, Miss., Oct. 7, 1910.

(3). JAMES RAY COOPER.—Born in Bogalusa, La., Mar. 17, 1918. Married Bernice Stone. Children: James Ray, Jr., (born May 26, 1949). They live in Bogalusa, La.

(4). MARTHA CHRISTINE COOPER.—Born in Bogalusa, La., Dec. 29, 1923. Married Paul Harris Murdoch July 6, 1946. Children: Deborah (born July 6, 1947), and Paul Harris, Jr. (born Apr. 12, 1949), and Scott Alan (born in Long Beach, Cal., Nov. 17, 1950).

They live in Long Beach, Cal.

(5). ELIZABETH JANE COOPER.—Born in Bogalusa, La., Apr. 4, 1926. Unmarried. Lives in Bogalusa, La.

(6). MARJORIE ELAINE COOPER.—Born in Bogalusa, La., Aug. 14, 1930. Unmarried. Lives in Bogalusa, La.

b. WILLIAM OTTO BURRIS.—Born near Franklinton, La., Dec. 17, 1892. Married Eunice Foil, daughter of Dock Foil, in 1917. Children: Wilda Estelle, William Shelby, and Joseph Harold.

William Otto Burris (called Otto by most people) served in World War I as private, 64th Depot Brigade. He served continuously and efficiently as assessor of Washington Parish, La., from Jan. 1, 1933, to May 25, 1950. He broke all records in Washington Parish in being elected this many times to the same public office. He died May 25, 1950, and was buried in the Ellis Cemetery in Franklinton, La.

(1). WILDA ESTELLE BURRIS.—Born near Franklinton, La., July 1, 1919. Married Hal Kilbourne of Clinton, La. Children: Don Burris (born June 29, 1943). They live in Clinton, La.

(2). WILLIAM SHELBY BURRIS.—Born near Franklinton, La., Aug. 18, 1921. Married Sarah Mabel Anglin, daughter of B. J. and Maggie (Alford) Anglin. Children: Ann (born Apr. 23, 1944).

William Shelby Burris served from June 25, 1942, to Dec. 28, 1945, as captain in 4th Infantry Division, during World War II. He was wounded twice in France. He lives in Baton Rouge, La.

(3). JOSEPH HAROLD BURRIS.—Born near Franklinton, La., Oct. 18, 1924. Married Gwendolyn Sylvest, daughter of Hezzie and Myrtle Sylvest, Dec. 27, 1945. Children: Sylvia Lynn (born Jan. 13, 1947), and William Joseph (born Nov. 1, 1949).

Gwendolyn Sylvest-Burris was born in Franklinton, La., Oct. 20, 1922.

Joseph Harold Burris lives near Franklinton, La. He is a deputy clerk in assessor's office.

c. WINCIE ORA BURRIS.—Born near Franklinton, La., July 21, 1894. Married William Andrew Page, Jr., son of William Andrew Page, Sr., of Morehouse Parish, La., Nov. 20, 1932, in Franklinton, La. Children: Virginia Ann (adopted).

Wincie Burris-Page taught school for many years before marrying.

They live in Bogalusa, La.

d. WALTER ADDISON BURRIS.—Born in Franklinton, La., Dec. 17, 1896. Married Electa Sylvest, daughter of James William Sylvest, Nov. 23, 1922, in Franklinton, La. Children: Kenneth James, Karl Hampton, Mary Lenora, and Walter Allen.

Electa Sylvest-Burris was born near Franklinton, La., Aug. 19, 1902.

They live near Franklinton, La.

(1). KENNETH JAMES BURRIS.—Born in Franklinton, La., Feb. 12, 1924. Married Jeanne Knight, daughter of Wilbur W. Knight, June 28, 1947, in Tylertown, Miss. No children.

Jeanne Knight-Burris was born in Franklinton, La., July 22, 1929.

Kenneth James Burris served in the U. S. Army Air Force during

World War II, from Dec. 3, 1942, to Mar. 14, 1946. He was a staff sergeant in the 356th Bombardment Squadron. He lives in Franklinton, La.

(2). KARL HAMPTON BURRIS.—Born in Franklinton, La., Mar. 22, 1927. Married Versie Viola Hodges, daughter of Aletha (Hines) and Ephrum H. Hodges. Served in the U. S. Navy as Seaman 1st Class during World War II from June 20, 1944, to June 8, 1946. Lives in Franklinton, La.

(3). MARY LENORA BURRIS.—Born in Franklinton, La., Mar. 14, 1930. Married Lavell Crain, son of J. A. Crain, Apr. 14, 1948, in Tylertown, Miss. Children: Dennis Lavell (born Dec. 6, 1949).

Lavell Crain was born in Pine, La., Mar. 15, 1929.

(4). WALTER ALLEN BURRIS.—Born in Franklinton, La., Nov. 28, 1935.

e. BENTON BLOCKER BURRIS.—Born in Franklinton, La., Aug. 2, 1901. Married Myrtle Pettitt, daughter of W. H. and Rose Lee (Pierce) Pettitt, Aug. 29, 1923, in Mt. Hermon, La. Children: Benny B. (adopted; born Feb. 9, 1945).

Myrtle Pettitt-Burris was born in Mt. Hermon, La., Aug. 30, 1906.

Benton Blocker Burris operates a farm near Franklinton, La.

f. HAMPTON BURRIS.—Born in Franklinton, La. Died when young.

2. BYRON BENTON BURRIS.—Born near Franklinton, La., Jan. 10, 1858. Married Lenora Graves, daughter of Nathaniel Graves. Children: Ralph Louie, Ollie, Nellie, William Nathaniel, Jesse Stallings, Inez, Belma Pearl, and Harvey Ellis.

Lenora Graves-Burris was born in Washington Parish, La., Mar. 24, 1860. She died Oct. 19, 1927, and was buried in Franklinton, La.

Byron Benton Burris lived in Washington Parish, La., all of his life. He was first a farmer, then a mill man. He died July 27, 1919, and was buried in Franklinton, La.

a. RALPH LOUIE BURRIS.—Born near Franklinton, La., in 1885. Died in 1937, and was buried in Franklinton, La.

Ralph Louie Burris was a railway employee all of his life. He held the position of fireman, engineer, and flagman. He was run over by a train and killed near Slidell, La.

b. OLLIE BURRIS.—Born near Franklinton, La., in 1887. Married Otis B. Bradley of Georgia in 1903. Children: Otis B., Jr., Milton, Mildred, and Jesse Allen.

Otis B. Bradley came from Georgia to Washington Parish, La., in 1903 to teach a small country school near Franklinton, La. He met Ollie Burris shortly after his arrival in Washington Parish; and, after a short acquaintance, married her. After teaching school one year in Washington Parish, Otis B. Bradley and family moved to Georgia, where he taught school for many years in various places in Georgia.

Ollie Burris-Bradley died in 1919, and was buried in Georgia. She was the mother of two sets of twins. One of her twins—Jesse Allen's brother—died shortly after birth.

(1). OTIS B. BRADLEY, JR.—Born in Georgia Dec. 28, 1904. Married Wilda McAnulty Oct. 2, 1932, in Bartow, Fla. Children: Wilda Ann (born Sept. 21, 1936).

Wilda McAnulty-Bradley was born in Barnsboro, Pa., June 1, 1911.

Otis B. Bradley, Jr., lives in Lake City, Fla.

(2). MILTON BRADLEY.—Born in Euharlee, Ga., Jan. 11, 1910. Married Dorothy Lee Show, daughter of Ruby Dobbs Show, Nov. 20, 1937, in Atlanta, Ga. No children.

Dorothy Lee Show-Bradley was born in Atlanta, Ga., Apr. 16, 1915.

Milton Bradley is a twin brother of Mildred Bradley. He lives in Atlanta, Ga.

(3). MILDRED BRADLEY.—Born in Euharlee, Ga., Jan. 11, 1910. Married Otho Bunyan Stansell, son of W. K. Stansell, June 1, 1934, in Fort Meade, Fla. Children: Linda Lou (born in Bartow, Fla., Oct. 20, 1943), and Otho Bunyan, Jr. (born in Wauchula, Fla., Jan. 3, 1947).

Otho Bunyan Stansell was born in Alexandria City, Ala., Jan. 29, 1903.

(4). JESSE ALLEN BRADLEY.—Born in Collins, Ga., Oct. 11, 1918. Unmarried. Jesse Allen Bradley lives in Norfolk, Va., and operates a two-chair barber shop. He is a graduate of the Tampa, Fla., Business College, also of the Norfolk Barber College. He is a veteran of World War II, having served in the U. S. Army in Africa and Sicily.

c. NELLIE BURRIS.—Born near Franklinton, La., in 1899. Married Paul E. Greenlaw, son of Lawrence D. and Dora (Runnells) Greenlaw, in 1908, in Franklinton. Children: Dorothy Alice, Katherine Russell, Eleanor Ruth, and Lawrence Dade.

Paul E. Greenlaw was born in Hazlehurst, Miss., Mar. 18, 1887. He died June 2, 1948, and was buried in Franklinton, La. He was a pioneer automobile dealer in Washington Parish, La.

Nellie Burris-Greenlaw has lived in Franklinton, La., all of her life. She lives in the old Greenlaw residence.

(1). DOROTHY ALICE GREENLAW.—Born in Franklinton, La., Aug. 18, 1909. Married Harold O'Neil Marquart, son of E. L. and Lelia (Vincent) Marquart, Apr. 6, 1931. Children: Paul Emerson, Dianne Runnells, Sidney Suzanne, Harold O'Neil, Jr., and Michael Vincent.

Harold O'Neil Marquart was born in Lake Arthur, La., Oct. 3, 1908. He attended L. S. U. and took the engineering course.

Dorothy Alice Greenlaw-Marquart attended Mississippi Woman's College and the Mississippi State College for Women.

They live in Franklinton, La.

(a). PAUL EMERSON MARQUART.—Born in Franklinton, La., Dec. 8, 1932. Attending college.

(b). DIANNE RUNNELLS MARQUART.—Born in Franklinton, La., May 18, 1935. Married James Clayton Moore, son of James Albert and Ina (McDaniel) Moore, in 1951.

James Clayton Moore was born Dec. 1, 1929. He is a graduate of Molar Barber College of New Orleans, La. He attended L. S. U. for a short time. He is a member of the Louisiana National Guard.

They live in Franklinton, La.

(c). SIDNEY SUZANNE MARQUART.—Born in Baton Rouge, La., No. 11, 1938. Lives in Franklinton, La., with her parents.

(d). HAROLD O'NEIL MARQUART, JR.—Born in Baton Rouge, La., Jan. 3, 1945. Lives in Franklinton, La., with his parents.

(e). MICHAEL VINCENT MARQUART.—Born in Franklinton, La., Dec. 29, 1947. Lives in Franklinton, La., with his parents.

(2). KATHERINE RUSSELL GREENLAW.—Born in Franklinton, La., July 20, 1914. Married Coleman Simmons, son of C. Willis Simmons, Jan. 6, 1933, in Tylertown, Miss. Children: Sara Michael (born in Franklinton, La., Jan. 27, 1943).

Coleman Simmons was born in Mt. Hermon, La., May 25, 1911. He operates an automobile body shop in Franklinton, La.

Katherine Greenlaw-Simmons studied bookkeeping and business administration by correspondence, and is an excellent bookkeeper.

They live in Franklinton, La.

(3). ELEANOR RUTH GREENLAW.—Born in Franklinton, La., Jan. 20, 1922. Married George Lewis Brown, son of George D. and Frankie (Bickham) Brown, July 28, 1946, in Franklinton, La. Children: George Lewis, Jr. (born in Pensacola, Fla., Oct. 23, 1948).

George Lewis Brown was born in Franklinton, La.

(4). LAWRENCE DADE GREENLAW.—Born in Franklinton, La., Feb. 7, 1913. Died Mar. 9, 1913, and was buried in Franklinton, La.

d. WILLIAM NATHANIEL BURRIS.—Born near Franklinton, La., Apr. 2, 1891. Married Bessie Hale. No children. William Nathaniel Burris is a graduate of the Louisiana State University, being awarded the B.A. Degree from that institution in 1915. He has been working for various plumbing manufacturers in the U. S. for many years. At present he is head of the plumbing department of the M. J. Gibbons Supply Co. of Dayton, Ohio. He is a twin brother of Jesse Stallings Burris.

e. JESSE STALLINGS BURRIS.—Born near Franklinton, La., Apr. 2, 1891. Married Addie Bruce Campbell, daughter of Howard P. and Olie (Cross) Campbell, Nov. 19, 1932, in Oakdale, La. No children.

Addie Bruce Campbell-Burris was born in Concordia Parish, La., June 6, 1904.

Jesse Stallings Burris has taught school all of his life. He has been principal of a junior high school, an assistant principal of a high school, principal of a high school, and is at present superintendent of schools of Concordia Parish, La., which position he has held since Mar. 18, 1933. He has been teaching school thirty-three years. He is a veteran of World War I, with seven months' service overseas, in France. They live in Vidalia, La.

f. INEZ BURRIS.—Born near Franklinton, La., in 1893. Died in 1896, and buried in the Hayes Creek Church Cemetery in Washington Parish, La.

g. BELMA PEARL BURRIS.—Born near Franklinton, La., in 1895. Unmarried.

Belma Pearl Burris has lived in Franklinton, La., all of her life. After finishing high school in 1913, she taught school in Washington Parish, La., for four years. She has been doing clerical work for the past several years.

h. HARVEY ELLIS BURRIS.—Born near Franklinton, La., Oct. 17, 1898. Married Marguerite Forrester of New Orleans, La., in 1922. No children.

Harvey Ellis Burris died Feb. 1, 1924, and was buried in Franklinton, La. He was a veteran of World War I. He was clerk in the New Orleans Great Northern Railway office in Bogalusa, La., for several years prior to his death.

3. EDMUND ANDREWS BURRIS.—Born near Franklinton, La., Mar. 6, 1864. Married Ruth Bateman, daughter of Hugh Bateman. Children: Hugh Addison, (a son who died in infancy), Flora Elma, Robert Hampton and Beatrice Olivia.

Ruth Bateman-Burris was born in Franklinton, La., Nov. 26, 1871. She died in the 1940's, and was buried in Franklinton, La.

Edmund Andrew Burris, known generally as Ed Burris, was named for his great grandfather, Edmund Andrews of Liberty, Miss. He was first a farmer, his farm being a portion of the William A. Burris Place, located about three and one-half miles north of Franklinton, La. In early life, he left the farm and moved to Franklinton, where he did various kinds of work and held various positions, among which was that of town marshall and deputy sheriff.

Ed Burris was the most widely known and popular of the early generations of Burrises in Washington Parish, La. He died Aug. 20, 1935, and was buried in Franklinton, La.

a. HUGH ADDISON BURRIS.—Born near Franklinton, La., Oct. 11, 1889. Died Apr. 13, 1899, during a flu epidemic, and was buried in Franklinton, La.

b. . . . . (A son—unnamed).—Born near Franklinton, La., Mar. 24, 1892. Died Mar. 31, 1892, and buried in Franklinton, La.

c. FLORA ELMA BURRIS.—Born in Franklinton, La., Aug. 13, 1898. Died Apr. 11, 1899, and buried in Franklinton, La.

d. ROBERT HAMPTON BURRIS.—Born near Franklinton, La., Dec. 25, 1891. Married Ophelia Pope, daughter of I. L. Pope, Nov. 2, 1919. Children: Dorothy Louise, and Elaine.

Ophelia Pope-Burris was born near Franklinton, La., Oct. 15, 1892.

Robert Hampton Burris did clerical work in Bogalusa, La., most of his life. For the last several years of his life he was an invalid, being afflicted with arthritis. He was a veteran of World War I. He died Oct. 17, 1948, and was buried in Franklinton, La.

(1). DOROTHY LOUISE BURRIS.—Born in Bogalusa, La., Jan. 19, 1923. Married Warren W. Seal, son of William Andrew and Martha Louise (Wheat) Seal, Nov. 5, 1938, in Poplarville, Miss. Children: Judith Lennon (born Feb. 21, 1940), Rebecca Ann (born Nov. 16, 1942), and Robert Warren (born Dec. 17, 1945).

Warren W. Seal was born in Varnado, La., June 21, 1918.

They live in Bogalusa, La.

(2). ELAINE BURRIS.—Born in Bogalusa, La., Aug. 4, 1925. Married Gradon Eldred Mongar, son of Jesse Paul and Freda V. (Cunningham) Mongar, Aug. 14, 1945, in Santa Monica, Cal. Children: Carol Ann (born Sept. 19, 1948).

Gradon Eldred Mongar was born in Beverly, Neb., Oct. 6, 1923. They live in Visalia, Cal.

e. BEATRICE OLIVIA BURRIS.—Born in Franklinton, La., Aug. 14, 1906. Married Joseph Newton Magee, son of E. L. Magee, Dec. 22, 1929, in Franklinton, La. Children: Patricia Ruth (born in Franklinton, La., Aug. 2, 1931), and Joseph Edmund (born in Franklinton, La., Nov. 10, 1934).

Joseph Newton Magee was born in Franklinton, La. He died in Bogalusa, La., May 26, 1950.

Beatrice Olivia Burris-Magee died Dec. 7, 1937, and was buried in Franklinton, La.

4. SARAH (SALLIE) BURRIS.—Born near Franklinton, La., Sept. 24, 1866. Married Daniel McSween Wadsworth, son of John Wadsworth, Dec. 23, 1886, in Franklinton, La. Children: Lucy Lavonia, John Addison, Winnie Davis, Iddo Franklin, William Hamilton, Sarah Margaret, Daniel McSween, Jr., Flora, and Jane.

Daniel McSween Wadsworth was born in Franklinton, La., July 17, 1863. He was a bookkeeper and a merchant. He held positions in Franklinton, La., Covington, La., Bogalusa, La., and Columbia, Miss. He died Dec. 9, 1926, and was buried in Franklinton, La.

Sarah (Sallie) Burris-Wadsworth died Sept. 10, 1942, and was buried in Franklinton, La.

    a. LUCY LAVONIA WADSWORTH.—Born in Columbia, Miss., Oct. 27, 1887. Never married. Did clerical work most of her life. Died Jan. 8, 1933, and was buried in Franklinton, La.

    b. JOHN ADDISON WADSWORTH.—Born in Columbia, Miss., Oct. 4, 1889. Married Emily Bateman, daughter of Milton Bateman, Jan. 1, 1934, in Franklinton, La. Children: Sarah Elizabeth (born in Franklinton, La., Apr. 7, 1935), and James Addison (born in Franklinton, La., Oct. 10, 1939).

Emily Bateman-Wadsworth was born in Franklinton, La., Sept. 3, 1911. She died Oct. 12, 1948, and was buried in Franklinton.

John Addison Wadsworth has done bookkeeping and general clerical work most of his life. He has worked for railway companies largely. He lives in Bogalusa, La.

    c. WINNIE DAVIS WADSWORTH.—Born in Columbia, Miss., Feb. 3, 1894. Married H. E. Rester. Children: Ruth, Henri Etta, and Winnie Marie.

Winnie Davis Wadsworth-Rester died Dec. 14, 1943, and was buried in Bogalusa, La.

    (1). RUTH RESTER.—Born in Bogalusa, La., Mar. 9, 1917. Unmarried. Lives in Bogalusa, La.

    (2). HENRI ETTA RESTER.—Born in Poplarville, Miss., Oct. 9, 1920. Married John Gates Seaman Mar. 7, 1946, in New Orleans, La. Children: John Gates, Jr. (born in Houston, Tex., Feb. 27, 1947).

    (3). WINNIE MARIE RESTER.—Born in Bogalusa, La., July 30, 1922. Married Wilbur Eugene Lyon of Missouri Jan. 28, 1944, in New Orleans, La. Children: Linda Gene (born in Dallas, Tex., July 20, 1945), Ann Marie (born in Dallas, Tex., May 4, 1947), and John Alan (born in Dallas, Tex., Nov. 1, 1948).

    d. IDDO FRANKLIN WADSWORTH.—Born in Columbia, Miss., Jan. 26, 1896. Married Ruby Moak, daughter of Tom Moak, July 5,

1923, in Bogalusa, La. No children. Ruby Moak-Wadsworth was born in Johnson Station, Miss., Oct. 30, 1897.

Iddo Franklin Wadsworth is a veteran of World War I, with twenty-one months' service in the U. S. Navy. He lives in Jackson, Miss.

e. WILLIAM HAMILTON WADSWORTH.—Born in Covington, La., Sept. 21, 1907. Unmarried. Served three years in the U. S. Navy, in the Pacific Area, during World War II. Lives in Bogalusa, La.

f. SARAH MARGARET WADSWORTH.—Born in Columbia, Miss., Dec. 10, 1900. Unmarried. Has taught school most of her life, and most, if not all of which has been done in the Bogalusa, La., city schools. Received her M. A. Degree in 1950 from Mississippi Southern College.

g. DANIEL MCSWEEN WADSWORTH, JR.—Born in Covington, La., Dec. 20, 1904. Married Eileen Coakley, daughter of John and Ann (Maughan) Coakley, Oct. 27, 1943, in Bogalusa, La. No children.

Eileen Coakley was born in Terre Haute, Ind., June 21, 1904. They live in Bogalusa, La.

h. FLORA WADSWORTH.—Born in Columbia, Miss., Dec. 4, 1890. Died Nov. 18, 1896, and was buried in Franklinton, La. Just before her death, Flora was lost for a day and night once. Her mother sent her from the peach orchard to the house to get her bonnet. She got lost in the tall cotton stalks along the way and wandered into the swamps. She was found the next day by a Negro man, several miles from home, after a community-wide search. She lived several months after this experience.

i. JANE WADSWORTH.—Born in Covington, La., Oct. 4, 1898. Died Oct. 21, 1898, and was buried in Franklinton, La.

5. ROBERT LEE BURRIS.—Born near Franklinton, La., Feb. 24, 1870. Married Martha Clotilde Wood, daughter of Press Wood, Nov. 22, 1895, in Franklinton, La. Children: Nathan Benton, Hugh Preston, Jesse Daniel, Flora Mae, Emma Gay, Alma Ernestine, James Wilson, William Addison, Roy Lee, and Roberta (Bobbie). Robert Lee Burris died Sept. 11, 1931, and was buried in Franklinton, La. He was killed when his mule team ran away with him enroute to Franklinton, not far from the place where his brother, James William, was killed in a similar way thirty years before. Robert Lee Burris was a

highly successful farmer and dairyman. He lived on his father's old place.

a. NATHAN BENTON BURRIS.—Born near Franklinton, La., Oct. 3, 1897. Married Gladys Bateman, daughter of Robert Bateman. Children: Robert Nathan.

Gladys Bateman-Burris was born near Franklinton, La., Dec. 8, 1898.

Nathan Benton Burris died Nov. 26, 1929, and was buried in Franklinton, La.

(1). ROBERT NATHAN BURRIS.—Born in Franklinton, La., June 1, 1925. Married Keitha Cassonova. No children.

Keitha Cassonova was born Sept. 3, 1928.

Robert Nathan Burris served in the U. S. Navy during World War II, from Oct. 14, 1942, to June 1, 1946, as Technician Mate, Third Class.

b. HUGH PRESTON BURRIS.—Born near Franklinton, La., Feb. 8, 1901. Married Velma Bateman, daughter of Robert H. Bateman, Jan. 29, 1925, in Franklinton, La. Children: Harvey Hugh, and Olive Velma.

Velma Bateman-Burris was born near Franklinton, La., Apr. 13, 1902.

Hugh Preston Burris has been engaged in farming and dairying most of his life. He lives on a part of his father's place, which is a part of the Old William Addison Burris Place.

(1). HARVEY HUGH BURRIS.—Born near Franklinton, La., Nov. 6, 1925. Married Agnes Aylene Wood, daughter of Minnie (Braun) and Robert Austin Wood. Served in the U. S. Navy during World War II, from June 27, 1944, to June 6, 1946, as Storekeeper, Third Class. Lives near Franklinton, La.

(2). OLIVE VELMA BURRIS.—Born near Franklinton, La., Jan 22, 1928. Unmarried. Lives with her parents near Franklinton, La.

c. JESSE DANIEL BURRIS.—Born near Franklinton, La., Sept. 21, 1899. Never married. Died Jan. 17, 1930, and was buried in Franklinton, La. While constructing a barn, Jesse Daniel Burris fell from the top of it and died of head injuries.

d. FLORA MAE BURRIS.—Born near Franklinton, La., July

5, 1903. Unmarried. Flora Mae Burris is a graduate of Northwestern State College of Natchitoches, La. She holds the B. A. Degree from that institution. She is one of the co-authors of this family history. She lives in Franklinton, La., and is a teacher in the Franklinton Elementary School.

e. EMMA GAY BURRIS.—Born near Franklinton, La., Apr. 6, 1905. Unmarried. Emma Gay Burris is a graduate of Scarritt College of Nashville, Tenn. She holds an M. A. Degree (in Sociology) from that institution. She has been a church and missionary worker for the Methodist Church since graduation. She was director of Marcy Center of Chicago, Ill., for several years. She is now located in New York, N. Y.

f. ALMA ERNESTINE BURRIS.—Born near Franklinton, La., Feb. 10, 1908. Married Lamar Merriot Richardson, son of Stephen Pinkney Richardson, June 20, 1937. Children: Lamar Merriot II (born in Baton Rouge, La., Nov. 1, 1949).

Lamar Merriot Richardson was born near Franklinton, La., Sept. 18, 1906.

Alma Burris-Richardson taught school for several years before her marriage. They live in Franklinton, La.

g. JAMES WILSON BURRIS.—Born near Franklinton, La., Jan. 19, 1913. Married Mary Margaret Watts, daughter of Walter Lee and Gladys (Saint) Watts, Dec. 27, 1947, in Hammond, La. Children: James Wilson (Jimmy), Jr. (born near Franklinton, La., Oct. 26, 1949), and Jesse Daniel (born near Franklinton, La., May 9, 1952).

Mary Margaret Watts-Burris was born in Hammond, La., Oct. 6, 1920.

James Wilson Burris served in the U. S. Navy during World War II, from Oct. 15, 1942, to Nov. 29, 1945. He made the Normandy invasion on the Omaha beachhead. He was in the first wave, and was commended by the commanding officer for his efficient job as PhMIC aboard landing ship. He lives near Franklinton, La., and operates a dairy.

h. WILLIAM ADDISON BURRIS.—Born near Franklinton, La., Jan. 29, 1919. Married Margie Ann Bickham-Williams, daughter of Benton Edgar Bickham, Dec. 19, 1948. Children: William Addison II (born Dec. 19, 1950). Margie Ann Bickham-Williams-Burris was born in Franklinton, La., Mar. 30, 1922.

William Addison Burris served in the U. S. Navy as Seaman First Class from Apr. 27, 1942, to June 15, 1945, during World War II. He served in the Pacific Area on the heavy cruiser San Francisco. He was wounded at Guadalcanal Nov. 13, 1942, and was given the Purple Heart Decoration. For gallantry in action, he received a Presidential Unit Citation. He lives in Franklinton, La., and operates a dairy.

i. ROY LEE BURRIS.—Born near Franklinton, La., July 24, 1910. Married Wilda Eugene Breland, daughter of E. Y. Breland, Aug. 8, 1940, in Franklinton, La. Children: Martha Jean (born Oct. 6, 1942), and Roy Lee, Jr. (born Jan. 5, 1949).

Wilda Eugene Breland-Burris was born in Pine, La., July 2, 1914. Roy Lee Burris holds a B. A. Degree in Agriculture from L. S. U. He taught school for several years, but is now operating a cleaning and pressing business in Ponchatoula, La.

j. ROBERTA (BOBBIE) BURRIS.—Born near Franklinton, La., July 9, 1915. Married Andrew Griffith Johnson, son of Delos R. Johnson, Aug. 25, 1940, in Franklinton, La. Children: Andrew Griffith, Jr. (born Apr. 12, 1942). Bobbie Burris-Johnson graduated from Whitworth College of Brookhaven, Miss., and taught school one year. After this, she worked two years for the Methodist Church in Tampa and Key West, Fla.

Andrew Griffith Johnson was born in Franklinton, La., July 9, 1915. He lives in Franklinton, La., and operates an insurance business.

I. AMANDA CAROLINE BURRIS.—Born in Amite County, Miss., Mar. 2, 1838. Married George Magee. Children: John William, Dora, Ollie, Earnest, and Sidney.

George Magee was born Oct. 30, 1829. He was a brother of Mrs. James Madison Burris and Mrs. Hampton Burris; he was also a first cousin of Mrs. William Addison Burris. Amanda Caroline Burris-Magee married at the age of 13, after returning from Alabama with her mother, Mariah Burris-Hamilton, according to a nephew of hers. This nephew also said that James Madison Burris, Amanda's oldest brother, ran his horse to death in an attempt to overtake Amanda and George and stop the marriage, as he thought Amanda was too young (only 13) to marry and he wanted to send her to school in Alabama. She died in Kentwood, La., and was buried there.

George Magee died Mar. 5, 1877, at the age of 47 years and 4 months.

1. JOHN WILLIAM MAGEE.—Born in Washington Parish, La., in 1853. Married Ellen Rebecca Daniels. No children. Died Oct. 28, 1883, at the age of 30.

2. DORA MAGEE.—Born in Washington Parish, La., in 1856. Married W. J. Brumfield. Children: George, William, Fleet, Hampton Addison, Anna, and an infant son (born Aug. 10, 1875; died in infancy).

Dora Magee-Brumfield died July 22, 1930, at the age of 74. She was living in Bogalusa, La., at the time of her death.

a. GEORGE BRUMFIELD.—Born in Washington Parish, La., Aug. 5, 1878. Married, first, Una Mizell. Children: Ollie. Married, second, Tella Sylvest. Children: Max Oliver and Bert.

George Brumfield died Apr. 28, 1941.

(1). OLLIE BRUMFIELD.—Married Robert W. Prescott. Children: Edrie LaUna, Evelyn Dora, Robert W., Jr., and George O. They live in Magnolia, Miss.

(a). EDRIE LAUNA PRESCOTT.—Married Thomas Wilkins. No children. Edrie LaUna Prescott-Wilkins keeps house. Her husband is the Gulf Company's gasoline distributor. They live in McComb, Miss.

(b). EVELYN DORA PRESCOTT.—Married Cliff Lawrence. No children. Evelyn Dora Prescott-Lawrence served as first lieutenant in the W. A. C. during World War II. She is a school teacher now, and lives with her mother in Magnolia, Miss.

(c). ROBERT W. PRESCOTT, JR.—Married Laura Marie .... No children. Served in the Army in Burma and China, during World War II. Engaged in farming now.

(d). GEORGE O. PRESCOTT.—Enlisted in the Navy and is stationed in California.

(2). MAX OLIVER BRUMFIELD.—Married Matalee Phares. Children: Max Oliver, Jr. (born Apr. 24, 1938), and Martha Ann (born Mar. 9, 1942).

Max Oliver Brumfield is a farmer and lives near Franklinton, La.

(3). BERT BRUMFIELD.—Married Mildred Foy. Children: Lenora Sue (born Mar. 2, 1942), and Bert, Jr. (born Oct. 7, 1943).

Bert Brumfield served as Petty Officer in the Seabees during

World War II. He is now working in the U. S. Department of Agriculture.

b. WILLIAM BRUMFIELD.—Born in Washington Parish, La., Apr. 22, 1881. Married, first, Corinne Brumfield. Children: William, Jr., and Clyde and Helen (twins). Married, second, Lillian .... No children.

William Brumfield died May 22, 1937.

c. FLEET BRUMFIELD.—Born in Washington Parish, La., May 24, 1886. Died May 21, 1899, being killed on a railroad hand-car.

d. HAMPTON ADDISON BRUMFIELD.—Born in Washington Parish, La., Aug. 29, 1892. Married Mattie Simmons. Children: Virgie, Hampton Addison, Jr., and Maudene.

They live in Bogalusa, La.

(1). VIRGIE BRUMFIELD.—Born Sept. 4, 1917. Married Charles Blount. Children: Charles Edward (born Dec. 22, 1937), Mattie Sandra (born July 3, 1939), Golda Rae (born Aug. 2, 1941), Lucy Dora (born Mar. 3, 1946), and Danny Craig (born May 14, 1949).

(2). HAMPTON ADDISON BRUMFIELD, JR.—Born Mar. 8, 1919. Died Dec. 25, 1939, and buried in Baughton Cemetery, Washington Parish, La.

(3). MAUDENE BRUMFIELD.—Born Sept. 30, 1921. Married Louis Leland Bush. No children.

e. ANNA BRUMFIELD.—Born in Washington Parish, La., June 3, 1895. Married Jim Buntin. No children.

f. .... (a son; died in infancy).

3. OLLIE MAGEE.—Born in Washington Parish, La., in 1860. Never married. Died Aug. 16, 1881, at the age of 21.

4. EARNEST MAGEE.—Born in Washington Parish, La., in 1865. Died Mar. 23, 1879, at the age of 14.

5. SIDNEY MAGEE.—Born in Washington Parish, La., Nov. 24, 1869. Married Amanda May (born May 6, 1887). Children: George (born Sept. 17, 1905), Clayton (born July 5, 1907), Albert William (born Jan. 31, 1910; married Jemima Roberts and has the following children: Albert William, Jr., born Apr. 5, 1945, and Patricia Ann, born Sept. 7, 1946), Mary (born Oct. 6, 1917), and Mamie (born July 16, 1904; died Nov. 18, 1908). Sidney Magee died

Oct. 18, 1942. His wife died June 15, 1940. They were both buried in Kentwood, La.

II. HARRIETT ALMIRA BURRIS

Harriett Almira Burris was the daughter of Samuel and Mary (Myers) Burris. She was born in South Carolina in 1793. She migrated to Amite County, Miss., with her parents in 1809. She married Samuel B. Simmons (stepson of James Chandler) Oct. 7, 1810. They had the following children: Amanda Melvina, Mary, Almina, Ann Eliza, Samuel Eccles, Catherine Elizabeth, Martha Jane, James Smith, John, Harriett Adeline, and Margaret.

The following is the tract of land on which Samuel B. Simmons first settled in Amite County, Miss.: The north half of section 27, township 3, range 5 east, which contained 320 acres, and was bought from the U. S. Government Dec. 2, 1811. This land lies one mile west of the East Fork of Amite River, some of it extending across the river, and one-half mile north of the Liberty-McComb Highway.

Harriett Almira Burris-Simmons died Aug. 15, 1837, and was buried in Amite County, it is thought.

After Harriett Almira's death, Samuel B. Simmons married Eliza W. Dunn Aug. 29, 1839. It is not known whether or not they had any children.

About Civil War time Samuel B. Simmons moved to Holmes County, Miss. He took his two sons, Samuel Eccles and James Smith, with him. It is not known which of his other children he took with him, as some of them had married and settled in Amite County, but it appears that he took his daughters Ann Eliza, Catherine Elizabeth, Martha Jane, and Margaret with him. His brother, Isiah M. Simmons, went with him also.

Sometime after moving to Holmes County, Samuel B. Simmons and C. S. Skidmore appear to have purchased the following lands, which were known as Gum Grove Plantation, and which are located in the southwestern section of Holmes County: Lots 1, 2, 3, 5, 6, and 7 of section 8; lots 1, 2, 3, 6, and 7 of section 17; lot 1 of section 20; and the northwest quarter and west half of SW¼ of section 9, all in township 14, range 2 west, containing 1166 acres.

After the death of Samuel B. Simmons, of his son James Smith Simmons, and of C. S. Skidmore, a dispute over the ownership of this property, arose among the heirs of Samuel B. Simmons and C. S. Skidmore. The dispute was carried to court, and the court ordered

144

the property sold at public auction. It was sold Feb. 3, 1868, for $5000.00 to the following heirs: Samuel E. Simmons, Ann E. Blake, Amanda Smith, Mary McKnight, Catherine E. Simmons, and Margaret H. Doyle each purchased an undivided one-eighth interest in said lands; Crosby S. Simmons, Gus B. Simmons, and David Jett Simmons purchased jointly an undivided interest of one-eighth in said lands; and William Frith and Martha Mock purchased an undivided one-eighth interest in said lands.

Samuel B. Simmons died about 1862, and was buried in Holmes County, Miss., it is thought.

WILL OF SAMUEL B. SIMMONS

In the name of God, Amen!

I, Samuel B. Simmons, being sound in mind and memory, do make this my last will and testament, as follows, to-wit:

Article 1. It is my will and desire that, after my death that my body be decently interred and that all of my just debts be paid out of my estate that I shall have left.

Article 2. It is my desire that my three Negroes, Jeff, Susan, and John, and the child of Susan, be appraised by three freeholders and that my daughter shall receive them at their valuation as so much money of her share of my estate.

Article 3. It is my desire that my daughter, Catherine E. Simmons, shall receive my boy Frank and that he shall be valued by three freeholders and that she receive him at the said appraisement as so much money of her share in my estate.

Article 4. It is my desire that, after my death, my Negro woman, Patsy, be set free and that I. M. Simmons shall see that this provision of my will be carried out, and that he act as her agent and guardian to see that she is well taken care of.

Article 5. It is my will and desire that my property, both real and personal, be equally divided between my children without reference to any former advancement that I have heretofore made.

Article 6. I do hereby nominate Isiah M. Simmons as my sole executor of this my last will and testament to execute these means according to the provisions above specified and that she shall not be required to give security as such executor.

Signed, sealed, and acknowledged this Sept. 4th, 1862.

Attest: S. B. Simmons

    J. T. Freeman
    J. E. Frizelo
    J. H. Mitchell

A. AMANDA MELVINA SIMMONS.—Born in Amite County, Miss., Dec. 1, 1811. Married, first, William Frith Aug. 11, 1831. Children: Charles Henderson, and Victoria Adeline. Married, second, Wm. S. Smith, Aug. 27, 1856. No children.

WILL OF WILLIAM FRITH

(Copied from Amite County, Miss., records)

The last will and testament of William Frith of the County of Amite and State of Mississippi, revoking all wills and testaments made by me:

1st. I will that all my just debts and funeral and testamentary expenses be paid by my executors hereinafter named with all convenient speed after my decease, and I do hereby subject, charge and make liable all and every of my real and personal estate and effects whatsoever to and with the payment of the same.

2nd. I will and desire that all my property of every kind be kept together on my plantation whereon I now reside and worked to the best advantage, under the direction of my executors until such time as hereinafter decided to be divided.

3rd. I will and desire that whenever the net proceeds of my farm shall amount to enough to purchase one or more Negroes that my executors lay it out to the best advantage in Negroes, and put them on my plantation to be worked and divided as that I now own.

4th. It is my will that my two children, Victoria Adeline and Charles Henderson Frith have a liberal and classical education and that the expenses of the same be out of the proceeds of my farm by my executors.

5th. I will that, whenever my daughter, Victoria Adeline Frith, marries, or whenever she desires, after she becomes of age, that all my property of every description, except land, be appraised by three commissioners appointed by the Probate Court of Amite County, and divided into three equal shares and one share drawn and set apart to her and said share so drawn I will to her and the heirs of her body. And, in the event of her dying without issue, or should she leave children and they die, in either case, it is my will that the property so allotted and set of her and increase thereof, return in equal shares to my wife, Amanda Melvina Frith, and my son, Charles Henderson Frith, and in the event of the death of either of them, the survivor to receive the whole amount.

6th. I will that the two remaining shares be kept together on my plantation and worked under the direction of my executors for the benefit of my wife, Amanda M. Frith, and my son, Charles H. Frith.

146

7th. I will that, whenever my son, Charles Frith, marries, or may desire, after he comes of age, the property then remaining on my plantation, all be appraised, except my land, by three commissioners appointed by the Probate Court of Amite County, and divided into two equal shares and allotted and set off to my wife, Amanda M. Frith, and my son, Charles H. Frith, and the shares so made and set off to my son, as aforesaid, I will to him and his heirs, and, in the event of his death without children, or should he leave children and they die, in either case, the property so allotted and set off, and the successor thereof is to return to my wife, Amanda M. Frith, and daughter, Victoria A. Frith, in equal shares. And, in the event of the death of either of them, the survivor is to receive the whole amount.

8th. I will that my wife, Amanda M. Frith, have and receive one share of my personal property as directed to be made out by the seventh item of this will as her own and separate property, subject to her disposal.

9th. I will that my wife, Amanda, own, hold, and use the plantation whereon I now reside, with all the privileges and approval announced there unto belonging, for her own separate use, after the division is made, as directed by the seventh item of this will, during her natural life.

10th. I will, after the death of my wife, Amanda M. Frith, that all my property and real estate be appraised by three commissioners appointed by the Probate Court of Amite County, and that my son, Charles H. Frith, have and receive the whole of my real estate so appraised, and that he pay my daughter, Victoria A. Frith, one-half the amount of the appraisement so made out. And, in the event of his death, my daughter, Victoria A. Frith, is to receive and hold all my real estate.

11th. I do hereby nominate, constitute, and appoint my wife, Amanda M. Frith, and John S. Robinson executors of this, my last will and testament.

In testimony whereof, I hereunto set my hand and affirm my seal this 24th day of July, 1852.

William Frith   (Seal)

In accordance with the fifth item of the above will, the following men were appointed commissioners by the Probate Court of Amite County: Dudley W. Bonds, R. P. Smiley, and Stephen Jackson. They appraised the value of the property, except the land, to be $25,742.00, and divided it into the following three equal shares:

Lot No. 1 .... $8571.00
Lot No. 2 ....   8586.00
Lot No. 3 (to Victoria A. Frith-Anderson)   8585.00

This document was dated Dec. 16, 1854.

And, in accordance with the seventh item of the above will, the following men were appointed commissioners by the Probate Court of Amite County: Stephen Jackson, G. B. McLain, and R. L. Huff. They appraised the value of the personal estate of Wm. Frith to be $26,124.00, and divided it into the following two equal shares:

Share No.1 (to Amanda M. Frith-Smith) $13,162.00

Share No. 2 (to Charles H. Frith) 13,062.25

1. CHARLES HENDERSON FRITH.—Born in Amite County, Miss., in 1838. Married Martha C. Turnipseed Jan. 31, 1866. Children: George Dardon, Will H., Susie, John Turnipseed, Lida, and Charles Henderson, Jr.

Charles Henderson Frith was a veteran of the Civil War, and in later years represented Amite County in the State Legislature.

a. GEORGE DARDON FRITH.—Born in Amite County, Miss., July 24, 1883. Married Rosalie Woodall, daughter of Robert Woodall, Oct. 16, 1924. No children.

George Dardon Frith died Nov. 15, 1951, and was buried in the Robinson Cemetery, near Peoria, Miss. He was a farmer, and his place, which is the old Turnipseed Place, is located about one mile south of the Liberty-McComb Highway, on the east side of the East Prong of Amite River.

b. WILL H. FRITH.—Born in Amite County, Miss. Never married. Died in 1920.

c. SUSIE FRITH.—Born in Amite County, Miss. Married Will Simmons.* Children: Carl, Earl, Mattie, and Katie.

(1). CARL SIMMONS.

(2). EARL SIMMONS.—Born near East Fork, Miss., in 1894. Married Vera Hughey. Children: Catherine.

Vera Hughey-Simmons was born near East Fork, Miss., in 1900.
Earl Simmons works in Philadelphia, Penn. His home is in McComb, Miss.

(a). CATHERINE SIMMONS.—Born Apr. 20, 1922. Married Murray Seal Apr. 19, 1946. Children: Eddie (born in McComb, Miss., Mar. 2, 1947), and Catherine Jean (born June 18, 1948). They live in McComb, Miss.

---

*Said by members of the family to be Susie Frith's cousin, and thought to be Samuel Eccles Simmons's son.

Addison and Rebecca (Ogden) Burris
*The Original Burris Parents
of East Baton Rouge (La.)*

THE HAMPTON BURRIS FAMILY

One of the early Burris families of Amite County (Miss.). Picture taken around 1900.
Left to right—seated: Ernest Burris, Enos Pinkney Burris, Thomas R. Burris, Maggie Burris, J. Addison Burris, Fleet Burris, Erasmus T. Burris.
Standing—back row: Mrs. Eros P. Burris, Mrs. Thomas P. Burris, Mrs. Hampton Burris, Mrs. Addison Burris, Mrs. Fleet Burris, Mrs. Erasmus T. Burris.

(3). MATTIE SIMMONS.

(4). KATIE SIMMONS.

d. JOHN TURNIPSEED FRITH.—Born in Amite County, Miss., May 3, 1871. Never married. Lives on his brother George Dardon's place, near Liberty, Miss.

e. LIDA FRITH.—Born in Amite County, Miss. Married Frank Spurlock. Children: Annie, Hazel, Mildred, Carroll, and Edwin.

Lida Frith-Spurlock died May 3, 1950, and was buried in Watson, Ark., where she was residing at the time of her death.

(1). ANNIE SPURLOCK.—Married ....
Children: ...., ...
They live in Watson, Ark.

(2). HAZEL SPURLOCK.—Married ....
Children: ....
They live in Santa Meda, Tex.

(3). MILDRED SPURLOCK.—Born Apr. 23, 1910. Married Ed Newlin. Children: Geraldine (born in Watson, Ark., Mar. 16, 1931), Edwin (born in Watson, Ark., July 22, 1945), and Shirley Jean (born in Watson, Ark., Mar. 4, 1936). They live in Watson, Ark.

(4). CARROLL SPURLOCK.—Died when young.

(5). EDWIN SPURLOCK.—Died when young.

f. CHARLES HENDERSON FRITH, JR.—Born in Amite County, Miss., May 9, 1879. Married Allie Denman in 1917. Children: Herbert Denman, William T., Aline Gwendoline, Gerald Howard, Bobby Ray, and Faye Elizabeth.

Allie Denman-Frith died Dec. 30, 1950, and was buried in the Robinson Cemetery, near Peoria, Miss.

They live near Terry, Miss., on route 2.

(1). HERBERT DENMAN FRITH.—Born in Liberty, Miss., Sept. 18, 1917. Married Nell Hall. Children: Herbert Edward (Eddie) (born in Jackson, Miss., June 5, 1942), and Ronald Kent (Ronnie) (born in Jackson, Miss., Oct. 24, 1946).

Herbert Denman Frith is a veteran of World War II. He is doing carpenter work now.

They live near Terry, Miss.

(2). WILLIAM T. FRITH.—Born in Liberty, Miss., Feb. 4, 1919.

(3). ALINE GWENDOLINE FRITH.—Born in Liberty, Miss., Sept. 5, 1921. Married Lonnie N. Smith, Jr. Children: Richard Grant (born in Jackson, Miss., July 5, 1946), Louis Terrill (born in Natchez, Miss., Dec. 22, 1947), and Stephan Alan (born in Little Rock, Ark., Aug. 31, 1949).

Lonnie N. Smith, Jr., was born in Silver Creek, Miss., Oct. 13, 1914. He served in World War II, and for his outstanding service was awarded the Bronze Star and Purple Heart. He is now assistant manager of the Swift Company's branch house in Little Rock. Ark., where he and his family reside.

(4). GERALD HOWARD FRITH.—Born in Port Neches, Tex., July 8, 1930.

(5). BOBBY RAY FRITH.—Born in Monroe, La., July 16, 1933.

(6). FAYE ELIZABETH FRITH.—Born in Liberty, Miss., Dec. 9, 1935.

2. VICTORIA ADELINE FRITH.—Born in Amite County, Miss., in 1836. Married James F. Anderson, Aug. 10, 1850.

James F. Anderson was reported to be very wealthy.

DEMOCRATIC AND STATE RIGHTS MEETING

(Published in The Piney Woods Planter of Liberty, Miss., in 1830's)

A meeting of the Democratic and State Rights Party will be held in Liberty on the 17th of Oct., by the expressed wish of those citizens whose names are affixed, for the purpose of electing delegates to the Democratic and State Rights Convention, to be held in Jackson in Jan. next.

All those friendly to the Sub-Treasury, and opposed to the elevation of H. Clay to the presidency, and the establishment of a U. S. Bank are requested to attend.

(John E. and William Frith's, and William Burris's names were listed.)

B. MARY SIMMONS.—Born in Amite County, Miss., Nov. 15, 1813. Married Thos. E. McKnight Mar. 15, 1833. Children: Leonard, Thomas J., James, Robert, Harriett A., Mary G. (Katherine), Margaret Alma (Maggie), Adelia, Nathan, ... (a boy), and .... (a girl).

Thos. E. McKnight was born in 1810. He was clerk pro tem of the Liberty, Miss., Baptist Church in 1850.

Mary Simmons-McKnight joined the Liberty, Miss., Baptist Church in 1842.

1. LEONARD MCKNIGHT.—Born in Amite County, Miss. Married Blanche Moore. Children: W. Bryant, Lois, Annie, Leonard, Jr., Ray, and Hosea B.

a. W. BRYANT MCKNIGHT.—Married Allie Marsalis. Children: J. B. They live in Sondheimer, La.

(1). J. B. MCKNIGHT.—Married Bertha Garley. Children: Julia Ann (born in Tallulah, La., Nov. 29, 1945), Linda Darline (born in Tallulah, La., July 3, 1948), and John Wayne (born in Tallulah, La., Jan. 8, 1951).

J. B. McKnight is a farmer and lives near Tallulah, La.

b. LOIS MCKNIGHT.—Married Leslie Bates. Children: Elldred.

c. ANNIE MCKNIGHT.—Married Joe Denman. Children: Annie Ray (dead), Eloise (married Fred McDaniel, and has one child; lives in Summit, Miss.), and W. B. (unmarried).

d. LEONARD MCKNIGHT, JR.—Married Mattie McCann. Children: Yvonne, Dorsie, and Jim.

e. RAY MCKNIGHT.—Married Bernice Marsalis. Children: Evie Lee Felder (adopted; married Winton Burris*).

Ray McKnight is a farmer and lives near Peoria, Miss.

f. HOSEA B. MCKNIGHT.—Married Inez Quin. Children: James Leonard (Married), Billy, and H. B.

2. THOMAS J. MCKNIGHT.—Born in 1841. Married Rebecca Cain. Children: Charlie, and Katie (married Eddie Campbell).

3. JAMES MCKNIGHT.—Born in 1834. Killed in Civil War.

4. ROBERT MCKNIGHT.—Born in 1845.

5. HARRIETT A. MCKNIGHT.—Born in 1838. Married Henry Bates Mar. 25, 1858. Children: Harriett (Shug).

a. HARRIETT (SHUG) BATES. — Married Maurice Allen Brashear. Children: Mary Etha, Samuel Vernon, Wiley Eddie, Dollie Elzine, Catherine Vella, Henry Maurice, and Bessie Louise. They live in McComb, Miss.

(1). MARY ETHA BRASHEAR.—Died at the age of 17.

----

*Interfamily marriage. Children listed under husband.

(2). SAMUEL VERNON BRASHEAR.—Dead.

(3). WILEY EDDIE BRASHEAR.—Married Stella Iris Ditto. Children: Ellis Allen (married Mae Tolar, and has one child, Amanda Lynn; lives in McComb, Miss.), George Miller (married Nolene Brady, and has three children, George Miller, Jr., Harriett Ann, and Edna Nolene), and Lester Merrill (married Georgene Mobley; lives in McComb, Miss.).

(4). DOLLIE ELZINE BRASHEAR.—Unmarried.

(5). CATHERINE VELLA BRASHEAR.—Unmarried.

(6). HENRY MAURICE BRASHEAR.—Unmarried.

(7). BESSIE LOUISE BRASHEAR.—Married Davis Lee Berryhill. No children.

6. MARY G. (KATHERINE) McKNIGHT.—Born in Liberty, Miss., May 24, 1846. Married James E. Bates, son of Richard Bates, June 9, 1864. Children: James, E., Jr., Lee, Mary Beulah, and Hattie.

James E. Bates was born July 4, 1823. He died Mar. 17, 1898.

Mary G. (Katherine) McKnight-Bates died Apr. 14, 1882, and was buried in Felder's Cemetery, Liberty, Miss.

They lived near Liberty, Miss.

a. JAMES E. BATES, JR.—Married, first, Mattie Robinson. Children: .... (died an infant). Mattie Robinson-Bates died shortly after child was born. James E. Bates, Jr., married, second, Betty Graves. Children: Beulah (died an infant).

b. LEE BATES.—Married Lillie .... Children: Raymond (married and has two children; lives in S. C.), Robert Lee (unmarried), and Carl (dead).

c. MARY BEULAH BATES.—Born in Amite County, Miss., Mar. 14, 1868. Married Pleasant Culpepper Webb, Jr., son of Pleasant Collinsworth and Mary (Smarr) Webb, in Amite County. Children: Carl Vernon, Winchester Merrill (Chess), James Leroy, Alma Lee, Charles Carey, Katie Lou, and Edgar Culpepper.

Pleasant Culpepper Webb, Jr., was born at Glading, in Amite County, Miss., Oct. 9, 1862. He died Oct. 21, 1922, and was buried in Felder's Cemetery, Liberty, Miss.

Mary Beulah Bates-Webb died Aug. 9, 1901, and was buried in Felder's Cemetery, Liberty, Miss.

They lived at Bates' Mill, near Liberty, Miss.

(1). CARL VERNON WEBB.—Born at Dickey's Mill in Amite County, Miss., Apr. 15, 1886. Married Myrtis Simmons, daughter of E. A. and Annie Simmons, Oct. 21, 1909, in Progress, Miss. Children: Elsie (married J. D. Brabham and has one child, James Vernon, by him; divorced J. D. Brabham and married Maurice Catha and has two children by him, Maureen, and George Russell; divorced Maurice Catha; lives in McComb, Miss.), Edward Collinsworth (married Pauline . . . .; lives in Mobile, Ala.), and Mary Adelia (married Rev. Otis Varnado, and has one child, Mary Margaret; lives in Menden, Tex.).

(2). WINCHESTER MERRILL (CHESS) WEBB.—Born at Dickey's Mill in Amite County, Miss., Mar. 20, 1888. Married Frances Smith, daughter of Langdon Quin and Cornelia Smith, Jan. 23, 1910, in Peoria, Miss. Children: Beulah Cornelia (married J. O. Lanier, and has three children, John Merrill, Frank Webb, and William; lives in McComb, Miss.), and James Buford (married Wilda Stokes, and has two children, Jimmy Dale, and Joseph Hilton; lives in McComb, Miss.).

Frances Smith-Webb was born near Peoria, Miss., July 16, 1887. She died Oct. 13, 1918.

Winchester Merrill (Chess) Webb lives in McComb, Miss.

(3). JAMES LEROY WEBB.—Born at Bates Mill, in Amite County, Miss., July 4, 1891. Married Ouida Mae Taylor, daughter of John and Hettie Taylor, July 13, 1920, in Gillsburg, Miss. Children: John Culpepper (married Lillian Young; lives in Clarksdale, Miss.), James Leroy, Jr. (lives in Leland, Miss.), Taylor (lives in Leland, Miss.), and Bae (married Joseph P. Brent, son of Sam A. Brent, and has one child, James Preston; lives in St. Louis, Mo.).

Ouida Mae Taylor-Webb was born in Gillsburg, Miss., Dec. 14, 1892. She died July 17, 1933, and was buried in the Hollywood Cemetery in McComb, Miss.

James Leroy Webb lives near Peoria, Miss., on route 1.

(4). ALMA LEE WEBB.—Born at Bates Mill in Amite County, Miss., Oct. 18, 1893. Married Julian Purser Noland, son of Jermiah and Eliza Noland, Jan. 16, 1926, in McComb, Miss. No children.

Julian Purser Noland was born in Norwood, La., June 28, 1878. He died May 25, 1949, and was buried in the Hollywood Cemetery in McComb, Miss.

Alma Lee Webb-Noland lives in McComb, Miss.

(5). CHARLES CAREY WEBB.—Born at Bates Mill in Amite County, Miss., July 4, 1895. Married Reine Georges, daughter of Firme Georges and Eugenia Horiot Georges, Nov. 1, 1918, in Bourbonne, Les Bains-Haute Marne, France. Children: James Merrill (married Patricia . . . ., and has one child, Victoria Rene; lives in McComb, Miss.), Eugenia Alma (married C. L. Klotz, and has three children, Carey, Eugene, and Clifton; lives in McComb, Miss.), Charles Firmin (married Katherine Rowe, and has two children, Robert Charles, and Leslie; lives in Hattiesburg, Miss.), and Claudette Reine (lives in McComb, Miss.).

Reine Georges-Webb was born in Serquex, France, May 30, 1894.

Charles Carey Webb served in the U. S. Army during World War I as a private. He served overseas from 1916 to Oct. 1919.

They live in McComb, Miss.

(6). KATIE LOU WEBB.—Born at Bates Mill in Amite County, Miss., Apr. 7, 1897. Died Nov. 20, 1905. Buried in Felder's Cemetery, Amite County, Miss.

(7). EDGAR CULPEPPER WEBB.—Born at Bates Mill in Amite County, Miss., Sept. 24, 1899. Married Myrtle Bloodsworth, daughter of W. J. and Ellen Bloodsworth, July 20, 1932, in Floresville, Tex. No children.

Myrtle Bloodsworth-Webb was born in Fairdale, Tex., Sept. 17, 1897.

Edgar Culpepper Webb served in the armed forces of the U. S. during World War I and II. He retired Oct. 16, 1950, after thirty years' service in the U. S. Air Force.

They live near Floresville, Tex., on route 2.

d. HATTIE BATES.—Married Sidney McElveen. Children: Grace, Herbert, Beulah, Edna, and Winnie.

(1). GRACE MCELVEEN.—Married James Q. Cain. Children: Jimmie Lou (married E. H. Hurst, and has five children: Sidney Jean, Margaret Ann, E. H., Jr., Martha Jane, and Billy Joe; none of the children is married), Irma (married, first, Henry Burns, and has one child, Henry Lou; married, second, Laverne Dixon; no children), and Elois (married Carl Helm, and has two children, Carlene, and George).

(2). HERBERT MCELVEEN.—Married Edna Wilkinson. Children: Frances (married Buddy Ford, and has one child, Christy).

(3). BEULAH MCELVEEN.—Married Hallie Barron. No children.

(4). EDNA MCELVEEN.—Married, first, Lee Mayers. Children: Raymond, and Marlene. Married, second, Edgar Whittington. No children.

(5). WINNIE MCELVEEN.—Married Herman Wilson. Children: Dorothy Ann.

Herman Wilson is dead.

7. MARGARET ALMA (MAGGIE) MCKNIGHT.—Born in Amite County, Miss., Jan. 21, 1850. Married Dr. Christopher Harbert Bates, son of James E. and Eletha (Frith) Bates, Nov. 22, 1871, at the McKnight home. Children: Maude Alma, Dr. William Harbert, Allie Ann, Christopher Ellison, Margaret Eloise, and Randolph.

Dr. Christopher Harbert Bates was born at Bates Mill in Amite Country, Miss., April 7, 1847. He was buried in Osyka, Miss.

Margaret Alma (Maggie) McKnight-Bates died in 1928, and was buried in Osyka, Miss.

a. MAUDE ALMA BATES.—Born Aug. 3, 1874. Died Sept. 12, 1888.

b. DR. WILLIAM HARBERT BATES.—Born at Bates Mill in Amite County, Miss., Aug. 16, 1877. Married Laura Miller, daughter of Robert Davies and Mattie E. (Granberry) Miller, June 5, 1907, in Clinton, Miss. Children: Margaret E., William Harbert, Jr., and Martha Miller.

Laura Miller-Bates was born in Learned, Miss., Ap. 4, 1884.

Dr. William Harbert Bates graduated from Tulane University in 1900. He practiced medicine with his father in Osyka, Miss., for ten years. In 1918 he moved to Gilbert, La., and practiced medicine there until his death June 28, 1928. He purchased a farm and engaged in farming, also operated a store while he lived in Gilbert. He was buried in Osyka, Miss.

His widow lives in the old home in Gilbert, La.

(1). MARGARET E. BATES.—Born in Osyka, Miss., Jan. 11, 1909. Married William Horace Jervis, son of H. B. F. Jervis of Holton, Maine, Aug. 29, 1930, in Gilbert, La. Children: John Vincent

155

(born in Vicksburg, Miss., Nov. 30, 1933), and William Horace, Jr. (born in Vicksburg, Miss., Dec. 5, 1934).

William Horace Jervis is a graduate of Yale University. He has done postgraduate work at Massachusetts Institute of Technology. He is a consultant engineer.

They live in Los Angeles, Calif.

(2). WILLIAM HARBERT BATES, JR.—Born in Osyka, Miss., Aug. 26, 1910. Married Grace Martin, daughter of H. J. Martin, Nov. 20, 1938, in Vicksburg, Miss. Children: William Harbert III (born in Vicksburg, Miss., Aug. 26, 1941), and Christopher Martin (born in Vicksburg, Miss., Jan. 9, 1943).

William Harbert Bates, Jr., is employed by the Martin Marble Co. of Vicksburg, Miss. He manages his mother's farm in Gilbert, La., also.

They live in Vicksburg, Miss.

(3). MARTHA MILLER BATES.—Born in Osyka, Miss., Aug. 13, 1912. Married Xavia Milton Holt, son of T. H. Holt, June 11, 1931, in Gilbert, La. Children: Xavia Milton, Jr. (born in Baton Rouge, La., May 11, 1932).

Xavia Milton Holt is an ex-mayor of Gilbert, La. He is now engaged in dairying in Wisner, La.

Martha Miller Bates-Holt is a teacher in the Gilbert High School. They live in Wisner, La.

c. ALLIE ANN BATES.—Born Mar. 4, 1879. Died Oct. 4, 1883.

d. CHRISTOPHER ELLISON BATES.—Born Feb. 12, 1881. Died Oct. 21, 1883.

e. MARGARET ELOISE BATES.—Born at Bates Mill in Amite County, Miss., Jan. 6, 1884. Married D. Eugene Newman, son of James Newman, Nov. 20, 1907, in Osyka, Miss. Children: Christine.

D. Eugene Newman was born in Gillsburg, Miss., June 16, 1872.

Margaret Eloise Bates-Newman died Mar. 7, 1933, and was buried in Osyka, Miss., where she lived.

(1). CHRISTINE NEWMAN.—Born in Osyka, Miss. Married Mort Ray. Children: Derrell Walter (born Sept. 7, 1941), and Roland Everett (born Nov. 8, 1937).

They live in McComb, Miss.

f. RANDOLPH BATES.—Born Oct. 12, 1887. Died May 31, 1890.

8. ADELIA MCKNIGHT.—Born June 1851. Married Scott Cockerham in 1872. Children: Myrtis, Claude Lafayette, Epho, Robert, Zula, Tommye (a girl), and Vola.

Adelia McKnight-Cockerham died Sept. 1, 1928.

a. MYRTIS COCKERHAM.—Married Will Wilson. Children: Matha, Leo, Herman, and Charles.

(1). MATHA WILSON.—Married Bernard H. Burris.*

(2). LEO WILSON.—Married Eva Robinson in East Fork, Miss. Children: Vernon (married Freddie Garner; no children; lives in McComb, Miss), and Clayton (unmarried).

Leo Wilson is a prosperous dairyman. They live in Liberty, Miss.

(3). HERMAN WILSON. — Married Winnie McElveen. Children: (Listed under wife's name, as this is an interfamily marriage).

Herman Wilson died in Chicago, Ill., Apr. 1950, and was buried in East Fork, Miss.

(4). CHARLES WILSON.—Married Ann Darwin. No children.

They live in Philadelphia, Pa.

b. CLAUDE LAFAYETTE COCKERHAM.—Born in East Fork, Miss., Mar. 4, 1879. Married Winnie Anders, daughter of Calvin Anders, Apr. 16, 1910, near Liberty, Miss. Children: Scott Ross, George Lane, Claude Lafayette, Jr., Lewyl, and Winnie B.

Winnie Anders-Cockerham was born in Amite County, Miss., Jan. 30, 1889.

Claude Lafayette Cockerham died Dec. 6, 1948, and was buried in East Fork, Miss.

(1). SCOTT ROSS COCKERHAM.—Born in East Fork, Miss., Feb. 7, 1912. Married Christine Coleman, daughter of J. H. Coleman, Oct. 18, 1936, in Jackson, Miss. Children: Jerry Ross (born in McComb, Miss., Apr. 18, 1937), and John Cresley (born in Gloster, Miss., Jan. 8, 1943).

Christine Coleman-Cockerham was born at Zion Hill, near Liberty, Miss., Nov. 18, 1914.

*Interfamily marriage. Children listed under husband.

Scott Ross Cockerham served two and one-half years in the U. S. Navy as a Seabee during World War II. He was a barber and stationed on the Island of Guam. He is a barber now in Gloster, Miss.

(2). GEORGE LANE COCKERHAM.—Born in East Fork, Miss., Apr. 10, 1914. Married Elsie Eugenia Sharp Dec. 16, 1936, in Liberty, Miss. Children: Linda Lane (born Dec. 24, 1937), and Wilda Dean (born July 27, 1942).

Elsie Eugenia Sharp-Cockerham was born near New Zion in Amite County, Miss., June 10, 1916.

George Lane Cockerham is a cattle dealer.

They live near Liberty, Miss., on route 1.

(3). CLAUDE LAFAYETTE COCKERHAM, JR.—Born in Liberty, Miss., May 17, 1920. Married Katherine Brown, daughter of John Brown, Feb. 22, 1941, in McComb, Miss. Children: Claude Lafayette II, and Katherine Cecilia (dead).

Claude Lafayette Cockerham, Jr., is employed by the I. C. Railway Co., as a machinist in their shops in Vicksburg, Miss. He served two and one-half years in the U. S. Navy during World War II.

They live in Vicksburg, Miss.

(4). LEWYL COCKERHAM.—Born in Liberty, Miss., Nov. 15, 1922. Married Anna Katharine Lutz Apr. 7, 1949, in Jefferson County, Miss. Children: Lewyl Glenn (born June 22, 1950).

Anna Katharine Lutz-Cockerham was born in Jefferson County, Miss., June 18, 1926.

Lewyl Cockerham is employed by the I. C. Railway Co., as a machinist in their shops in Vicksburg, Miss. He served two and one-half years in the U. S. Army, in an armored division of the Third Army, in Europe, during World War II.

They live in Vicksburg, Miss.

(5). WINNIE B. COCKERHAM.—Born in East Fork, Miss., Dec. 18, 1916. Married Rufus Houston Hagan May 17, 1936, in Woodville, Miss. Children: Richard Nores (born June 7, 1938), Sharon Wynn (born Jan. 1, 1943), and Janis Lou (born Apr. 14, 1947).

Rufus Houston Hagan was born in Tangipahoa, La., Dec. 25, 1906.

They live in Baker, La.

. c. EPHO COCKERHAM.—Married John J. Newman. Children: John J., Jr., Marjorie, Harold R., Warren H., and Eloyse.

They live in Bude, Miss.

(1). JOHN J. NEWMAN, JR.—Born in Glading, Miss., May 12, 1907. Married Mary Lee Cooper, daughter of Rev. W. R. Cooper of Tylertown, Miss., July 16, 1939, in Tylertown, Miss. No children.

They live in Vicksburg, Miss.

(2). MARJORIE NEWMAN.—Born in Brookhaven, Miss., Nov. 28, 1908. Married John A. Gerard, Jr., son of J. A. Gerard, of Natchez, Miss., Jan. 2, 1927, in Bude, Miss. Children: Jeanne, Carol Ann, and Jere.

They live in Bude, Miss.

(a). JEANNE GERARD.—Born in McComb, Miss., May 10, 1929. Married Lester L. Scarborough, son of Lester V. Scarborough, of Bude, Miss., Dec. 28, 1947, in Bude, Miss. Children: Lester L., Jr. (born in McComb, Miss., Dec. 6, 1948).

They live in Dallas, Tex.

(b). CAROL ANN GERARD.—Born in Bude, Miss., May 20, 1937. Lives in Bude, Miss.

(c). JERE GERARD.—Born Nov. 28, 1945. Lives in Bude, Miss.

(3). HAROLD R. NEWMAN.—Born in Brookhaven, Miss., Dec. 11, 1911. Married Mildred Laird, daughter of J. H. Laird, Nov. 28, 1932, in Brookhaven, Miss. Children: Linda Kay (born in Centreville, Miss., Sept. 14, 1939), and Harold R., Jr., (born in Centreville, Miss., Aug. 12, 1947).

They live in Centreville, Miss.

(4). WARREN H. NEWMAN.—Born in Bude, Miss., Feb. 22, 1914. Unmarried. Lives in Bude, Miss.

(5). ELOYSE NEWMAN.—Born in Bude, Miss., Sept. 26, 1917. Married John Glenn Hollingsworth, son of J. C. Hollingsworth of Brookhaven, Miss., June 20, 1940, in Bude, Miss. Children: John Glenn, Jr. (born in Brookhaven, Miss., Mar. 15, 1945).

They live in Bude, Miss.

d. ROBERT COCKERHAM.—Married Alice Nunnery. Children: Robbie, Pascal, and Geraldine.

They live in McComb, Miss.

(1). ROBBIE COCKERHAM.—Married, first, Cecil Hyer. Children: Virginia. Married, second, Pollard Hayes. No children. They live in McComb, Miss.

(2). PASCAL COCKERHAM.—Married Marjorie Leddy. No children.

(3). GERALDINE COCKERHAM.—Married .... Magee. No children.

e. ZULA COCKERHAM.—Married, first, Kirk Turner. Children: Kirk Hilton (born near East Fork, Miss., Aug. 26, 1916). Married, second, Gaines Bates. No children.

They live in Peoria, Miss.

f. TOMMYE COCKERHAM.—Married Proby Cloy. Children: James Alfred. They live in Bude, Miss.

g. VOLA COCKERHAM.—Married, first, Elliot Bates. Children: Frances. Married, second, Boyd Williams. Children: A. Boyd. They live near Liberty, Miss.

(1). FRANCES BATES.—Married, first, Merkel Brady. Children: Kathryn. Married, second, W. S. McDaniel. No children.

(2). A. BOYD WILLIAMS.—Married Ora Lee Graves. Children: Sandra Gene, Quin Dale, and Ronnie.

9. NATHAN McKNIGHT.—Born in 1833. Married Fannie Cockerham. Children: Sidney, Ansel, Eva, Naomi, Ira, Chris, and Lucy.

a. SIDNEY McKNIGHT.—Married, first, Cora Barron. Children: Henry Nathan. Married, second, Maud Barron. Children: Carrie Lee, Robert, Annie Belle, Earl, and Jewell V.

They live in Summit, Miss.

(1). HENRY NATHAN McKNIGHT.—Married Jewel Moak. Children: Imagene. They live in Summit, Miss.

(2). CARRIE LEE McKNIGHT.—Married Elbert Kirby. No children. They live in Summit, Miss.

(3). ROBERT McKNIGHT.—Unmarried.

(4). ANNIE BELLE MCKNIGHT.—Married J. P. Davis. Children: Sidney Lee, Jerry Alton, and Sandra Faye.

(5). EARL MCKNIGHT.—Married Johnnie Mozelle Anderson. Children: (listed under wife's name, as this is an interfamily marriage).

They live in Summit, Miss.

(6). JEWELL V. MCKNIGHT.—Married Onzell B. Ford. No children.

b. ANSEL MCKNIGHT.—Dead. Never married.

c. EVA MCKNIGHT.—Married, first, John Rutland. Children: Monroe Roosevelt (married Annie Reid, and has four children: Horace, Melvin, James, and Geraldine; lives in Eva, Miss.). Married, second, Armiston Reid. No children.

d. NAOMI MCKNIGHT.—Married Ivy Blue. Children: Houston (married Louella Fletcher, and has two children, Carloss, and Fletcher).

e. IRA MCKNIGHT.

f. CHRIS MCKNIGHT.

g. LUCY MCKNIGHT.—Married, first, Houston Terrell. Children: Gladys. Married, second, James Carroll. Children: Leroy. Married, third, Grover Oliphant. Children: Robert, Nathan, E. L., and Leroy.

(1). GLADYS TERRELL.—Married Elvin Marsdale. Children: Joyce (married Eddie Rainey, and has one child, Samuel), and Samuel Alton.

(2). LEROY CARROLL.—Married Avvie Michon. Children: Garry Lee.

Leroy Carroll is dead.

(3). ROBERT OLIPHANT.—Unmarried.

(4). NATHAN OLIPHANT.—Married Nelda Davis. No children.

(5). E. L. OLIPHANT.—Unmarried.

(6). LEROY OLIPHANT.—Unmarried.

10. .... (a boy—died in infancy).

11. .... (a girl—died in infancy).

C. Almina Simmons.—Born in Amite County, Miss., Jan. 4, 1816. Married John E. Frith Dec. 18, 1832. Children: Jno. E. Frith, Jr., Wm. Frith, Harbert Frith, Rebecca Ann (Bates).

The Last Will and Testament of John E. Frith*

(Copied from Amite County, Miss., records)

In the name of God, Amen! I, John E. Frith, of Amite County and State of Mississippi, being of sound mind and disposing memory, but weak in body, and believing that I may shortly die, do make, ordain, publish, and declare this to be my last will and testament, in manner and form following, that is to say—

To my beloved son, John E. Frith, I will and bequeath as follows: One Negro man, Charles; one Negro man, Stephen; one Negro boy, Saul; one Negro woman, Fanny; one Negro girl, Maria.

To my beloved son, William Frith, I give and bequeath one Negro man, Jack; one Negro boy, Tom; one Negro boy, Adam; one Negro woman, Hannah; one Negro girl, Eliza.

I further will and bequeath to my son, William Frith, the northwest quarter of section one in township two of range four east, containing one hundred and fifty three acres and eighty-five hundredths of an acre, lying and being in the County of Amite and State aforesaid.

To my son, John E. Frith, I will and bequeath the southwest quarter of section thirty-six in township three of range four east, containing one hundred and fifty three acres, and eighty-seven hundredths of an acre. The said land being and lying in the County and State aforesaid.

To my wife, Mary Frith, I give and bequeath as her dower, my lot or parcel of ground on which I lately resided, in or about three miles from Liberty in Amite County, together with all the houses and improvements thereon, containing nineteen acres, being the same, more or less, which I purchased of John Thompson. And after her death I will and bequeath said nineteen acres to my son, William Frith.

Item. I will and bequeath to my two sons, John E. Frith, and William Frith, the three lots of ground which I own in the Town of Liberty, known and designated as lots number one and two, in square ten, in the plan of said Town; and lot number two in square nine, together with the buildings, and privileges, for the said John E. and William Frith, to share equally in the profits arising from said lots, until my son William arrives at the age of twenty-one. Then it is my will that said lots and buildings be sold. And the proceeds arising from the sale be divided between my three sons, Harbert, John E., and William Frith.

---

*William Frith's and John E. Frith, Jr.'s father.

Item. I will and bequeath that my stock of cattle, hogs, and horses be kept together until my son William becomes of age, and then to be equally divided by my executors between my two sons, John E. and William Frith.

Item. I give to my son, Harbert Frith, one feather bed and furniture. The balance of my household furniture I wish to be kept together until my son William is of age, when I will that it be equally divided between my sons, John and William.

Item. It is my last will and testament that my sons, John E. and William Frith, do dutifully and comfortably support Mary Frith, their mother, and afford her everything necessary for her comfort during her natural life.

Item. To my daughter, Rebecca Ann Bates, and her heirs, Mary A. Jones, and Jane Robinson, I leave nothing, having already given them all I ever intended.

Lastly, I nominate, constitute and appoint my wife, Mary Frith, and my son, Harbert Frith, executors of this, my last will and testament, hereby revoking all former wills by me made.

In testimony whereof I have hereunto set my hand and seal, this 20th day of January, 1829.

his
John   X   E. Frith
mark

Signed, sealed, published, and declared
this my last will and testament in presence of
Morgan Davis
Ed Carroll
V. T. Crawford

D. ANN ELIZA SIMMONS.—Born in Amite County, Miss., Jan. 7, 1821. Married William Blake. Children: Jim Ella.

Ann Eliza Simmons-Blake joined the Liberty Baptist Church in 1842.

1. JIM ELLA BLAKE.—Married James Theodore Hammond, son of Edwin and Mary Missouri (Duncan) Hammond, about 1890, in Clinton, Miss. No children.

James Theodore Hammond was born in Kershaw Dist., S. C., Oct. 10, 1835. He died Apr. 4, 1912, and was buried in Kosciusko, Miss.

Jim Ella Blake-Hammond died July 24, 1928, and was buried in Kosciusko, Miss., where she was residing at the time of her death.

E. SAMUEL ECCLES SIMMONS.—Born in Amite County, Miss., Mar. 3, 1818.

F. CATHERINE ELIZABETH SIMMONS.—Born in Amite County, Miss., Oct. 3, 1827.

G. MARTHA JANE SIMMONS—Born in Amite County, Miss., Oct. 7, 1825. Married . . . . Mock.

H. JAMES SMITH SIMMONS.—Born in Amite County, Miss., Jan. 4, 1830. Married Augusta Skidmore, daughter of Crosby Skidmore of Flora, Miss. Children: Crosby Skidmore, Daniel Jett, James Echols, and C. Augustus.

James Smith Simmons served in the Civil War. He died during the war of pneumonia. Prior to the war he was a farmer in Holmes County, Miss.

JAMES SMITH SIMMONS' WILL

(Copied from the Holmes County, Miss., records)

Knowing the uncertainty of human life, and with a firm reliance in the justice of Him who giveth and taketh away our earthly existence, I ordain this my last will and testament.

Know ye, all men by these presents, That I, James S. Simmons, of the County of Holmes, State of Mississippi, do ordain this my last will and testament. I wish all of my property to be equally divided as follows among my four children, Crosby S. Simmons, C. Augustus Simmons, D. Jett Simmons and James Eccles Simmons. The property is to be kept together until my oldest child becomes of age or marries, then to be valued and he be allowed to draw his share, one-fourth, the balance is to remain for the support of the other children, to be again divided as each child becomes of age or marries.

My watch I wish given to my son, Crosby Simmons.

I appoint my father, Samuel B. Simmons, as my administrator, and it is my desire that he shall not be required to give any security.

It is my desire that my administrator shall erect a tombstone over my deceased wife as soon as the condition of affairs in his opinion justifies him in doing so.

Signed this 23rd day of Mar., 1862, in the presence of L. Lambert, Harris M. Brooks, A. S. Hillman,

James S. Simmons.

1. CROSBY SKIDMORE SIMMONS.—Born in Madison Station, Miss. Married, first, Julia Vinson. Children: Nola Augusta, and Ernie Estelle. Married, second, Dec. 18, 1889, Mary Gassaway, daughter of Dr. S. M. Gassaway of Centreville, Miss., in Belzoni, Miss.

Children: Nannie Belle, Crosby Samuel, Birdie Mae, James Echols, Roy Skidmore, Thomas Mark, and Mary Louise.

Julia Vinson was a school teacher.

Mary Gassaway was born in Centreville, Miss., Mar. 20, 1870. She died Apr. 23, 1950, and was buried in Belzoni, Miss. She was a school teacher.

Crosby Skidmore Simmons was a farmer. He was a member of the Board of Supervisors when the present courthouse in Indianola, Miss., was built. He died Aug. 19, 1914, and was buried on Sky Lake Bend Plantation, Miss. He lived in Belzoni, Miss.

      a. NOLA AUGUSTA SIMMONS.—Born in Madison Station, Miss., Feb. 6, 1880. Married Joshua Killebrew Toler, son of Joshua and Julia Toler, Oct. 189-, near Belzoni, Miss. Children: Julia Gaynelle, and Paul.

Joshua Killebrew Toler was born in Tolerville, Miss. He died Mar. 5, 1945, and was buried in Belzoni, Miss.

Nola Augusta Simmons-Toler died Aug. 6, 1916, and was buried in Belzoni, Miss., where she resided.

      (1). JULIA GAYNELLE TOLER.—Born near Belzoni, Miss., Sept. 4, 1898. Married Richard Lister, son of Pat Lister, Aug. 6, 1921, in Yazoo City, Miss. Children: Richard Toler.

Richard Lister was born in Jackson, Tenn., Mar. 29, 1898. He died Mar. 4, 1943, and was buried in Jackson, Tenn. He was a county employee.

Julia Gaynelle Toler-Lister lives in Belzoni, Miss.

      (a). RICHARD TOLER LISTER.—Born in Memphis, Tenn., Oct. 23, 1926. Married Lila Mae Brannon, daughter of C. H. and Lillian Jane Brannon, Apr. 20, 1946, in Starkville, Miss. Children: Lillian Jane (born in Belzoni, Miss., Aug. 6, 1947), and Richard Toler, Jr. (born in Brookhaven, Miss., July 28, 1951).

Lila Mae Brannon was born Jan. 29, 1927.

Richard Toler Lister is a sergeant in the U. S. Army, and is stationed in Camp Atterbury, Ind.

      (2). PAUL TOLER.—Born in Belzoni, Miss., July 27, 1905. Married Laura Lee Hollingsworth, daughter of Robert Hollingsworth, in Jackson, Miss. No children.

Laura Lee Hollingsworth was born in Yazoo City, Miss.

Paul Toler is a salesman and lives in Memphis, Tenn.

b. ERNIE ESTELLE SIMMONS.—Born in Madison Station, Miss., Feb. 2, 1882. Died Oct. 26, 1903, and was buried near Belzoni, Miss.

c. NANNIE BELLE SIMMONS.—Born in Belzoni, Miss., Nov. 23, 1890. Married Bias Wells Webb, son of Steve Webb, Sept. 23, 1911, in Jackson, Miss. Children: Crosby Steve.

Bias Wells Webb was born in Star, Miss., Aug. 25, 1880. He died Feb. 13, 1934, and was buried in Star, Miss.

Nannie Belle Simmons-Webb is postmistress at Swiftown, Miss. She is also the O. E. S. Conductress in the lodge there. She is a land owner, and owner of other rental property. She secured the data on this branch of the family. She lives in Swiftown, Miss.

(1). CROSBY STEVE WEBB.—Born in Star, Miss., Apr. 28, 1915. Married Margaret Case, daughter of Mrs. Lucille Case, in Belzoni, Miss. Children: Virginia Dianne (born in Hollandale, Miss., Feb. 20, 1946).

Crosby Steve Webb is a merchant in Belzoni, Miss.

d. CROSBY SAMUEL SIMMONS.—Born near Belzoni, Miss., Feb. 21, 1892. Married Lena Wixon, daughter of Duke and Ida Wixon, Apr. 9, 1915, in Belzoni. Children: Lena Louise, Lois Juanita, Katherine Samuel, and Crosby Samuel, Jr.

Lena Wixon-Simmons was born in Cary, Miss., Jan. 12, 1894.

Crosby Samuel Simmons served in the U. S. Navy four years. He is owner of a plantation, a cattleman, and has been member of the Board of Supervisors for eight years. He lives in Inverness, Miss.

(1). LENA LOUISE SIMMONS.—Born in Belzoni, Miss., Nov. 17, 1915. Married Charles Edward Rode, son of William and Ida Rode, Jan. 3, 1937, in Inverness, Miss. Children: Sandra Ilene (born Feb. 6, 1937).

Charles Edward Rode was born in Cleveland, Miss., July 1, 1911. They live in Greenville, Miss.

(2). LOIS JUANITA SIMMONS.—Born in Belzoni, Miss., Dec. 3, 1917. Married William Alsie Jones, son of Alsie and Ethel Jones, Aug. 26, 1935, in Greenville, Miss. Children: William Crosby (born July 22, 1937), and Duke Wixon (born June 12, 1943).

William Alsie Jones was born in Eupora, Miss., Dec. 18, 1914.

They live in Greenville, Miss.

(3). KATHARINE SAMUEL SIMMONS.—Born in Belzoni, Miss., Oct 12, 1919. Married Edward McWilliams Jones, son of Edward Jones, Mar. 22, 1946, in Inverness, Miss. Children: Rose Mary (born Apr. 23, 1951).

They live in Shreveport, La., at the Barksdale Air Force Base.

(4). CROSBY SAMUEL SIMMONS, JR.—Born in Greenville, Miss., Dec. 14, 1928. Married Martha Turner, daughter of Robert and Maud Turner, Mar. 19, ..., in Inverness, Miss. Children: Martha Lynn (born Jan. 3, 1951).

Crosby Samuel Simmons, Jr., played football at Starkville College. He is a planter.

They live in Inverness, Miss.

e. BIRDIE MAE SIMMONS.—Born near Belzoni, Miss., Jan. 29, 1894. Married Paul Krivos in Greenwood, Miss. No children.

Paul Krivos was born in Budapest, Hungary, Jan. 1, 1872. He died May 24, 1931, and was buried in Greenwood, Miss.

Birdie Mae Simmons-Krivos is a merchant of Swiftown, Miss.

f. JAMES ECHOLS SIMMONS.—Born near Belzoni, Miss., Jan. 4, 1897. Married Anna Laura Brown, daughter of Robert Brown, Sept. 14, 1925, in Belzoni, Miss. Children: James Robert, Wiley Hardy, and Marion Lamar.

Anna Laura Brown-Simmons was born in Benton, Miss., Sept. 1899.

James Echols Simmons died Mar. 24, 1949, and was buried in Yazoo City, Miss. He was a plantation owner. His family lives in Carter, Miss.

(1). JAMES ROBERT SIMMONS.—Born in Lampkin, Miss., Aug. 24, 1926. Married Livie Posey Steinreide Oct. 1947 in Yazoo City, Miss. Children: James Robert Jr., and William Mark.

James Robert Simmons served in World War II. He was in the Military Police Corps, and saw overseas duty.

They live in Carter, Miss.

(2). WILEY HARDY SIMMONS.—Born near Belzoni, Miss., July 24, 1928. Died (was murdered) Aug. 20, 1949, and was buried in Yazoo City, Miss.

(3). MARION LAMAR SIMMONS.—Born in Carter, Miss., Sept. 1930. Is corporal in the U. S. Air Force, in cadet training now in Houston, Tex. His home address is Carter, Miss.

g. ROY SKIDMORE SIMMONS.—Born near Belzoni, Miss., Sept. 3, 1901. Married Emma Mason Apr. 1935 in Delhi, La. Children: Mary Hunt (born near Belzoni, Miss., Nov. 9, 1936; student in Belzoni High School).

Roy Skidmore Simmons is a merchant, plantation owner, beef-cattle owner, and has a share in a gin company and in the Delta Oil Co.

They live near Belzoni, Miss.

h. THOMAS MARK SIMMONS.—Born near Belzoni, Miss., Mar. 7, 1904. Married Nona Nell Ingold, daughter of Oscar Ingold, Nov. 1930, in Yazoo City, Miss. Children: Thomas Mark, Jr. (born in Swiftown, Miss., Nov. 23, 1933; student at Miss. State College).

Nona Nell Ingold-Simmons was born in Lexington, Miss., Sept. 23, 1904.

Thomas Mark Simmons is a plantation owner and cattle man. He is president of Farmers' Elevator and Delta Gin Co. He is also president of Humphreys County Livestock Association. He is director of Quin County Electric Association, and of the Dusting Corporation. He is connected with the Federal Land Bank.

They live near Belzoni, Miss.

i. MARY LOUISE SIMMONS.—Born near Belzoni, Miss., June 12, 1908. Married James Willie Gammons, son of Samuel Gammons, Nov. 27, 1927, in Belzoni. Children: Billie Marie (born in Calhoun, Ky., Aug. 24, 1928; is a school teacher), Dwayne Simmons (born in Kingston, Tenn., Nov. 11, 1930; in the U. S. Army in Korea with the rank of master sergeant), and Thomas Roy (born in Swiftown, Miss., Jan. 10, 1933; is a student at Miss. State College).

They live in Belzoni, Miss.

2. DANIEL JETT SIMMONS.—Born in Madison Station, Miss., Mar. 30, 186... Married Mary Lillian Huffstickler, daughter of John Able Huffstickler, Jan. 15, 188.., on Sky Lake Bend Plantation. Children: Esma, Samuel Skidmore, Johnie Erin, Anna Augusta, Daniel Jett, Jr., William Jennings Bryan, Isaac Herbert, Ivor, Beatrice, and Eston.

Mary Lillian Huffstickler-Simmons was born on Sky Lake Bend

Plantation Mar. 23, 1871. She died Mar. 20, 1936, and was buried on Sky Lake Bend Plantation.

Daniel Jett Simmons died Aug. 19, 1913, and was buried on Sky Lake Bend Plantation. He was a justice of the peace for twenty years; was a farmer and bookkeeper.

a. ESMA SIMMONS.—Born on Sky Lane Bend Plantation, Miss., Mar. 1889. Died Sept. 1889, and was buried on Sky Lake Bend Plantation.

b. SAMUEL SKIDMORE SIMMONS.—Born on Sky Lake Bend Plantation, Miss., Sept. 3, 1891. Married Katherine Bartling Mar. 1914 in the Methodist Church at Four-Mile Lake, Miss. Children: Katherine Sue (born in Itta Bena, Miss., Jan. 4, 1919; married J. W. Roberts in Jackson, Miss.; lives in Jackson), Mavis, Samuel Skidmore, Jr., and Harry Daniel.

Katherine Bartling-Simmons was born in Berclair, Miss., Apr. 15, 1889.

Samuel Skidmore Simmons served four years in the U. S. Navy. He is a farmer.

They live near Carter, Miss.

c. JOHNNIE ERIN SIMMONS.—Born near Four-Mile Lake, Miss., Jan. 27, 1894. Married Robert Corden McKewen, son of Andrew Jackson and Ever (Grenlee) McKewen, May 11, 1914, in Itta Bena, Miss. Children: Robert Corden (Red), Jr.

Robert Corden McKewen was born in Hermanville, Miss., Nov. 21, 1884. He has a business in Isola, Miss., and rental property in Greenwood, Miss. He went to junior college one year.

They live in Greenwood, Miss.

(1). ROBERT CORDEN (RED) MCKEWEN, JR.—Born in Swiftown, Miss., May 6, 1915. Married May Lynn Ricketts, daughter of Curtis and Exie Ricketts, May 3, ..., in Columbus, Miss. Children: Robert Michael.

Mary Lynn Ricketts-McKewen was born in Macon, Miss., May 18, ...

Robert Corden (Red) McKewen, Jr., served as a pilot with the rank of captain on a B-29 during World War II. He is in the U. S. Air Force now, and is stationed in England.

a. ANNA AUGUSTA SIMMONS.—Born on Sky Lake Bend Plantation, Miss., Jan. 22, 1895. Married William Arnold Switzer, son of Lynn Switzer, Dec. 24, 1916, in Swiftown, Miss. Children: Frances, and William Arnold, Jr.

William Arnold Switzer was born in Four-Mile Lake, Miss., Aug. 20, 1887. He lives in Isola, Miss.

(1). FRANCES SWITZER.—Born in Isola, Miss., Aug. 20, 1918. Married George Henry Shuey, Jr., son of George Henry Shuey, Dec. 8, 1945, in Lake City, Fla. Children: George Henry III (born in Jacksonville, Fla., Sept. 15, 1946), and Anna Karen (born in Isola, Miss., Mar. 6, 1948).

George Henry Shuey, Jr., was born in Chicago, Ill., Oct. 26, 1919.
Frances Switzer-Shuey graduated from Delta State Teachers College, and taught school six years. She served from 1942 to 1944 in the WAVE Corps of the U. S. Navy during World War II. They live in Long Branch, N. J.

(2). WILLIAM ARNOLD SWITZER, JR.—Born in Isola, Miss., Jan. 15, 1921. Married Mervin Crawford, daughter of Hilton Crawford, Mar. 2, 1941, in Arcola, Miss. Children: Dennis Ray (born in Isola, Miss., June 30, 1946), and Lynn (born in Isola, Miss., July 24, 1948).

Mervin Crawford-Switzer was born in Sunflower, Miss., Feb. 27, 1925.

William Arnold Switzer, Jr., served with the rank of private first class in World War II. He was a prisoner in Germany for twenty-one months. He is a farmer.

They live in Isola, Miss.

e. DANIEL JETT SIMMONS, JR.—Born Mar. 6, 1897. Married Rena Martin in 1928 in Belzoni, Miss. No children. Died Aug. 30, 1930, and was buried in Sky Lake Bend Plantation, Miss.

Daniel Jett Simmons, Jr., served six months in World War I. He was a farmer. He lived near Belzoni, Miss.

f. WILLIAM JENNINGS BRYAN SIMMONS.—Born on Sky Lake Bend Plantation, Miss., Oct. 27, 1899. Never married. Died of malaria fever Oct. 27, 1920. Lived near Belzoni, Miss.

g. ISAAC HERBERT SIMMONS.—Born in Sunflower County, Miss., Oct. 27, 1902. Married Doris Inez Calhoun, daughter of William D. and Elizabeth (Ballard) Calhoun, Dec. 1922, in Hollandale, Miss. Children: Lucille Elizabeth, Herbert Aaron, Lillie Erin, Inez

LaRue, Sammie Kathryn, William Duncan, Augusta Frances, and Sylvia Maude.

Doris Inez Calhoun-Simmons was born in Humphreys County, Miss., July 7, 1906.

Isaac Herbert Simmons died Apr. 2, 1947, and was buried in Doddsville, Miss.

(1). LUCILLE ELIZABETH SIMMONS. — Born in Isola, Miss., Mar. 18, 1924. To be married Aug. 27, 1952, in Shelby County, Tenn., to John Prescott McGoldrick, son of Walter L. McGoldrick of Memphis, Tenn.

Lucille Elizabeth Simmons lives in Memphis, Tenn.

(2). HERBERT AARON SIMMONS.—Born in Sunflower County, Miss., May 29, 1925. Married Dorothy Irene McKie, daughter of Raymond McKie, Oct. 24, 1947, in Sardis, Miss. Children: Marijett (born in Memphis, Tenn., Oct. 25, 1948), and Herbert Aaron II (born in Memphis, Tenn., Nov. 2, 1950).

Dorothy Irene McKie-Simmons was born in Tyro, Miss., May 15, 1923.

They live in Memphis, Tenn.

(3). LILLIE ERIN SIMMONS.—Born in Sunflower County, Miss., May 29, 1925. Married Harold James Blessitt July 9, ..., in Indianola, Miss. Children: Gwendolyn Murray (born in Drew, Miss., Apr. 20, 1947), and Harold James II (born in Leland, Miss., Feb. 1950).

They live in Memphis, Tenn.

(4). INEZ LaRUE SIMMONS.—Born in Indianola, Miss., May 20, 1927. Married Jesse Floyd Brown, Jr., son of Jesse Floyd Brown, Sr., Feb. 13, 1951, in Senatobia, Miss. No children.
Jesse Floyd Brown, Jr., was born Feb. 23, 1926.
They live in Doddsville, Miss.

(5). SAMMIE KATHRYN SIMMONS.—Born in Medicine Lodge, Kan., Aug. 19, 1929. Married Willie Clyde Alford, son of Leonard Alford, Mar. 11, 1950, near Doddsville, Miss. Children: Terry Linn (born in Greenville, Miss., Mar. 15, 1951), and Harry Glynn (born in Indianola, Miss., Feb. 1952).

They live in Indianola, Miss.

(6). WILLIAM DUNCAN SIMMONS.—Born in Isola, Miss.,

Aug. 31, 1931. To be married in June 1952 to Carol Lee Farish of Leland, Miss., daughter of Lee Farish.

William Duncan Simmons lives in Doddsville, Miss.

(7). AUGUSTA FRANCES SIMMONS.—Born in Indianola, Miss., July 11, 1937. Lives near Doddsville, Miss.

(8). SYLVIA MAUDE SIMMONS.—Born in Indianola, Miss., May 4, 1940. Died Nov. 12, 1945, and was buried in the Roundaway Community, Doddsville, Miss.

h. IVOR SIMMONS.—Born on Sky Lake Bend Plantation, Miss., July 6, 1908. Married, first, O. McDaniel in Yazoo City, Miss. Children: Mavis Ray. Married, second, Percy Haynes Apr. 1938. No children.

They live in Greenwood, Miss.

(1). MAVIS RAY McDANIEL.—Born on Four-Mile Lake, Miss., Dec. 18, 1923. Married Joe McBride Jan. 1949 in Oxford, Miss. Children: Percy Haynes (born in Greenwood, Miss., Oct. 1950), and Joe, Jr. (born in Greenwood, Miss., Nov. 1951).

Mavis Ray McDaniel-McBride attended the University of Miss. for three and one-half years. They live in Greenwood, Miss.

i. BEATRICE SIMMONS.—Born on Sky Lake Bend Plantation, Miss., Aug. 29, 1909. Married Eston Switzer, son of Lynn Switzer, Sept. 14, 1927, at the residence on Four-Mile Lake. Children: Eston Linwood (born on Sky Lake Bend Jan. 4, 1931; in the U. S. Marines and stationed at Quantico, Va.), and Dannie Hall (born on Sky Lake Bend May 13, 1946).

They live near Belzoni, Miss.

j. ESTON SIMMONS.—Born on Sky Lake Bend Plantation, Miss., Mar. 7, 1905. Married Artie Brazwell of Boyle, Miss. Children: Nettie Helen (born in Boyle, Miss., in 1928; married . . . . McClure in Boyle; lives in Boyle, Miss.), and Elizabeth Ann Simmons (born in Merigold, Miss., in 1933; lives in Merigold).

Eston Simmons was killed by lightning May 14, 1937, and was buried near Belzoni, Miss. He was a farmer and lived near Shaw, Miss.

3. James Echols Simmons.—Thought by members of the family to have died when very young.

4. C. AUGUSTUS SIMMONS — Thought by members of the family to have died when about eight years of age.

I. JOHN SIMMONS.—Born in Amite County, Miss., June 29, 1823. Died Feb. 28, 1833.

J. HARRIETT ADELINE SIMMONS.—Born in Amite County, Miss., July 21, 1832.

K. MARGARET SIMMONS.—Born in Amite County, Miss., Feb. 11, 1834. Married .... Doyle.

III. JOHN BURRIS

John Burris was the son of Samuel and Mary (Myers) Burris. It is thought that he was born in South Carolina, and that he was one of the older children (perhaps in his 'teens), when his parents migrated to Amite County, Miss., in 1809. Nothing to indicate that he was ever married, or when he died, was found, and for a while there was some question of a son by this name. In a few instances his name appeared in the records. In his father's (Samuel Burris's) will, he bequeaths "to my son, John Burris, my shotgun." His name appears again in the Amite County, Miss., marriage records, as bondsman for James Denman, who married Elizabeth M. Burris, his sister. In the U. S. Census of 1810 of Amite County, Miss., Samuel Burris's (John Burris's father) family is listed as consisting of one male over 21 years, seven males under 21, one female over 21, and three females under 21—a total of 12, including himself and wife. Since the youngest child, Addison Burris, was born in 1811, one year after this census was taken, this census verifies the fact that there were eight sons in the family, and doubtless John was the name of the eighth son, as the names of the other seven are established. The following document, copied from the Amite County, Miss., records, establishes unquestionably the existence of John Burris:

GUARDIAN BOND

(For Hampton Burris, minor)

State of Mississippi
Amite County

         Know all men by these presents that we, John Burris and Samuel B. Simmons, are held and firmly bound unto John R. Browne, Judge of Probate of said County, and his successors in office, in the final sum of six hundred dollars, which payment well and truly to be made, we bind ourselves, our heirs, executors, and administrators, jointly and severally, by these presents.

Sealed with our seals and dated the 26th day of November, 1827.

The condition of the above obligation is such, that, if the

above bounden John Burris as guardian to Hampton Burris, a minor of Amite County, shall faithfully account with the Orphans' Court of Amite County, as directed by law for the management of the property and estate of the orphan under his care, and shall deliver up the said property, agreeably to the order of the said Court, or the direction of law, and shall in all respects perform the duty of guardian to the said Hampton Burris, according to law, then the above obligation shall cease; it shall otherwise remain in full force and virtue in law.

Signed, sealed and delivered
in the presence of V. T. Crawford

John Burris (Seal)
Samuel B. Simmons (Seal)

Another good indication that there was a son named JOHN lies in the fact that such a large number of the male descendants of this family were, or are, named JOHN.

IV. ELIZABETH (BETSY) BURRIS

Elizabeth (Betsy) Burris was the daughter of Samuel and Mary (Myers) Burris. She was born in South Carolina in 1897. She married, first, James Wilson Jan. 14, 1814, in Amite County, Miss. They had one child, a son named Bruce Myers. She married, second, James Denman Aug. 18, 1825, and they had two children, Martha Ann, and Samuel James.

MARRIAGE LICENSE OF JAMES DENMAN AND ELIZABETH M. BURRIS

(Copied from Amite County, Miss., records)

State of Mississippi
Amite County

Know all men by these presents, that we, James Denman and John Burris, of said County, are held and firmly bound unto Walter Leake, Esq., governor of State aforesaid, or his successors in office, in the sum of two hundred dollars, lawful money of said State, to which payment will and truly be made to the governor, for the time being, or his successors in office, we bind ourselves, our heirs, executors, and administrators, each and every one of us and them jointly and severally, firmly, by these presents.

Sealed with our seals, and dated this 15th day of August eighteen hundred and twenty-five.

The condition of the above obligation is such that, whereas, a marriage is shortly intended to be celebrated between the above bound James Denman and Elizabeth M. Burris.—Now, if there

174

is lawful cause to obstruct the said marriage, then this obligation is to be void, otherwise, to remain in full force and virtue.

Signed, sealed, and delivered in my presence,

James Denman
John Burris

James Denman's homestead was the west half of the northeast quarter of section 6, township 3, range 6 east, containing 79.87 acres, which he bought from the U. S. Government Jan. 3, 1922. This land is located in the Thompson Community. He bought considerable land later from the U. S. Government, on the Mars Hill-McComb Highway, about half way between these two places, and settled there.

In the list of County Officers, published in The Piney Woods Planter of Liberty, Miss., June 16, 1838, James Denman was listed as a member of the Board of Police of Amite County. His will, a copy of which follows, was probated Feb. 24, 1841, and this was doubtless shortly after his death.

The Last Will and Testament of James Denman

(Copied from Amite County, Miss., records)

State of Mississippi
Amite County
In the name of God, Amen!

I, James Denman, of the County and State aforesaid, being weak of body but of perfect mind and memory, calling to mind the mortality of my body, and knowing that it is appointed to all men once to die, do make and ordain this and no other my last will and testament—that is to say, principally and first of all I commit and assign my soul to God, who gave it, with the hope of its salvation through the merits of Christ, my only redeemer, and my body I recommend to the earth to be buried at the discretion of my executors in a decent, Christian manner, and as touches such worldly goods, chattels, lands, and tenements as it hath pleased God to bless me with in this life. I bequeath, devise, and dispose of the same in the following manner, and form, viz.,

1st. All my just debts to be paid out of my estate after my decease, and before any other disposition is made of the same.

2nd. I will and bequeath to my beloved wife, Elizabeth Denman, the plantation whereon I reside, with all privileges and appurtenances thereunto belonging or in any ways appertaining to her, the said Elizabeth Denman, during her life, and, after her death, I wish it to be equally divided between my several lawful heirs. I further will and bequeath to my beloved wife, Elizabeth

Denman, five hundred dollars in cash, which she has at this time at her disposal, and my Negro girl, Caroline, aged about twenty-two.

3rd. It is my desire for my executors to sell my stock of horses, cattle, hogs, and sheep, and make an equal distribution of the proceeds, when collected, between my wife Elizabeth and my several children.

4th. It is my desire for the balance of my property, including my Negroes, namely, Tip, Mary, Doll, Billy, Nathan, and Sam, and their increase, if any, be sold by hereinafter constituted executors and the proceeds of which to be equally distributed between my beloved wife and children.

5th. It is my wish and desire that my two youngest children, Martha Ann, and Samuel James Denman (both of whom are at this time minors) should remain with and be raised and educated by my wife, Elizabeth Denman, the provisions in this, my last will and testament for my beloved wife being deemed by me a full compensation for the same.

Lastly, I hereby nominate and appoint as executors to this my last will and testament, my beloved wife, Elizabeth Denman, and, with her, my brother, Thomas Denman, jointly.

Signed, sealed, pronounced, and declared by the aforesaid James Denman as his last will and testament, the tenth of August, in the year of our Lord one thousand eight hundred and thirty-eight.

James Denman

The words *my*, on the first page, and *wife*, on the second page, entered before signing.

In the presence of

T. J. Spurlock

Baxter McMorris

FINAL SETTLEMENT

(Published in The Liberty Advocate Sept. 27, 1845)

At the November term, 1945, of the Probate Court of Amite, I will present my account as Executrix of the estate of James Denman, deceased, for final settlement.

Elizabeth Denman, Exec.

———

Elizabeth Denman died Nov. 1848, and the following is a copy of her will, which was probated Dec. 18, 1848:

The Last Will and Testament of Elizabeth Denman, Dec'd

(Copied from Amite County, Miss., records)

State of Mississippi }
Amite County }

Be it known that I, Elizabeth Denman, of the County and State aforesaid, being of sound mind and memory, do make and establish this my last will and testament, hereby revoking all other wills by me at any time made.

1st. It is my will and desire for my funeral expenses, together with all liabilities against me, to be paid by my hereinafter constituted and appointed executor, out of such worldly goods and chattels as it has pleased God to bestow me with.

2nd. I will and bequeath to my beloved son, Bruce Myers Wilson, one cow and calf.

3rd. I will and bequeath to my beloved daughter, Martha Ann Stricklin, one cow and calf and bed clothing for one bed.

4th. I will and bequeath to my beloved son, Samuel James Denman, my saddle horse, one bed and furniture, one yoke of oxen, which oxen his guardian may sell if he thinks best, charging himself with the sale of the same, and as to his bed and furniture, it is my desire for my brother Hampton Burris to keep it until my son Samuel James as aforesaid shall become of age or marry. Then I desire said bed and furniture to be delivered to him.

5th. And as to the balance of my goods, chattels and personal estate and rights of whatsoever kind of which I may be in possession, I desire that it shall be sold and disposed of as follows—viz.—I will and bequeath to my brother, George N. Burris, in trust for my beloved daughter, Martha Ann Stricklin, one half of the net proceeds of the sale of the property above described, he, the said George N. Burris, to receive, keep in trust and pay out to my beloved daughter, Martha Ann Stricklin, as aforesaid, whatever amount annually in his judgment he may think she requires for her comfort, he not being liable for any interest upon no sum or sums whatsoever that may come into his hands as trustee for said Martha Ann, as aforesaid.

6th. I will and bequeath to my beloved son, Samuel James Denman, the balance of my personal estate, above alluded to, it being one half of the net proceeds of the sale above mentioned.

And, I, the said Elizabeth Denman, as aforesaid, do hereby nominate, constitute and appoint my brother, George Nelson Burris, my executor, to this my last will and testament.

Given under my hand and seal this 6th day of March A. D. 1846.

"Being of sound mind and memory" interlined before signing on the first page and third line.

Elizabeth Denman (Seal)

Signed in the presence of

T. G. Spurlock

Francis Wrigley

Baxter McMorris

A. BRUCE MYERS WILSON.—Married Saline Andrews. Children: Rose, Malena, and Mattie.

Bruce Myers Wilson sold Hampton Burris, his uncle, the following tracts of land July 24, 1866, for $100: Northeast quarter of northeast quarter, section 4, township 3, range 6 east, 39.76 acres. Also the northwest quarter of northwest quarter; northwest quarter of southeast quarter; northeast quarter of southwest quarter of section 4, township 3, range 6 east, 119.26 acres. This was perhaps his old homestead. It is located from one to two miles east of Thompson, on the Tangipahoa-McComb Road.

Bruce Myers Wilson joined the East Fork Baptist Church Sept. 1841.

1. ROSE WILSON.—Married Lawrence Robinson. Children: Eugene, Maude, Alma, Helen, Maggie, and Laurence (a girl).

a. EUGENE ROBINSON.—Dead.

b. MAUDE ROBINSON.—Born in Amite County, Miss. Married H. P. Moseley. Children: H. P., Jr. (married Cenie Hargrove; no children). They live in McComb, Miss.

c. ALMA ROBINSON.—Dead. Never married.

d. HELEN ROBINSON.—Married Jerry Walker. Children: Rosalyn (dead), and Wiley (unmarried). They live in McComb, Miss.

e. MAGGIE ROBINSON.—Married A. Storm. Children: Jane (lives in Jackson, Miss.). A. Storm is dead.

They live in McComb, Miss.

f. LAURANCE ROBINSON (a girl).—Married B. T. Walker. Children: Bill, and Jerry T.

They live in McComb, Miss.

(1). BILL WALKER.—Married Gussie Reed. Children: Oma Belle, and Betsy. They live in McComb, Miss.

(2). JERRY T. WALKER.—Eleven years old.

2. MALENA WILSON.—Born in Amite County, Miss., Aug. 17, 1841. Married Marshall Enos Burris Dec. 5, 1867. Children: (Listed under Marshall Enos Burris's name as this is an interfamily marriage).

Malena Wilson-Burris joined the Mars Hill Baptist Church May 21, 1866.

3. MATTIE WILSON.—Married John Robinson. Children: Rose Ella, Emma, John, Jr., Thomas J., Ammie, Eddie, and Charlie.

a. ROSE ELLA ROBINSON.—Married Ira Wyatt Oct. 17, 1897. Children: Eddie Lee, and Eugene. They live in Columbia, Miss.

(1). EDDIE LEE WYATT.—Born Oct. 13, 1898. Married Willie Carr of Laurel, Miss., Aug. 20, 1922. Children: Barbara Jean (born May 30, 1936).

(2). EUGENE WYATT.—Born Oct. 6, 1901. Married Hilda Beaner of Chicago, Ill., Mar. 27, 1926. Children: Robert Eugene (born Nov. 11, 1938), and William Lee (born Apr. 25, 1945).

b. EMMA ROBINSON.—Married, first, Walter Brumfield in 1903. Children: Etta Mae, Lucille, and Hilda. Married, second, J. W. Butler in 1922. No children. They live in Liberty, Miss.

(1). ETTA MAE BRUMFIELD.—Married Bennett Butler. No children. They live in Summit, Miss.

(2). LUCILLE BRUMFIELD.—Married Dr. D. T. Brock. No children. They live in Jackson, Miss.

(3). HILDA BRUMFIELD.—Married Jack H. Ewing. Children: Lucy Claire (age 14), and Jack Hilton (age 11). They live in Jackson, Miss.

c. JOHN ROBINSON, JR.—Born in Amite County, Miss., May 1, 1878. Married Kate Holmes, daughter of W. Holmes of Tylertown, Miss., Apr. 3, 1905, in McComb, Miss. Children: Atwood, Marguerite, Juanita, Seth Eugene, and Dean Carlton. They live in Tylertown, Miss.

(1). ATWOOD ROBINSON.—Born in McComb, Miss., Feb. 18, 1905. Married Loucerna Williams Oct. 1939 in Texas. No children.

Atwood Robinson is a druggist and lives in Strawn, Tex.

(2). MARGUERITE ROBINSON. — Born in China Grove,

Miss., Apr. 19, 1907. Married Stanton Key Calhoun, son of Daniel Calhoun, Jan. 3, 1933, in Tylertown, Miss. Children: Stanton Key, Jr.

Stanton Key Calhoun was born in Mt. Olive, Miss., Sept. 7, 1898. He died Aug. 23, 1945, and was buried in Arlington National Cemetery, Arlington, Va.

Marguerite Robinson-Calhoun is a school teacher and lives in Arlington, Va.

(3). JUANITA ROBINSON.—Born in Tylertown, Miss., Dec. 4, 1914. Unmarried. She is a school teacher and lives in Arlington, Va.

(4). SETH EUGENE ROBINSON.—Born in Tylertown, Miss., Apr. 9, 1917. Married Edith Pope, daughter of Joe Pope, Aug. 1942, in Columbus, Ga. Children: Gloria Jean, and Dean Carlton.

Seth Eugene Robinson is a druggist and lives in Tupelo, Miss.

(5). DEAN CARLTON ROBINSON.—Born in Tylertown, Miss., Feb. 25, 1920. Died Dec. 2, 1924.

d. THOMAS J. ROBINSON.—Married Bessie Elizabeth Turnipseed. Children: Carl, Jerry, Laurence, Hugh Marvin, and Ira Lee.

They live in Smithdale, Miss.

(1). CARL ROBINSON.—Married Ira Belle Caraway. Children: Betty Jean (age 18), Peggy Lanelle (age 14), and Carl Douglas (age 7).

(2). JERRY ROBINSON.—Married Ella Lee Touchstone. Children: Jerry Wyatt (age 17), Cynthia Kay (age 12), Cheryl Faye (age 5), and John Hardy (died at the age of 16 months).

They live in Liberty, Miss.

(3). LAURENCE ROBINSON.—Married Essie Ray Pray. Children: Thomas Ray (age 11), Elizabeth Ann (age 8), and Jimmie Louis (age 5).

They live in Smithdale, Miss.

(4). HUGH MARVIN ROBINSON.—Married Daisy Christine Raley. Children: Hugh (age 7).

(5). IRA LEE ROBINSON.—Married Hazel Touchstone. Children: Anna Margaret (age 3).

e. AMMIE ROBINSON.—Born in Amite County, Miss., Aug.

20, 1883. Married Harry Butler, son of Hugh Butler, Oct. 17, 1909, in Amite County, Miss. Children: Caro Lee, Marjorie, and Grace.

Harry Butler was born in Amite County, Miss., Nov. 11, 1876. He died Sept. 17, 1932, and was buried in the Mars Hill Cemetery. Ammie Robinson-Butler lives in Smithdale, Miss.

(1). CARO LEE BUTLER.—Born in Amite County, Miss., Feb. 20, 1915. Married Oscar Lee Wells, son of Ray Wells, Nov. 30, 1930, in Magnolia, Miss. Children: Martha Ann (age 19; married Merwin Burris),* Rita Rose (age 13), and Harry Butler (age 9). They live in Smithdale, Miss.

(2). MARJORIE BUTLER.—Born in Amite County, Miss., Aug. 6, 1917. Married L. E. Wolfe, Jr., son of L. E. Wolfe, Sr., Sept. 23, 1941, in Louisiana. Children: Carolyn (born in McComb, Miss., Apr. 23, 1946).

L. E. Wolfe, Jr., was born in Arkansas Sept. 11, 1917. He is a veteran of World War II, having served in this war two years. He was a nose gunner on a B-24 bomber. His plane was shot down by the Germans and, when he bailed out, he broke his ankle. He was captured by the Germans, and was imprisoned for eleven months.

They live in Smithdale, Miss.

(3). GRACE BUTLER.—Born in Amite County, Miss., July 15, 1920. Married Earl Gillis, Jr., son of Earl Gillis, Sr., Mar. 7, 1943, in Brookhaven, Miss. Children: Cary Wayne (born in McComb, Miss., July 13, 1948).

They live in McComb, Miss.

f. EDDIE ROBINSON.—Born in Amite County, Miss., Sept. 24, 1889. Married Eva Louise Hinton, daughter of W. F. Hinton of McComb, Miss., Oct. 13, 1913, in McComb, Miss. Children: Edith Frances, and Evelyn Lorraine.

They live in Baton Rouge, La.

(1). EDITH FRANCES ROBINSON.—Married Harrell Lane Sisson. Children: Nelda Carolyn (age 11), and Michael Lane (age 4).

They live in Natchitoches, La.

(2). EVELYN LORRAINE ROBINSON.—Married Dr. James A. Avant. Children: Lorraine Adair (age 9), Ruth Victoria (age 6), and Frances Evelyn (age 4).

*An interfamily marriage.

They live in New Orleans, La., where Dr. Avant is specializing in pediatrics at the Charity Hospital.

g. CHARLIE ROBINSON.—Born in Amite County, Miss. Married Ruth Darville. Children: Charles Ray.

They live in McComb, Miss.

(1). CHARLES RAY ROBINSON. — Married Mary Alice Stockman. Children: Charla Mary (age 4), Charles Ray, Jr. (age 2), and Mary Elizabeth (born Nov. 8, 1950).

B. MARTHA ANN DENMAN.—Born in Amite County, Miss., in 1829. Married Dr. Jacob Burton Strickland Jan. 18, 1884. Children: Cade Drew (Dick), John Spencer, Jane Elizabeth, Ruth Victoria, Jeptha Joe, Henry Willis, James Denman.

Martha Ann Denman-Strickland died in 1885. She was buried in St. Helena Parish, La.

Dr. Jacob Burton Strickland was born in St. Helena Parish, La., Jan. 27, 1825. He was shot and killed at Kirksville, La., July 10, 1860. He was buried in St. Helena Parish, La.

1. CADE DREW (DICK) STRICKLAND.—Born in St. Helena Parish, La., May 16, 1845. Married, first, Lucinda Wright. Children: Delila. Married, second, Ary Poole. Children: Ruth, Lucy, Lena, Nita, and Jacob (Jake).

Cade Drew (Dick) Strickland moved to LaSalle Parish, La., about 1867. It was said by his son Nita that he came over on horseback. He bought 160 acres of land from Jake Womack, near Jena, the parish seat.

Ary Poole was born Dec. 14, 1857. She died Mar. 7, 1925.

a. DELILA STRICKLAND.—Born near Jena, La., Oct. 16, 1873. Married John Coleman. Children: Jesse, Ted, Roy, Lou, and Mamie. Delila Strickland-Coleman is dead. She was buried near Jena, La.

(1). JESSE COLEMAN.—Born in LaSalle Parish, La. Married Adie Perchard. Children: Octavia, Arthur, Grace, and Loyd.

Jesse Coleman is a farmer. They live near Jena, La.

(a). OCTAVIA COLEMAN.—Born in LaSalle Parish, La. Married Other Taylor. Children: Leon, Wilbur, and Francis. Leon and Wilbur are twins.

Other Taylor is a farmer. They live near Jena, La.

(b). ARTHUR COLEMAN.—Dead.

(c). GRACE COLEMAN.—Born in LaSalle Parish, La. Married Buster Cooper. Children: Margaret. They live in Jena, La.

(d). LOYD COLEMAN.—Born in LaSalle Parish, La. Married and in the U. S. Army.

(2). TED COLEMAN.—Born in LaSalle Parish, La., in 1901. Married Mary Smith, daughter of H. B. and Ruth (Strickland) Smith. Children: Airlea, Mildred, Catherine, and Donald.

Ted Coleman is an oil field worker. He and his wife are half first cousins. They live in Jena, La.

(a). AIRLEA COLEMAN. Born in LaSalle Parish, La., Aug. 7, 1926. Married U. V. Taylor. Children: Charles (born Dec. 28, 1944).

They live in Olla, La.

(b). MILDRED COLEMAN.—Born in LaSalle Parish, La., May 30, 1928. Married C. B. Kirl. Children: Runia (born Apr. 23, 1950).

C. B. Kirl is a service station attendant. They live in Alphin, Tex.

(c). CATHERINE COLEMAN.—Born in LaSalle Parish, La., Sept. 4, 1935. Unmarried. Lives near Jena, La.

(d). DONALD COLEMAN.—Born in LaSalle Parish, La., Jan. 30, 1949. Lives near Jena, La.

(3). ROY COLEMAN.—Born in LaSalle Parish, La. Died a boy.

(4). LOU COLEMAN.—Born in LaSalle Parish, La. Married Putman Thomas. No children.

Putman Thomas is a farmer, and lives near Jena, La.

(5). MAMIE COLEMAN.—Born in LaSalle Parish, La. Married Jesse Neal. Children: Jewel (born in LaSalle Parish, La.; married Elmo Eubanks, and has two children, David, and Glinda Sue. Elmo Eubanks is an oil-field worker, and lives in Jena, La.), Daisy, Velma, Betty Lou, and Robert.

Jesse Neal is a farmer, and lives near Jena, La.

b. RUTH STRICKLAND.—Born in LaSalle Parish,La., Sept. 14, 1877. Married Henry Butler Smith. Children: Cade, James (Jimbo), Lena, and Mary.

183

Henry Butler Smith is a blacksmith, and lives near Jena, La.

(1). CADE SMITH.—Born in LaSalle Parish, La., Mar. 18, 1903. Married Mary Smith, daughter of Lewis and Genie (Young) Smith, Sept. 7, 1924, in Jena, La. Children: Lucy (born Aug. 1, 1926), and Allen Cade (born Oct. 1, 1927; in the U. S. Air Corps).

They live in Jena, La.

(2). JAMES (JIMBO) SMITH.—Born in LaSalle Parish, La., Aug. 27, 1910. Married Sallie Love. No children.

James (Jimbo) Smith is an electrician and salesman, and lives in Corpus Christi, Tex.

(3). LENA MAY SMITH.—Born in LaSalle Parish, La., Aug. 12, 1905. Unmarried.

(4). MARY SMITH.—Born in LaSalle Parish, La., Mar. 14, 1908. Married Ted Coleman (her half-first cousin). Children: (Listed under Ted Coleman as this is an interfamily marriage). They live near Jena, La.

c. LUCY STRICKLAND.—Born in LaSalle Parish, La., Aug. 14, 1886. Married Charles Smith. Children: Jettie. Lucy Strickland-Smith died (from child-birth) Nov. 17, 1904. She was buried in Jena, La.

Charles Smith is a farmer, and lives near Jena, La.

(1). JETTIE SMITH.—Born in LaSalle Parish, La., in 1906. Married Eula Neal. Children: Adrian (A. D.), and Maurice (a girl).

Jettie Smith's mother died when he was born, and he was reared by his uncle, Nita Strickland. He is a farmer, and lives near Jena, La.

(a). ADRIAN (A. D.) SMITH.—Born in LaSalle Parish, La., in 1926. Unmarried. Lives near Jena, La.

(b). MAURICE SMITH (a girl).—Born in LaSalle Parish, La., in 1928. Married Otis Decker. Children: Adrian (born 1946), and Linda Dianne (born 1948).

Otis Decker is an oil field worker, and lives in Brookhaven, Miss.

d. LENA STRICKLAND.—Born in LaSalle Parish, La., Apr. 14, 1891. Unmarried. Lives with her brother, Nita, near Jena, La.

e. NITA STRICKLAND.—Born in LaSalle Parish, La., Jan. 7, 1883. Unmarried. He is a farmer and lives near Jena, La., on his father's old place.

f. JACOB (JAKE) STRICKLAND.—Born in LaSalle Parish, La., Jan. 17, 1897. Died Jan. 8, 1913. Buried in Jena, La.

2. JOHN SPENCER STRICKLAND.—Born in St. Helena Parish, La., July 15, 1857. Married Emma C. Powell. Children: Martha Ann, Elizabeth, Mildred, Annie, Velma Pinkie, Dewitt, John Spencer, Jr., and Cade Drew.

John Spencer Strickland died May 27, 1896, and was buried in St. Helena Parish, La. He was a deacon and superintendent of the Sunday School in the New Zion Baptist Church.

a. MARTHA ANN STRICKLAND.—Married, first, Tom Beatty. Children: Richard, Cordia, Hugh, and Anna. Married, second . . . . . . McElveen. No children.

b. ELIZABETH STRICKLAND.—Married . . . . Williams, thought to be Alex Wattley Williams, grandson of Addison Burris, which would make this an interfamily marriage. The children are listed under the husband.

c. MILDRED STRICKLAND.—Married John T. Newman. Children: Blanche, Hazel, and Mildred.

Mildred Strickland-Newman is dead.

d. ANNIE STRICKLAND.—Born in St. Helena Parish, La., Dec. 21, 1887. Married John T. Newman, son of M. A. and Delion E. (Amacker) Newman, Sept. 22, 1904, in St. Helena Parish. Children: Leon Thomas, John Strickland, Joseph C., Annie Laura, Robert Reed, and Carl Kennon.

John T. Newman married Annie Strickland after her sister Mildred's death. They live near Kentwood, La.

(1). LEON THOMAS NEWMAN.—Born in St. Helena Parish, La., Dec. 20, 1905. Died Apr. 13, 1906, in St. Helena Parish.

(2). JOHN STRICKLAND NEWMAN.—Born in St. Helena Parish, La., Mar. 6, 1907. Married Martha Ida Wall, daughter of Willie and Mary Wall, Feb. 16, 1942, in St. Helena Parish. Children: Mary Annie, Martha Emma, Marie Alice, Henry Earl, and Dudley John.

(3). JOSEPH C. NEWMAN.—Born in St. Helena Parish, La., Oct. 25, 1917. Married Jacqueline Arp, daughter of Lillian Arp, Apr. 3, 1941, in Reno, Nevada. Children: Joseph C., Jr.

Joseph C. Newman served as first lieutenant in the U. S. Air Corps during World War II. He was awarded five bronze stars, significant of service in five major campaigns in the European Theatre of Operations. His unit was the 438th Troop Carrier Group, which performed troop carrier operations in the areas of Northern France, Southern France, Normandy, Rome-Arno, and Germany. This group was cited for its successful fulfillment of airborne operations on D-Day in Normandy. After which, this group carried out thousands of re-supply and air evacuation missions between combat sorties. He is serving in the U. S. Air Corps overseas, and was promoted to captain in 1951.

(4). ANNIE LAURA NEWMAN.—Born in St. Helena Parish, La., Nov. 13, 1920. Married August Mikkola June 1949, in Detroit, Mich. Children: Arthur.

(5). ROBERT REED NEWMAN.—Born in St. Helena Parish, La., Dec. 12, 1923.

Robert Reed Newman enlisted in the U. S. Air Corps Feb. 15, 1945, during World War II. He served in the 82nd Airborne Division. He was discharged Nov. 30, 1946. He lives with his mother near Kentwood, La.

(6). CARL KENNON NEWMAN.—Born in the Sixth Ward of St. Helena Parish, La., Jan. 4, 1927. Enlisted in the U. S. Army Mar. 14, 1945, during World War II. Served with the 267th Air Group. Re-enlisted in the U. S. Army Air Corps July 3, 1950, and was stationed in Great Falls, Montana.

e. VELMA PINKIE STRICKLAND.—Married Judson Emmett Martin. Children: (Listed under husband—an interfamily marriage). Velma Pinkie Strickland-Martin is dead.

f. DEWITT STRICKLAND.—Dead.

g. JOHN SPENCER STRICKLAND, JR.—Dead.

h. CADE DREW STRICKLAND.—Married Elizabeth Phillips. Children: Bruce, Cade Drew, Jr., Fay, Thelma, and Betty.

Cade Drew Strickland and his wife are dead. They were buried in the family cemetery on the old John Newman Place.

3. JANE ELIZARETH STRICKLAND.—Born in St. Helena Parish, La., in 1851. Married Hardy S. Bridges, son of Jackson J. Bridges. Children: Jackson J., Jimmie, Martha, Bessie, Henry, and Hardy S., Jr.

Jane Elizabeth Strickland-Bridges and her husband were buried in the New Zion Cemetery in the Sixth Ward of St. Helena Parish.

a. JACKSON J. BRIDGES.—Born in St. Helena Parish, La. Married Martha (Sis) Grice, daughter of Dave Grice. Children: Zellie, Geneva (dead), Harry, Kelly, Willard, and Kitty.

Martha (Sis) Grice-Bridges was born in St. Helena Parish, La. She is dead. She was buried in the New Zion Cemetery in the Sixth Ward of St. Helena Parish.

Jackson J. Bridges died in 1951.

b. JIMMIE BRIDGES.—Born in St. Helena Parish, La. Married Dave White. No children.

Jimmie and Dave White are dead.

c. MARTHA BRIDGES.—Born in St. Helena Parish, La. Married, first, Bud Womack. Children: Janie (married Charlie Harrell and has one child, Troy. Janie died Mar. 11, 1951, and was buried in the New Zion Cemetery), Nettie (married Albert Harrell of Liverpool, La., and has five children, Eudora, Hazel, Jessie Mae, Victor, and Phillip), Abner, and Euna Cook. Married, second, Hanse Simmons. No children.

Martha Bridges-Womack-Simmons is dead.

d. BESSIE BRIDGES.—Born in St. Helena Parish, La. Married Tom Burch. Children: Clyde, Read, and O. W.

Bessie and Tom Burch are dead. They were buried in the New Zion Cemetery of St. Helena Parish.

e. HENRY BRIDGES.—Born in St. Helena Parish, La. Married Daisy Sandifer. Children: Hosey, Jewell, Alvin, Claud (dead), Valley (dead), and Ruby.

Henry Bridges is dead. He was buried in the New Zion Cemetery of St. Helena Parish, La. His folks live in Michigan.

f. HARDY S. BRIDGES, JR.—Born in St. Helena Parish, La. Married Jessie Bridges. Children: Launa Pearl, and Otis Virgil.
Hardy S. Bridges, Jr., is dead. He was buried in the New Zion Cemetery of St. Helena Parish. His folks live in Kentwood, La.

4. RUTH VICTORIA STRICKLAND.—Born in St. Helena Parish, La., in 1850. Married Peter F. Hutchinson. Children: Sallie, Mary, Martha, Merritt, and Jake.

Ruth Victoria Strickland-Hutchinson died in 1923, and was buried in the family cemetery on the old Hutchinson Place, Sixth Ward of St. Helena Parish, La.

a. SALLIE HUTCHINSON.—Born in St. Helena Parish, La. Married Boykin Bridges, son of Wilson and Sallie (Hutchinson) Bridges. No children.

Sallie Hutchinson-Bridges and her mother-in-law were first cousins, and had the same names.

They live near Kentwood, La.

b. MARY HUTCHINSON.—Born in St. Helena Parish, La. Married Willie Guy. Children: Ruth Elizabeth (married Willie T. Allen of Greensburg, La.; no children).

Mary and Willie Guy are dead.

c. MARTHA HUTCHINSON.—Born in St. Helena Parish, La. Married Josh Guy. Children: Ola, Sallie, Lora (married Clyde Strickland; an interfamily marriage; children are listed under husband), and Georgia.

Martha and Josh Guy are dead. They were buried in Day's Church Cemetery in the Second Ward of St. Helena Parish, La.

d. MERRITT HUTCHINSON.—Born in St. Helena Parish, La. Married Aryie Newman. Children: Sitman, Grace, Daisy, Helen, L. T., and Carrie.

Merritt Hutchinson is dead. He was buried in the Hutchinson Cemetery in St. Helena Parish. His family lives near Kentwood, La.

e. JAKE HUTCHISON.—Born in St. Helena Parish, La. Married Rosa Branch. Children: Preston, Jake Henry, and Tisha Mae.

Jake Hutchinson is dead. He was buried in the Hutchinson Cemetery in St. Helena Parish. His family lives near Kentwood, La.

5. JEPTHA JOE STRICKLAND.—Born in St. Helena Parish, La., Apr. 19, 1855. Married Ida Elizabeth Taylor Mar. 2, 1881. Children: Charles Richmond, John Taylor, Joseph Quincy, Ida Roberta, and James Wirt.

Jeptha Joe Strickland died Jan. 29, 1920.

a. CHARLES RICHMOND STRICKLAND.—Born near Greensburg, La., July 3, 1882. Married Cassie C. Wales June 27, 1912, near Greensburg, La. Children: Clayton Clifton, and Clyde Dayton.

Charles Richmond Strickland was a retired farmer and lived near Greensburg, La., at the time of his death, Jan. 24, 1951. He was the Strickland Family Historian, and assisted with this history. He was buried in the Wales Cemetery, near Greensburg, La.

(1). CLATON CLIFTON STRICKLAND.—Born near Greensburg, La., June 24, 1915. Married Grace Hurst in 1934. Children: Clovis (age 15), C. Grace (age 9), and Robert C. (age 2).

They live near Greensburg, La.

(2). CLYDE DAYTON STRICKLAND.—Born near Greensburg, La., Sept. 29, 1918. Married Lora Guy, daughter of Josh and Martha (Hutchinson) Guy, Jan. 15, 1949.* Children: Bettie Lee (age 5 months).

Lora Guy-Strickland is a direct Burris-Denman descendant. She and her husband are third cousins. They live near Greensburg, La.

b. JOHN TAYLOR STRICKLAND.—Born near Greensburg, La., Aug. 27, 1885. Married Mary E. Blades. Children: Herbert Burton, Glynn E., and Clyde C. Mary E. Blades-Strickland was born Dec. 1, 1889. John Taylor Strickland works for a railway company. They live in Vicksburg, Miss.

(1). HERBERT BURTON STRICKLAND.—Born in St. Helena Parish, La., Dec. 11, 1910. Married Janie Webb of Vicksburg, Miss., July 1938, in Vicksburg, Miss. Children: John (age 14), Mary L. (age 11), and Burton (age 9).

Herbert Burton Strickland was employed as personnel clerk by the Government before entering military service during World War II. He was killed in action in France in 1944.

(2). GLYNN E. STRICKLAND.—Born in St. Helena Parish, La., Apr. 22, 1912. Married Lucille Furrow, daughter of J. Furrow, Oct. 1937, in Chicago, Ill. Children: Carol Ann (age 11), Rosie Myre (age 6), Joe G. (age 4), and Helen Anita (age 2).

Lucille Furrow-Strickland was born in Vicksburg, Miss., Nov. 1911.

Glynn E. Strickland is employed by the U. S. Government as a civil engineer.

(3). CLYDE C. STRICKLAND.—Born in McComb, Miss., Mar. 17, 1914. Married Erna Voss, daughter of E. Voss, Dec. 14, 1941, in Natchez, Miss. Children: Roy Clifton (age 8), and Elizabeth Ann (age 6).

Erna Voss-Strickland was born in Copenhagen, Denmark, Sept. 7, 1909.

---

*Interfamily marriage.

Clyde C. Strickland is employed by the Illinois Central Railway Co. as a civil engineer.

c. JOSEPH QUINCY STRICKLAND.—Born near Greensburg, La., Sept. 5, 1893. Married Etta Smith. Children: Lehman Erwin.

Etta Smith-Strickland was born Oct. 9, 1894.

They live on West Mason St., Baton Rouge, La.

(1). LEHMAN ERWIN STRICKLAND.—Born Feb. 25, 1921. Married Margie Bennett. No children.

Lehman Erwin Strickland is a fireman at the city powerhouse. They live in Baton Rouge, La.

d. IDA ROBERTA STRICKLAND.—Born near Greensburg, La., in the Sixth Ward of St. Helena Parish, Dec. 3, 1898. Married Merritt G. Allen, son of Thomas H. Allen, Oct. 28, 1917, in Greensburg, La. Children: Hulon Merritt, Thomas Gaylon, Vera Mae, Evelyn Geraldine, Gladys Leona, Hubert Price, and Ernie Joe.

Merritt G. Allen was born in Liverpool, La., Apr. 13, 1886.

They live near Greensburg, La.

(1). HULON MERRITT ALLEN.—Born in Liverpool, La., Sept. 27, 1918. Married Anna Belle Landry, daughter of Alfred Landry, Dec. 17, 1938, in Liverpool, La. Children: Shirley Ann (age 10), Hulon David (age 5), and Frances Fay (age 2).

Anna Belle Landry-Allen was born in Charenton, La., Oct. 1914.

Hulon Merritt Allen was trained in the 120th general hospital, Camp Van Dorn, Miss., during World War II. He served in the South Pacific, New Guinea, the Philippines, and Japan. He was awarded the Asiatic-Pacific Campaign Medal with two bronze stars. He was also awarded the Philippine Liberation ribbon; the Good Conduct medal; the Meritorious Unit award; and the World War II Victory medal. His rank was private first-class. He served six months in the U. S., and eighteen months and twenty-three days overseas. His occupation is oilfield worker; however, at present he is attending a trade school for veterans.

They live in Charenton, La.

(2). THOMAS GAYLON ALLEN.—Born in New Orleans, La., Oct. 26, 1922. Married Rainer Estelle Cox, daughter of Raymond C. and Mary (Hill) Cox, Oct. 14, 1946, in Kentwood, La. Children: Raymond Gaylon (age 2).

Rainer Estelle Cox-Allen was born in Booneville, Miss., Mar. 27, 1930.

Thomas Gaylon Allen entered service during World War II, Nov. 17, 1942. He was an electrician, 2nd class, with duty under the Naval Air Command on Guadalcanal. He was discharged Jan. 16, 1946. His present occupation is electrician and plumber. They live in Liverpool, La.

(3). VERA MAE ALLEN.—Born in Liverpool, La., Nov. 4, 1926. Married Johnny Lee Hodges, son of John Robert and Birdie Cecille (Martin) Hodges, Dec. 25, 1947, in Baton Rouge, La. Children: Dennis Ralph, and Daryll Allen (twins—born Nov. 2, 1951).

Johnny Lee Hodges was born in Hammond, La., Oct. 31, 1922. He enlisted in the U. S. Air Force, during World War II, Oct. 19, 1942. He served in the 9th Bombardment Squadron, 7th Bombardment Group, 10th Air Force—B-24 Flight Engineer. His rank was sergeant. They live in Baton Rouge, La.

(4). EVELYN GERALDINE ALLEN. — Born in Liverpool, La., June 28, 1929. Married Clifford N. Battles, son of Nathan Clifford and Lucille (Bennett) Battles, Jan. 30, 1948, in Magnolia, Miss. Children: Judith Kay (born Apr. 16, 1949), June Lynette (born July 8, 1950).

Clifford N. Battles was born in Amite, La., Mar. 24, 1923. He served two and one-half years as corporal in the First Cavalry Division, in the South Pacific, during World War II. They live in Amite, La.

(5). GLADYS LEONA ALLEN.—Born in Liverpool, La., Aug. 11, 1931. Married Lea Toler Hanks, son of Clarence E. and Louise (Bridges) Hanks, Feb. 11, 1949, in Magnolia, Miss. Children: Connie Lea (born Aug. 13, 1951).

Lea Toler Hanks was born in Jackson, La., Nov. 14, 1926. They live in Amite, La.

(6). HUBERT PRICE ALLEN.—Born in Liverpool, La., Sept. 27, 1918. Died Feb. 21, 1919. Was Hulon Merritt's twin brother.

(7). ERNIE JOE ALLEN.—Born in Liverpool, La., Apr. 18, 1934. Married Alvin Clifton Thompson, son of Johnny Ray and Katie (Hardy) Thompson, May 12, 1951.

Alvin Clifton Thompson was born in the Fifth Ward of St.

Helena Parish July 1, 1926. He operates a dairy and lives near Liverpool, La.

e. JAMES WIRT STRICKLAND.—Born in St. Helena Parish, La., Nov. 1891. Married Janie Venable. Children: Wilbur Burke (age 26), Aline Elizabeth (age 24), Vernone Leroy (age 21), and Edith Marion (age 16).

Janie Venable-Strickland was born in Liverpool, La. They live in Kentwood, La.

6. HENRY WILLIS STRICKLAND.—Born in St. Helena Parish, La., in 1847. Died in 1861. Never married.

7. JAMES DENMAN STRICKLAND.—Born in St. Helena Parish, La., in 1848. Died near Jena, La., in 1913. Never married.

C. SAMUEL JAMES DENMAN.—It was reported by a member of the family that James Denman (probably Samuel James Denman) served in the Civil War. He was mustered into service in April, 1861. He was a member of the Summit Rifles. What became of him after the Civil War, if he survived it, is unknown.

V. JAMES BURRIS

James Burris was the son of Samuel and Mary (Myers) Burris. It is thought that he was born in South Carolina and was only a few years old when his parents migrated to Amite County, Miss., in 1809. Nothing to indicate that he was ever married has been found. His will was probated in the Amite County courts Feb. 20, 1837, which was doubtless shortly after his death.

WILL OF JAMES BURRIS—DEC'D.

(Copied from Amite County, Miss., records)

State of Mississippi ⎰
Amite County ⎱

In the name of God, I, James Burris, of the State and County aforesaid, being very weak of body, but of perfect mind and memory, do make and ordain this and no other, by last will and testament; that is to say—Principally, and first of all, I wish at my decease my body be buried in a decent, Christian-like manner, and touching my worldly goods, my will that the whole of my estate be equally divided amongst my four brothers, and three sisters, namely: William Burris, George N. Burris, Hampton Burris, Addison Burris, Elizabeth Denman, Harriett Simmons, and Anna Smith, equally—my two sisters, Elizabeth and Anna, I wish their part to be secured to them, and their children, exclusively and entirely, in my estate, consisting principally of money.

192

And I do hereby acknowledge and assign this my last will and testament, and none other.

In witness whereof I have hereunto set my hand this 20th day of February, 1837.

James Burris (L. S).

In the presence of us:

Charles F. Felder

Alexander M. Morris

Baxter M. Morris

ADMINISTRATORS' BOND OF THE ESTATE OF JAMES BURRIS, DEC'D

(Copied from Amite County, Miss., records)

State of Mississippi }
Amite County }

Know all men by these presents that we, George N. Burris, Samuel B. Simmons, and Edmund Smith, are held and firmly bound unto John Walker. Esquire, Judge of Probate of Said County, and in the sum of three thousand dollars to be paid the Said Judge of Probate Court or his successors in office or their certain attorney or assigns, to which payment well and truly to be made, we bind ourselves and every one of us and every one of our heirs, executor and administrators, for the whole and in the whole, jointly and severally, firmly, by these presents, sealed with our seals, and dated this 27th day of March, Anno Domini, one thousand eight hundred and thirty-seven.

The condition of this obligation is that of the Said George N. Burris, administrator, with the will annexed of James Burris, deceased, do make a true and perfect inventory of all and singular the goods, chattels and credits of the said deceased, which have or shall come to the hands or possession of any other person or persons for him and the same do make, do exhibit to the Probate Court of Amite County at such time as he shall be there as required, to obey the Said Court, and the same goods, chattels and credits do well and truly administer according to law and make a just and true account of his actings and doings when thereby required by the Court, and further, do well and truly pay and deliver all the legacies contained and specified in the said will as far as the said goods, chattels and credits will expand according to the value thereof and of the law shall charge him, then this obligation to be void, or else to remain in full force and virtue.

Signed, sealed and delivered in the presence of S. R. Davis, Clk.

G. N. Burris

Samuel B. Simmons

Edmund Smith

The Administration Account and Final Settlement of G. N. Burris, Administrator of James Burris, Deceased

(Copied from Amite County, Miss., records)

The administrator charges himself with the following amount,

This amount ....$ 3496.02

The administrator prays allowange for the following disbursements:

1.	Paid W. C. Butler, as per receipt ....$	8.25
2.	" Gordon Y. Tillston, as per receipt................................	5.19
3.	" William Spinks " " "	3.00
4.	" J. Walker, J. Probate " "	6.00
5.	" S. R. Davis " "	7.50

Total	3454.08
6. " William Burris, as per receipt..................................	494.86
7. " Hampton Burris " " "	494.86
8. " Edmund Smith & Wife " "	494.86
9. " Samuel Burris " "	494.86
10. " Addison Burris " "	494.86
11. " James Denman & Wife " "	494.86
	2969.16

Deduct J. Probate fees for this account	484.92
	2.50
In Administrator's hand	482.42

Probate Court, June Term, 1838

George N. Burris says on oath that the above account is just and true, as he verily believes,

Geo. N. Burris

Sworn to this 20th day of
June, 1838, S. R. Davis, Clk.

VI. SAMUEL BURRIS, JR.

Samuel Burris, Jr., was the son of Samuel and Mary (Myers) Burris. He was born in South Carolina in 1800. He migrated to Amite County, Miss., in 1809 with his parents. He married Julia Ann Everett Apr. 1, 1830. They had the following children: John, Mary, Harriett, Victoria, Ellen Elizabeth, Julia, Judson, Amanda, Alice, Alma, and Adeline.

Samuel Burris, Jr. first settled on the northwest quarter of the southeast quarter of section 6, township 3, range 6 east, containing

39.94 acres, which he bought from the U. S. Government Feb. 7, 1834. This land is located on the East Fork of Amite River, about halfway between East Fork and the Thompson Community. He bought 240 acres of the Estate of Jas. W. and Susanna Weeks, Jan. 10, 1835, and settled there. This land is located on the East Fork of Amite River, part of it running across the river, and about one mile south of the old James Chandler Place. Later, he bought land near Gillsburg, Miss., and moved there. Still later, Nov. 10, 1855, he bought seventy-one acres of land from Thos. W. Day of St. Helena Parish, La., for $265—$110 in cash and the balance in note—and moved there. This land is located on the east side of the Tickfaw River, near Liverpool, La. About a year later, Feb. 20, 1856, he bought thirty-five acres of land for $135 cash, also located on the east side of the Tickfaw River, near the tract he bought from Thos. W. Day. When Samuel Burris, Jr. died his estate in St. Helena Parish consisted of 420 acres, which was located in section 62, township 2, range 5 east, east of Tickfaw River, and near Liverpool, La. It was sold to B. D. Rand Nov. 26, 1890, for $390.

Julia Ann Everett-Burris joined the East Fork Baptist Church Nov. 1841. She transferred her membership to the Jerusalem Baptist Church (located near Gillsburg, Miss.) Oct. 1859.

Samuel Burris, Jr. was buried in the Anglin Cemetery, near Liverpool, La.

A. JOHN BURRIS.—Born in Amite County, Miss., in 1832. Married Nancy Anglin. Their children all died young.

John Burris was a farmer.

B. MARY BURRIS.—Born in Amite County, Miss., in 1834. Married Lafayette Swearingen Mar. 19, 1855. Children: George Washington, Dora, Joseph Lafayette, Hattie, Piney Jane, Mattie, Rosalie, Mary, and J. Monroe.

Lafayette Swearingen was born in Amite County in 1836.

Mary Burris-Swearingen was buried in the old Anglin Cemetery in St. Helena Parish, La.

1. GEORGE WASHINGTON SWEARINGEN.—Born near Gillsburg, Miss. Married Mary Jane (Mollie) Wall, daughter of Addie Stewart-Wall, Feb. 17, 1876, in Gillsburg, Miss. Children: Octavia, Ida, Ella, George Monroe, Lafayette, Willie, Benjamin Everett, and Seborn Elbert.

Mary Jane (Mollie) Wall-Swearingen was born near Mt. Vernon

Church, in Amite County, Miss., in 1856. She died in 1916 and was buried in Wall's Cemetery, Amite County, Miss.

George Washington Swearingen died in 1923, and was buried in Wall's Cemetery.

a. OCTAVIA SWEARINGEN.—Born near Amite River Church, Amite County, Miss. Married Tom Redmond. Children: Ada Lou.

Tom Redmond was buried in Kentwood, La.

Octavia Swearingen-Redmond died in 1911, and was buried in Wall's Cemetery, Amite County, Miss.

(1). ADA LOU REDMOND.—Born June 1909. Married George Tidwell. Children: Lillie Mae (born in 1925), Norma (married Bob Christopher, and has two children: Bob, Jr., and Perry; lives in San Pedro, Calif), and Evonne.

b. IDA SWEARINGEN.—Born in Amite County, Miss., near Gillsburg, Miss. Never married. Dead. Buried in Wall Cemetery, Amite County, Miss.

c. ELLA SWEARINGEN.—Born near Amite River Church, Amite County, Miss., Feb. 4, 1889. Married Fred Varnado, son of R. S. Varnado, Apr. 11, 1914, in Osyka, Miss. Children: R. F., Helen Marie, Willie Ray, Mary Frances, Alton Lamar, and Ella Grace.

Fred Varnado was born in Greenlaw, La., May 14, 1889.

They live in Osyka, Miss.

(1). R. F. VARNADO.—Born in Greenlaw, La., Feb. 8, 1915. Married Thelma Geraldine Williams of Cairo, Ill. Children: Laura Ella (dead—lived one year).

R. F. Varnado served four and one-half years in the armed forces of the U. S. during World War II. He is now attending the University of Mississippi. They live in Osyka, Miss.

(2). HELEN MARIE VARNADO.—Born in Osyka, Miss., Sept. 27, 1917. Married Cecil Paul Young of Sikeston, Mo. Children: Jerry Dianne (born Nov. 5, 1947).

(3). WILLIE RAY VARNADO.—Served four years and twenty days in the armed forces of the U. S. during World War II.

(4). MARY FRANCES VARNADO.

(5). ALTON LAMAR VARNADO.—Served two years in the armed forces of the U. S. during World War II.

(6). ELLA GRACE VARNADO.—Died at the age of one year.

d. GEORGE MONROE SWEARINGEN. — Born in Gillsburg, Miss., Sept. 16, 1888. Married Ada Florine Jordan, daughter of Marion A. and Henrietta Jordan, Dec. 6, 1916, in Marshall, Tex. Children: Constance Gene, and George Monroe, Jr.

Ada Florine Jordan-Swearingen was born in Long Branch, Tex., Apr. 19, 1896.

They live in Marshall, Tex.

(1). CONSTANCE GENE SWEARINGEN.—Born in Marshall, Tex., Apr. 9, 1923. Married John William Casey, III, son of John William and Cecile Casey, Nov. 19, 1948. No children.

John William Casey III, was born in Theresa, N. Y., June 29, 1924.

They live on 63rd Road, Forest Hills, Long Island, New York.

(2). GEORGE MONROE SWEARINGEN, JR.—Born in Marshall, Tex., Feb. 16, 1925. Unmarried. Lives on Lefferts Blvd., Richmond Hill, Long Island, New York.

e. LAFAYETTE SWEARINGEN. — Born near Amite River Church, in Amite County, Miss., May 28, 1885. Married Vesta Alford, daughter of Jesse B. Alford, Mar. 1, 1906, in Washington Parish, La. Children: Velo B., Benamay, Leveta, Marie, Quentin, and Loudean.

Vesta Alford-Swearingen was born in Washington Parish, La., Aug. 29, 1882.

They live in Osyka, Miss.

(1). VELO B. SWEARINGEN.—Born in Washington Parish, La., Feb. 12, 1908. Married Tincie Strickland. Children: Jerry (born Feb. 2, 1936; blind—caused by dynamite cap explosion; in blind school in Baton Rouge, La.), and Norman (born Nov. 19, 1938).

Velo B. Swearingen served three years in the armed forces of the U. S. during World War II. They live near Osyka, Miss., on Route 3.

(2). BENAMAY SWEARINGEN.—Born Aug. 24, 1911. Married Iley Simmons. Children: I. W. (born Jan. 6, 1935), and Bennie Gaylan (born Feb. 1, 1941).

They live near Osyka, Miss., on Route 3.

(3). LEVETA SWEARINGEN.—Born Apr. 24, 1914. Married Downey Miller. Children: Dennis Wayne (born Oct. 1944), and Carolyn Ann (born Oct. 1946).

They live near Osyka, Miss., on Route 3.

(4). MARIE SWEARINGEN.—Born Mar. 14, 1916. Married Leslie Roberts. Children: Donald (born Aug. 31, 1944).
They live in Kentwood, La.

(5). QUENTIN SWEARINGEN.—Born Nov. 29, 1920. Married Della Gohram of Sparfish, S. Dakota. Children: Beverly Jean (born Oct. 8, 1947), and Connie Sue (born Sept. 9, 1950).

Quentin Swearingen served two years in the armed forces of the U. S. during World War II. They live near Osyka, Miss.

(6). LOUDEAN SWEARINGEN.—Born Apr. 11, 1922. Married Jewel Simpson (born Oct. 14, 1919). Children: Glynn Elbert (born Apr. 29, 1946), Sandra (born June 6, 1947), and Kenneth Wayne (born June 18, 1948). They live near Osyka, Miss.

f. WILLIE SWEARINGEN.—Born near Amite River Church, Amite County, Miss., July 3, 1896. Married Lucille Sumerall, daughter of John Sumerall. Children: Evelyn, Inez (married), Nolan, Clayton, and Richie.

Lucille Sumerall-Swearingen was born in Kentwood, La.

Willie Swearingen served one year in the armed forces of the U. S. during World War I. He is dead. He was buried near Foley, Fla.

g. BENJAMIN EVERETT SWEARINGEN.—Born near Gillsburg, Miss., Dec. 23, 1880. Married Mollie Darden Bell, daughter of James Allison and Fannie (Corley) Bell, Aug. 30, 1905, in Marshall, Tex. Children: Lillie Opal, Lola Bell, Benjamin Everett, Jr., Acey Avolea, Michael Darden, Arra Marie, and Iris Ella.

Mollie Darden Bell-Swearingen was born in Scottsville, Tex., June 15, 1888. She died Apr. 25, 1937, and was buried in Marshall, Tex.

Benjamin Everett Swearingen operates a machine shop in Marshall, Tex.

(1). LILLIE OPAL SWEARINGEN.—Born in Marshall, Tex., Aug. 23, 1906. Married David Pinkney Edwards, son of David Pinkney Edwards, Sr., Feb. 16, 1945, in Lorssburg, New Mexico. No children.

David Pinkney Edwards, Jr. was born in Charlotte, N. Carolina, July 4, 1907. They live in Phoenix, Ariz.

(2). IOLA BELL SWEARINGEN.—Born in Marshall, Tex., July 13, 1908. Married Albert Lewis Moeschle, son of Lewis P. Moeschle, Apr. 5, 1942, in Marshall, Tex. No children.

Albert Lewis Moeschle was born in Marshall, Tex., Oct. 16, 1898.

They live in Marshall, Tex.

(3). BENJAMIN EVERETT SWEARINGEN, JR.—Born in Marshall, Tex., July 3, 1910. Married Mary Hellen Smith, daughter of John Smith, Sept. 30, 1936, in Tucson, Ariz. Children: Benjamin Everett III (born Sept. 23, 1937).

Mary Hellen Smith-Swearingen was born in Easton, Penna., Jan. 14, 1906. They live in Texarkana, Tex.

(4). ACEY AVOLEA SWEARINGEN.—Born in Marshall, Tex., Nov. 3, 1913. Married Emma Jean Greenwood, daughter of John C. and Maudie Bell (Owens) Greenwood, Nov. 20, 1950, in Texarkana, Tex. No children. Emma Jeane Greenwood-Swearingen was born in Hickory Ridge, Ark., July 30, 1927. They live in Pine Bluff, Ark.

(5). MICHAEL DARDEN SWEARINGEN.—Born in Marshall, Tex., May 25, 1916. Married Eunice Loyce Whitted, daughter of T. C. Whitted, Jan. 2, 1942, in Texarkana, Tex. Children: Michael Darden, Jr. (born Nov. 3, 1942), Molly Inez (born Sept. 8, 1943), and Patricia Loyce (born Dec. 15, 1945).

Eunice Loyce Whitted-Swearingen was born in Wheatley, Ark., Sept. 16, 1919. They live in Gladewater, Tex.

(6). ARRA MARIE SWEARINGEN.—Born in Marshall, Tex., May 22, 1919. Married Harry Edwin Overlock, son of Harry Edwin and Ellen (Farrel) Overlock, Nov. 21, 1940, in Yuma, Ariz. Children: Harry Edwin, Jr. (born in Alhambra, Calif., July 12, 1942), Mary Ann (born in Alhambra, Calif., June 5, 1944), and Timothy Lee (born in Alhambra, Calif., Oct. 13, 1946).

Harry Edwin Overlock was born in Douglas, Ariz., May 22, 1916. He is the grandson of Charles Alton Overlock, one of the founders of Douglas, Ariz.

Arra Marie Swearingen-Overlock was graduated from the Arizona State College in Tempe, Ariz., in 1940 with a bachelor of arts degree in education. She owns and operates a nursery school in Temple City, Calif.

They live in Temple City, Calif.

(7). IRIS ELLA SWEARINGEN.—Born in Marshall, Tex., Sept. 3, 1921. Married, first, Cortney C. Morrison, son of Alonzo Davis and Alice Marie (Brown) Morrison, July 11, 1942, in Las Vegas, Nevada. Children: Penelope Marie (born in Texarkana, Ark., June 10, 1944), and Phoebe Jean (born in Texarkana, Ark., May 4, 1946).

Cortney C. Morrison was born in Covington, Ky., July 21, 1919.

Iris Ella Swearingen-Morrison was divorced from Cortney C. Morrison in New Boston, Tex., Feb. 11, 1948. She married, second, Ollie (Jack) Strickland, son of L. and Willie Etta (Banks) Strickland, Feb. 14, 1948, in Henderson, Tex. Children: Idona Iris (born Jan. 9, 1949).

Ollie (Jack) Strickland was born in Cushing, Tex., July 6, 1912.

They live in Gladewater, Tex.

h. SEBORN ELBERT SWEARINGEN.—Born in Gillsburg, Miss., Sept. 8, 1892. Married Eva Hodges, daughter of R. F. Hodges, July 23, 1920, in Memphis, Tenn. Children: Geraldine and Glenn Elbert.

Eva Hodges-Swearingen was born in Memphis, Tenn., Nov. 16, 1901.

They live in Jefferson, Tex.

(1). GERALDINE SWEARINGEN. — Born Nov. 29, 1922. Married Charles Wells. Children: Charles Seborn (born July 31, 1945, and Beverly Jean (born Mar. 31, 1950).

They live in Jefferson, Tex.

(2). GLENN ELBERT SWEARINGEN.—Born Oct. 17, 1936. Lives in Jefferson, Tex.

2. DORA SWEARINGEN.—Married Theodore Brabham. Children: Lafayette, Eugene (Bud), Charlie, T. M. (Mack), Emmett, Mary (Sis), Estelle, Anna, Pearl, Minnie, Ola, and Irene.

Dora and Theodore Brabham are dead.

a. LAFAYETTE BRABHAM.—Married, first, Flora McDonald. Children: Dora, Ludie, Gladys, Eula, Mabel, Julius, and Dewitt. Married, second, Kate Bellue. No children.

Lafayette and Flora Brabham are dead.

(1). DORA BRABHAM.—Married Reuben Matthews. Children: R. L. (married and has two children, Harold, and Murel), Ethel Linda (married James Lea, and has two children, Jamie, and . . . .), Donald (married; no children), Mavis (married, and has three children), Larry, Hattie Pearl, and Elena.

They live in McComb, Miss.

(2). LUDIE BRABHAM.—Married Elliott Bates. Children: Richard, Milford, Dewitt, Murray (in service of the U. S.), E. C. (married . . . . Burnett, and has one child, Bernice), Marjorie (lives in Baton Rouge, La.), Beatrice (married T. F. Randall, and has three children, T. F., Jr., Evonne, and Gary; lives in Liberty, Miss.), Henry Marshall (married, and has two children, Buddy, and Pat), and Theodore (lives in Texas).

Elliott Bates died in 1947, and was buried in Liberty, Miss.

(3). GLADYS BRABHAM.—Married Earl Bryant. Children: Roy, and Alton (married and has two children, Buddy, and . . . . ; lives in Baton Rouge, La.).

(4). EULA BRABHAM.—Born in Gillsburg, Miss., Oct. 4, 1904. Married, first, John Earl Blalock, son of John James Blalock, Jan. 10, 1923, in Liberty, Miss. Children: Florine Earline, Kathryn Irene, Henry Earl, William Kenneth, Paul Julius, Ivey Bell, Avery Nell, and John Hilton. Married, second, Marvin Beasley Aug. 6, 1941, in Magnolia, Miss. Children: Linda Faye.

They live near Liberty, Miss., on route 1-A.

(a). FLORINE EARLINE BLALOCK.—Born in Liberty, Miss., Jan. 31, 1924. Married Willie Lea Newcomb, son of W. E. Newcomb, Feb. 1941, in Liberty. Children: Guindal Lee (born Dec. 21, 1946), Ester Gale (born Aug. 23, 1948), Ivey Earline (born June 11, 1950), and Avery Louise (born Aug. 30, 1951).

Willie Lea Newcomb served in the armed forces of the U. S. during World War II. He was wounded in the shoulder, and was awarded the Purple Heart.

They live in Liberty, Miss.

(b). KATHRYN IRENE BLALOCK. — Born in Detroit, Mich., Apr. 27, 1925. Married Floyd L. Tarver, son of Percy Tarver, Nov. 8, 1941, in Liberty, Miss. Children: Floyd Earl (born Nov. 19, 1944).

Floyd L. Tarver was born in Liberty, Miss., June 9, 1923. He was a veteran of World War II. He was killed in action in Japan, and was buried in Liberty. His family lives near Tylertown, Miss., on route 6.

(c). HENRY EARL BLALOCK.—Born in Detroit, Mich., Feb. 3, 1927.

Henry Earl Blalock is a veteran of World War II. He is still serving in the armed forces of the U. S., serving now in Frankfurt, Germany. He has been in service eight years. His home address is Liberty, Miss., Route 1-A.

(d). WILLIAM KENNETH BLALOCK.—Born in Liberty, Miss., Nov. 25, 1928. Unmarried.

William Kenneth Blalock served in the armed forces of the U. S. during World War II three years. He is now living near Liberty, Miss., on route 1-A.

(e). PAUL JULIUS BLALOCK.—Born in Liberty, Miss., Aug. 26, 1931. Unmarried. Lives near Liberty on route 1-A.

(f). IVEY BELL BLALOCK.—Born in Liberty, Miss., June 2, 1933. Unmarried. Lives in Liberty.

(g). AVERY NELL BLALOCK.—Born in Liberty, Miss., June 12, 1935. Lives near Liberty on route 1-A.

(h). JOHN HILTON BLALOCK.—Born in Liberty, Miss., Aug. 6, 1937. Lives near Liberty on route 1-A.

(i). LINDA FAYE BEASLEY.*—Born in Crosby, Miss., Oct. 8, 1944. Lives near Liberty on route 1-A.

(5). MABEL BRABHAM.—Married Reuben Kirkland. Children: William (married Marie Granger, and has two children, Sue and Billie; lives in Baton Rouge, La.), Juanita (married Robert Earl Ogle; lives in Baton Rouge, La.), Reuben, Jr., Julius, and Janie Mae.

(6). JULIUS BRABHAM.—Married Bertha Ellen Hodges. Children: Arie Jean, Herbert, Quin, Dewitt, Oliver, and Alexzene.

(7). DEWITT BRABHAM.—Married Mabell ....
Children: Betty (adopted).

They live in Arkansas.

---

*Daughter by her second marriage, to Marvin Beasley.

b. EUGENE (BUD) BRABHAM. — Married Minnie Hurst. Children: Lorena (married and lives in New Orleans, La.).

They live in Jackson, Miss.

c. CHARLIE BRABHAM.—Married Mim Jones. Children: C. M., Dale, Hugh, Eunice, Ethel, Inez, Mim, and Bonnie.

Charlie Brabham is dead.

The family lives in Baton Rouge, La.

d. T. M. (MACK) BRABHAM.—Born in Amite County, Miss., Feb. 14, 1889. Married Betty Powell, daughter of W. A. and Margaret (Waller) Powell, Dec. 18, 1910, in Amite County, Miss. Children: Grace, Alawee, Theodore, and Marjorie.

Betty Powell-Brabham was born in Amite County, Miss., Apr. 30, 1889.

T. M. (Mack) Brabham was first a farmer, then a salesman for the Robinson Co. of Centreville, Miss. In 1936 he was elected sheriff of Amite County and served four years in this office. He died Aug. 5, 1940, just prior to the end of his term as sheriff. He was buried in Liberty, Miss.

His wife lives in Liberty, Miss.

(1). GRACE BRABHAM.—Born in Liberty, Miss., Nov. 12, 1911. Married Guy Rosary Serio, son of Anthony and Bernice (Zucconi) Serio, Sept. 25, 1938, in Vidalia, La. Children: Grace Louise (born in Ferriday, La., Oct. 3, 1939), Guy Rosary, Jr. (born in Ferriday, La., Apr. 17, 1942), Betty Lynn (born in Ferriday, La., May 24, 1944), and Margie Joyce (born in Ferriday, La., July 31, 1951).

Guy Rosary Serio was born in Newellton, La., Oct. 13, 1906. He operates a modern grocery store in Ferriday, La. He has been alderman and mayor protem of the town of Ferriday for the past twelve years.

They live in Ferriday, La.

(2). ALAWEE BRABHAM.—Born in Liberty, Miss., Aug. 6, 1913. Married Howard Melton, son of J. B. Melton, Oct. 13, 1933, in Centreville, Miss. Children: Howard, Jr. (born in Jackson, Miss., Oct. 29, 1934), and Frances (born in Greenville, Miss., May 1, 1941).

Howard Melton was born in Rionzi, Miss., July 12, 1909.

They live in Greenville, Miss.

(3). THEODORE BRABHAM.—Born in Liberty, Miss., July 1, 1918. Married Evelyn Day, daughter of C. E. (Clyde) and Jessie (Turnbough) Day, Jan. 8, 1943, in Denver, Colo. Children: Mack (born in McComb Miss., Jan. 6, 1945), Joe and Jack (twins; born in Vicksburg, Miss., Oct. 4, 1950).

Evelyn Day-Brabham was born in Brookhaven, Miss., Sept. 9, 1916.

Theodore Brabham works for a wholesale feed, flour and produce store in Vicksburg, Miss. He served three years in the Army Air Force during World War II.

They live in Vicksburg, Miss.

(4). MARJORIE BRABHAM.—Born in Liberty, Miss., Feb. 10, 1923. Married J. T. Walsh, son of Will A. and Myrtis (Short) Walsh, Feb. 2, 1941, in Rolling Fork, Miss. Children: Tommy Jean (born in Liberty, Miss., Apr. 5, 1942), and Ronnie (born in Clinton, La., July 21, 1947).

J. T. Walsh was born in Liberty, Miss., July 29, 1919. He operates the Chevrolet Agency of Liberty. He served three years in the U. S. Army during World War II.

They live in Liberty, Miss.

e. EMMETT BRABHAM.—Married Gertrude Schilling. Children: Dudley (dead—casualty of World War II), Sam, Mary, and Maudie.

Emmett Brabham is dead. His family lives in Centreville, Miss.

f. MARY (SIS) BRABHAM.—Married, first, Kim Brame. Children: Murel (married Fleet Williams; no children; dead). Married, second, Eugene Dickey. Children: Bonnie B. (married Edwin Simmons, and has one child, Dorothy), Minnie Mae (married Curtis Raborn; no children), and T. C. (married Mary Cutrer, and has two children, Tom and Mary Ann; lives in Osyka, Miss.).

g. ESTELLE BRABHAM.—Born in Amite County, Miss., Apr. 5, 1882. Married Alva R. Hughes. Children: Merble, James Floyd, Edyce, Charlie, Minnie, Hettie, Blanche, A. R., Ray, Roy, and Hilda Estelle.

Alva R. Hughes was born in Amite County, Miss., Jan. 27, 1880. He died Nov. 18, 1949.

They live near Peoria, Miss.

(1). MERBLE HUGHES.—Born in Amite County, Miss., Mar. 31, 1903. Married Hollis Jones. Children: Dorothy Dell (married John D. Sudduth, and has one child, Nena Grace).

They live near Peoria, Miss.

(2). JAMES FLOYD HUGHES.—Born in Amite County, Miss., Sept. 27, 1905. Married Grace Cook. No children. They live in Leland, Miss.

(3). EDYCE HUGHES.—Born in Amite County, Miss., Jan. 2, 1907. Married James Little. Children: Ary Jean (married Ralph Helton; lives in New Orleans, La.; no children).

They live in New Orleans, La.

(4). CHARLIE HUGHES.—Born in Amite County, Miss., Apr. 27, 1908. Married Eulalie Schneider. Children: Barbara Jo, and Noel.

They live in McComb, Miss.

(5). MINNIE HUGHES.—Born in Amite County, Miss., Nov. 5, 1910. Married Julius Little. Children: Freddie LaNell (married Paul Campbell, and has one child, Beverly Jean; lives in New Orleans, La.), and Kenneth. They live in Liberty, Miss.

(6). HETTIE HUGHES.—Born in Amite County, Miss., Oct. 22, 1912. Married Aubrey LeGette. Children: Mary Ellen, Alvanell, and John Carl.

They live in Liberty, Miss.

(7). BLANCHE HUGHES.—Born in Amite County, Miss., July 24, 1914. Married Elmer Minks. Children: Jimmy, Roy Hughes, and Sharon Sue.

They live in Liberty, Miss.

(8). A. R. HUGHES.—Born in Amite County, Miss., Apr. 5, 1916. Married Claudine Conerly. Children: Renny (adopted).

They live in New Orleans, La.

(9). RAY HUGHES.—Born in Amite County, Miss., July 10, 1919. Married Burkett Burnyce Wall. Children: Hugh Ray, H. A., Frances Jane, and James Floyd.

They live near Peoria, Miss.

(10). ROY HUGHES.—Born in Amite County, Miss., Nov. 5, 1921. Died Jan. 31, 1925, and was buried in Amite County.

(11). HILDA ESTELLE HUGHES.—Born in Amite County, Miss., Jan. 12, 1924. Married Charles Womack. Children: Michael, Darryl, and Robin Faye.

They live in McComb, Miss.

h. ANNA BRABHAM.—Married Robert Wall. Children: Velma, Evelyn, Clytie, Merle, R. J., and Morris.

Their address is Liberty, Miss., Route 5.

i. PEARL BRABHAM.—Married Johnnie Bean. Children: Lillie Opal, and Oville.

j. MINNIE BRABHAM.—Married Buck Simmons. Children: Audrey, and Joyce Ann.

They live in San Francisco, Calif.

k. OLA BRABHAM.—Married Frank Allison. No children. Lives in Beaumont, Tex.

l. IRENE BRABHAM.—Married Robert Lindsey. Children: T. W., Lamar, James, Hughey, Shirley Joyce, and Betty Jo.

They live in Greensburg, La.

3. JOSEPH LAFAYETTE SWEARINGEN. — Born in Gillsburg, Miss., Feb. 26, 1872. Married, first, Dora Jones, daughter of Jake and Kate Jones, Feb. 16, 1896, near Liberty, Miss., Route 2. Children: Everett, Iris, Myrtis, Jewel, Thelma, Clifton, and Nolan. Married, second, Auline Tucker Coney. No children.

Dora Jones-Swearingen was born in Amite County, Miss., in 1868. She died in 1929, and was buried in the Amite River Church Cemetery.

Joseph Lafayette Swearingen died Aug. 7, 1947, and was buried in the Amite River Church Cemetery.

a. EVERETT SWEARINGEN.—Born near Liberty, Miss., on Route 2, Oct. 21, 1898. Married Lottie Lee Wilkinson, daughter of Tom and Lunie Wilkinson, Sept. 3, 1934, in McComb, Miss. No children.

Lottie Lee Wilkinson-Swearingen was born in Liberty, Miss., Jan. 3, 1905.

Everett Swearingen served one year in the armed forces of the U. S. during World War I.

b. IRIS SWEARINGEN.—Born near Liberty, Miss., on Route

2, Feb. 17, 1897. Married Carl Lea, son of Wilford Lea, in 1920, in Liberty. Children: Helen (married T. J. Pluscett; no children; lives in Baton Rouge, La.), and Hilda Jean (married Dr. J. L. Custer; no children; lives in Shreveport, La.)

Carl Lea was born in Liberty, Miss. They live in Centreville, Miss.

c. MYRTIS SWEARINGEN.—Born near Liberty, Miss., on Route 2, Nov. 20, 1911. Unmarried. Lives in Jackson, Miss., and is manager of the Paramount Theatre there.

d. JEWEL SWEARINGEN.—Born near Liberty, Miss., on Route 2, Nov. 25, 1900. Married Tracey Rice, daughter of George and Nannie Rice, Dec. 24, 1940, in Liberty, Miss. Children: Joe Ann (born Mar. 24, 1944).

Tracey Rice-Swearingen was born in Liberty, Miss., Mar. 3, 1909.

They live in Liberty, Miss.

e. THELMA SWEARINGEN.—Born near Liberty, Miss., on Route 2, Oct. 7, 1907. Married Frank Batterford in 1941. Children: Frankie (8 yrs. old). They live in New Orleans, La.

f. CLIFTON SWEARINGEN.—Born near Liberty, Miss., on Route 2, Feb. 8, 1909. Married Janette Keith, daughter of Denver Keith, Aug. 1936, in Liberty. Children: Malcolm (born Sept. 1, 1941), Rachel (born Aug. 31, 1943), and Dora Joe (born Feb. 1948).

Janette Keith-Swearingen was born in Smithdale, Miss.

They live in Meade, Kan.

g. NOLAN SWEARINGEN.—Born near Liberty, Miss., on Route 2, Aug. 7, 1914. Married Vera Rapp Green Dec. 31, 1940. No children.

Vera Rapp Green-Swearingen was born in Dequion, Ill.

Nolan Swearingen served four years in the armed forces of the U. S. during World War II. They live in Liberty, Miss.

4. HATTIE SWEARINGEN.—Born in Gillsburg, Miss., Aug. 15, 1876. Married J. S. Simmons, son of Jim Simmons, in 1904, in Greensburg, La. No children.

J. S. Simmons was born in Pike County, Miss., Aug. 29, 1856. He is dead. He was buried in Kentwood, La.

Hattie Swearingen-Simmons died Feb. 28, 1942, and was buried in Kentwood, La.

5. PINEY JANE SWEARINGEN.—Born in Gillsburg, Miss., Mar. 18, 1874. Married, first, Dan Westbrook, son of Albert Newton Westbrook, in 1902, near Liberty, Miss., on Route 2. Children: Elbert (born near Liberty, Miss., Apr. 30, 1903; married Martha Davidson; no children; lives in Texas), Irma (born June 18, 1905), and Joe (born Apr. 12, 1907). Married, second, Will Lambert. No children.

Dan Westbrook was born in the northern part of Amite County, Miss. He died in 1914, and was buried in the Westbrook Cemetery, near Mt. Olive Church, Amite County, Miss.

Will Lambert is dead. He was buried in the Amite River Church Cemetery.

Piney Jane Swearingen-Westbrook-Lambert lives near Liberty, Miss.

6. MATTIE SWEARINGEN.—Born in Gillsburg, Miss., May 8, 1867. Unmarried. Lives in Houston, Tex.

7. ROSALIE SWEARINGEN.—Died young.

8. MARY SWEARINGEN.—Married Winfield White. Children: Ellis (married, first, Annie Kirkland, and has four children, Clyde, Hewitt, Annie Mae, and Walton Ellis; married, second, Mrs. Maud White; lives in Kentwood, La.).

9. J. MONROE SWEARINGEN.—Married Mary E. Newman. Children: John Neafus, Bessie L., George Washington, David L., Lea Bridewell, May Irene, Albert Jesse, Doyle Denver, and Ellis Arville.

J. Monroe and Mary E. (Newman) Swearingen are dead.

a. JOHN NEAFUS SWEARINGEN.—Born in Mississippi April 21, 1885. Married, first, Carrie Epperson Dec. 22, 1905, in Louisiana. Children: May Irene. Married, second, Lizzie Maud Devereux Dec. 17, 1919, in Louisiana. Children: John Neafus, Jr.

Carrie Epperson-Swearingen was born in Mississippi Feb. 21, 1877. She died July 7, 1919, and was buried in Mississippi.

Lizzie Maud Devereux-Swearingen was born in Mississippi Feb. 18, 1885.

(1). MAY IRENE SWEARINGEN.—Born in Ringgold, La., Dec. 10, 1912. Died Dec. 11, 1912, and was buried in Mississippi.

(2). JOHN NEAFUS SWEARINGEN, JR.—Born Nov. 30, 1920. Lives in Fresno, Calif. Unmarried.

John Neafus Swearingen, Jr., served in the U. S. Army during

World War II from June 26, 1942, to Oct. 1945. He participated in the Tunisian Campaign. He was awarded the Bronze Star for meritorious service and the Purple Heart for wounds in this campaign. He landed in Sicily, in the first wave, July 10, 1943. He participated in the assault on Million Dollar Hill, and was a member of the unit that captured Messina. He landed at Salerno, Italy, Sept. 1943, in support of the 36th Division, and he crossed the Volturno River Oct. 1943. He landed at Anzio Beachhead Jan. 22, 1944, in the second wave. He was a member of the battalion that was reduced from 1000 men to 35 in 24 hours. He was wounded Mar. 6, 1944, in the Germans' attempted drive to the sea. He was sent home June 1944, and was discharged Oct. 1945. The other awards he received were: Two clusters on Purple Heart, Victory Medal, Presidential Citation, and Croix de Guerre. He was a member of the 168th Infantry Regiment, 34th Division, and Headquarters Company, Infantry Regiment, 3rd Division.

At present he is an accounting student in a college in Fresno, Calif.

b. BESSIE L. SWEARINGEN.—Born in Mississippi Nov. 6, 1886. Married Lyman Oscar Casebier, son of Jacob and Eliza Casebier, June 21, 1903, in Louisiana. No children. Lyman Oscar Casebier was born in Illinois Oct. 7, 1879. They live on a ranch near Fresno, Calif.

c. GEORGE WASHINGTON SWEARINGEN.—Born in Mississippi Dec. 30, 1888. Married Parthenia Ophelia Van in Mississippi. No children. Died July 24, 1941, and was buried in Osyka, Miss.

Parthenia Ophelia Van-Swearingen was born in Mississippi. She died Dec. 8, 1941, and was buried in Osyka, Miss.

d. DAVID L. SWEARINGEN.—Born in Mississippi Sept. 14, 1891. Married Emily Josephine Wall, daughter of John and Elizabeth Wall, Mar. 25, 1917, in Mississippi. Children: Mary D.

Emily Josephine Wall-Swearingen was born in Mississippi Oct. 11, 1893.

They live in Fresno, California.

(1). MARY D. SWEARINGEN.—Born in Mississippi Jan. 23, 1918. Married Melvin A. Figeroid, son of Anthony P. Figeroid, Nov. 1, 1944, in California. Children: Nancy Jo (born in Sacramento, Calif., Nov. 13, 1950).

They live in Sacramento, Calif.

e. LEA BRIDEWELL SWEARINGEN.—Born in Louisiana Jan. 10, 1894. Died Nov. 21, 1894, and was buried in Mississippi.

f. MAY IRENE SWEARINGEN.—Born in Louisiana May 9, 1896. Died Sept. 4, 1896, and was buried in Mississippi.

g. ALBERT JESSE SWEARINGEN.—Born in Louisiana July 3, 1897. Married, frist, ... (a widow) ; no children. Divorced, and married, second, ... ; no children. Divorced.

Albert Jesse Swearingen served in Company L, 9th Infantry Regiment, 2nd Division, from Sept. 1917, to July 1919, during World War I. He took part in several battles during his period of service. He lives in Las Vegas, Nevada.

h. DOYLE DENVER SWEARINGEN.—Born in Louisiana Feb. 18, 1902. Unmarried. Lives in Boulder City, Nevada.

i. ELLIS ARVILLE SWEARINGEN.—Born in Mississippi Aug. 23, 1904. Married Marie Stahl, daughter of R. D. Stahl, Nov. 1, 1941, in Reno, Nevada. Children: Cheryl Ann (born in Portland, Oregon, May 3, 1944), and James Ellis (born in Portland, Oregon, Aug. 8, 1948).

Ellis Arville Swearingen was a sailor on U. S. Ship Marcus.

C. HARRIETT BURRIS.—Born in Amite County, Miss., in 1836. Married Harvey D. Martin Dec. 22, 1861, in Amite County. Children: Eugene, Melissa (Mickie), Judson Emmett, Mary Julia (Mollie), Della, and Oceola (Babe).

Harriett Burris-Martin is dead. She was buried in the Anglin Cemetery in St. Helena Parish, La.

Harvey D. Martin died July 3, 1918, and was buried in the Red Bluff Church Cemetery in St. Helena Parish, La.

1. EUGENE MARTIN.—Born in St. Helena Parish, La., Sept. 1862. Married Nina Marsalis. Children: Guidry (deceased), and Delsie (lives in Beaumont, Tex.).

Eugene Martin is dead. He was an employee of the I. C. Railway Company, and lived in McComb, Miss.

2. MELISSA (MICKIE) MARTIN.—Born in St. Helena Parish, La., Sept. 1864. Married J. C. Stuart. No children.

Melissa (Mickie) Martin-Stuart is dead. She was buried in Bogalusa, La., where she was living at the time of her death.

3. JUDSON EMMETT MARTIN.—Born in St. Helena Parish, La.,

Mar. 1868. Married Velma Pinkie Strickland, his cousin. Children: Emma, June (dead), and Ada. Judson Emmett Martin lives in Texas.

4. MARY JULIA (MOLLIE) MARTIN.—Born in St. Helena Parish, La., Dec. 1, 1872. Married Chas. Wall. Children: Eula (married Lawrence Jones; no children; dead), and Earnest (adopted). Mary Julia (Mollie) Martin lives in St. Helena Parish with her adopted son, Earnest.

5. DELLA MARTIN.—Born in St. Helena Parish, La., in 1877. Married August Sturkins. No children (August is the father of some children by a former marriage).

Della Martin-Sturkins died in New Orleans, La.

6. OCEOLA (BABE) MARTIN.—Born in St. Helena Parish, La., in 1879. Married Willie Thomas Bridges, son of William and Pauline (Travis) Bridges. Children: Gracie, Nellie, Lena, William V., Thomas E., Minnie Lou, Ruby, Lucy, Wilma, and Virginia.

Willie Thomas Bridges was born in St. Helena Parish, La., Sept. 1869. He died Sept. 1948, and was buried in Baton Rouge, La.

Prior to her death, Feb. 1948, Oceola (Babe) Martin-Bridges lived in Baton Rouge, La. She was buried in Baton Rouge.

a. GRACIE BRIDGES.—Born in St. Helena Parish, La., in 1899. Married Pierce Phillips, son of William and Jane (Lea) Phillips, in Kentwood, La. Children: Christina, Willie Pierce, Joe, and Wilda.

Pierce Phillips was born in St. Helena Parish, La., in 1897.

They live in Tangipahoa, La.

b. NELLIE BRIDGES.—Born in St. Helena Parish, La., in 1900. Married Lawrence Jones. Children: Quinn, Denzel, Newt, and Wilva Nell.

They live in New Orleans, La.

c. LENA BRIDGES.—Born in St. Helena Parish, La., in 1901. Married, first, Charlie Phillips. Children: Percy, and Charles, Jr. Married, second, Setman Sims. No children.

They live in Port Arthur, Tex., and are engaged in the real estate and brokerage business under the name of Lena B. and Setman Sims.

d. WILLIAM V. BRIDGES.—Born in St. Helena Parish, La., Feb. 1912. Unmarried. William V. Bridges holds the B. A. and M. S. W. degrees from Louisiana State University, which he received in

1934 and 1942, respectively. He taught school seven years. Presently he is Rehabilitation Supervisor for Blind in the Louisiana State Welfare Department. He served as lieutenant in U. S. Navy for four years during World War II, as Public Relations Officer. He received Presidential Unit Citation during World War II.

While a student in Louisiana State University he was elected president of the graduate students in 1942. In 1950, he was elected president of the L. S. U. Social Welfare Alumni.

He lives in Baton Rouge, La.

e. THOMAS E. BRIDGES.—Born in St. Helena Parish, La., Apr. 1916. Married Nathalie Ryan, daughter of Clayton and Lucille Ryan, in 1937, in Baton Rouge, La. Children: Donald (adopted).

Nathalie Ryan-Bridges was born in Florida in 1920.

Thomas E. Bridges served in the U. S. Army during World War II as Operations Supervisor at the Ethyl Corporation in Baton Rouge, La. He received the B. S. degree in Petroleum Engineering from L. S. U. in 1938.

They live in Baton Rouge, La.

f. MINNIE LOU BRIDGES.—Born in St. Helena Parish, La., in 1905. Married B. T. Young, son of Burgess and Doshie (Newman) Young, in Kentwood, La. Children: Geraldine, Evelyn, Burgess, Jr., and Adrienne.

B. T. Young was born in St. Helena Parish, La.

They live in Houston, Tex.

g. RUBY BRIDGES.—Born in St. Helena Parish, La., in 1910. Married, first, George Kippers, in New Orleans, La. Children: George, Jr. Married, second, Amos Taushey, in Baton Rouge, La. No children.

They live in Baton Rouge, La.

h. LUCY BRIDGES.—Born in St. Helena Parish, La., in 1908. Married Arthur Guerra in New Orleans, La. Children: Arthur, Jr.

They live in Baton Rouge, La.

i. WILMA BRIDGES.—Born in St. Helena Parish, La., in 1903. Married Tom Blackwell in Bogalusa, La. No children.

They live in Bogalusa, La.

j. VIRGINIA BRIDGES.—Born in St. Helena Parish, La., in

1916. Married William W. McGinity in 1932 in New Orleans, La. Children: William W., Jr.

Virginia Bridges-McGinity was selected as the outstanding Junior Club woman of New Orleans in 1948. She was the recipient of the Benson Trophy.

They live in New Orleans, La.

D. VICTORIA BURRIS.—Born in Amite City, Miss., in 1839. Married William Lee. Children: Regina.

Victoria Burris-Lee died in Dennis Mills, La., in 1881.

1. REGINA LEE.—Born in Dennis Mills, La., May 6, 1878. Married J. G. DeArmond, son of Green Joshua and Minerva (Neely) DeArmond, Dec. 21, 1898, in Dennis Mills, La. Children: Velfort Judson, Maple Joshua, Virgil Lee, Lorena Bell, Willie Donald, Maurice Lewis, Stanley Adrian, and Reymond Houston.

J. G. DeArmond was born in Stony Point, La., Apr. 26, 1872. He died in Baywood, La., where he lived most of his life, Oct. 1, 1949, and was buried in Baywood.

Regina Lee-DeArmond lives in Baywood, La.

a. VELFORT JUDSON DEARMOND.—Born in Dennis, Mills, La., Sept. 24, 1899. Married Madge M. Brown, daughter of A. P. and Oliva (Williams) Brown, Dec. 24, 1917, in Port Allen, La. Children: V. J., Jr., Dorothy Marie, Alfred Josh, and Barbara Ann.

Madge M. Brown-DeArmond was born in Harrisburg, Ill., July 10, 1899.

They live near Greenwell Springs, La.

b. MAPLE JOSHUA DEARMOND.

c. VIRGIL LEE DEARMOND.—Born in Dennis Mills, La., Dec. 11, 1904. Married Eunice Daigle, daughter of Louis Joseph Daigle, June 29, 1940, in Port Allen, La. Children: Lance, Donald, and Dane.

Eunice Daigle-DeArmond was born in Brusly, La., June 22, 1908.

They live in Baton Rouge, La., at 3060 N. Blvd. St.

d. LORENA BELL DEARMOND.

e. WILLIE DONALD DEARMOND.—Born in Dennis Mills, La., Nov. 15, 1912. Married Shirley Lunsford. Children: Arthur (age 2 years).

f. MAURICE LEWIS DEARMOND.—Born in Dennis Mills, La.,

Feb. 7, 1914. Married Virginia Jackson. Children: Wayne (adopted; age 2 years).

      g. STANLEY ADRIAN DEARMOND.

      h. REYMOND HOUSTON DEARMOND.

E. ELLEN ELIZABETH BURRIS.—Born in Amite County, Miss., in 1840. Married Leroy Bellue, son of William and Harriett (Pettiss) Bellue. Children: William Howard, Samuel Wayne, Emma, Mollie, Lee, Pinkie, and Maude.

Leroy Bellue was born Feb. 8, 1839. He died Apr. 22, 1903, and was buried in the Anglin Cemetery in St. Helena Parish, La.

Ellen Elizabeth Burris-Bellue died Nov. 11, 1918, and was buried in the Anglin Cemetery.

      1. WILLIAM HOWARD BELLUE.—Left home when young and was never heard from.

      2. SAMUEL WAYNE BELLUE.—Born in St. Helena Parish, La., Feb. 6, 1874. Married Phoebe Starch Fluker in St. Helena Parish. Children: Percy I., Carl, Woodrow, James, Webb, Effie Rae, Addie, Maydelle, and Julius.

Phoebe Starch Fluker-Bellue was born in St. Helena Parish in 1881. She died in 1936 and was buried in the Red Bluff Church Cemetery, St. Helena Parish, La.

Samuel Wayne Bellue died Oct. 26, 1942, and was buried in the Red Bluff Church Cemetery in St. Helena Parish.

      a. PERCY I. BELLUE.—Born in St. Helena Parish, La., Aug. 19, 1901. Married Mabel Beatrice Stewart, daughter of Willie J. and Julia (Easley) Stewart, Aug. 2, 1924, in St. Helena Parish. Children: James Derrell, Julia Laverne, Mavourleen, Willie Mae, Charles Irwin, Phebia Lanell, and Peggy Ruth.

Mabel Beatrice Stewart-Bellue was born in Amite County, Miss., Jan. 25, 1907.

They live near Peoria, Miss., on route 1.

      (1). JAMES DERRELL BELLUE.—Born in Livingston Parish, La., July 31, 1925. Married Madge Elizabeth Causey, daughter of Lloyd J. and Gladys (Wilson) Causey, July 31, 1946, in Amite County, Miss. Children: Eula Elizabeth (Beckie) (born Sept. 1947).

They live in Baton Rouge, La.

      (2). JULIA LAVERNE BELLUE.—Born in Livingston Parish, La., June 3, 1927. Married Cleon Earl Allen Apr. 23, 1942, in Pike County, Miss. Children: Merwin Earl (born Sept. 21, 1944), and Beverly Diane (born Feb. 1948).

They live in Port Lavaco, Tex.

(3). MAVOURLEEN BELLUE.—Born in Livingston Parish, La., Aug. 31, 1929. Married Sheldon Derwood Bean, son of Nephus R. and Hazel (Stephenson) Bean, June 1, 1946, in Pike County, Miss. Children: Richard Lane (born July 8, 1947), Constance Marie (born Aug. 30, 1948), and Robert Irwin (born Dec. 10, 1949). Sheldon Derwood Bean was born in Amite County, Miss., June 17, 1926.

They live near Peoria, Miss., on route 1.

(4). WILLIE MAE BELLUE. — Born in Amite County, Miss., May 24, 1932.

(5). CHARLES IRWIN BELLUE.—Born in Amite County, Miss., Nov. 11, 1934.

(6). PHEBIA LANELL BELLUE.—Born in Amite County, Miss., Oct. 1, 1939.

(7). PEGGY RUTH BELLUE.—Born in Amite County, Miss., Feb. 7, 1943.

b. CARL BELLUE.—Married Maggie Lee Frazier. Children: Carline (married Rudolph Jenkins and has two children: Carl Wayne, two years old, and a baby son three months old), Betty Jean, Bennie Belton, Naomi Dell, Donald, and Patricia Ann (killed by an automobile at the age of six).

Carl Bellue is dead. His family lives in Bogalusa, La.

c. WOODROW BELLUE.—Born in St. Helena Parish, La., Aug. 5, 1915. Married Mary Idelle Lea, daughter of Sam and Sarah (Allen) Lea, Oct. 20, 1938, in St. Helena Parish. Children: Helen Willena (born Nov. 7, 1939), Edna Ruth (born Apr. 16, 1941), Bennie Ray (died an infant), Samuel Wayne (born Aug. 26, 1944), and Wm. Howard (died an infant).

Mary Idelle Lea-Bellue was born in St. Helena Parish, La., Jan. 12, 1920.

Their address is Osyka, Miss., Route 3.

d. JAMES BELLUE.—Scalded to death at the age of seven years.

e. WEBB BELLUE.—Married Eunice Watson. No children. Lives in Greensburg, La.

f. EFFIE RAE BELLUE.—Born in St. Helena Parish, La. Married Joe C. Allen, son of "Bud" Allen, in St. Helena Parish. Children: Ellzey (born Apr. 17, 1932; serving in the U. S. Army), and Morris (born in 1934).

They live in Jackson, La.

g. ADDIE BELLUE.—Born in St. Helena Parish, La. Unmarried. Lives in Baton Rouge, La., where she is employed as bookkeeper.

h. MAYDELLE BELLUE.—Born in St. Helena Parish, La. Married Jack Asbeck. Children: Eddie Wayne, and . . . . (a baby born in Tokyo, Japan).

Jack Asbeck was born in Edna, Tex. He has served seven years in the U. S. Air Corps as aviator. He is a test pilot now. His family lives in Nashville, Tenn.

i. JULIUS BELLUE.—Born in St. Helena Parish, La. Unmarried. Veteran of World War II. A patient now in the Veterans' Hospital in New Orleans, La. His home address is Osyka, Miss., Route 2.

3. EMMA BELLUE.—Born in St. Helena Parish, La. Married Adolphus Frazier. Children: Vernon, Gladys, Tollie, Claude, and Clifton.

a. VERNON FRAZIER.—Married . . . . Davis. Children: . . . . (dead). Is a retired army veteran and lives in Pensacola, Fla.

b. GLADYS FRAZIER.—Married . . . . Bernard. Children: Alfred. Gladys Frazier-Bernard died in 1950.

c. TOLLIE FRAZIER.—Born in St. Helena Parish, La. Married Doris Brabham in St. Helena Parish. Children: Evelyn (married . . . . . . Whitehead of Kentwood, La.), Estelle, and Roy.

They live in Kentwood, La.

d. CLAUDE FRAZIER.—Born in St. Helena Parish, La. Married, first, Mollie Davidson, in St. Helena Parish. No children. Mollie Davidson-Frazier was born in Chesbrough, La. Married, second, Irma Lee Goldman. Children: Hulon, Margaret Ellen, James Adolphus, Emma Mae, Roy Douglas, Thelma Lea, Vernon Allen, and Clifton Lamar.

They live in Kentwood, La.

e. CLIFTON FRAZIER.—Born in St. Helena Parish, La. Married Maggie Lee, daughter of Sam and Sarah (Allen) Lee, in 1936, in St. Helena Parish. Children: Jeanette, Jackie (died at the age of two years), and Charles.

Their address is Osyka, Miss., Route 2.

4. MOLLIE BELLUE.—Born in Amite County, Miss., Jan. 20, 1880. Married James Osburn Lee, son of James Osburn and Nancy (Allen) Lee, Dec. 27, 1897, in St. Helena Parish, La. Children: Minnie Irene, Hollis, Homer, and Howard.

James Osburn Lee was born in St. Helena Parish, La., Mar. 28, 1866. He died Mar. 31, 1935, and was buried in the Red Bluff Church Cemetery.

Mollie Bellue-Lee lives near Osyka, Miss.

a. MINNIE IRENE LEE.—Born in Louisiana June 3, 1899. Married Atkerson Frazier, son of Tom and Mary (Wall) Frazier. Children: Prentiss E. (married Annette McDaniel and has four children: Judy Gayle, born July 3, 1948; Janice Ann, born Aug. 21, 1949; Prentiss E., Jr., born Sept. 5, 1950, and Ronnie Keith, born Nov. 28, 1951), Grace (born Oct. 5, 1922; unmarried, and lives in Baton Rouge, La.), Elbert (dead), and Reed (dead).

They live near McComb, Miss.

b. HOLLIS LEE.—Born in St. Helena Parish, La., June 29, 1902. Married Velma Lee Frazier, daughter of A. J. and Lydia Mae (Lee) Frazier, Nov. 29, 1924, in St. Helena Parish. Children: Leopold, Yvonne, Eudora, and Herbert.

Velma Lee Frazier-Lee was born in St. Helena Parish, La., June 3, 1908. They live near Osyka, Miss., on route 2.

(1). LEOPOLD LEE.—Born Apr. 10, 1926.

(2). YVONNE LEE.—Born in St. Helena Parish, La., Dec. 29, 1927. Married Alex Sibley, son of Louis and Martha Sibley, Apr. 16, 1949, in the Red Bluff Church. No children.

Alex Sibley was born in Livingston Parish, La., Dec. 24, 1928.

They live near Osyka, Miss., on route 2.

(3). EUDORA LEE.—Born June 23, 1931. Unmarried.

(4). HERBERT LEE.—Dead.

c. HOMER LEE.—Born Sept. 27, 1900. Unmarried.

d. HOWARD LEE.—Died in infancy.

5. LEE BELLUE.—Married Effie Smiley. Children: Zack, Howard, ... (a son; died in infancy), Hughey, Everett, Margaret Ellen (a nurse; veteran of World War II, as nurse), Sybil, Willie (a girl), Starr (a girl), and Stone (a boy).

6. PINKIE BELLUE.—Died when an infant. She and Samuel Wayne were twins.

7. MAUDE BELLUE.—Dead. Never married.

F. JULIA BURRIS.—Born in Amite County, Miss., in 1846. Married Nathaniel (Nat) Dykes. Children: Napoleon, Estelle, and Fred N.

Julia Burris-Dykes is dead. She was buried in Kentwood, La.

1. NAPOLEON DYKES.—Born in Tangipahoa Parish, La., Feb. 8, 1876. Married Fannie Marshall, daughter of John and Mary Elizabeth (Oneal) Marshall, Oct. 22, 1901, in Hattiesburg, Miss. No children.

Fannie Marshall-Dykes was born in Wesson, Miss., Sept. 15, 1884. They live in Kentwood, La.

2. ESTELLE DYKES.—Born in Tangipahoa Parish, La., in 1892. Married Dr. A. G. Root in Kentwood, La. Children: A. G., Jr.

Dr. A. G. Root was born in Kentwood, La., in 1883. He died in 1937, and was buried in Kentwood.

Estelle Dykes-Root died Apr. 11, 1949, and was buried in Kentwood.

a. A. G. ROOT, JR.—Born in Kentwood, La. Married Gladys Travis, daughter of Dr. W. B. and Lena (Yarborough) Travis, in Kentwood, La. Children: A. G. III, and Barrett.

Gladys Travis-Root was born in Kentwood, La.

A. G. Root, Jr., is a graduate of Louisiana State University. He served four years as radar operator in the armed forces of the U. S. during World War II, and held the rank of captain. He lives in Bogalusa, La.

3. FRED N. DYKES.—Born in Tangipahoa Parish, La., Apr. 3, 1884. Married Iona Tillery, daughter of John Bunyan and Ethel (Cobb) Tillery, Mar. 8, 1918, in Columbia, Miss. Children: Fred N., Jr.

Iona Tillery-Dykes was born in Wilkinson County, Miss., Oct. 15, 1895.

Fred N. Dykes died Apr. 21, 1936, and was buried in Bogalusa, La.

a. FRED N. DYKES, JR.—Born in Kentwood, La., Dec. 18, 1918. Married Alice Mary Clark, daughter of A. B. and Alice (Higgins) Clark, June 6, 1942, in New Orleans, La. Children: Frederick James (born July 7, 1943), and Michael Clark (born July 18, 1944).

Alice Mary Clark-Dykes was born in Algiers, La., Sept. 9, 1918.

Fred N. Dykes, Jr., served in the U. S. Navy Air Corps during World War II from July 1941 to Oct. 1945, two years of which was served overseas in the Pacific Theatre. He was graduated from Loyola University of New Orleans, La., in 1941. He is airline pilot for the Chicago and Southern Airlines.

They live in Covington, La.

G. JUDSON BURRIS.—Born in Amite County, Miss., in 1844. Married Sarah (Sallie) Rand. Children: Charles Levy (died in infancy), and two daughters who died young.

Judson Burris was a farmer. He was buried near Liverpool, La.

LAND TRANSFERS OF JUDSON BURRIS

(Copied from the St. Helena Parish, La., records)

Judson Burris of St. Helena Parish, La., bought 420 acres of land from Mrs. Mary E. Hub of New Orleans, La., for $700 June 5, 1881. A down payment of $100 was made on this land. It was bounded by the Tickfaw River on the east; by land of B. D. Rand and vendor on the north; by lands of W. K. Carruth and Reubin Lee on the south; and by lands of W. G. Prescott on the west.

Mrs. Sarah J. Burris bought 420 acres of land from B. D. Rand May 14, 1891, for $600. This was the Judson Burris homestead. This land is located on the west side of Tickfaw River. It is the northern part of section 63, township 2, SR 5 E, in St. Helena Parish, La. (This appears to be the same place as the above. Judson Burris probably died before paying the balance due on it, and the mortgagor, B. D. Rand, took possession of it.)

H. AMANDA BURRIS.—Born in Amite County, Miss., in 1848. Never married. Died young with malaria fever. Buried in the Anglin Cemetery in St. Helena Parish, La.

I. ALICE BURRIS.—Born in Amite County, Miss., June 1853.

Married Hardy Dekalk Travis Dec. 23, 1877. Children: Lelia, Lance, Myrtis Udora, Herman Hardy, Richard Everett, and William Lee.

Hardy Dekalk Travis was born near the Red Bluff Church in St. Helena Parish, La., Feb. 21, 1862. He died Dec. 5, 1925, and was buried in the New Zion Church Cemetery in St. Helena Parish, La.

Alice Burris-Travis died Feb. 5, 1924, and was buried in the New Zion Church Cemetery, St. Helena Parish, La.

1. LELIA TRAVIS.—Born in St. Helena Parish, La., June 29, 1884. Married John Seaborn (Bruce) Brabham, son of W. C. and Ada (Wall) Brabham, in 1907, in St. Helena Parish, La. Children: Jewel Travis, John Hardy, and Alice Lanelle.

Lelia Travis-Brabham died Mar. 25, 1932, and was buried in the New Zion Cemetery, St. Helena Parish, La.

a. JEWEL TRAVIS BRABHAM.—Born in St. Helena Parish, La., Jan. 30, 1908. Married Charles George Dupree in 1930 in Port Arthur, Tex. Children: L. D. (born in 1932), and Charles George, Jr. (born in 1934).

They live in Texas City, Tex.

b. JOHN HARDY BRABHAM.—Born in Kentwood, La., July 4, 1918. Married Joyce .... in Texas City, Tex. Children: Judy Kay, Vickie Cheryl, and John Neil.

They live in Wichita, Kan.

c. ALICE LANELLE BRABHAM.—Married J. E. McIntyre. No children. They live in Houston, Tex.

2. LANCE TRAVIS.—Born in 1886, and died in 1886.

3. MYRTIS UDORA TRAVIS.—Born in St. Helena Parish, La., Jan. 16, 1888. Married Enos James Newman, son of A. J. and Mattie (Stewart) Newman, Dec. 20, 1908, in St. Helena Parish, La. Children: Ella Mae, Louise, William Lee, Fred Firman, Albert Dekalk, Leonard Enos, and Enos James, Jr.

They live near Kentwood, La.

a. ELLA MAE NEWMAN.—Born Sept. 22, 1909. Married Herman Newman. Children: Louise Lurline (born Aug. 20, 1935), and Christine Sue (born Dec. 27, 1944).

b. LOUISE NEWMAN.—Born Jan. 9, 1911. Married Earl Williams. No children.

c. WILLIAM LEE NEWMAN.—Born Mar. 9, 1913. Married

Dicy Neva Smith. Children: Myrtis Lou (born Oct. 19, 1941), and William Lee, Jr. (born Sept. 30, 1943).

d. FRED FIRMAN NEWMAN.—Born Jan. 29, 1915. Married Pearl Blades. Children: Fred Firman, Jr. (born Feb. 23, 1927).

e. ALBERT DEKALK NEWMAN.—Born Dec. 8, 1919. Married Maydell Frazier. Children: Albert Dekalk, Jr. (born Aug. 17, 1943), and Carolyn Warnell (born Aug. 7, 1946).

f. LEONARD ENOS NEWMAN.—Born Aug. 25, 1926. Married Faye Goings. Children: Leonard James (born Oct. 28, 1947).

g. ENOS JAMES NEWMAN, JR.—Born Sept. 25, 1928. Unmarried.

4. HERMAN HARDY TRAVIS.—Born in St. Helena Parish, La., Aug. 27, 1913. Married Ethel Brabham, daughter of William Hardy and Malisse (Brumfield) Brabham, Dec. 1911, in St. Helena Parish. Children: Hardy Virgil, Herman Hardy, Jr., Ethel Velma, Irma Estelle, Maye Aline, Richard Everett, Willie Reid, and Vivian.

Ethel Brabham-Travis was born in St. Helena Parish, La., in 1893. She died in 1934, and was buried in the New Zion Cemetery, St. Helena Parish.

Herman Hardy Travis died Sept. 6, 1922, and was buried in the New Zion Cemetery.

a. HARDY VIRGIL TRAVIS.—Born in St. Helena Parish, La., Aug. 30, 1912. Married Ethel Marie Rutland, daughter of Valentine O. and Bertha (Martin) Rutland, Apr. 2, 1938, in Plaquemine, La. Children: Gary Virgil and Gilbert Hardy.

Ethel Marie Rutland-Travis was born in St. Helena Parish, La., Mar. 20, 1913.

They live in Roseland, La.

b. HERMAN HARDY TRAVIS, JR.—Born in St. Helena Parish, La., Jan. 25, 1914. Unmarried. Lives in New Orleans, La.

c. ETHEL VELMA TRAVIS.—Born in St. Helena Parish, La., Feb. 26, 1915. Married Vernell Leon Hendry, son of Elmo and Kate (Bennett) Hendry, Sept. 24, 1938, in Amite, La. Children: Richard Vernell.

Vernell Leon Hendry was born near Roseland, La., Jan. 16, 1906.

Their address is Roseland, La., Route 1.

d. IRMA ESTELLE TRAVIS.—Born in St. Helena Parish, La., Apr. 10, 1916. Unmarried.

e. MAYE ALINE TRAVIS.—Born in St. Helena Parish, La., Jan. 26, 1918. Married James Marion Norsworthy II, son of James Marion and Alma (Dawson) Norsworthy, July 4, 1942, in Woodville, Miss. Children: Vivian Elizabeth, and James Marion III.

James Marion Norsworthy II was born in Jackson, La., Oct. 26, 1913.

f. RICHARD EVERETT TRAVIS.—Born in St. Helena Parish, La., May 21, 1919. Unmarried. Served in World War II. Lives in New Orleans, La.

g. WILLIE REID TRAVIS.—Born in St. Helena Parish, La., Mar. 15, 1921. Married Marguerite Wilkinson, daughter of Claude and Ellen Wilkinson, in Roseland, La. Children: Arthur Reid, Douglas, and Marilyn.

Marguerite Wilkinson-Travis was born in McComb, Miss., May 12, 1923.

Their address is Kentwood, La., Route 2.

h. VIVIAN TRAVIS.—Born in St. Helena Parish, La., Oct. 1922. Unmarried.

5. RICHARD EVERETT TRAVIS.—Born in St. Helena Parish, La., Aug. 27, 1893. Unmarried. Lives near Magnolia, Miss.

6. WILLIAM LEE TRAVIS.—Born in St. Helena Parish, La., July 8, 1895. Married Eula Eugenia Powell, daughter of William Alfred and Sarah (Easley) Powell, Dec. 27, 1924, in Magnolia, Miss. Children: William Lee II (born Jan. 5, 1927; graduate of L. S. U.; attending Tulane University medical school at present), and Eugenia Powell Travis (born Apr. 7, 1928; married Donald Arthur Bousquet Jan. 27, 1951; graduate of L. S. U.; was a school teacher before marrying; lives in New Orleans, La.)

Eula Eugenia Powell-Travis was born Nov. 20, 1898.

William Lee Travis is a retired naval commander. He is a veteran of World Wars I and II. He lives near Kentwood, La.

J. ALMA BURRIS.—Born in St. Helena Parish, La. Never married. Died in Jackson, La., and was buried there.

K. ADELINE BURRIS.—Born in St. Helena Parish, La. Married

Thomas Melton. Children: Benton Burris, Ada, Fleta, Serena, and Effie Marian.

Adeline Burris-Melton is dead. During her young womanhood, she taught school, it was said.

1. BENTON BURRIS MELTON.—Never married. Killed by a Negro.

2. ADA MELTON.—Married Adolphus Frazier. No children.

3. FLETA MELTON.—Unmarried. Lives in St. Helena Parish.

4. SERENA MELTON.—Died young.

5. EFFIE MARIAN MELTON.—Born in the Sixth Ward of St. Helena Parish, La., Mar. 22, 1877. Married Albert Bunyan Raborn Mar. 3, 1901. Children: Percy Melton, Helen Eloise, Addie Mae, Thomas Bunyan, and Fleta Estelle.

They live in Zachary, La.

a. PERCY MELTON RABORN.—Born in St. Helena Parish, La., Dec. 31, 1901. Married Lucille Denham in Baton Rouge, La. No children.

b. HELEN ELOISE RABORN.—Born in St. Helena Parish, La., July 30, 1905. Unmarried. Employed and lives in Baton Rouge, La.

c. ADDIE MAE RABORN.—Born in St. Helena Parish, La., July 6, 1908. Married Clifton D. Turner of Zachary, La., in Baton Rouge, La. Children: Elbert Ray, Beverly, Glynn, Harold, Christine, Gloria Mae, Catherine and Janelle.

d. THOMAS BUNYAN RABORN.—Born in St. Helena Parish, La., Nov. 2, 1911. Married Verna Achord. Children: Thomas Ronald, Kenneth Dale, and Nelda Sue.

e. FLETA ESTELLE RABORN.—Born in Tangipahoa Parish, La., July 10, 1915. Married Francis I. Whiting Feb. 23, 1946, in Baltimore, Md. No children.

Fleta Estelle Raborn-Whiting sailed Nov. 23, 1949, for Guam, where her husband is stationed. She is a registered nurse.

VII. ANN BURRIS.—

Ann Burris was the daughter of Samuel and Mary (Myers) Burris. She was born in South Carolina Apr. 1, 1803. She married, first, Phillip Raiford of Camden, S. C., and they had one child, a son named Phillip, Jr. After Phillip Raiford's death, Ann married Judge Edmund Smith Sept. 8, 1827. They had the following children: William Burris, James Harley, George Kinnebrew, Samuel Pinkney, Seaborn, and Ann.

Judge Edmund Smith was born in Oglethorpe County, Ga., in 1790, and moved from there to Amite County, Miss. He bought the southwest quarter of section 17, township 4, range 6 east, Dec. 31, 1811; and the southeast quarter of the same section July 28, 1818, from the U. S. Government. These tracts comprised the original Edmund Smith homestead in Amite County. They are located near Mars Hill, and extend across the river there. Later, he bought the north half of section 5, township 4, range 6 east, and the northeast, southeast, and northwest quarters of section 6, township 4, range 6 east, all of which contain 520 acres. This land is located about two and one-half miles north of Mars Hill and borders on the Lincoln and Franklin County lines.

Judge Edmund Smith served in the Mississippi State Legislature as representative from Amite County in 1826, 1828, 1831, 1838, and 1839. He left Amite County in 1840 and moved to Hinds County, Miss. His daughter, Ann, was born there. He owned property in or near Jackson, Miss. Millsaps College is on the site of one piece of land owned by him, and the old asylum is on, or nearby, another piece of land owned by him. He left Hinds County and moved to Yazoo County, near Way, Miss. He went to the State Legislature as representative from Sunflower County, and died in 1854, while in the Legislature. Both House and Senate adjourned to attend the funeral. He was buried in Jackson, Miss.

Ann Burris-Smith died Apr. 14, 1864, and was buried in Indianola, Miss.

Judge Edmund Smith and his wife, Ann, donated the site on which the Mars Hill Baptist Church is located. The following is a copy of the deed covering this donation, which was copied from the Amite County, Miss., records:

State of Mississippi ⎞
Amite County ⎭

Know all men by these presents that we, Edmund Smith and Ann Smith, his wife, of the State and County aforesaid, being at all times anxious to promote the preaching of the gospel, by all denominations of Christians, have given and granted, and by these presents, do give, grant, bargain and confirm, unto the trustees of Mars Hill Baptist Chuch and their successors in office, two acres of land, to be taken from the southeast corner of the southwest quarter of section 17, in township

4, of range 6 east; to be laid off so as to include the meeting house of said Church, and so that the south and east lines of said quarter section shall constitute the south and east lines of the above described lot of two acres, which said lot or parcel of land, containing two acres, together with all the rights, privileges, and appurtenances thereunto belonging, or in any wise appertaining, we, the said Edmund Smith and Ann, his wife, for ourselves, our heirs and assigns, do warrant and defend unto the said trustees and their successors in office, in trust for the use and accommodation of the Baptist Church, as a place of public worship forever, against all legal demands whatever. It being understood that, if the said Church shall cease to be or change their faith to any licentious or unscriptual form, then and in that case this deed to be void, and the said two acres of land, above described, to revert to the said Edmund Smith and Ann, his wife, their heirs, or assigns.

In testimony whereof we have hereunto subscribed our names this 23rd of May, 1835.

Attest:

Edward Winfield	Edmund Smith (Seal)
Peter A. Marsalis	Ann Smith (Seal)

It was said that the postoffice, located near the Mars Hill Baptist Church and named Smithdale after Judge Edmund Smith, was originally established by him. Edmund Smith was appointed Associate Justice for Amite County Jan. 21, 1824. The following is a copy of the commission, which was copied from the Amite County records:

THE STATE OF MISSISSIPPI

To all who shall see these presents, greeting:

Know ye that reposing special trust and confidence in the integrity and ability of Edmund Smith, we do appoint him an associate justice for Amite County—and do authorize and empower him to execute and fulfill the duties of that office according to law and to have and to hold the said office with all the powers, privileges, and emoluments to the same right appertaining therefrom the day of the date hereof for the term prescribed by the constitution.

In testimony whereof, I, Walter Leake, governer of the State aforesaid, have caused these letters to be made patent and the great seal of the State to be hereunto affixed. Given under my hand at the town of Jackson the 21st. day of January in the year of our Lord one thousand eight hundred and twenty-four and of the independence of the United States of America, the forty-eighth.

By the Governor,   Walter Leake
    John A. Gruinball,
        Secretary of State.

An Old Letter of Judge Edmund Smith's

(Published in The Piney Woods Planter, June 2, 1838)*

J. Tothill, Esq.

Dear Sir:—

Your note of the 6th inst. has been received, and in compliance with your request, I have read the article in the Advocate to which you direct my attention. I do not recollect the particular conversation alluded to by Mr. Graves, but have no doubt the expression imputed to me was made. Divest this matter of the unkindness which Mr. Graves seems to feel toward you, and his own inference, and I see no harm in it; for it is evident that I spoke of the opinions which I understood you to entertain of the original institution of slavery as a moral problem. I never considered you an abolitionist;—on the contrary, I have understood you to maintain that you did not consider the inhabitants of the Southern States responsible for the introduction of slavery amongst them; that it had been forced on them by the cupidity of a Tyrannical Government over which they had no control;—and that it had now taken such deep root that it could not be eradicated but by a convulsion which would destroy the Union, and inflict a greater evil on the community than those sought to be removed. I have understood you to say that such misapprehension prevailed both in Europe and the Northern States, as to the condition and treatment of slaves, and that, if they could be convinced that the African race in the United States were in a better situation and happier than thousands of themselves, it would tend much to allay the excitement among them; and I know that you frequently spoke of writing on this subject.

My feelings toward yourselves and the conductors of the Advocate are kind and friendly and it has been a source of much regret to me, that either party should feel it their duty to introduce my name into the debate between you. Your connection with me justifies your appeal, and the fidelity with which you have discharged your engagements, and the correctness of your department while a member of my family entitles you to a frank declaration of any fact of which I may have any knowledge and in which you may have any interest.

I hope that yourselves and your antagonists may feel at liberty to bring your controversy to a speedy close, as it is evidently becoming too personal to be agreeable to the parties or their friends.

Yours with sincere esteem,

E. Smith

---

*Published in Liberty, Miss.

A. PHILLIP RAIFORD, JR.—The following old document, copied from the Amite County, Miss., records, pertains to his guardianship:

State of Mississippi ⎱
Amite County ⎰

It appearing to the satisfaction of the Judge of Probate that it is better and more convenient to the interest of Phillip Raiford, a minor of said County under age of fourteen years, that Edmund Smith should become guardian of said minor. It is, therefore, ordered and decreed that the letters of guardianship formerly granted Ann Raiford, now Ann Smith, on the person and estate of said minor, be rescinded and that the said Edmund Smith be appointed guardian to the said minor, Phillip Raiford, on his entering into bond with Wm. Burris, his security, in the sum of twenty-five hundred dollars, for the faithful performance of his guardianship.

Edmund Smith entered into bond and security, which was approved, whereupon it is ordered that Edmund Smith be appointed guardian of said minor.

A. T. Crawford,
Judge Probate.

B. WILLIAM BURRIS SMITH.—Born in Amite County, Miss., in 1831. Married, first, Peninna Gillespie. Children: Georgia Ann, and Eugenia. Married, second, Hattie Ingraham Boyer. Children: William Burris, Jr., Samuel Pinkney, and Homer.

William Burris Smith, Sr. served in the Civil War. He was a captain. He was buried in Indianola, Miss.

1. GEORGIA ANN SMITH.—Born in Indianola, Miss., in 1866. Married Dr. William Benjamin Martin of Copiah County, Miss. Children: Nina and Monroe. Georgia Ann Smith-Martin was reared and educated at Whitworth College, Brookhaven, Miss. She died in 1930, and was buried in Indianola, Miss.

Dr. William Benjamin Martin is a prominent physician of Indianola, Miss.

a. NINA MARTIN.—Married Dr. Cecil Dickerson. Children: Dr. Cecil Dickerson, Jr. (was a flight surgeon in World War II with the rank of major), and Dr. Martin Dickerson.

Dr. Cecil Dickerson, Sr. is a prominent surgeon and physician of Conway, Ark.

b. MONROE MARTIN.—Unmarried.

2. EUGENIA SMITH.—Born in Indianola, Miss., in 1868. Mar-

ried Robert Moore. No children. Robert Moore is dead. Eugenia Smith-Moore died Nov. 22, 1951, and was buried in Indianola, Miss.

3. WILLIAM BURRIS SMITH, JR.—Born in Indianola, Miss., in 1876. Married, first, Ione (Onie) Stubblefield in 1901. Children: William Burris III, and Robert Stubblefield. Married, second, Elvira .... Children: Francis, James P., Paul F., David M., Marvin M., ..., ..., and .... All of these sons, except Robert Stubblefield, served in the armed forces during World War II, and had the following ranks: William Burris III, captain; Francis, killed in 1944; James P., technician; Paul F., lieutenant; David M., corporal; and Marvin M., private. They were called "The Fighting Smiths".

William Burris Smith, Jr., died Jan. 18, 1927, and was buried in Greenville, Miss.

4. SAMUEL PINKNEY SMITH.—

5. HOMER SMITH.—

C. JAMES HARLEY SMITH.—Born in Amite County, Miss., Nov. 7, 1828. Married Frances Ann Stubblefield, daughter of Wm. Henry and Agnes (Etheridge) Stubblefield, Jan. 31, 1850. Children: Edmund Harley, James David, Addison Burris, Mary Elizabeth, and Raiford.

Frances Ann Stubblefield-Smith was born in Georgia. She died Apr. 4, 1885, and was buried in Indianola, Miss.

James Harley Smith was a druggist in Benton, Miss. He served in the Confederate Army in Kentucky, during the Civil War. He was detailed as escort of the corpse of a soldier killed in action. From exposure and hardships suffered on the journey, he contracted pneumonia and died Mar. 5, 1862. He was buried in Benton, Miss. His widow moved to Indianola, Miss., where she reared her sons.

1. EDMUND HARLEY SMITH.—Born in Benton, Miss. Married Mabel Barker. Children: Julia (married Pembroke Stubblefield; no children).

Edmund Harley Smith was a highly respected citizen of Indianola, Miss. He bought the old home place, engaged in farming, and was successful. He died in 1923.

2. JAMES DAVID SMITH.—Born in Benton, Miss. Married Mabelle Moseley. Children: Mabelle Moseley, George Kinnebrew, Rebecca, Ann, and Marion.

Hampton and Mary (Turner) Burris and their sons, Enos Pinkney *left* and Tom *right*. Hampton's second family.

The Hampton Burris Home at Smithdale, Mississippi. *Built before the turn of the century.*

James David Smith was a prominent merchant of Greenville, Miss., and later of Indianola, Miss. He was manager of the firm, Starling-Smith Co. also of Indianola Supply Co. His wife was a member of a very prominent and aristocratic family. He died in 1917.

a. MABELLE MOSELEY SMITH.—Married William Garrard of Greenwood, Miss. Children: William, Jr., James, Mabelle, Robert, and Mary Jane.

William Garrard is head of the Staple Cotton Cooperative Association. They live in Greenwood, Miss.

b. GEORGE KINNEBREW SMITH.—Married Ella Faison. Children: Elinor, Mabelle, George, Richard, Jack, and Garrard.

George Kinnebrew Smith works for the Gilmer Grocery Co. of Greenwood, Miss.

c. REBECCA SMITH.—Married James Moseley Hairston. Children: Katherine, and James Moseley, Jr.

James Moseley Hairston was adjutant general on Governor Bilbo's staff.

They live in Jackson, Miss.

d. ANN SMITH.—Married Earnest H. Tanner. No children. Earnest H. Tanner is cashier of the Bank of Indianola, Miss.

e. MARION SMITH.—Married Dr. James Rives of New Orleans, La. Children: . . . .

Dr. Rives is a prominent physician of New Orleans.

3. ADDISON BURRIS SMITH.—Born in Benton, Miss., Feb. 16, 1858. Married, first, Beatrice Holt, daughter of William J. and Mary (Harrison-Hudson) Holt, Nov. 29, 1888. Children: Mary Augusta, and Cromwell Orrick.

Beatrice Holt-Smith was born July 23, 1871. She died Sept. 20, 1893.

William J. Holt served in the Confederate Army throughout the Civil War, and was wounded twice.

Addison Burris Smith married, second, Ada Love, Jan. 1897. Children: DeWitt Love. Married, third, Mamie Pollock, June 18, 1904. Children: Addison Burris, Jr., Frances Pollock, and Allen Harley.

Addison Burris Smith died Oct. 7, 1927, and was buried in Indianola, Miss. He was a pioneer builder of Indianola. He was a merchant, planter, banker, and general business man.

a. MARY AUGUSTA SMITH.—Born in Indianola, Miss., Jan. 3, 1890. Married Simon Peter Stubblefield in Indianola, Sept. 27, 1911. Children: Mary Elizabeth, Gloria, and Ann Augusta.

Simon Peter Stubblefield was secretary to John Sharp Williams, U. S. Senator from Mississippi. He has served three terms in the Mississippi Senate. He is in the cotton business.

Mary Augusta Smith-Stubblefield is one of the outstanding descendants of Ann Burris-Smith. She assisted in the preparation of this family history. They live in Vaughan, Miss.

(1). MARY ELIZABETH STUBBLEFIELD.—Born Feb. 18, 1913. Died in infancy.

(2). GLORIA STUBBLEFIELD.—Born May 16, 1915. Died June 21, 1917.

(3). ANN AUGUSTA STUBBLEFIELD.—Born Jan. 20, 1927.

b. CROMWELL ORRICK SMITH.—Born in Indianola, Miss., Nov. 21, 1891. Married Edith Scott Jan. 11, 1926. Children: Cromwell Orrick and Cromwell Scott (twins), and Addison Burris III.

Cromwell Orrick Smith, Sr. is a veteran of World War I. He was a lieutenant in the 114th Engineers Corps. He saw action in the battles of Saint Mihiel and Argonne Forest. He lives in New Orleans, La., and is in the insurance business.

(1). CROMWELL ORRICK SMITH, JR.—Born Nov. 8, 1926. Cromwell Orrick Smith, Jr., served in the U. S. Navy during World War II. He is now attending Tulane University.

(2). CROMWELL SCOTT SMITH.—Born Nov. 8, 1926. Twin brother of Cromwell Orrick.

Cromwell Scott Smith served in the U. S. Navy during World War II. He is now attending Louisiana State University.

(3). ADDISON BURRIS SMITH III.—Born Mar. 5, 1938.

c. DeWITT LOVE SMITH.—Born Sept. 10, 1897. Died Dec. 9, 1950. Was a cotton buyer in Yazoo City, Miss.

d. ADDISON BURRIS SMITH, JR.—Born Sept. 29, 1907. Unmarried. Served in the U. S. Ninth Army, with the rank of sergeant, during World War II. Participated in the Battle of the Bulge and was wounded. Is now an auto sales manager in New Orleans, La.

e. FRANCES POLLOCK SMITH.—Born Oct. 11, 1909. Married Jeff Collins Feb. 1937. Children: Frances Ann, and Jeff, Jr.

Jeff Collins is a public relations man for a sulphur company of Louisiana. They live in White Plains, N. Y.

f. ALLEN HARLEY SMITH.—Born Oct. 30, 1911. Married Mary Elizabeth Mitchell Nov. 1941. Children: Harley, Ann, and Petrie.

Allen Harley Smith is an employee of the Federal Bureau of Investigation. He lives in Monterey Park, Cal.

(4). MARY ELIZABETH SMITH.—Born in 1851. Died in infancy.

(5). RAIFORD SMITH.—Born in 1860. Died at the age of 12. Buried in Indianola, Miss.

D. GEORGE KINNEBREW SMITH.—Born in Yazoo City, Miss., Dec. 25, 1844. Married Augusta Heathman. Children: Minnie Heathman, Faison Heathman, James Martin, Mabelle Augusta, and Edmund Burrage.

Augusta Heathman-Smith was born in Wilkes County, N. C. She died Dec. 1929, and was buried in Indianola, Miss.

George Kinnebrew Smith was one of the most illustrious and respected of the Ann Burris-Smith descendants. He died in 1913, and was buried in Indianola, Miss.

1. MINNIE HEATHMAN SMITH.—Born in Indianola, Miss., Apr. 11, 1878. Married Warner J. Holt, son of William J. and Mary (Harrison-Hudson) Holt, Dec. 30, 1903. Children: Addison Heathman, and Warner J., Jr.

Minnie Heathman Smith-Holt is a member of Chi Omega Sorority and the D. A. R. She is a graduate of the University of Mississippi, and is one of the most illustrious members of the Ann Burris-Smith descendants. Most of the data in this history, on these descendants, was secured and compiled by her.

Warner J. Holt died May 8, 1927, and was buried in Indianola, Miss. His mother, Mary Harrison Hudson-Holt, was born in Oglethorpe County, Ga., in 1844.

a. ADDISON HEATHMAN HOLT.—Born in Oxford, Miss., Sept. 1904. Is a captain in the U. S. Army Air Force.

b. WARNER J. HOLT, JR.—Born Oct. 14, 1916. Married Vivian Settlemyre of Charlotte, N. C., Nov. 1941, in Salina, Kan. Children: Richard Wayne, and Dianne Julene.

Warner J. Holt, Jr. served as captain in the U. S. Army Air Corps during World War II. He is now a permanent captain in the U. S. Air Corps and is serving in a rescue squadron at McDill Field.

2. FAISON HEATHMAN SMITH.—Born in Indianola, Miss., Nov. 30, 1879. Married Jessye Gooch. Children: George Kinnebrew, Faison Heathman, Jr., and Jessye.

Although a young man at the time of his death, Mar. 14, 1926, Faison Heathman Smith had made quite a success in the cotton business. He was a graduate of the University of Mississippi, and was a member of the Phi Delta Fraternity. His wife is a descendant of the Shelby Family, for which Family Shelby County, Tenn., is named. He was buried in Indianola, Miss.

a. GEORGE KINNEBREW SMITH.—Married Clendenning Baird. Children: Catchings, George, and Richard.

George Kinnebrew Smith is a cotton buyer of Greenwood, Miss.

b. FAISON HEATHMAN SMITH, JR.—Married Elizabeth McKnight of Temple, Tex. Children: Faison Heathman III, and Robin (a girl).

They live in Greenwood, Miss.

c. JESSYE SMITH.—Married Gordon Grantham. Children: Jessye, ... (a daughter), and .... (a daughter).

Jessye Smith-Grantham is a graduate of Washington and Lee University, and joined the Chi Omega Sorority while attending this institution.

Gordon Grantham graduated from the University of Mississippi in law. During World War II he was an outstanding F. B. I. agent. He is practicing law now, and lives in Jackson, Miss.

3. JAMES MARTIN SMITH.—Born in Heathman, Miss., June 19, 1882. Married Anne Gourley Lombard Fowlkes of Clarksdale, Miss. Children: Amy, Martin Robert, and Edmund.

James Martin Smith was a graduate of the University of Mississippi and of Tulane University. He was a member of Phi Delta Theta Fraternity. He was a cotton buyer. He died Mar. 1928.

a. AMY SMITH.—Married Jerry Porter. Children: ......, ...

Amy Smith-Porter is a graduate of Sophie Newcomb College of

New Orleans, La. She is a member of Phi Mu Sorority, and won the Phi Beta Kappa key while in college. They live in Memphis, Tenn.

b. MARTIN ROBERT SMITH.—Married Mary Glenn Yeager of Terre Haute, Ind. Martin Robert Smith holds B.S. degree from Miss. State College, and Master's Degree from Mass. Institute of Technology. He is a member of Phi Eta Sigma and Kappa Mu honorary societies; and of Pi Kappa Alpha Fraternity. He is connected with the M. W. Kellog Co. of New York, N. Y.

c. EDMUND SMITH.—

4. MABELLE AUGUSTA SMITH.—Born in Greenville, Miss., Aug. 30, 1884. Married Herman Glenn, son of Thomas and Lily (Hohlebohn) Glenn. Children: Lillian and Mary Elizabeth.

Mabelle Augusta Smith-Glenn is a member of the D. A. R., also of the Chi Omega Sorority. Herman Glenn is a partner in the Nelson Dry Goods Co. of Oxford, Miss., one of the oldest department stores in Mississippi. It was established in 1837.

a. LILLIAN GLENN.—Married Robert Payne. Children: Robert Glenn. Lillian Glenn-Payne is a graduate of the University of Mississippi, and a postgraduate of Emory College (in Library Science). She is a member of the Chi Omega Sorority.

Robert Payne is a captain in the U. S. Army Engineers.

b. MARY ELIZABETH GLENN.—Married William C. Cox. Children: Glenn.

Mary Elizabeth Glenn-Cox is a graduate of the University of Mississippi. She is a member of the Chi Omega Sorority.

William C. Cox is a graduate of the University of Mississippi. He is a member of the Delta Kappa Epsilon Fraternity. He served as major in the U. S. Marine Air Corps during World War II.

5. EDMUND BURRAGE SMITH.—Born in Indianola, Miss., in 1888. Married Winnie Vance. Children: Martha Vance (married Capt. Richard Denman Crow of Shreveport, La. Martha Vance is a graduate of Sullins College and the University of Mississippi. She is a member of the Chi Omega Sorority).

Edmund Burrage Smith wa a graduate of the University of Mississippi. He was a member of the Phi Delta Theta Fraternity. He died in 1917, and was buried in Indianola, Miss. After his death his wife married Edwin L. Bass. They live in Grenada, Miss.

E. SAMUEL PINKNEY SMITH.—Born in Yazoo City, Miss., in 1842. Never married.

Samuel Pinkney Smith died in 1862, while serving in the Confederate Army during the Civil War, and was buried in Richmond, Va. He was an honor student in the University of Mississippi at the time of his enlistment in the Confederate Army in 1861. He was a member of the Delta Psi Fraternity.

F. SEABORN SMITH.—Died in 1858. No children.

G. ANN SMITH.—Born in Hinds County, Miss., in 1840. Married, first, John Waites, son of Eli Waites, sheriff of Sunflower County, Miss. No children. She married, second, George W. Faison. Children: Walter, Edmund, James, Adelaide, and William Murff.

Ann Smith-Faison died in 1888, and was buried in Indianola, Miss.

1. WALTER FAISON.

2. EDMUND FAISON.—Married Gertrude Hardy in 1911. Children: Ann Elizabeth (born in 1912; married Jack Gordon of Oxford, Miss., and has a daughter named Faison), and Edmund Gertrude (born in 1914).

Edmund Faison died in 1926.

3. JAMES FAISON.

4. ADELAIDE FAISON.—Married .... McMahon. Children: Edward.

They live in Conway, Ark.

5. WILLIAM MURFF FAISON.—Married Janie Birdsong. Children: William (died in Memphis, Tenn.), and Janie (married Clayton Tolar of Moorehead, Miss.).

VIII. GEORGE NELSON BURRIS.—

George Nelson Burris was the son of Samuel and Mary (Myers) Burris. He was born in South Carolina Apr. 10, 1805. He married Elizabeth Thompson Jan. 12, 1832, in Amite County, Miss. They had the following children: Mary Ann Catherine, Salina Jane, Marshall Enos, Harriett Malinda, (Minnie), Thomas J., William Alexander, Ivy J. L., Amanda Eunice, Jaheel Jasper (Dock), Emily A., Almine Rosetta, Nancy L., and George Nelson, Jr.

Elizabeth Thompson-Burris was born in Amite County, Miss.,

Apr. 18, 1813. She died June 1, 1880. She was a member of the Liberty, Miss., Presbyterian Church.

George Nelson Burris's original homestead seems to have been a part of his mother's old homestead, which he owned jointly with his brother, Enos. Later, Feb. 19, 1834, he bought 80 acres from the U. S. Government, and moved there. This land is located about two miles south of the Liberty-McComb Highway and four miles east of the East Fork of Amite River. It is known as the Old George Nelson Burris Homestead. George Nelson Burris died Oct. 2, 1869, and he and his wife were buried in the family graveyard on the Old George Nelson Burris Homestead. He was an elder in the Liberty, Miss., Presbyterian Church.

A. MARY ANN CATHERINE BURRIS.—Born in Amite County, Miss., Dec. 14, 1832. Married Dr. William Jones, son of Henry and Mary (Spurlock) Jones, Jan. 12, 1849. Children: Alice Elizabeth, Seaborn Tecumseh, and Mary Emily.

Dr. William Jones was born in Amite County Apr. 11, 1827. He died Oct. 10, 1898, in Osyka, Miss. Mary Ann Catherine Burris-Jones died July 6, 1855, in Osyka, Miss.

1. ALICE ELIZABETH JONES.—Born Nov. 6, 1849. Died Jan. 4, 1854, of scarlet fever. Buried by her mother.

2. SEABORN TECUMSEH JONES.—Born in Osyka, Miss., Feb. 12, 1852. Married Nancy Josephine Lea Oct. 16, 1872, in Amite County, Miss. Children: Catherine Lea (Katie), Alice Gertrude, Emily Ella (Nell), Leonidas Ludwell, Harry Aldrich, James Monroe, Josephine Viola, and William Reed.

Nancy Joephine Lea-Jones was born in Amite County, Miss., Aug. 5, 1849. She died Apr. 4, 1911, in McComb, Miss., and was buried in the Hollywood Cemetery, Houston, Texas.

Seaborn Tecumseh Jones died Jan. 4, 1917, in Houston, Texas.

a. CATHERINE LEA (KATIE) JONES.—Born Apr. 12, 1874. Married William Franklin Holmes Dec. 25, 1901. Children: Katie Nell (adopted).

Catherine Lea (Katie) Jones-Holmes lives with her daughter and son-in-law in Vicksburg, Miss. It was she who started this family history and secured much of the data for it.

(1). KATIE NELL HOLMES.—Married T. J. Ogletree. Children: William Clay, and Linda and Brenda (twins).

They live in Vicksburg, Miss.

b. ALICE GERTRUDE JONES.—Born June 2, 1875. Married Henry Clay Fuller Oct. 16, 1889. Children: Deyette, Bryan, Brand, Henry Clay, Jr., Seaborn, Townsend, and Katie Lea.

c. EMILY ELLA (NELL) JONES.—Born Sept. 4, 1877. Married Thomas J. Donahue Mar. 23, 1897. Children: Catherine and Thomas J., Jr.

(1). CATHERINE DONAHUE.—Married Dewitt Estess. Children: Emily, Dewitta, Nell, and .... (a daughter).

They live in McComb, Miss.

(2). THOMAS J. DONAHUE, JR.

d. LEONIDAS LUDWELL JONES.—Born May 19, 1881. Married Hattie Nix Mar. 18, 1906. Children: Harry and Leonidas Ludwell, Jr.

e. HARRY ALDRICH JONES.—Born Jan. 11, 1884. Married Annie Nix Mar. 20, 1919. Children: Louise and Harry Aldrich, Jr.

f. JAMES MONROE JONES.—Born Mar. 19, 1887. Married Bertha Rosa Ott June 12, 1911. Children (Listed under Bertha Rosa Ott, as this is an inter-family marriage). Died Nov. 25, 1923.

g. JOSEPHINE VIOLA JONES.—Born Feb. 2, 1890. Married, first, Clyde Wesley Brumfield. No children. Married, second, David White. Children: .... (an adopted daughter). They live in Kentwood, La.

h. WILLIAM REED JONES.—Born Apr. 6, 1880. Died Apr. 15, 1880.

3. MARY EMILY JONES.—Born in Osyka, Miss., Oct. 8, 1853. Married Thomas Charles Ott Feb. 18, 1874, in Osyka. Children: Charles Monroe, Thomas Edward, William Jones, Annie Eleanor, Carrie Pearl, Bertha Rosa, Seaborn Grover, and Harry Leon.

Thomas Charles Ott was born Jan. 25, 1854. He died in Oct. 1928.

Mary Emily Jones-Ott died Jan. 27, 1924.

a. CHARLES MONROE OTT.—Born Feb. 21, 1875. Married Gertrude McMillan Aug. 5, 1906. Children: Ronald Howard, Mildred Bertha, and Clifford Davis.

Charles Monroe Ott is retired and lives near Osyka, Miss., on Route 2.

(1). RONALD HOWARD OTT.—Married Irene Hunt. Children: William, James, and Peggy Sue.

Ronald Howard Ott lives in Amarillo, Texas.

(2). MILDRED BERTHA OTT.—Married William W. Brown. Children: Mildred Louise and William W., Jr.

They live in Memphis, Tenn.

(3). CLIFFORD DAVIS OTT.—Married Hortense Harrell. Children: Carol Jean, William, Clifford Davis, Jr., Wendell H., Steve Edward, Charles Philip, and Linda Ann.

Clifford Davis Ott is a dairy farmer, and lives near Osyka, Miss.

b. THOMAS EDWARD OTT.—Born July 3, 1876. Married Ella Shattuck Jan. 21, 1903. Children: Clara Belle and Paul Shattuck.

They live in Lake Charles, La.

(1). CLARA BELLE OTT.—Married Paul Zeigler. Children: Eleanor, Paul, Jr., and Edward.

They live in Baton Rouge, La.

(2). PAUL SHATTUCK OTT.—Salesman for Murray-Brooks Oil Supplies, and lives in Harvey, La.

c. WILLIAM JONES OTT.—Born Apr. 11, 1878. Married Margaret Ott Nov. 29, 1900. Children: Marguerite, Azel Jaston, William Jones, Jr., Ruby Mae, and Thomas Truett. William Jones Ott is dead.

(1). MARGUERITE OTT.—Married Wallace Forshag. No children. They live in Whitfield, Miss.

(2). DR. AZEL JUSTIN OTT.—Married Frances Phipps. Children: Helen Judith, and Mary Frances. Dr. Azel Justin Ott is a dentist and is located in Tallahassee, Fla.

(3). DR. WILLIAM JONES OTT, JR.—Married Mary Carlton. Children: Carol (adopted). Dr. William Jones Ott, Jr., is a dentist and is located in Tallahassee, Fla.

(4). RUBY MAE OTT.—Married Joe Stubbs. Children: Susan Little, and A. J., Jr. They live in Houston, Tex.

(5). THOMAS TRUETT OTT.—Married Anita Williamson. Children: Sandra and Thomas Truett, Jr. Thomas Truett Ott is serving in the armed forces of the U. S. His family lives in Tampa, Fla.

d. ANNIE ELEANOR OTT.—Born Sept. 18, 1880. Married J.

L. Slay Aug. 5, 1909. Children: Mary Catherine (married C. S. Sykes and has two children, Margaret Ann and John Ott).

They live in Jackson, Miss.

e. CARRIE PEARL OTT.—Born May 11, 1882. Never married. Is a school teacher in the Osyka, Miss., school.

f. BERTHA ROSA OTT.—Born Feb. 21, 1886. Married James Monroe Jones June 12, 1911. Children: Hettie Ott, Landon Lea, and William.

They live in Osyka, Miss.

(1). HETTIE OTT JONES.—Married Marvin Zipp. Children: Eric Stoll.

They live in Arlington, Va.

(2). LANDON LEA JONES.—Married Mary Edna Jones. Children: Landon Booth.

Landon Lea Jones is employed by the Gulf Oil Co. of Houston, Tex., as a geologist. He served in the U. S. Army, on limited duty, as a geologist during World War II, with technical sergeant rating.

(3). WILLIAM JONES.—Married Alice Graham. No children. Is a major in the U. S. Air Corps.

g. SEABORN GROVER OTT.—Born July 8, 1888. Died June 23, 1890.

h. HARRY LEON (JACK) OTT.—Born Sept. 24, 1889. Married Mabel DeBhrul June 25, 1911. Children: Polly, Pearl Ernestine, Harry Leon, Jr., and Mary Thomas.

Harry Leon (Jack) Ott is a mechanic and lives in Osyka, Miss.

(1). POLLY OTT.—Married Sam Magee. No children.

(2). PEARL ERNESTINE OTT.—Married Robert Raborn. Children: Robert, Jr., and Gene Ott. They live in Houston, Tex.

(3). HARRY LEON (JACK) OTT, JR.—Unmarried. Is a captain in the U. S. Air Corps, and is stationed at Keesler Field, Biloxi, Miss.

(4). MARY THOMAS OTT.—Unmarried. Is a registered nurse, and lives in New Orleans, La.

B. SALINA JANE BURRIS.—Born Jan. 27, 1834. Married Thad Gray, Oct. 23, 1849. Children: Mary Elizabeth, Sherrod Nelson, Mijamon Lafayette (Max), Lelia Salina, Minnie, Thomas, Ary, and Burris.

Thad Gray died about 1890 in Headsville, Limestone County, Texas.

Salina Jane Burris-Gray united with East Fork Baptist Church June 1859.

1. MARY ELIZABETH GRAY.—Born in Amite County, Miss., in 1850. Married Daniel W. Dooley in 1870, in Amite County. Children: Elizabeth (married J. N. Butler and lived in Decatur, Ala. No children), John (died in infancy), Daniel (died in infancy), and Annie.

2. SHERROD NELSON GRAY.—Dead.

3. MIJAMON LAFAYETTE (MAX) GRAY.—Married .... White. Was overseer on a farm in Texas and was shot from ambush.

4. LELIA SALINA GRAY.—Married Frank Cook. Died Dec. 9, 1923.

5. MINNIE GRAY.—Married John Price.

6. THOMAS GRAY.—Married Anna Smith. When heard from last his address was Deleon, Texas, Route 2.

7. ARY GRAY.—Married Robert Harper.

8. BURRIS GRAY.—Married Laura Hobbs. Died in 1915, with tuberculosis. Laura Hobbs-Gray died in 1916.

C. MARSHALL ENOS BURRIS.—Born in Amite County, Miss., Dec. 13, 1835. Married Malena Wilson*, his second cousin, Dec. 5, 1867. Children: Minnie, Lucy Ora, Pearla Nelson, George Enos, and Ada.

Malena Wilson-Burris was born in Amite County Aug. 17, 1841. She died Apr. 25, 1918, and was buried in Amite County.

Marshall Enos Burris died Aug. 3, 1879, and was buried in Amite County. He was a member of the Liberty, Miss., Presbyterian Church.

1. MINNIE BURRIS.—Born in Amite County May 3, 1869. Married Rev. W. K. Anderson May 8, 1883. Children: Lucy (born Sept. 17, 1885; never married).

Rev. W. K. Anderson was born May 10, 1860. He died in 1946, and was buried in Liberty, Miss.

Minnie Burris-Anderson died May 3, 1899, and was buried at East Fork, Miss.

2. LUCY ORA BURRIS.—Born in Amite County Jan. 15, 1871.

---

*Malena Wilson was the daughter of Bruce Myers Wilson, who was the son of Samuel and Mary (Myers) Burris's daughter Elizabeth.

Married Thos. M. Honea Mar. 24, 1888. Children: Pearla Lutishia, Enos, Monette Minnie, Lelia, Marshall Leslie, Ruth, and Thomas Leon. Lucy Ora Burris-Honea died in 1950, and was buried in the family plot in Glading, Miss. She lived in Magnolia.

a. PEARLA LUTISHIA HONEA.—Born in Amite County Jan. 10, 1890. Married Frank E. Stocklin May 10, 1920. No children. Died in 1948. Frank E. Stocklin was born Aug. 7, 1877.

b. ENOS HONEA.—Born in Amite County Sept. 16, 1889. Married Myrtis McDaniel July 4, 1908. Children: Morris E., Wilma, James, Ernestine, and Paul. They live in Magnolia, Miss.

(1). MORRIS E. HONEA.—Born July 1909. Married Mary Cutrer in 1938. Children: James Shelton (died at the age of 4), Thomas Edward (born in 1941), Harold Clifton (died at the age of one month), Morris E., Jr., George Randolph, Michael McDaniel, and Jack Hughes.

(2). WILMA HONEA.—Born June 7, 1913. Married Frank Martin. Children: Frank, Jr., and Wilma Louise. They live in Magnolia, Miss.

(3). JAMES HONEA.—Born June 11, 1914. Married Marie Schwing. Children: Patty Lou. They live in Panama City, Fla.

(4). ERNESTINE HONEA.—Born Apr. 1926. Married Hollis Griffin. Children: Jerry Wayne, and Donald George. They live in Magnolia, Miss.

(5). PAUL HONEA.—Unmarried. Lives in Santiago, Cuba.

c. MONETTE MINNIE HONEA.—Born in Amite County Jan. 8, 1896. Married Jewell Anderson Aug. 18, 1917. Children: Jewell, Jr., Mamie, Thomas H., Virginia, Wilma Frank, and Betty Jean.

Jewell Anderson was born Apr. 21, 1896. They live in Magnolia, Miss.

(1). JEWELL ANDERSON, JR.—Born in Amite County May 3, 1918. Married Louise Brumfield. No children. Lives in Magnolia, Miss.

(2). MAMIE ANDERSON.—Born in Amite County Jan. 28, 1920. Married Henry L. Ross, a dental technician. Children: John Lamar, and Jimmie. They live in Magnolia, Miss.

(3). THOMAS H. ANDERSON.—Born in Amite County Oct. 13, 1921. Died Jan. 21, 1923.

(4). VIRGINIA ANDERSON.—Born in Amite County Oct. 26, 1923. Married James Cook. No children.

(5). WILMA FRANK ANDERSON.—Born in Amite County Mar. 20, 1926. Married Earl Scott. Children: Sandra K.

(6). BETTY JEAN ANDERSON.—Married Bernard Cook. Children: A. Darrel. They live in McComb, Miss.

d. LELIA HONEA.—Born in Amite County July 16, 1897. Married Lonnie Anderson Aug. 23, 1917. Children: Johnnie Mozelle, Pearl Louise, George Leon, W. L., ... (a son; dead), and Geraldine.

Lonnie Anderson was born in Glading, Miss., Jan. 21, 1894.

(1). JOHNNIE MOZELLE ANDERSON.—Born in Glading, Miss., Sept. 7, 1920. Married Earl McKnight Dec. 21, 1941, in Glading, Miss. Children: Beverly Lou (born in Glading, Miss., Sept. 12, 1942), and Dicky Lynn (born in East Fork, Miss., Jan. 4, 1947).

(2). PEARL LOUISE ANDERSON.—Born in Glading, Miss., Jan. 27, 1922. Unmarried. Lives in McComb, Miss.

(3). GEORGE LEON ANDERSON.—Born in Glading, Miss., Nov. 24, 1924. Married Elaine Powell Apr. 16, 1946. Children: George Wesley (born in Glading Mar. 5, 1947), Gary Winston (born Dec. 31, 1948; died in 1949; buried in the Honea Cemetery in Glading), Charlotte, and James Oliver. They live near Magnolia, Miss.

(4). W. L. ANDERSON, JR.—Born in Glading, Miss., Aug. 19, 1925. Married Laverne Thomas, Feb. 8, 1948, in Glading. Children: Billy Joe (born in Baton Rouge, La., Nov. 28, 1948), and Martha Lynn. They live in Baton Rouge, La.

(5). .... (A son who died in 1919 and was buried in Glading, Miss.)

(6). GERALDINE ANDERSON.—Born in Glading, Miss., July 10, 1929. Married Sidney Blailock. Children: Michael (born Mar. 6, 1951), and Teresa (born Feb. 1952). They live in McComb, Miss.

e. MARSHALL LESLIE HONEA.—Born in Amite County, Miss., Mar. 20, 1892. Married Elma Barron Nov. 1917. Children: Leroy (born July 1923), and Leslie Moore. They live in Magnolia, Miss.

f. RUTH HONEA.—Born in Amite County, Miss., Aug. 10, 1893. Married Wiley Williams Dec. 27, 1909. Children: Floyd, Julia Mae, Laurence, Lynelle, and Charles.

Wiley Williams was born in Wesson, Miss., Feb. 10, 1885.

Ruth Honea-Williams is dead. She was buried in Glading, Miss.

(1). FLOYD WILLIAMS.—Born Sept. 1, 1912. Married Teresa Brown. Children: Ava Lou, Jettie Ruth, Mary Ann, Floyd Lamar, and Martha Sue. They live in Fernwood, Miss.

(2). JULIA MAE WILLIAMS.—Born Feb. 11, 1914. Died Apr. 29, 1915.

(3). LAURENCE WILLIAMS.—Born Mar. 23, 1916. Married Margie Westbrook. No children.

(4). LYNELLE WILLIAMS.—Born Nov. 29, 1920. Married Maurice McDaniel. No children. They live in Centreville, Miss.

(5). CHARLES WILLIAMS.—Born Apr. 29, 1922. Unmarried.

g. THOMAS LEON HONEA.—Born in Amite County, Miss., Sept. 11, 1902. Married Lillian Smith Sept. 1924. Children: Ruby Mae, John Norman, and Phyllis. They live in Baton Rouge, La.

(1). RUBY MAE HONEA.—Born Apr. 28, 1925. Married Hamp Lee. Children: Patricia. They live in Magnolia, Miss.

(2). JOHN NORMAN HONEA.—Unmarried. Lives in Magnolia, Miss.

(3). PHYLLIS HONEA.—Unmarried. Lives in Magnolia, Miss.

3. PEARLA NELSON BURRIS.—Born in Amite County, Miss., Sept. 13, 1873. Married John Wolf Nov. 1893. Children: Madeline (born in Amite County Oct. 6, 1897; married Kirby Payne and has eight children, Joe Frank, John Nelson, Bee, Mary Ellen, Henry (a girl), Hilda Mae, Eva, and Jeanette), Grace (born in Amite County May 16, 1901), Minnie (born in Amite County Oct. 18, 1904), Hilton (born in McComb, Miss., Nov. 28, 1908), and Pearla Mae (born in Fernwood, Miss., Aug. 13, 1911).

John Wolf died in Fernwood, Miss., Aug. 2, 1923.

Pearla Nelson Burris-Wolf died in Fernwood, Miss., Apr. 7, 1912.

4. GEORGE ENOS BURRIS.—Born in Amite County, Miss., July 17, 1876. Married Hattie Barron Nov. 2, 1899. Children: Velma A., Mable L., Omer E., Etta Mae, Agnes R., Georgie P., Marshall Randolph, Juanita, and Raiford G.

Hattie Barron-Burris was born Sept. 17, 1882.

George Enos Burris lives near the old George Nelson Burris homestead, which is located near Liberty, Miss. He is one of the outstanding citizens of Amite County. He took an active interest in, and assisted with the preparation of this family history.

a. VELMA A. BURRIS.—Born in Amite County, Miss., Oct. 21, 1900. Married Vernon Y. Felder Feb. 20, 1933. No children.

Vernon Y. Felder was born in Summit, Miss., Mar. 13, 1883.

They live near Magnolia, Miss., on Route 1.

b. MABLE L. BURRIS.—Born in Amite County, Miss., Sept. 1, 1902. Married Roy Newman Sept. 27, 1925, in Gillsburg, Miss. Children: Flora Nell, Ruby Joyce, and Paul.

Roy Newman was born in Amite County Apr. 25, 1900.

They live in Liberty, Miss.

(1). FLORA NELL NEWMAN.—Born in Glading, Miss., Feb. 13, 1927. Married Kenneth Gordon Oct. 15, 1948, in Liberty, Miss. No children.

Kenneth Gordon was born in Liberty, Miss., Feb. 28, 1925. They live in Liberty, Miss.

(2). RUBY JOYCE NEWMAN.—Born in Glading, Miss., Feb. 17, 1931. Married John Davis Tynes May 10, 1947. Children: Johnnie Lee (born in Centreville, Miss., Dec. 25, 1948), and David Michael (born in Amite County, Miss., Apr. 1, 1951).

John Davis Tynes was born in Liberty, Miss., Sept. 22, 1925. They live in Liberty, Miss.

(3). PAUL NEWMAN.—Born in Glading, Miss., Jan. 8, 1933. Unmarried. Lives in Liberty, Miss.

c. OMER E. BURRIS.—Born in Amite County, Miss., July 31, 1904. Married Hilda Bostick Sept. 20, 1925. Children: Edwin E., and Barbara.

Hilda Bostick-Burris was born in Amite County Nov. 25, 1906.

They live near Magnolia, Miss., on Route 2.

(1). EDWIN E. BURRIS.—Born in Glading, Miss., July 8, 1926. Married Johanna McDaniel Mar. 15, 1947, in McComb, Miss. No children. Johanna McDaniel-Burris was born in McComb, Miss., Nov. 9, 1927.

Edwin E. Burris is a veteran of World War II. He was inducted into service at Camp Shelby, Hattiesburg, Miss., Dec. 7, 1944. He was trained 15 weeks and sent overseas to Germany Apr. 20, 1945. He served in the army of occupation. He was staff sergeant of Company 301, 9th Infantry Division.

They live near Magnolia, Miss., on Route 2.

(2). BARBARA BURRIS.—Born in Peoria, Miss., Nov. 26, 192-. Married Wyman Raborn July 25, 1948. Children: Sylvia Dianne (born June 28, 1949), and Mary Camille (born Mar. 14, 1951).

Wyman Raborn was born in Progress, Miss., Jan. 15, 1923.

They live in Progress, Miss.

d. ETTA MAE BURRIS.—Born in Amite County, Miss., July 28, 1906. Died July 8, 1922, and was buried in the East Fork Cemetery.

e. AGNES R. BURRIS.—Born in Amite County, Miss., Oct. 19, 1908. Married M. T. Causey Apr. 26, 1947, in Magnolia, Miss. No children.

M. T. Causey was born in Liberty, Miss., Dec. 26, 1913.

They live in Baton Rouge, La.

f. GEORGIE P. BURRIS.—Born in Amite County, Miss., Mar. 31, 1913. Married Louis Wells Dec. 18, 1936, in McComb, Miss. Children: Janice (born in Liberty, Miss., July 4, 1940), and Raymond (born in Osyka, Miss., Feb. 7, 1943).

Louis Wells was born in Amite County, Miss., Sept. 28, 1911.

They live in Osyka, Miss.

g. MARSHALL RANDOLPH BURRIS.—Born in Amite County, Miss., July 26, 1915. Married Myrtis Velma Wall Dec. 25, 1938, in Natalbany, La. Children: Thomas (born in Magnolia, Miss., June 19, 1940).

Myrtis Velma Wall-Burris was born in Woodhaven, La., May 10, 1911.

They live near Magnolia, Miss., on Route 2.

h. JUANITA BURRIS.—Born in Amite County, Miss., July 27, 1917. Married Dallas Stevenson Dec. 14, 1940, in Hattiesburg, Miss. Children: James (born in Centreville, Miss., Dec. 27, 1945).

Dallas Stevenson was born in Sandy Hook, Miss., Apr. 8, 1912.

They live near Liberty, Miss., on Route 5.

i. RAIFORD G. BURRIS.—Born in Amite County, Miss., June

30, 1919. Married Wanza Rimes June 4, 1945. Children: Raiford G., Jr. (born in Magnolia, Miss., May 28, 1946), and George Arthur (born in Magnolia, Miss., Sept. 13, 1948).

Wanza Rimes was born in Progress, Miss., Jan. 6, 1923.

Raiford G. Burris is a veteran of World War II. He was inducted into service Oct. 21, 1942, at Camp Shelby, Hattiesburg, Miss. He was sent overseas Mar. 23, 1944, and served in Company G, 90th Infantry Division, Third Army, as sergeant. He was in a number of battles and was wounded once, July 4, 1944, in northern France. He received two awards. He was discharged May 20, 1945.

They live in Progress, Miss.

5.   ADA BURRIS.—Born in Amite County, Miss., Aug. 3, 1879. Married Thos. Pray June 13, 1899.   No children.

Thos. Pray was born in Amite County Aug. 1, 1881. He died Nov. 2, 1926, and was buried in Amite County.

Ada Burris-Pray died Feb. 27, 1924, and was buried in Amite County.

D.   HARRIETT MALINDA (MINNIE) BURRIS.—Born in Amite County, Miss., Oct. 2, 1837. Never married. Died Oct. 9, 1866. Was a member of the Liberty, Miss., Presbyterian Church.

E.   THOMAS J. BURRIS.—Born in Amite County, Miss., Apr. 22, 1840. Never married. Died Sept. 21, 1863. Was a member of the Liberty, Miss., Presbyterian Church.

Thomas J. Burris was killed in the battle of Chickamauga, Tenn., during the Civil War. He served, first, in the 33rd. Miss. Regiment, Army of the West, and was later transferred to the 7th Miss. Regiment, Army of Tenn. He was in love with Miss Lizzie Wells when he was killed. When he enlisted, he was a school teacher, and the following were his pupils: D. B. and D. O. McMorris; John, S. E., Dora and David Lea; Jane Bradham; Monroe Thompson; C. E. Davis, Albert and Charles Cook, J. P., H. H., Louisa, and J. M. Garner; J. J., E. A., and R. A. Burris; Mary, S. N., and M. L. Gray; N. T. and S. E. Butler; John and Georgia Wilson.

The schoolhouse was located near the old George Nelson Burris home, in Amite County, Miss.

F.   WILLIAM ALEXANDER BURRIS.—Born in Amite County, Miss., Feb. 10, 1842. Married Nora Marsalis Jan. 7, 1867. No children. Died in 1870. William Alexander Burris joined the Mars Hill Baptist Church Aug. 29, 1864.

G. IVY J. L. BURRIS.—Born in Amite County, Miss., Jan. 5, 1844. Died Sept. 4, 1851, at the age of seven.

H. AMANDA EUNICE BURRIS.—Born in Amite County, Miss., Apr. 12, 1846. Married J. Merritt Taylor Dec. 24, 1877. Children: Cassie Lou (born Feb. 12, 1879; died Sept. 7, 1882), and Louie (born Jan. 5, 1882; died Sept. 20, 1883). Amanda Eunice Burris was a member of the Liberty, Miss., Presbyterian Church.

J. Merritt Taylor was born Mar. 21, 1857.

I. JAHEEL JASPER (DOCK) BURRIS.—Born in Amite County, Miss., Oct. 15, 1849. Married Julia Marsalis Feb. 8, 1871, in Amite County, Miss. Children: Stella (dead), Nora (dead), Bessie, Virgie, Claude, and George.

Julia Marsalis-Burris united with the East Fork (Miss.) Baptist Church by experience Oct. 1841. Jaheel Jasper (Dock) Burris was a member of the Liberty, Miss., Presbyterian Church.

Jaheel Jasper (Dock) Burris moved to East Feliciana Parish, La., about 1878. He bought a place containing 275.8 acres with all buildings and other improvements from W. J. Taylor of Amite County, Miss., July 27, 1878. The place is located about 10 miles east of Clinton, La. He transferred a place in Amite County, Miss., as part payment for this property. Later, in 1881, he and W. J. Taylor (of Avoyelles Parish, La.) made a division of a tract of land owned jointly by them in East Feliciana Parish, La. He sold Silas M. Rogers a part, 40 acres, of his land in East Feliciana Parish, La., Dec. 10, 1888. Sometime later Jaheel Jasper (Dock) Burris of Limestone County, Texas, appointed Geo. W. White of East Feliciana Parish, his attorney, with full power to sign his name and sell certain of his property in East Feliciana Parish. This property consisted of 200 acres of land and buildings and other improvements.—(Taken from the East Feliciana Parish, La., records).

Jaheel Jasper (Dock) Burris died Apr. 15, 1911, and is presumed to have been buried in Texas.

J. EMILY A. BURRIS.—Born in Amite County, Miss., Sept. 26, 1850. Married William J. (Bill) Taylor Oct. 8, 1874, in Amite County. Children: Adella May, and Lyda Lou.

Emily A. Burris-Taylor died Mar. 15, 1882. She was a member of the Liberty, Miss., Presbyterian Church.

1. ADELLA MAY TAYLOR.—Born in Amite County, Miss., July 17, 1875. Married Dave T. Smith Apr. 25, 1908. Children: Mamie (born May 20, 1909), and Thomas Lee (born July 11, 1911).

Adella May Taylor-Smith died Mar. 25, 1912, in Merryville, La.

2. LYDA LOU TAYLOR.—Born Sept. 20, 1878. Died Oct. 9, 1882.

K. ALMINE ROSETTA (ABBIE) BURRIS.—Born in Amite County, Miss., Apr. 22, 1852. Married Rev. Wilborn Monroe Thompson Jan. 8, 1874, in Amite County. Children: Winchester Monroe, Leslie Lea, Ivy Finch, Minnie Eudora, Bessie Ida, and Augustus Allen.

Rev. Wilborn Monroe Thompson was a Baptist Minister. He was born in Greensburg, La., Aug. 17, 1853. He died in Westlake, La., Aug. 20, 1891.

Almine Rosetta (Abbie) Burris-Thompson died in Lewis, La., May 26, 1925, and was buried in Lake Charles, La.

1. WINCHESTER MONROE THOMPSON.—Born Nov. 10, 1874. Died Aug. 24, 1882.

2. LESLIE LEA THOMPSON.—Born Apr. 22, 1876. Married Lucy D. Creighton Dec. 13, 1900, in Lake Charles, La. Children: Wilborn Monroe (born Sept. 21, 1902), and Ida Pearl (born Mar. 17, 1904; married June 13, 1924, in Lafayette, La.)

Lucy D. Creighton-Thompson was born Nov. 2, 1882.

3. IVY FINCH THOMPSON.—Born Aug. 28, 1878. Died Sept. 29, 1883.

4. MINNIE EUDORA THOMPSON.—Born Nov. 22, 1885. Died Aug. 24, 1887.

5. BESSIE IDA THOMPSON.—Born May 31, 1889. Married George Ashford May 22, 1910, in Merryville, La. No children.

George Ashford was born in Grimes County, Texas, Sept. 25, 1884.

When last heard from they were living in Lewis, La.

6. AUGUSTUS ALLEN THOMPSON.—Born May 11, 1891. Died Dec. 1, 1891.

L. NANCY L. BURRIS.—Born in Amite County, Miss., Sept. 7, 1854. Died Sept. 19, 1854.

M. GEORGE NELSON BURRIS, JR.—Born Nov. 7, 1858. Died Nov. 21, 1858.

IX. ENOS BURRIS.—

Enos Burris was the son of Samuel and Mary (Myers) Burris. He was born in South Carolina, in the 1790's, it is estimated. He settled first in Amite County, Miss., on a portion of his mother's place, and later in West Feliciana Parish, La. He never married.

WILL OF ENOS BURRIS—DEC'D.

(Copied from Amite County, Miss., records)

State of Louisiana }
Parish of West Feliciana }

In the name of God this 13th of September A. D. 1831, I, Enos Burris, formerly of the State of Mississippi, I now a resident of the State and Parish, aforesaid, being at this time sound in mind and memory do make this my last will and testament, first after all my just debts, being paid, I give and bequeath to my brothers and sister, to-wit: Addison Burris, Hampton Burris, James Burris, George N. Burris, and Harriett Simmons all my real and personal estate to have and hold forever. I also give and bequeath to Addison Burris one rifle gun and watch, and a little mare to Bruce Wilson.

In witness whereof I set my hand and seal in the presence of the undersigned witnesses.

Enos Burris   (Seal)

Babruk Mueller
Edmd. V. Collier
Jno. Whittaker
Thos. A. Hamilton
John A. Hamilton

———

This will of Enos was probated in the Amite County courts Sept. 13, 1831, which was doubtless shortly after his death.

BOND OF SAMUEL B. SIMMONS AND JAMES BURRIS, ADMINISTRATORS OF WILL OF ENOS BURRIS, DEC'D

(Copied from Amite County, Miss., records)

State of Mississippi }
Amite County }

Know all men by these presents that we, Samuel B. Simmons, James Burris, and William A. Knox are held and firmly bound unto Van Tromp Crawford, Esquire, Judge of Probate of Said County, in the sum of two thousand dollars, to be paid to the Said Judge of Probate, or his successors in office, or their certain attorney, or assigns, to which payment well and truly to be made, we bind ourselves and every one of us and every one of our heirs, executors and administrators, for the whole and in the whole, jointly and severally, firmly by these presents, sealed with our seals and dated this 17th day of October, Anno Domini, one thousand eight hundred and thirty-one.

The condition of the above is—That, if the Said Samuel B. Simmons, and James Burris, administrators of Enos Burris, deceased, do make a true and perfect inventory of all and singular the goods, chattels and credits of the said deceased, which have or shall come to the hands, possession, or knowledge of them, the Said Samuel B. Simmons and James Burris, or into the hands or possession of any other person or persons for them, and the same so made, do exhibit to the Orphans Court of Amite County, at such time as they shall be thereto required by the Said Court, and the same goods, chattels and credits do well and truly administer according to law and make a just and true account of their actings and doings, when thereunto required by the Said Court, and further do well and truly pay and deliver all legacies contained and specified in the said Will, as far as the said goods, chattels and credits will extend according to the value thereof, as the law shall charge them, then this obligation to be void, or else to remain in full, force and virtue.

Signed, sealed, and delivered in the presence of W. Baker, Reg.

Samuel B. Simmons

James Burris

William A. Knox

Account of Sales of the Personal Property Belonging to the Estate of Enos Burris, Deceased

Sold according to law the 26th day of December, 1831.

(Copied from Amite County, Miss., records)

George N. Burris, Dr.
    16 head of cattle............................$ 59.62

Addison Burris, Dr.
    1 set of razors.............................. 2.00
    Do, 1 pair saddlebags........................ 3.00
    Do, 1 bed & furniture........................ 2.00
    Do, 1 watch 15.00
    Do, 1 rifle gun.............................. 15.00
George N. Burris, Dr.
    1 bay mare................................... 22.75
Samuel Burris, Dr.
    1 boy, Hardy................................. 487.00

        Total amount of sales   624.37

State of Mississippi ⎰
Amite County ⎱

      Personally appeared in open court Samuel B. Simmons, administrator of Enos Burris, dec'd, and made oath that the within account of sales are true as he verily believes,

Sworn to and subscribed,   Samuel B. Simmons
July 16th, 1832, W. Baker, Reg.

LAND TRANSFER (DEED) OF GEORGE N. BURRIS AND ENOS BURRIS TO WM. BURRIS

(Copied from Amite County, Miss., records)

Know all men by these presents that we, George N. Burris and Enos Burris, of the State of Mississippi and County of Amite, in consideration of the sum of $700, paid us by Wm. Burris, of the State and County aforesaid, the receipt whereof we do hereby acknowledge, do hereby give, grant, bargain, sell, and convey to the said Wm. Burris, his heirs and assigns forever, certain tracts of land known by the northwest quarter of section 7, of township 3 in range 6 E of the basic meridian line, also the northeast quarter of section 12 in township 3 of range 5 E, containing in the whole 325 acres and .18 of an acre. To have and hold the said granted and bargained premises with the privileges, appurtenances thereof to him, the said Wm. Burris, his heirs and assigns forever to his and their use and behoof forever, and we the said George N. Burris and Enos Burris for ourselves, our heirs, executors and administrators do covenant with the said Wm. Burris, his heirs and assigns that we are lawfully seized in the fee of the premises that they are free of all incumbrances; that we have good right to sell and convey the same to the said Wm. Burris, to hold as aforesaid and that we will warrant and defend the same to the said Wm. Burris, his heirs and assigns forever against the lawful claims and demands of all persons.

    In witness whereof we have hereunto set our hands and seals this 31st. day of Jan. 1829. Signed, sealed, and delivered in the presence of us

    James Denman   (George N. Burris
    Allen Spurlock   (
    Prestridge Denman   (Enos Burris

X. HAMPTON BURRIS.—

Hampton Burris was the son of Samuel and Mary (Myers) Burris. He was born in Amite County, Miss., July 3, 1809.* He married,

---

*He may have been born in South Carolina.

first, Mary (Polly) Magee Dec. 20, 1838, and they had the following children: Mary Elizabeth, John Addison, William Louis, Jacob Fleet, Erasmus Theodore, Sarah Jane, and James Nelson. After Mary (Polly) Magee's death Aug. 4, 1857, Hampton Burris married Mary Turner Mar. 1, 1859, and they had the following children: Thomas Raiford, Enos Pinkney, George Ernest, and Maggie Elizabeth.

From The Liberty Advocate of Jan. 3, 1839, James Smiley, Editor, the following was copied:

Married—On the 20th inst., by the Hon. Mr. Richardson, Mr. Hampton Burris, of this county, to Miss Mary Magehee of Washington Parish, La.

Mary (Polly) Magee was a sister of Rebecca (Becky) Magee, and of George Magee. Rebecca (Becky) Magee was James Madison Burris's first wife, and George Magee was Amanda Caroline Burris's husband. They were first cousins of Flora Lavonia Magee, who was William Addison Burris's (Hampton's nephew) wife. Mary (Polly) Magee-Burris was buried in the Burris Cemetery, near Smithdale, Miss.

Hampton and Mary (Polly) Magee-Burris often visited their relatives in Washington Parish, La., both the Burrises and the Magees, and they were highly regarded, it was said.

Mary Turner was born in Pike County, Miss., Feb. 15, 1835. She died Jan. 11, 1917, and was buried in the Mars Hill Cemetery.

In his early manhood days, Hampton Burris disposed of his share of his father's old place, and bought the following land,† which lies north of his father's place, and on both sides of the East Prong of Amite River, near Smithdale, Miss.: In 1840, he bought the following lands from John Wilson: The west half of the southeast quarter of section 30, t4n, r6e, containing 80 acres; the southwest quarter of section 30, t4n, r6e, containing 160 acres; and the northwest quarter of northeast quarter of section 31, t4n, r6e, containing 40 acres. In 1850 he bought from John Knight the northeast quarter of section 30, t4n, r6e, containing 160 acres. In 1853 he bought from the U. S. Government the southeast quarter of southwest quarter of section 25, t4n, r5e, containing 40 acres. In 1854 he bought the following lands from the U. S. Government: Southwest quarter of southeast quarter, and southeast quarter of southeast quarter of section 25, t4n, r5e, containing 80 acres; and the southeast quarter of the southeast quarter, and

---

† Copied from Amite County, Miss., records.

northeast quarter of southeast quarter of section 30, t4n, r6e, containing 80 acres. Also in 1854 he bought from Thomas Hewitt the southwest quarter of northwest quarter of section 30, t4n, r6e, containing 40 acres. From 1840 to 1854 he bought a grand total of 680 acres.

About the time of his death this land was divided up amongst his several children, who, in turn, divided their shares amongst their children. A large number of Hampton Burris's grand and great-grandchildren are living on this property today, and it is still in possession of his descendants.

THE LAST WILL AND TESTAMENT OF HAMPTON BURRIS

(Copied from Amite County, Miss., records)

In the name of God, Amen!

I, Hampton Burris, being sound in body and mind, do make and detail this to be my last will and testament, that is to say, after my death.

1st.   I will all of my just debts paid.

2nd.   I will and bequeath to my beloved wife, Mary M. Burris, all of real estate east of the east prong of the Amite River, to include my last place of residence; all of my personal property, consisting of horses, mules and cattle, hogs, sheep, household and kitchen furniture.

3rd.   I will that my wife, Mary M. Burris, to have the sole use and benefit of the above mentioned property during her natural life and then all of the above mentioned property to be divided between the heirs of her body, that she should have born her said husband, Hampton Burris, share and share alike.

4th.   I will that my grandson, Charles E. Gatlin, and granddaughter, Mary E. Gatlin, have each ten dollars, when they arrive at the age of 21 years, to be paid out of my estate, in addition to what their mother, Mary E. Gatlin, has already received.

5th.   I have given to four eldest children, to-wit: J. A. Burris, Sarah Jane Walker, J. F. Burris, and E. T. Burris all of real estate west of the East prong of Amite River as their distributive shares, as will be seen in a deed of conveyance.

6th.   I appoint my wife, Mary M. Burris, my executrix, of this will and testament.

7th.   I will that my wife, Mary M. Burris, not be required to execute any bond.

8th.   The word property mentioned in the 3rd clause before signing.

Given under by hand and seal this, the 23rd day of December 1873.

H. Burris

Jas. A. Jenkins
Israel Rogers

A. MARY ELIZABETH BURRIS.—Born in Amite County, Miss., Nov. 8, 1839. Married John Gatlin Jan. 12, 1858. Children: Mary Elizabeth, and Charlie (Sonny).

Mary Elizabeth Burris-Gatlin died June 1862, and was buried in the Burris Cemetery near Smithdale, Miss.

1. MARY ELIZABETH GATLIN.—Born in Mississippi. Married W. F. Ellzey. Children: Myrtis, Edgar John, Eric Watt, Rodger T., Grady, Smithy Vernon, Lois, Mamie Eudine, and William Clyde.

Mary Elizabeth Gatlin-Ellzey died Nov. 15, 1900, and was buried in the Silver Springs Church Cemetery. W. F. Ellzey died Apr. 8, 1945.

a. MYRTIS ELLZEY.—Born Dec. 24, 1884. Married Willie J. F. Fortenberry Jan. 6, 1905. Children: Eric, Lucille, Jackson V., Mildred, and William Harold.

Willie J. F. Fortenberry was born Nov. 18, 1879.

(1). ERIC FORTENBERRY.—Born July 24, 1906. Married Leone Bardwell. Children: Jimmie (dead), Jerry, Glyn, Betty Sue, and Charles.

(2). LUCILLE FORTENBERRY.—Born June 20, 1908. Unmarried.

(3). JACKSON V. FORTENBERRY.—Born Sept. 11, 1911. Married Clarence Bennett. Children: Anita.

(4). MILDRED FORTENBERRY.—Born Jan. 20, 1920. Married Johnnie Brumfield. Children: Harold Edwin.

(5). WILLIAM HAROLD FORTENBERRY.—Born Jan. 13, 1925. Married Selma Bennett. Children: Joe Kenneth.

b. EDGAR JOHN ELLZEY.—Born Dec. 15, 1885. Married, first, Bertha Tullos. Children: Evelyn Devoyx (born Aug. 30, 1912; died Sept. 14, 1923, and was buried in Bogalusa, La.), and LaVerne (born Dec. 14, 1914; married Belle Milner and has two children, Barbara and John).

Bertha Tullos-Ellzey died Sept. 20, 1920, and was buried in Bogalusa, La.

Edgar John Ellzey married, second, Lorene Tullos Feb. 3, 1922. Children: Audimese (born Dec. 14, 1924; died in 1925, and was buried in Bogalusa, La.), and Betty Gene (born Mar. 7, 1930; unmarried).

    c. ERIC WYATT ELLZEY.—Born June 3, 1888. Died Aug. 13, 1892, and was buried in the Silver Springs, Miss., Church Cemetery.

    d. RODGER T. ELLZEY.—Born Feb. 9, 1890. Married, first, Lottie Brumfield. Children: Bertile, Rodger T., Jr., Wayland, Cecil, Gertrude, Mary Ellen, Thomas, and Charles Lindy. Married, second, Monie Branch. No children. They live in Tylertown, Miss.

    (1). BERTILE ELLZEY.—Born in Pike County, Miss., May 10, 1913. Married Earl Fortenberry, son of W. T. and Clara (McElveen) Fortenberry, Aug. 27, 1932, in Tylertown, Miss. Children: Glynn (born Jan. 24, 1935), and Bobby Earl (born Nov. 13, 1936).

Earl Fortenberry was born Apr. 22, 1907.

    (2). RODGER T. ELLZEY, JR.—Born in Pike County, Miss., June 30, 1915. Married Edith Breland, daughter of L. E. and Otera (May) Breland, Apr. 1934, in Cedar Rapids, Iowa. Children: Patricia Ann (born Jan. 25, 1937), Betty Lou, and Nancy.

Rodger T. Ellzey, Jr., died May 7, 1945, and was buried in Tylertown, Miss.

    (3). WAYLAND ELLZEY.—Born in Walthall County, Miss., Mar. 7, 1918. Married Gwin Brumfield. Children: Susan (born Oct. 1, 1944), and Wayland Alan (born June 26, 1948). They live in Tylertown, Miss.

    (4). CECIL ELLZEY.—Born Sept. 11, 1919. Married Margie Nell Brumfield. No children.

    (5). GERTRUDE ELLZEY.—Born in Walthall County, Miss., Aug. 19, 1921. Married Ford McKenny, son of B. F. and Mary (Seal) McKenny. Children: Billy, Barbara Ellen, and Bobby Bert.

    (6). MARY ELLEN ELLZEY.—Born Nov. 3, 1923. Married James Carlise. Children: .... (Died in infancy).

    (7). THOMAS ELLZEY.—Born in Walthall County, Miss., Nov. 27, 1925. Unmarried.

    (8). CHARLES LINDY ELLZEY.—Born in Walthall County, Miss., June 26, 1928. Unmarried.

    e. GRADY ELLZEY.—Born Dec. 14, 1891. Married Bertha Fortenberry. Children: Wesley, Odean, Carroll, and Ellen.

(1). WESLEY ELLZEY.—Married Elaine Johnson. Children: Michael Wesley, and Randall Clyde.

They live in California.

(2). ODEAN ELLZEY.—Married Lamar Simmons. Children: Gayle Dean and Jimmie Lamar.

(3). CARROLL ELLZEY.—Married June Prescott. Children: Sherra Ann, and Daniel James.

(4). ELLEN ELLZEY.—Married James McDaniel. Children: James Conrad.

f. SMITHY VERNON ELLZEY.—Born Jan. 24, 1894. Married, first, Rose Wooster. Children: Vernon (born Jan. 1925), and Evelyn Sue (born in 1927). Married, second, Margeria Ferris. Children: Yvonne, Nancy Lee, and Margeria Ann.

They live in Rochester, N. Y.

g. LOIS ELLZEY.—Born Feb. 1, 1896. Married Laney L. Pope. Children: Mary Eleanor, Zelma, Nelson Winston, Hansford, Everett, Wilda, Clayton, and Maxine.

Laney L. Pope is a farmer and dairyman.

They live in Osyka, Miss.

(1). MARY ELEANOR POPE.—Born Sept. 11, 1916. Married Brown Simmons. Children: Sherra (age 15), Joyce (age 11), Bill (age 9), and Mavis (age 7).

Brown Simmons is a hotel clerk. They live in Baton Rouge, La.

(2). ZELMA POPE.—Born Aug. 29, 1918. Married Lloyd Roberts. Children: Tilford Lane (age 11), Jimmie (age 9), and John (age 7). Lloyd Roberts is a dairyman and electrician. They live in Summit, Miss.

(3). NELSON WINSTON POPE.—Born Sept. 14, 1920. Married Sybil McElveen. Children: .... (a daughter—died in infancy), and Sammy Nelson (age 4). Nelson Winston Pope is a salesman.

They live in Baton Rouge, La.

(4). HANSFORD POPE.—Born Jan. 6, 1923. Married Sadie Rose Robinson. Children: Sylvia Jo (age 10 mos.).

They live in Jackson, Miss.

(5). EVERETT POPE.—Born Mar. 18, 1925. Unmarried. Dairyman. Lives with his parents near Osyka, Miss.

(6). WILDA POPE.—Born Jan. 31, 1927. Married Eugene Rhodes. Children: Michael Eugene (age 4). Eugene Rhodes is a dairyman. They live in Magnolia, Miss.

(7). CLAYTON POPE.—Born June 3, 1930. Unmarried. Attending college.

(8). MAXINE POPE.—Born May 11, 1932. Unmarried. Working at the G.E. Plant in Jackson, Miss.

h. MAMIE EUDINE ELLZEY.—Born Apr. 15, 1897. Married Joe Minton. Children: Joseph Eugene, Bernell, Charles, and Marlan Clyde.

(1). JOSEPH EUGENE MINTON.—Born Mar. 21, 1923. Married Lucille Bruner. Children: Jimmie, and Edwin.

(2). BERNELL MINTON.—Born Apr. 28, 1926. Married Ralph Conerly. Children: Mary Elizabeth, and Ralph, Jr.

(3). CHARLES MINTON.—Born Mar. 4, 1929. Unmarried.

(4). MARLAN CLYDE MINTON.—Born Sept. 3, 1932. Unmarried.

i. WILLIAM CLYDE ELLZEY.—Born Nov. 4, 1900. Married Ruth Miller. Children: Marilyn (born Apr. 5, 1931), Carol Lee (born Apr. 9, 1933), and Sandra (born July 5, 1935). All of the children are unmarried.

They live in Camden, N. J.

2. CHARLIE (SONNY) GATLIN.—Died at the age of 7 years.

B. JOHN ADDISON BURRIS.—Born in Amite County, Miss., Dec. 5, 1842. Married Laura Toler. Children: Lois Saton, Mary Blanche, Willie, Lucius Toler, Lillie Mae, Jacob Oscar, Joe A., Hugh Chilson, Bryant Eugene, Laura Estella, Gertrude, John Hampton, and James M.

John Addison Burris was a prosperous farmer and a highly respected citizen of Amite County. He served in the Civil War under Gen. Joseph E. Johnson. He died Mar. 18, 1922, and was buried in the Mars Hill Cemetery. Laura Toler-Burris died in 1939, and was buried in the Mars Hill Cemetery.

1. LOIS SATON BURRIS.—Died in 1869.

2. MARY BLANCHE BURRIS.—Died in 1870. Was a member of the Mars Hill Baptist Church.

3. WILLIE BURRIS.—Born in Amite County, Miss., in 1870. Married Hattie Hewett. Children: Lillie Belle, Ollie, Thelma, Maureen, and Annie Hewett.

Hattie Hewett-Burris was born Feb. 5, 1871.

Willie Burris was a rural mail carrier for a number of years. He was buried in the Mars Hill Cemetery.

a. LILLIE BELLE BURRIS.—Born in Amite County, Miss., in 1892. Died in infancy.

b. OLLIE BURRIS.—Born in Smithdale, Miss., Oct. 19, 1894. Married Vertram C. Westbrook. Children: Lillie Belle, Olga Addie, Rema, Vertram C., Jr., Orien, Eunice, R. E., Nellie Rae, and Hattie Anita.

They live in Smithdale, Miss.

(1). LILLIE BELLE WESTBROOK.—Born in Smithdale, Miss., Mar. 10, 1914. Married George Temple. Children: Mary Olive (born Apr. 15, 1937).

(2). OLGA ADDIE WESTBROOK.—Born in Smithdale, Miss., Dec. 20, 1915. Married Roy Temple. Children: L. D. (born 1935), Annie Lethia (born 1937), Addie Laura (born 1938), Mavis and Grace (twins; born 1940).

(3). REMA WESTBROOK.—Born in Smithdale, Miss., June 30, 1919. Unmarried.

(4). VERTRAM C. WESTBROOK, JR.—Born in Smithdale, Miss., May 8, 1921. Married Eurlene Steele. Children: Dianne.
Vertram C. Westbrook, Jr., is a veteran of World War II.

(5). ORIEN WESTBROOK.—Unmarried. Is a veteran of World War II.

(6). EUNICE WESTBROOK.—Died young.

(7). R. E. WESTBROOK.—Unmarried.

(8). NELLIE RAE WESTBROOK.—Born in Smithdale, Miss., Dec. 5, 1930. Married James Trueman Hodge. Children: Alice Dell (born Sept. 30, 1945).

(9). HATTIE ANITA WESTBROOK.—Born in Smithdale, Miss., Sept. 30, 1917. Married Fosby Laird. Children: Glynn (born

1936), Willie V. (born 1938), Phillip W. (born 1939), Hilda Anita (born 1944), and Joe Estess (born 1948).

     c. THELMA BURRIS.—Born in Smithdale, Miss., Nov. 24, 1901. Married Corbet Edward Ratcliff. Children: Emily, William Benjamin, Ned, Corbet Edward, Jr., Joseph, and Paul Clyde.

Corbet Edward Ratcliff, Sr., died in 1930, at the age of 36.

     (1). EMILY RATCLIFF.—Born in Amite County, Miss. Married J. C. Kersten. Children: Jimmy (born 1942; dead).

Emily Ratcliff-Kersten was a graduate nurse. She and her son, Jimmy, were killed in an automobile accident in 1942. They were buried in the Mars Hill, Miss., Cemetery.

     (2). WILLIAM BENJAMIN RATCLIFF.—Born in Amite County, Miss., June 21, 1920. Married Zella Smith Dec. 1945. Children: Peggy (born Nov. 20, 1946), and William Edward (born Sept. 12, 1949).

William Benjamin Ratcliff is a veteran of World War II.

Zella Smith was born Sept. 3, 1924. They live in Baton Rouge, La.

     (3). NED RATCLIFF.—Born in Amite County, Miss., Feb. 9, 1923. Married Neva Stockhouse Feb. 24, 1945. Children: James Arthur (born May 18, 1949).

Neva Stockhouse was born Feb. 11, 1924.

Ned Ratcliff is a veteran of World War II.

     (4). CORBET EDWARD RATCLIFF, JR.—Born in Amite County, Miss., Nov. 19, 1925. Unmarried.

     (5). JOSEPH RATCLIFF.—Born in Amite County, Miss., Dec. 25, ... Unmarried.

     (6). PAUL CLYDE RATCLIFF.—Born in Amite County, Miss., Mar. 17, ... Unmarried.

     d. MAUREEN BURRIS.—Born in Smithdale, Miss., Apr. 14, 1908. Unmarried.

Maureen Burris is a registered nurse and lives in Hattiesburg, Miss.

     e. ANNIE HEWITT BURRIS.—Born in Smithdale, Miss., Aug. 27, 1911. Unmarried.

Annie Hewitt Burris is a school teacher. She is teaching at this time in the public schools of Hattiesburg, Miss.

4. LUCIUS TOLER BURRIS.—Born in Smithdale, Miss., Jan. 14, 1874. Married Willie Hudson Gunby June 11, 1902. Children: Jeannette Laura, Hubert Marvin, Eileen Errol, Lucius Harold, Dorothy Pearl, and Lionel Toler.

Willie Hudson Gunby-Burris died Dec. 20, 1941.

Lucius Toler Burris was a teacher in the public schools of Mississippi for many years. He was also a prosperous farmer. He is now retired and living in the Berwick Community of Amite County, Miss. He is a friend to every one.

a. JEANNETTE LAURA BURRIS.—Born in Amite County, Miss., July 23, 1903. Married John Buren Nobles Aug. 18, 1929. Children: Wilhelmina Rebecca (born Nov. 12, 1932). Jeannette Laura Burris-Nobles teaches mathematics in the Gloster, Miss., High School.

b. HUBERT MARVIN BURRIS.—Born in Amite County, Miss., Feb. 14, 1905. Married Eleanor James Mar. 7, 1930. Children: Marvin Eugene (born Apr. 3, 1933), and Lilliace Ann (born Apr. 23, 1935).

Hubert Marvin Burris is a veteran of World War II.

c. EILEEN ERROL BURRIS.—Born in Amite County, Miss., Nov. 30, 1907. Married Leland Lyle Stokes Aug. 30, 1934. Children: Leland Lyle, Jr (born July 1, 1937), James Lucius (born Feb. 2, 1940), and Richard Wayne (born Sept. 2, 1946).

d. LUCIUS HAROLD BURRIS.—Born in Amite County, Miss., Dec. 8, 1910. Married Adelyn Lavender Sept. 1, 1940. Children: Betty Ann (born June 8, 1945), Gloria (born Mar. 28, 1948), and Lucius Harold, Jr. (born Nov. 20, 1949).

Lucius Harold Burris is a veteran of World War II.

e. DOROTHY PEARL BURRIS.—Born in Amite County, Miss., Nov. 15, 1915. Married Fred Dixon Robertson June 28, 1942. Children: Fred Dixon, Jr. (born Sept. 23, 1946), William Lucius (born Sept. 28, 1949), and James Lee (born Apr. 28, 1952).

They live in Gloster, Miss.

f. LIONEL TOLER BURRIS.—Born in Amite County, Miss., July 3, 1921. Married Lillian Hendrix Nov. 17, 1947. Children: Sherry Lynn (adopted) (born July 24, 1949).

Lionel Toler Burris is a veteran of World War II. His service record follows: Inducted into service Aug. 20, 1943, as private. Served as Technician Fifth Class with the 1308th Army Engineers. Did demolition work. Participated in the following battles: Northern France, Ardennes, and Rhineland. Served in the Pacific Area also. Discharged Jan. 10, 1946.

5. LILLIE MAE BURRIS.—Born in Amite County, Miss., Jan. 3, 1876. Married William Benjamin Dickerson Feb. 27, 1902. Children: Hilton Burris, Henry Addison, Willie Mae, Benjamin Howard, and Frank C.

William Benjamin Dickerson died Jan. 14, 1946.

Lillie Mae Burris-Dickerson, in her girlhood days, was one of a charming set of girls. She had a sunny disposition and a kind word for every one. She made a splendid housewife. They live in Hattiesburg, Miss.

a. HILTON BURRIS DICKERSON.—Born Apr. 6, 1903. Married Margaret Law of Atlanta, Ga., Dec. 3, 1938. Children: Beverly Jean (born Jan. 3, 1940), and Hilton Burris, Jr. (born July 6, 1943).

b. HENRY ADDISON DICKERSON.—Born Feb. 26, 1906. Married Margaret Blanche Leap Aug. 17, 1935. Children: Margaret Scott (born Apr. 23, 1940), and Jane Addison (born Aug. 3, 1943).

c. WILLIE MAE DICKERSON.—Born Feb. 26, 1909. Married Fant Ewing Hulsey Aug. 7, 1929. Children: Mikell Patricia (born Aug. 28, 1935), and Fant Ewing, Jr. (born Aug. 15, 1941).

d. BENJAMIN HOWARD DICKERSON.—Born in Hattiesburg, Miss., Aug. 8, 1911. Married Elizabeth Hassett Jan. 31, 1942. Children: Jeffery Hilton (born Dec. 15, 1942), and Janet Susan (born July 11, 1945).

e. FRANK C. DICKERSON.—Born Jan. 3, 1915. Married Doris Roberts Apr. 10, 1942. Children: Judith Lynn (born Feb. 2, 1943).

Frank C. Dickerson is a veteran of World War II.

6. JACOB OSCAR BURRIS.—Born in Smithdale, Miss., in 1878. Married, first, Stella Patterson. Children: .... (a son), Annie Idelle, James Oscar, Fay Avanelle, Hugh Benton, and Thomas Donald.

Stella Patterson-Burris was born in 1891. She died in 1936, and was buried in the Mars Hill, Miss., Cemetery.

Jacob Oscar Burris married, second, Ethel Wilkinson-Burris, widow of Julius Burris, deceased. No children. Jacob Oscar Burris

William Addison Burris
One of the two first progenitors of the Burris name in Washington Parish (La.)

Mrs. William Addison Burris (seated)

With her are three of her sons, one grandson-in-law, two daughters-in-law, two grandchildren and three great grandchildren.

was a rural mail carrier, but he is now retired on a pension. He is a leading citizen of the Mars Hill Community.

a. .... (a son).—Born in Smithdale, Miss., Jan. 18, 1912. Died Apr. 23, 1912.

b. ANNIE IDELLE BURRIS.—Born Oct. 16, 1909. Married E. M. Newman. Children: James, and Tommie. They live in Cheyenne, Wyo.

(1). JAMES NEWMAN.—Born in Chicago, Ill., Apr. 11, 1931. Married Sammie Harris Sept. 2, 1950, in Cheyenne, Wyo. Children: Terry Lee. They live in Cheyenne, Wyo.

(2). TOMMIE NEWMAN.—Born in Chicago, Ill., Aug. 22, 1933.

c. JAMES OSCAR BURRIS.—Born in Smithdale, Miss., Feb. 11, 1913. Married Anne Ruth King, June 30, 1939. Children: Louise Ann (born Oct. 1, 1940), and James Oscar, Jr. (born Apr. 21, 1944). They live in Hattiesburg, Miss.

d. FAY AVANELLE BURRIS.—Born in Smithdale, Miss., July 8, 1915. Married Burton Coulter Sept. 2, 1940. Children: Frances Ann (born Sept. 21, 1943). They live in Chicago, Ill.

e. HUGH BENTON BURRIS.—Born in Smithdale, Miss., Sept. 27, 1918. Married Margaret Catherine Mulcay June 28, 1942. Children: Marsha Lynn (born Dec. 25, 1943), Hugh Benton, Jr. (born Mar. 1947), and Sue Ellen (born in Sunny Vale, Calif., July 28, 1951). They live in Sunny Vale, Calif.

Hugh Benton Burris enlisted in the U. S. Navy in August, 1941, during World War II, and served in the European Area. He is still in the Navy and is a lieutenant.

f. THOMAS DONALD BURRIS.—Born in Smithdale, Miss., Aug. 22, 1922. Married Miriam Ott Dec. 20, 1944. No children.

Thomas Donald Burris enlisted in the U. S. Naval Air Corps in July 1943, and served in the Pacific Area during World War II. He was discharged in 1945.

7. JOE A. BURRIS.—Born in Smithdale, Miss., in 1883. Married Madge Hall May 26, 1909. Children: Burmah, Barbara, Joe A., Jr., Malcolm, and Mary.

Joe A. Burris, Sr., was a teacher in the public schools of Mississippi for many years. He served one term as county superintendent of schools of Amite County, Mississippi. He is operating a business of his own now in Clinton, Miss.

a. BURMAH BURRIS.—Born in Mississippi in 1910. Unmarried.

b. BARBARA BURRIS.—Born in Mississippi in 1912. Married Jack Ritchey in 1940. Children: Jackie, Jr. (born in 1941), Joe (born in 1943), Jimmie (born in 1945), and Jerry (born in 1947).

c. JOE A. BURRIS, JR.—Born in Mississippi in 1915. Married Katherine Rogers in 1942. Children: Martha Madge (born in 1947). Joe A. Burris, Jr., is a veteran of World War II.

d. MALCOLM BURRIS.—Born in Mississippi in 1918. Married Sarah Prichard Dec. 1946. No children.

Dr. Malcolm Burris is a veteran of World War II. He is now a member of the staff of Ochsner Clinic of New Orleans, La.

e. MARY BURRIS.—Born in Mississippi in 1918. Married Albert Green in 1937. Children: Albert, Jr. (born in 1938), and Burmah Kay (born in 1943).

8. HUGH CHILSON BURRIS.—Born in Smithdale, Miss., July 11, 1886. Married Edna Earle Gordon Dec. 26, 1919. Children: Gordon Douglas, Anna Loyd, and Betty Claire.

Hugh Chilson Burris is a teacher in the Mars Hill (Miss.) School.* He is a member of the Mars Hill Baptist Church and is a prosperous farmer of the Mars Hill Community.

a. GORDON DOUGLAS BURRIS.—Born in Smithdale, Miss., Sept. 11, 1920. Married Mary Scavelli Nov. 28, 1947. Children: Gordon John (born Oct. 19, 1948).

b. ANNA LOYD BURRIS.—Born in Smithdale, Miss., Jan. 4, 1922. Married Floyd C. Watts Dec. 11, 1948. Children: Anna Llewelynn (born Nov. 9, 1949).

c. BETTY CLAIRE BURRIS.—Born in Smithdale, Miss., Nov. 14, 1928. Married Daniel Orthillo Lewman June 9, 1948. No children.

9. BRYANT EUGENE BURRIS.—Born in Smithdale, Miss. Married, first, Retha Branch Dec. 23, 1915. Children: Wilda and Hilda (twins).

Married, second, Eva Tynes, Apr. 20, 1930. No children.

---

*Elected assessor of Amite County, Miss., in 1951.

Retha Branch-Burris died Nov. 25, 1918.

Bryant Eugene Burris served for a while as rural mail carrier. Before this he was engaged in farming. He lives in Liberty, Miss.

     a. WILDA BURRIS.—Born in Amite County, Miss., Nov. 22, 1918. Died July 24, 1938. She was Hilda Burris's twin sister.

     b. HILDA BURRIS.—Born in Amite County, Miss., Nov. 22, 1918. Married Alfred Bogen, Jr., Aug. 31, 1941. Children: Alfred III (born Mar. 28, 1947), and Vesta Ann (born in Baton Rouge, La., Aug. 31, 1950).

They live in Baton Rouge, La.

     10. LAURA ESTELLA BURRIS.—Born in Smithdale, Miss., Sept. 7, 1890. Married Fenton Lee Kenna Nov. 4, 1922. Children: William Burris, Miriam Evelyn, and Fenton Lee, Jr.

Laura Estella Burris-Kenna died in 1938, and was buried in the Mars Hill, Miss., Cemetery. She was John Addison Burris's youngest child.

     a. WILLIAM BURRIS KENNA.—Born in Summit, Miss., Apr. 30, 1924. Married Joyce Terrell in 1946. No children.

William Burris Kenna served three years in the U. S. Air Corps during World War II. He was a corporal and radio technician.

     b. MIRIAM EVELYN KENNA.—Born in Summit, Miss., Feb. 4, 1927. Married Gordon Covington, Jr., Oct. 15, 1948. No children.

Miriam Evelyn Kenna-Covington is a graduate of L. S. U.

     c. FENTON LEE KENNA, JR.—Born in Summit, Miss., Mar. 25, 1920. Unmarried. Is attending college now.

     11. GERTRUDE BURRIS.—Born in Smithdale, Miss., Feb. 19, 1872. Married Willie J. Branch Dec. 18, 1900. No children.

Gertrude Burris-Branch is a housewife. She is one of the finest characters in the Hampton Burris Family. She lives near Smithdale, Miss.

     12. JOHN HAMPTON BURRIS.—Born in Smithdale, Miss., May 3, 1881. Married Fannie Alford Jan. 15, 1911. Children: Hazel Juanita, Julius Addison, and Wilton Enoch.

John Hampton Burris was a prosperous farmer, and one of the leading citizens of the Thompson, Miss., Community. He was also one of the leading members of the Mars Hill, Miss., Baptist Church. He died in 1950 and was buried in the Mars Hill Cemetery.

a. HAZEL JUANITA BURRIS.—Born Nov. 29, 1911. Married George M. Cain Oct. 13, 1934. Children: Patricia Kirk (born May 2, 1936), and George Douglas (born June 10, 1938). They live near McCall Creek, Miss.

b. JULIUS ADDISON BURRIS.—Born Oct. 14, 1915. Unmarried.

Julius Addison Burris is a veteran of World War II. He is now an instructor in a G. I. Training School. He is a very capable young man.

c. WILTON ENOCH BURRIS.—Born Dec. 12, 1921. He was killed in action June 15, 1943, during World War II, and was first buried in Port Moresby, New Guinea. After the war, he was brought home and buried in the Mars Hill, Miss., Cemetery Mar. 10, 1948.

13. JAMES M. BURRIS.—Born in Amite County, Miss., Mar. 23, 1880. Died June 6, 1880.

C. WILLIAM LOUIS BURRIS.—Born in Smithdale, Miss., Sept. 22, 1844. Buried in the Burris Cemetery, near Smithdale, Miss. Was a member of the Mars Hill Baptist Church.

D. JACOB FLEET BURRIS.—Born in Amite County, Miss., Aug. 28, 1848. Married, first, Luretta Swearingen May 6, 1868. No children. Married, second, Amazon Cain Nov. 4, 1869. Children: Mollie E., Hardy H., Frank Horace, Sarah Alice, Luretta E., Amazon Rebecca, William A., Laura Lenorah, Dempsey Eddie, Luna Hall, Lula Ball, Jacob Fleet, Jr., and Ruby Ray.

Luretta Swearingen-Burris died Jan. 16, 1869, and was buried in Smithdale, Miss. Amazon Cain-Burris died Jan. 3, 1932.

Jacob Fleet Burris died June 27, 1911, and was buried in the Concord Church Cemetery in Franklin County, Miss. He was a farmer. He was a member of Mars Hill Baptist Church.

1. MOLLIE E. BURRIS.—Born Sept. 13, 1870. Married Cero Jones, son of Pink and Annie Jones, Jan. 21, 1892, in Franklin County, Miss. Children: Eslie, Lillian Lozaine, Emma Julia, and John.

Cero Jones was born in Franklin County, Miss., Mar. 29, 1868. He died Nov. 15, 1931, and was buried in McComb, Miss.

Mollie E. Burris-Jones died Feb. 29, 1924, and was buried in McComb, Miss.

a. ESLIE JONES.—Died May 27, 1946. Buried in McComb, Miss.

b. LILLIAN LOZAINE JONES.—Born in Franklin County, Miss., July 19, 1893. Married Dewitt Talmadge Foster, son of Thomas and Mary Foster, Sept. 10, 1911, in McComb, Miss. Children: Ray Louie, William Grady, Lucy Mae, John Talmadge, Lillian Emily, Clifton Cero, Marion Dewitt, and Lois Frances.

Dewitt Talmadge Foster was born in Attala County, Miss., May 12, 1888.

They live in Baton Rouge, La.

(1). RAY LOUIE FOSTER.—Born in McComb, Miss., Oct. 17, 1912. Married Gladys Lucille Myers, daughter of Jesse Myers, May 9, 1931, in McComb, Miss. Children: Edwin Earl (born May 23, 1932; served in the U. S. Army Air Force two and one-half years, has re-enlisted as private and is in Japan. Married to Mary Olivia Nicolosi), Charles Ray (born Aug. 4, 1936), and Nelda Kay (born July 6, 1943).

Gladys Lucille Myers-Foster was born in McComb, Miss., Mar. 9, 1912.

They live in Baton Rouge, La.

(2). WILLIAM GRADY FOSTER.—Born in McComb, Miss., Dec. 8, 1914. Married Lois Thelma Boyd, daughter of Jefferson and Polly Boyd Feb. 8, 1935, in Magnolia, Miss. No children.

Lois Thelma Boyd-Foster was born in Bogue Chitto, Miss., Mar. 22, 1902.

William Grady Foster served in the U. S. Navy, in the 129th Naval Construction Battalion, from July 1, 1943, to Mar. 25, 1945, as Chief Carpenter's Mate. He was stationed in the Hawaiian and Philippine Islands.

(3). LUCY MAE FOSTER.—Born in Monroe, La., Sept. 21, 1917. Died July 24, 1918, and buried in Franklin County, Miss.

(4). JOHN TALMADGE FOSTER.—Born in McComb, Miss., Mar. 14, 1920. Married Ellen Erwin, daughter of Molly and Ben Erwin, in 1936, in McComb, Miss. Children: John Talmadge, Jr., and Jerry Lynden.

John Talmadge Foster, Sr., served three years in the armed forces of the U. S. during World War II. He served in Camp Croft, S. C., and got his foot badly wounded. He is now in the Veterans' Hospital, Jackson, Miss.

He lives in McComb, Miss.

(5). LILLIAN EMILY FOSTER.—Born in Monroe, La., May 17, 1922. Died Jan. 24, 1924, and was buried in McComb, Miss.

(6). CLIFTON CERO FOSTER.—Born in McGehee, Ark., Jan. 9, 1927. Married Margaret Fern Gunby, daughter of S. W. Gunby, July 11, 1947, in Baton Rouge, La. Children: Larry Dana.

Margaret Fern Gunby-Foster was born in Centreville, Miss., Mar. 23, 1919.

Clifton Cero Foster served in the U. S. Navy, aboard U. S. S. Cross, as Gunner's Mate, Second Class, from Jan. 28, 1944, to May 27, 1946. He served in the Asiatic-Pacific Theatre. He lives in Baton Rouge, La.

(7). MARION DEWITT FOSTER.—Born in McComb, Miss., Nov. 18, 1932. Unmarried. Lives in McComb, Miss.

(8). LOIS FRANCES FOSTER.—Born in McComb, Miss., Dec. 10, 1934. Unmarried. Lives in McComb, Miss.

c. EMMA JULIA JONES.—Born in McComb, Miss., Jan. 22, 1898. Married Frank A. Williams, son of Alex D. Williams, July 14, 1916, in Summit, Miss. Children: Albert Luther, Frank Eslie, Fannie Lee, Bryant Jefferson, Mary Emily, Frances Ann, and Linda Sue.

Frank A. Williams was born in Raymond, Miss., Dec. 21, 1895. He is a carpenter and lives in Baton Rouge, La.

(1) ALBERT LUTHER WILLIAMS.—Born in Monroe, La., July 8, 1917. Married, first, Anna Mae Starr, daughter of Gilbert D. Starr, Feb. 22, 1941, in Woodville, Miss. Children: Linda Yvonne (born Aug. 15, 1942), and .... (a son, born dead Apr. 5, 1944). Married, second, Elizabeth Ruth Grigsby, daughter of Sam Grigsby, July 3, 1947. Children: Jack Melvin (born June 16, 1950).

Anna Mae Starr-Williams died Apr. 5, 1944, when the baby son was born, and was buried in Roselawn Cemetery, Baton Rouge, La.

Elizabeth Ruth Grigsby-Williams was born in Dallas, Texas.

Albert Luther Williams served in the U. S. Navy, Seabees, during World War II. He was stationed at Pearl Harbor, also in Japan and numerous other South Pacific islands. He lives in Baton Rouge, La.

(2). FRANK ESLIE WILLIAMS.—Born in McComb, Miss., Dec. 18, 1918. Married Edna Leoda Roth, daughter of James H. Roth, Oct. 24, 1941, in St. Francisville, La. Children: Frank Eslie, Jr. (age

7 years), Albert Louis (age 5 years), Ronald Charles (age 2 years), and Richard Earl (age 1 month).

Edna Leoda Roth-Williams was born in St. Francisville, La., Oct. 18, 1917.

Frank Eslie Williams is a carpenter, and lives in Baton Rouge, La.

(3). FANNIE LEE WILLIAMS.—Born May 8, 1921. Died May 27, 1921.

(4). BRYANT JEFFERSON WILLIAMS.—Born in McComb, Miss., Aug. 4, 1922. Married Alma Bell George, daughter of Earnest George, Dec. 30, 1942, in Baton Rouge, La. Children: John Dempsey (born Sept. 28, 1943), and Bryant Jefferson, Jr. (born Nov. 17, 1946).

Bryant Jefferson Williams served in the U. S. Navy, in the South Pacific, during World War II. He is a carpenter. They live in Deerford, La.

(5). MARY EMILY WILLIAMS.—Born in Tchula, Miss., June 30, 1928. Married Louis D. Cunningham, son of Mary Cunningham, Nov. 16, 1946, in Baton Rouge, La. No children.

Louis D. Cunningham was born in Kewanne, Ill., Oct. 8, 1916. He served in the U. S. Army, in the European Theatre, during World War II. He was wounded six times. He is now in the U. S. Air Corps, with T/Sgt. rating, and is stationed in the Burgerstrom Air Base, Austin, Tex.

(6). FRANCES ANN WILLIAMS.—Born Sept. 4, 1936.

(7). LINDA SUE WILLIAMS.—Born Nov. 29, 1940.

d. JOHN JONES.—

2. HARDY H. BURRIS.—Born in Franklin County, Miss., Mar. 9, 1872. Dead. Buried in the Concord Church Cemetery in Franklin County.

3. FRANK HORACE BURRIS.—Born in Franklin County, Miss., Dec. 31, 1873. Married Inez Jones Feb. 6, 1901. Children: Velma Lucille, Frank Rupert, Mabel Ivenora, Eugene Quitman, and Jacob Hampton.

Frank Horace Burris died in 1938, was buried in the Concord Church Cemetery in Franklin County. His wife lives in McCall Creek, Miss.

a. VELMA LUCILLE BURRIS.—Born in Franklin County, Miss., Feb. 27, 1903. Married Clarence Arnold Nov. 11, 1939. No children.

They live in Fayette, Miss.

b. FRANK RUPERT BURRIS.—Born in Franklin County, Miss., Nov. 6, 1904. Married Fay Brandon May 11, 1943. Children: Paul Brandon (born Dec. 24, 1943; died Dec. 25, 1943).

Frank Rupert Burris entered the armed forces of the U. S. May 18, 1942, during World War II. He was discharged Mar. 5, 1943. He lives near Baker, La.

c. MABEL IVENORA BURRIS.—Born in Franklin County, Miss. Never married.

d. EUGENE QUITMAN BURRIS.—Born in Franklin County, Miss., Aug. 6, 1909. Married Lola Jordan Dec. 13, 1929. Children: Eugene Quitman, Jr. (born Sept. 13, 1930), Mary Fay, and Lola Annette (born Feb. 13, 1935). Eugene Quitman Burris lives in Baton Rouge, La.

e. JACOB HAMPTON BURRIS.—Born in Franklin County, Miss., Sept. 18, 1912. Married Jimmie Orenne Mathews. Children: Russell Winford (born Oct. 11, 1935), and Relda Ann (born Mar. 15, 1939). Jacob Hampton Burris lives in Baker, La.

4. SARAH ALICE BURRIS.—Born in Franklin County, Miss., Feb. 21, 1876. Married Virgil Chisholm Mar. 10, 1901. Children: William Jewel (born Dec. 5, 1902; dead).

5. LURETTA E. BURRIS.—Born in Franklin County, Miss., May 25, 1878. Died Jan. 9, 1897. Buried in the Concord Church Cemetery, Franklin County.

6. AMAZON REBECCA BURRIS.—Born in Franklin County, Miss., Feb. 12, 1880. Married, first, Gus Cotton. Children: Jacob, Asa, and Rayford. Married, second, ... Poole.

They live in Baton Rouge, La.

7. WILLIAM A. BURRIS.—Born in Franklin County, Miss., July 22, 1881. Married Lillie Cotton Jan. 15, 1905. Children: Hardy, Claude, Lizzie, Leon, Ammie Lottie, Jim, Laura Alyce, Nolan, and John.

William A. Burris is a farmer and lives near McCall Creek, Miss.
a. HARDY BURRIS.—Born in Franklin County, Miss., Dec. 2,

1905. Married Nova Smith Jan. 14, 1933. Children: Nelda Jean (born Oct. 21, 1936), and Toba Faye (born July 23, 1939).

Hardy Burris is a farmer and lives near McCall Creek, Miss.

b. CLAUDE BURRIS.—Born in Franklin County, Miss., Sept. 22, 1907. Married Pauline McManus Apr. 10, 1937. Children: Aaron James (born Dec. 10, 1937; died Dec. 23, 1938).

Claude Burris is a farmer and lives near McCall Creek, Miss.

c. LIZZIE BURRIS.—Born in Franklin County, Miss., Feb. 17, 1909. Married C. C. Martin Mar. 8, 1925. Children: Leroy, and Earl. They live in McCall Creek, Miss.

(1). LEROY MARTIN.—Born in Franklin County, Miss., Jan. 1, 1926. Married Helen Cupit Apr. 9, 1946. No children.

Leroy Martin served in the U. S. Army as corporal during World War II. He is a farmer and lives near McCall Creek, Miss.

(2). EARL MARTIN.—Born in Franklin County, Miss., Aug. 25, 1932. Is a member of the U. S. Air Force, and is stationed at Chanute Field, Ill.

d. LEON BURRIS.—Born in Franklin County, Miss., Dec. 4, 1910. Married Gladys Arnold Jan. 1, 1931. Children: Bobbie Nell (born June 21, 1933), Carolyn Joyce (born Jan. 11, 1939), and Robert Leon (born Sept. 4, 1943). Leon Burris is a farmer and lives near McCall Creek, Miss.

e. AMMIE LOTTIE BURRIS.—Born in McCall Creek, Miss., Oct. 9, 1912. Married Thomas Eli Cupit, son of Leon L. Cupit, Apr. 20, 1934, in McCall Creek, Miss. Children: Claudell (age 14), Clayton Eli (age 10), Doris Glen (age 8), W. L. (age 4), and Nina Dale (age 2).

Thomas Eli Cupit was born in McCall Creek, Miss., Dec. 21, 1913. He is a farmer, and lives in McCall Creek, Miss.

f. JIM BURRIS.—Born in Franklin County, Miss., Feb. 9, 1914. Married Louise McGehee Dec. 8, 1936. Children: Jimmie (born Oct. 6, 1941). Jim Burris is a farmer and lives near McCall Creek, Miss.

g. LAURA ALYCE BURRIS.—Born in McCall Creek, Miss., Feb. 9, 1916. Married Warren Aaron Porter, son of Ella Porter, Apr. 27, 1935, in Summit, Miss. Children: Jo Nita (age 14), Tama Rea (age 12), Rodney Earl (age 9), LaVelle (age 7), Patsy Ella (age 4), and Warren Aaron, Jr. (age 2½).

Warren Aaron Porter, Sr. was born in Bude, Miss., Apr. 25, 1915. He is a carpenter, and lives near Meadville, Miss.

h. NOLAN BURRIS.—Born in Franklin County, Miss., Feb. 7, 1918. Married DeLores Pevey June 4, 1943. Children: Nolan Dee (born May 10, 1944), Kenney Bee (born Apr. 16, 1946), and Bruce Darryl (born Aug. 18, 1950).

Nolan Burris served in the armed forces of the U. S. during World War II, and held the rank of a sergeant. He has re-enlisted and holds the rank of T/Sgt. He is stationed in Biloxi, Miss.

i. JOHN BURRIS.—Born in Franklin County, Miss., Aug. 21, 1921. Married Golda Mae Smith Dec. 20, 1944. Children: Linda Sue (born Sept. 18, 1946). John Burris lives in McCall Creek, Miss., and does public work.

8. LAURA LENORAH BURRIS.—Born in Franklin County, Miss., Nov. 13, 1883. Married Clem Mullins. Children: William Prentiss, Eddie Fleet, Ray, Caroll, Lola Lenorah, Clement Leroy, Percy Hubert, and Rita Victoria.

They live in McCall Creek, Miss.

a. WILLIAM PRENTISS MULLINS.—Born in Franklin County, Miss., Jan. 28, 1906. Married Pearl Nesbit in 1936. Children: Carolyn E. (born in 1938), and William Prentiss, Jr. (born in 1947).

William Prentiss Mullens lives in Memphis, Tenn., and does public work.

b. EDDIE FLEET MULLINS.—Born in Franklin County, Miss., Apr. 25, 1908. Married, first, Ruby Laird Jan. 25, 1925. Children: Analo (married Merle Scott, and has two children, Merle, Jr., and Sue (born July 16, 1949), and Gus.

After Ruby's death, Eddie Fleet Mullins married Retha Ann Freeman Nov. 10, 1935. Children: LaNell and Eddie Glenn.

Eddie Fleet Mullins is a carpenter. He lives in McCall Creek, Miss.

c. RAY MULLINS.—Born in Franklin County, Miss., Jan. 17, 1911. Married Adee Almeda Lewis. Children: Billie Ray.

Ray Mullins is a plumber and lives in McCall Creek, Miss.

d. CARROLL MULLINS.—Born in Franklin County, Miss., June 8, 1913. Unmarried. Blind. Lives in McCall Creek, Miss.

e. LOLA LENORAH MULLINS.—Born in Franklin County,

Miss., July 30, 1915. Married Claude Quitman Bowlin. Children: Barbara Ann (born Apr. 2, 1936), Claude Quitman, Jr. (born Nov. 23, 1939), and Clement Wiley (born Nov. 6, 1946).

Claude Quitman Bowlin was born Jan. 4, 1909. He is a salesman for the Standard Coffee Co., and lives in Monticello, Miss.

f. CLEMENT LEROY MULLINS.—Born in Franklin County, Miss., June 12, 1917. Married Willie Mae Wallace July 24, 1941. Children: Clement Leroy, Jr. (born Aug. 25, 1942), Danny Wallace (born Nov. 24, 1946), and Harry Miller (born Sept. 29, 1951).

Willie Mae Wallace-Mullins was born Dec. 22, 1923.

Clement Leroy Mullins lives in Quentin, Miss., and does public work.

g. PERCY HUBERT MULLINS.—Born in Franklin County, Miss., Sept. 26, 1919. Unmarried. Lives in Memphis, Tenn., and does public work.

h. RITA VICTORIA MULLINS.—Born in Franklin County, Miss., Oct. 23, 1922. Married Raleigh Henley in 1941. Children: Raleigh, Jr. (born in 1946), and Richard Paul (born Jan. 9, 1951).

They live in Memphis, Tenn.

9. DEMPSEY EDDIE BURRIS.—Born in Franklin County, Miss., Jan. 23, 1886. Married Louvinia Elizabeth Coward Dec. 21, 1904. Children: Hazel Edith, William Linton, Jacob Fleet III, John Dempsey, James Ford, Aaron Henderson, and Hugh Vance. They live near Auburn, Miss.

a. HAZEL EDITH BURRIS.—Born in Franklin County, Miss., Sept. 14, 1907. Died Dec. 21, 1910.

b. WILLIAM LINTON BURRIS.—Born in Franklin County, Miss., July 9, 1909. Married Josie Mae Henderson Dec. 25, 1932. Children: William Dempsey (born Nov. 5, 1933), Mary Frances (born Oct. 2, 1935), and Joy Charldene (born June 12, 1948).

They live in Lucien, Miss.

c. JACOB FLEET BURRIS III.—Born in Franklin County, Miss., July 23, 1911. Died June 1912.

d. JOHN DEMPSEY BURRIS.—Born in Franklin County, Miss., Dec. 16, 1912. Married Fern Lewis Jan. 23, 1939. Children: Louvinia Odessa (born Dec. 21, 1940), and Jacqueline (born May 21, 1944).

They live in Florence, Miss.

e. JAMES FORD BURRIS.—Born in Franklin County, Miss., May 11, 1916. Married Mary Ileen Wells Oct. 21, 1939. Children: Juanita Faye (born in McComb, Miss., Dec. 12, 1940), and Pollard Ford (born in McComb, Miss., Dec. 5, 1944). James Ford Burris is a railway flagman, and lives in McComb, Miss.

f. AARON HENDERSON BURRIS.—Born in Franklin County, Miss., Feb. 17, 1920. Married Maidee Dillon. Children: Linda Dianne (born Feb. 15, 1949). They live in Natchez, Miss.

g. HUGH VANCE BURRIS.—Born in Franklin County, Miss., Dec. 2, 1924. Married Flora Mae Hambright Apr. 12, 1947. Children: Dew Wayne (born Nov. 20, 1950). They live in Monroe, La.

10. LUNA HALL BURRIS.—Born in Franklin County, Miss., Dec. 1, 1887. Married Holmes Smith Dec. 24, 1914. Children: Joseph Glen, Lennie Lenora, Sarah Dixie, and Ruby Lorelle.

Holmes Smith works for the Miss. Highway Department.

They live in Auburn, Miss.

a. JOSEPH GLEN SMITH.—Born in Franklin County, Miss., July 7, 1917. Married Margaret Baudauf Dec. 7, 1946. Children: Glenda Kay (born May 3, 1950). Joseph Glen Smith lives in Baton Rouge, La., and works for the telephone company there.

b. LENNIE LENORA SMITH.—Born in Franklin County, Miss., Nov. 10, 1919. Married Paul J. Freeman Dec. 21, 1942. No children.

They live in Brookhaven, Miss.

c. SARAH DIXIE SMITH.—Born in Franklin County, Miss., Apr. 23, 1922. Married Guy Richard Lovely May 5, 1944. Children: Guy Richard, Jr. (born May 17, 1945).

They live in Albuquerque, N. Mex.

d. RUBY LORELLE SMITH.—Born in Franklin County, Miss., Oct. 11, 1925. Married Robert Rodney LeBlanc Jan. 3, 1948. Children: Peggy Lynn (born Dec. 17, 1948). They live in Crowley, La.

11. LULA BALL BURRIS.—Born in Franklin County, Miss., Dec. 1, 1887. Married G. W. Lewis May 8, 1908. No children.

G. W. Lewis is a Primitive Baptist minister. Lula Ball Burris-

Lewis is a twin sister of Luna Hall Burris-Smith. They live in Auburn, Miss.

12. JACOB FLEET BURRIS, JR.—Born in Franklin County, Miss., Jan. 1, 1892. Married Lizzie Ratcliff July 12, 1912. Children: Rettie, Nellie, Addison, Albia, and Andrew.

Jacob Fleet Burris, Jr. is a farmer and lives in Franklin County.

a. RETTIE BURRIS.—Born in Franklin County, Miss., Apr. 18, 1913. Married Willie Watson Dec. 5, 1942. No children. They live in Brookhaven, Miss.

b. NELLIE BURRIS.—Born in Franklin County, Miss., Nov. 9, 1914. Married Meredith Corban Jan. 25, 1947. Children: Mary Elizabeth (born Nov. 14, 1947). They live in McCall Creek, Miss.

c. ADDISON BURRIS.—Born in Franklin County, Miss., Apr. 5, 1916. Unmarried. Is a farmer and lives near McCall Creek, Miss.

d. ALBIA BURRIS.—Born in Franklin County, Miss., Oct. 4, 1918. Married Monte Allred Oct. 8, 1938. Children: William Earl (born Sept. 10, 1939), Margie Louine (born Oct. 13, 1943), and James Randel (born Sept. 18, 1947). Albia Burris lives in Baton Rouge, La., and works in the Ethyl Plant as a machine operator.

e. ANDREW BURRIS.—Born in Franklin County, Miss., Aug. 6, 1929. Married Marilee Crumbly. Children: Andrew David (born June 10, 1950). Andrew Burris lives in Baton Rouge, La., and works for the Baton Rouge Creamery.

13. RUBY RAY BURRIS.—Born in Franklin County, Miss., Dec. 17, 1893. Married William Henderson Coward of Lincoln County, Miss., Apr. 18, 1914. Children: ...., Laurine Elmo, Willie Ray, Lula Ellen, Mavis Burris, and Norma Vernell. They live near Auburn, Miss.

a. ....—Born in Franklin County, Miss., Sept. 8, 1915. Died in infancy.

b. LAURINE ELMO COWARD.—Born in Franklin County, Miss., Feb. 23, 1917. Married Elmo McGehee Nov. 14, 1939. Children: Relda Joyce (born July 27, 1942), Wilda (born Aug. 30, 1944), Margie Ray (born Feb. 3, 1947), and Ward Lynn (born Feb. 7, 1948). They live in Bude, Miss.

c. WILLIE RAY COWARD.—Born in Franklin County, Miss., Oct. 10, 1919. Married Edna Smith Nov. 2, 1940. Children: William Henderson II (born Dec. 18, 1941), Pollard Ray (born Feb. 15, 1943),

Oscar (born Oct. 23, 1946), and Ellouise. Willie Ray Coward is a farmer and lives near Smithdale, Miss.

d. LULA ELLEN COWARD.—Born in Franklin County, Miss., Dec. 24, 1922. Unmarried. Works for the G. E. Company of Jackson, Miss.

e. MAVIS BURRIS COWARD.—Born in Smithdale, Miss., July 25, 1927. Married L. G. Young Dec. 15, 1946. No children. They live in Shannon, Miss.

f. NORMA VERNELL COWARD.—Born Aug. 28, 1932. Lives near Smithdale, Miss.

E. ERASMUS THEODORE BURRIS.—Born in Smithdale, Miss., Feb. 22, 1851. Married, first, Martinetta Gardner Dec. 8, 1870. Children: Mabel and Louis. Martinetta Gardner-Burris died Oct. 4, 1874, and was buried in the Burris Cemetery, Smithdale, Miss.

Erasmus Theodore Burris married, second, Eliza Toler Feb. 9, 1876. Children: Thomas Edgar (Eddie), J. Curtis, Mattie Lee, George Otis, Hampton, Frank, Morris Lane, Alton Graves, and Alvie Ray.

Erasmus Theodore Burris was a prosperous farmer of the Smithdale, Miss., Community. He was a member of the Mars Hill, Miss., Baptist Church. He died June 10, 1932, and was buried in the Mars Hill Cemetery.

1. MABEL BURRIS.—Born in Smithdale, Miss., Nov. 24, 1871. Married Jeffie J. Branch Jan. 2, 1896. Children: Nettie, Ruby, Joe Lawrence, Birdie, Frank Benjamin, Louis, Raiford Earl, Callie, and Ras Marshall.

Mabel Burris-Branch devoted the best years of her life to the rearing of her children, most of whom grew up to be school teachers. She made an ideal wife and mother. She lives near Smithdale.

a. NETTIE BRANCH.—Born in Smithdale, Miss., Dec. 12, 1896. Married Oscar Ellis Young Dec. 22, 1929. No children.

Nettie Branch-Young taught school for a number of years in Mississippi and Louisiana. She and her husband live with her mother in Smithdale, Miss. She is an active member of the Mars Hill, Miss., Baptist Church.

b. RUBY BRANCH.—Born in Smithdale, Miss., June 16, 1898. Married Floyd C. Young Dec. 27, 1923. Children: Fannie Lynn (born Apr. 24, 1929; is a college graduate).

Ruby Branch-Young taught school for a number of years in Mississippi. At present, she is keeping house.

c. JOE LAWRENCE BRANCH.—Born in Smithdale, Miss., Nov. 11, 1899. Married Georgina McNair May 1929. Children: Anne Haughton (born Mar. 18, 1933).

d. BIRDIE BRANCH.—Born in Smithdale, Miss., Sept. 28, 1901. Married William Richard Carroll June 15, 1927. Children: Kathryn, William Richard, Jr., and Charles Bryson.

(1). KATHRYN CARROLL.—Born in Smithdale, Miss., Sept. 20, 1928. Married Myron G. Grennell June 10, 1950, in Gainesville, Fla. No children.

Kathryn Carroll-Grennell graduated from Florida State University Mar. 1950. Myron G. Grennell graduated from the University of Florida in 1948. They live in Gainesville, Fla.

(2). WILLIAM RICHARD CARROLL, JR.—Born in Smithdale, Miss., July 7, 1932. Unmarried.

(3). CHARLES BRYSON CARROLL.—Born in Smithdale, Miss., Feb. 24, 1938.

e. FRANK BENJAMIN BRANCH.—Born in Smithdale, Miss., Oct. 25, 1907. Married Lennie Barnett, daughter of Dr. Silas L. and Josephine (Patterson) Barnett of Pace, Miss., Nov. 23, 1940. Children: Frank Benjamin, Jr. (born in Ackerman, Miss., Sept. 23, 1944).

Lennie Barnett-Branch received the B.A. Degree from Mississippi State College for Women in 1928. She did graduate work at the University of Mississippi. Prior to her marriage, she taught in the schools of Pace and Shaw, Miss. Since that time she has been a member of the Holmes Junior College faculty as teacher of French and English, with the exception of the two years they resided in Ackerman, Miss.

Frank Benjamin Branch received the B.A. Degree from Mississippi College in 1931, and the M.A. Degree from the University of Alabama in 1940. After teaching at Pace, Miss., from 1931 to 1937, he was employed to teach and coach in the Holmes Junior College of Goodman, Miss., where he has remained until the present time, with the exception of two years, 1943 and 1944, when he was superintendent of schools of Ackerman, Miss.

f. LOUIS BRANCH.—Born in Smithdale, Miss., Apr. 26, 1911. Unmarried.

g. RAIFORD EARL BRANCH.—Born in Smithdale, Miss., Dec. 27, 1915. Married Annie Jo Watson of Milan, Tenn., Dec. 22, 1944. Children: Beverly (born Apr. 28, 1947), and Raiford Earl, Jr. (born Jan. 24, 1950).

Raiford Earl Branch lives in Kosciusko, Miss., where he owns and operates the Attala Laundry and Cleaners. He was graduated from the University of Florida with the B.A. Degree in 1939.

h. CALLIE BRANCH.—Born in Smithdale, Miss., July 12, 1903. Unmarried.

Callie Branch is employed by the Southern Bell Telephone Co. of McComb, Miss., with whom she has worked for several years.

i. RAS MARSHALL BRANCH.—Born near Smithdale, Miss., Apr. 24, 1905. Married Nell Yarborough Mar. 1936. Children: Katherine (born July 10, 1937), and Betty (born Mar. 1941).

2. LOUIS BURRIS.—Born near Smithdale, Miss., April 27, 1874. Died in 1876. Buried in the Burris Cemetery, near Smithdale.

3. THOMAS EDGAR (EDDIE) BURRIS.—Born near Smithdale, Miss., Mar. 20, 1878. Married Lula Branch Mar. 3, 1903. Children: Ruth, Mildred, Fred, Elwin, Annie Mae, Hilburn, Norman, Mary, and Joyce.

Thomas Edgar (Eddie) Burris is a prosperous farmer and a leading citizen of the Smithdale Community. He is a member of the Mars Hill Baptist Church.

a. RUTH BURRIS.—Born near Smithdale, Miss., Jan. 29, 1905. Married, first, Noel Young. Children: Juanita.

Noel Young was electrocuted in New Orleans, La., Apr. 1927. Ruth Burris-Young married, second, James E. Weathersby Sept. 1939. No children.

James E. Weathersby is a merchant seaman. Ruth Burris-Weathersby is a beautician of McComb, Miss.

(1). JUANITA YOUNG.—Born Feb. 20, 1927. Married Roy L. Thompson Dec. 25, 1949, in McComb, Miss. Children: Marilyn Kay (born Feb. 27, 1952). They live in Pasadena, Texas.

b. MILDRED BURRIS.—Born near Smithdale, Miss., Oct. 22, 1906. Married Marvin Avara Dec. 25, 1945. No children.

Marvin Avara is an insurance salesman.

Mildred Burris-Avara has been a teacher in the schools of Mississippi for a number of years. At present she is principal of the Central Elementary School in Greenville, Miss.

c. FRED BURRIS.—Born in Smithdale, Miss., Oct. 25, 1908. Married Geneva Barron Dec. 1947. Children: Eddie Milton, and Charles Wilton (twins; born Mar. 1, 1950).

Fred Burris has been employed by the Fernwood Industries, Fernwood, Miss., for a number of years. He is timber inspector and buyer, and manager of one of their branches. He lives in Hammond, La.

d. ELWIN BURRIS.—Born in Smithdale, Miss., Oct. 19, 1910. Married Beatrice Strickland of Osyka, Miss., May 12, 1941. No children.

Elwin Burris is employed by the Fernwood Industries, Fernwood, Miss. He lives in Osyka, Miss.

e. ANNIE MAE BURRIS.—Born in Smithdale, Miss., Oct. 31, 1913. Married Jewel Williams May 26, 1933. Children: Tommie (adopted; born Aug. 7, 1940), and Sylvia (adopted; born July 1942).

Jewel Williams is bookkeeper for O. R. and R. E. Williams of Smithdale, Miss.

f. HILBURN BURRIS.—Born in Smithdale, Miss., Aug. 12, 1916. Married Emily Jane Barlow, daughter of C. L. Barlow, Nov. 11, 1949. Children: Roxie Ann (born Nov. 20, 1950).

Hilburn Burris is a veteran of World War II. He is farming now, and lives near Smithdale, Miss.

g. NORMAN BURRIS.—Born in Smithdale, Miss., July 1, 1919. Married Harvietta Gonzales Verdia Aug. 29, 1942. Children: Norman, Jr. (born Oct. 20, 1943), Susan (born Apr. 1947), and Dickie (born Sept. 1949).

Norman Burris is employed by the Fernwood Industries, Fernwood, Miss., as timber estimator and buyer. He lives in Fernwood, Miss.

h. MARY BURRIS.—Born in Smithdale, Miss., Sept. 26, 1921. Married Winnifred Johnston June 4, 1942. Children: Mary Ann (born June 2, 1943), and Kenneth (born Apr. 27, 1946).

Winnifred Johnston died in 1949, and was buried in the Mars Hill Cemetery.

Mary Burris-Johnston lives in Auburn, Miss., and operates a store.

      i. JOYCE BURRIS.—Born in Smithdale, Miss., Sept. 26, 1924. Married Corbett Boyd Mar. 8, 1946. Children: Mike (born Mar. 5, 1947), Thomas (born May 21, 1948), Corbett Wayne and Nita Jane (twins; born in Wyoming Apr. 1, 1950).

Corbett Boyd is in the U. S. Air Corps, and lives in Cheyenne, Wyo.

      4. J. CURTIS BURRIS.—Born in Smithdale, Miss., Dec. 1, 1879. Married Fannie Terry Nov. 3, 1901. Children: Pearl, Lena, Richard Alton, and Mattie Lexine.

They live near Smithdale, Miss.

      a. PEARL BURRIS.—Born in Smithdale, Miss., Sept. 12, 1904. Married Loyd C. Williams May 29, 1929. Children: James Loyd (born May 25, 1933), Jon Edward (born May 20, 1937), and Janice Pearl (born Feb. 5, 1944).

Loyd C. Williams lives in McComb, Miss., and operates the Williams Texaco Service Station.

      b. LENA BURRIS.—Born in Smithdale, Miss., Aug. 18, 1907. Married Leo McDaniel Dec. 21, 1924. Children: Carolyn Pearl, and June Roselyn.

Leo McDaniel lives in McComb, Miss., and works for the I. C. Railway Co.

      (1). CAROLYN PEARL MCDANIEL.—Born in McComb, Miss. Married Larcus McClelland May 2, 1948. Children: Larcus James (born June 14, 1950).

Larcus McClelland is a travelling salesman, and lives in Memphis, Tenn.

      (2). JUNE ROSELYN MCDANIEL.—Born in McComb, Miss. Married Buford Huffman Sept. 1947. No children.

Buford Huffman lives in Jackson, Miss., and works for the Miss. Power and Light Co.

      c. RICHARD ALTON BURRIS.—Born in Smithdale, Miss., Jan. 16, 1911. Married Claudia Moore Dec. 24, 1932. Children: Richard Alton, Jr. (born Oct. 25, 1933; married Sally Kathryn Moore of Gloster, Miss.), and Fannie Lexine (born Oct. 30, 1940).

Richard Alton Burris has been employed by the Illinois Central

Railway Co. for the past 25 years. His sidelines are farming and dairying. It was at his place that the Amite County Burris Association was organized and the family reunions held from 1947 to 1950. He lives near Smithdale, Miss.

d. MATTIE LEXINE BURRIS.—Born in Smithdale, Miss., Nov. 1914. Died in 1918. Buried in Mars Hill Cemetery.

5. MATTIE LEE BURRIS.—Born in Smithdale, Miss., Oct. 24, 1881. Died Jan. 14, 1906. Buried in Burris Cemetery, near Smithdale.

6. GEORGE OTIS BURRIS.—Born in Smithdale, Miss., Aug. 29, 1883. Married Gertrude Wilson Feb. 21, 1915. Children: Melba Gertrude, Mattie Lee, and Georgia Lynn.

George Otis is a farmer and lives near Smithdale, Miss.

a. MELBA GERTRUDE BURRIS.—Born in Smithdale, Miss., June 17, 1916. Died Sept. 14, 1920.

b. MATTIE LEE BURRIS.—Born in Smithdale, Miss., Nov. 11, 1918. Unmarried. Is a school teacher and is teaching this year in the Clinton, Miss., schools.

c. GEORGIA LYNN BURRIS.—Born in Smithdale, Miss., Feb. 24, 1924. Married Joe W. Albritton Dec. 24, 1943. Children: Jimmie Glynn (born Oct. 21, 1947).

Joe W. Albritton is a dairyman, and lives in Auburn, Miss.

7. HAMPTON BURRIS.—Born in Smithdale, Miss., July 18, 1885. Married Violet Moore, daughter of Cecil Moore, Dec. 21, 1913. Children: Aline, Golda, Bennie Loyd, Dorothy, Winton, and Bobbie Glen.

Hampton Burris once worked for the I. C. Railway Co., but he is disabled and is now living on his farm near Smithdale, Miss.

a. ALINE BURRIS.—Born in Smithdale, Miss., Oct. 10, 1914. Married Earl Wells Sept. 28, 1934. Children: Bobbie (born Nov. 14, 1935), Billie (born Dec. 18, 1937), Gloria Dean (born Dec. 18, 1939), and Paulette (born July 18, 1944).

Earl Wells is a farmer and lives near Smithdale, Miss.

b. GOLDA BURRIS.—Born in Smithdale, Miss., Oct. 16, 1916. Unmarried. Has been living in McComb, Miss., and working for the McCrory Store for the past several years.

c. BENNIE LOYD BURRIS.—Born in Smithdale, Miss., Oct. 16, 1919. Died Nov. 26, 1919.

d. DOROTHY BURRIS.—Born in Smithdale, Miss., Nov. 14, 1920. Married Billy Whittington Nov. 18, 1946. Children: Donald Glenn (born Aug. 5, 1948; died Aug. 6, 1948), and Kenneth Michael (born in Amite County).

Billy Whittington is a farmer and lives near Smithdale, Miss.

e. WINTON BURRIS.—Born in Smithdale, Miss., Apr. 15, 1923. Married Evie Lee Felder-McKnight* Apr. 30, 1942. Children: Johnnie Ray (born June 30, 1943).

Winton Burris is a farmer and lives near Peoria, Miss.

f. BOBBIE GLEN BURRIS.—Born in Smithdale, Miss., May 7, 1927. Died Feb. 26, 1928.

8. FRANK BURRIS.—Born in Smithdale, Miss., Sept. 19, 1887. Married Georgia Gerald, daughter of Emmett Gerald, Nov. 17, 1915. Children: Virgie Mae, Nellie Jean, Emmett F., and Jessie Maude.

Georgia Gerald-Burris was born in Smithdale, Miss., Mar. 11, 1895.

Frank Burris is an employee of the I. C. Railway Co. He lives in McComb, Miss., and is an active member of the East McComb Baptist Church.

a. VIRGIE MAE BURRIS.—Born in McComb, Miss., Apr. 15, 1917. Married Jewell D. Norman Dec. 24, 1934. Children: Morris Edwin (born May 2, 1941), and Jewell Eugene (born Feb. 15, 1949).

Jewell D. Norman lives in McComb, Miss., and works for the I. C. Railway Co.

b. NELLIE JEAN BURRIS.—Born in McComb, Miss., July 25, 1922. Married John Edward Newman Apr. 16, 1942. Children: Jeffery Edwin (born Feb. 26, 1943). John Edward Newman lives in McComb, Miss., and works for the I. C. Railway Co.

c. EMMETT F. BURRIS.—Born in McComb, Miss., Apr. 11, 1924. Married Kathleen Cullom Nov. 8, 1944. Children: Richard Gerald (born June 2, 1949).

Kathleen Cullom-Burris was born Feb. 26, 1926.

Emmett F. Burris lives in McComb, Miss., and works for the Southern Bell Telephone Co.

d. JESSIE MAUDE BURRIS.—Married Vaught Lenoir, Jr.

---

*An interfamily marriage.

Children: Ruth Elise (born June 17, 1950), and Lola Jean (born Apr. 3, 1952). Vaught Lenoir, Jr., is an attorney, and lives in McComb, Miss.

9. MORRIS LANE BURRIS.—Born in Smithdale, Miss., Dec. 21, 1889. Married Beulah Branch, daughter of Marshall Branch, Dec. 19, 1909. Children: Marion Lane, Elsie Lillian, Morris Grady, Mattie Lucille, Benjamin Ward, and Marshall Audry.

Marshall Branch was born in Amite County, Miss., Feb. 11, 1870.

Morris Lane Burris died Oct. 4, 1921, and was buried in the Mars Hill Cemetery.

a. MARION LANE BURRIS.—Born in Smithdale, Miss., Oct. 18, 1910. Died Dec. 22, 1910.

b. ELSIE LILLIAN BURRIS.—Born in Smithdale, Miss., Apr. 21, 1912. Married W. D. Parker Apr. 26, 1931. No children. Died Sept. 9, 1932, and was buried in the Mars Hill Cemetery.

c. MORRIS GRADY BURRIS.—Born in Smithdale, Miss., May 7, 1914. Married Nellie Rae Wells Apr. 19, 1943. Children: Randy Morris (born Dec. 15, 1945), Charles Windell (born Aug. 24, 1946), and James Larry (born Jan. 6, 1949). Morris Grady Burris is a farmer and lives in Belzoni, Miss.

d. MATTIE LUCILLE BURRIS.—Born in Smithdale, Miss., Dec. 1, 1917. Married Grover Smith, son of Otis Smith, Dec. 10, 1936. Children: Mary Catherine (born Dec. 16, 1938), Miriam Lanelle (born Dec. 17, 1940), and Grover Elton (born June 28, 1944).

Grover Smith is a farmer and lives at Smithdale, Miss.

e. BENJAMIN WARD BURRIS.—Born in Smithdale, Miss., Mar. 20, 1919. Married Doris Marie Scott Sept. 15, 1942. Children: Terry Lane (born Oct. 28, 1943), Tommy Gene (born Aug. 14, 1946), and Rita Elizabeth (born Aug. 26, 1949). Benjamin Ward Burris is a dragline operator and lives at Smithdale, Miss.

f. MARSHALL AUDRY BURRIS.—Born in Smithdale, Miss., Nov. 4, 1921. Married Betty Jean Greenlee June 4, 1946. Children: Betty Ann (born Aug. 30, 1947).

Marshall Audry Burris enlisted in the armed forces of the U. S. during World War II Sept. 17, 1942. He was overseas, in the South Pacific area, for twenty-two months. He was discharged Jan. 4, 1946. He lives in Fernwood, Miss., and works for the Fernwood Industries.

10. ALTON GRAVES BURRIS.—Born in Smithdale, Miss., Dec. 14, 1892. Married Alma Garner Dec. 25, 1915. Children: Loraine, Merwin, and Ola Marie. Alton Graves Burris is a twin brother of Alvie Ray Burris.

They live near Smithdale, Miss.

a. LORAINE BURRIS.—Born in Smithdale, Miss., Nov. 12, 1918. Married Forrest Edwards May 10, 1936. Children: Mary Marguerite (born July 26, 1940), Joseph Douglas (born Jan. 8, 1944), and Thomas James (born Nov. 7, 1947).

Forrest Edwards is a dairy farmer and lives at Smithdale, Miss.

b. MERWIN BURRIS.—Born in Smithdale, Miss., Oct. 16, 1921. Married Martha Ann Wells in 1949.* No children. Is a dairy farmer and lives near Smithdale, Miss.

c. OLA MARIE BURRIS.—Died in infancy.

11. ALVIE RAY BURRIS.—Born in Smithdale, Miss., Dec. 14, 1892. Married Alma Roberts, Feb. 2, 1921. Children: Raiford Earl and Melba Joy.

Alvie Ray Burris lives near Smithdale, Miss.

a. RAIFORD EARL BURRIS.—Born in Smithdale, Miss. Married Ruth Lurlyne Young Sept. 4, 1948. Children: Beverly Jean (born July 2, 1950).

Ruth Lurlyne Young-Burris was born Aug. 15, 1927. Raiford Earl Burris lives near Smithdale, Miss., and is employed by the I. C. Railway Co. He is a veteran of World War II.

b. MELBA JOY BURRIS.—Born in Smithdale, Miss., Dec. 12, 1931. Is a student at Southwest Junior College, Summit, Miss. Lives at Smithdale, Miss.

F. SARAH JANE BURRIS.—Born in Smithdale, Miss., June 18, 1846. Married William Ross Walker Dec. 21, 1868. Children: Seth E., Mary Alice, Hampton E., W. Alva, Annie R., M. Emma, and . . . . (an infant son).

Sarah Jane Burris-Walker died May 24, 1879, and was buried in the Walker Family Cemetery, Magnolia, Miss.

William Ross Walker joined the Mars Hill Baptist Church Aug. 24, 1864.

----

*An interfamily marriage.

1. SETH E. WALKER.—Born Mar. 27, 1870. Married Lillie Patrick June 15, 1902. Children: Seth E., Jr., Laverne (married M. L. Oliveira), and Ruth (married A. F. McWhorter of Hobbs, N. Mex).

Seth E. Walker was a merchant in Covington, La.

2. MARY ALICE WALKER.—Born Oct. 28, 1871. Never married. Died Dec. 8, 1888, and was buried in the Walker Family Cemetery, Magnolia, Miss.

3. HAMPTON E. WALKER.—Born July 20, 1873. Married Emma Prescott, Dec. 22, 1897. Children: Kenneth (married Ada Garner —no children). Hampton E. Walker died June 14, 1899.

4. W. ALVA WALKER.—Born in Pike County, Miss., Mar. 27, 1875. Married Rosa Belle Coney, Dec. 25, 1901. Children: Mildred, Wilma, Thelma, Mabel, W. Alva, Jr., Maude, Joe, Sarah Loyd, Bonnie Belle, Helen, and Ruth.

W. Alva Walker is a merchant, farmer, and ginner. He lives near McComb, Miss.

a. MILDRED WALKER.—Died at the age of one year.

b. WILMA WALKER.—Married Vince Barr. Children: V. W., Wilma Fay, Richard Wesley, Rodney, and Barbara Ann.

(1). V. W. BARR.—Married Charlene Ivey. Children: Wilson.

V. W. Barr is an employee of the I. C. Railway Co., and lives in McComb, Miss.

(2). WILMA FAY BARR.—Married Bernon Pounds. Children: Brenda Fay. They live in Magnolia, Miss.

(3). RICHARD WESLEY BARR.—Married Martha Lynn . . . . No children. They live in McComb, Miss.

(4). RODNEY BARR.

(5). BARBARA ANN BARR.

c. THELMA WALKER.—Married O. S. Reeves. Children: Henry Alva (married Emily Claire Havers; no children), and Russell.

They live in McComb, Miss.

d. MABEL WALKER.—Unmarried. Lives in Jackson, Miss.

e. W. ALVA WALKER, JR.—Married Eula Foil. Children: W. Alva III. They live near McComb, Miss., and operate a store.

f. MAUDE WALKER.—Married Clark Simmons. Children: Clark, Jr. They live in McComb, Miss.

g. JOE WALKER.—Married J. P. Creel. Children: Rosa Belle. They live in McComb, Miss.

h. SARAH LOYD WALKER.—Married B. L. Stacks. Children: Nancy Walker.

They live near McComb, Miss.

i. BONNIE BELLE WALKER.—Married Roy Sanders. Children: Linda Joe.

j. HELEN WALKER.—Died in 1932. Never married.

k. RUTH WALKER.—Married James H. Tucker. Children: James H., Jr. They live in McComb, Miss.

5. ANNIE R. WALKER.—Born Mar. 27, 1875. Married George Raborn Sept. 1, 1899. Children: Hollis, Lois, James Purser, Jessie D., and George L.

Annie R. Walker-Raborn died Nov. 26, 1938, and was buried in the Magnolia, Miss., Cemetery.

a. HOLLIS RABORN.—Born in Pike County, Miss., Sept. 1905. Married Lena Foster. Children: Hollis, Jr.

They live in Greensburg, La.

b. LOIS RABORN.—Born in Pike County, Miss., Dec. 1, 1903. Married Claude W. Holmes Aug. 6, 1924. Children: Virginia Ann.

They live in Summit, Miss.

(1). VIRGINIA ANN HOLMES.—Born in Pike County, Miss., Mar. 1, 1926. Married John P. Reeves Mar. 10, 1946. Children: John P., Jr. (born Sept. 9, 1947).

c. JAMES PURSER RABORN.—Born in Pike County, Miss., Mar. 13, 1913. Married Wilmuth Travis. Children: Lena Wilmuth (born Jan. 16, 1943). James Purser Raborn lives in Ferriday, La., and manages the Western Auto Stores there.

d. JESSIE D. RABORN.—Born in Pike County, Miss., Feb. 25, 1915. Married Cecil P. Cook. Children: Ann Dolores.

They live in Fernwood, Miss.

e. GEORGE L. RABORN.—Born in Pike County, Miss., June 29, 1907. Married Cecile Ghisaborti. Children: Carol Ann, and George L., Jr. Cecile Ghisaborti-Raborn died about 1949. They live in New Orleans.

6. M. EMMA WALKER.—Born June 7, 1877. Married Sidney Allen, Feb. 4, 1900. Children: Houston.

a. HOUSTON ALLEN.—Born Aug. 25, 1903. Married Lois Sandifer Jan. 10, 1924. Children: Nelda L., Betty S., V. Pansy, W. Wayne, and Warren S. They live in Edinburgh, Tex.

(1). NELDA L. ALLEN.—Born Feb. 10, 1925. Married John Pavlica May 5, 1944. Children: Janice L. (born Feb. 24, 1945), and J. Dale (born May 10, 1947).

(2). BETTY S. ALLEN.—Born Feb. 11, 1928. Married Verbon L. Anthony Nov. 30, 1945. Children: Norman L. (born Mar. 24, 1946).

(3). V. PANSY ALLEN.—Unmarried.

(4). W. WAYNE ALLEN.—Unmarried.

(5). WARREN S. ALLEN.—Unmarried.

7. .... (An infant son—died May 24, 1879).

G. JAMES NELSON BURRIS.—Born in Amite County, Miss., Mar. 10, 1854. Dead.

H. THOMAS RAIFORD BURRIS.—Born in Smithdale, Miss., May 21, 1860. Married Julia Pate, daughter of James Pate, Dec. 22, 1884. Children: Julius Alva, Raiford, Ross Miller, Lessie Lillian, Lawrence Homer, and Thomas Roy.

Thomas Raiford Burris died Feb. 22, 1934, and was buried in the Mars Hill Cemetery. He was a farmer. His farm is located in the Smithdale Community. He was a quiet, and an unassuming citizen and was respected and revered by all who knew him.

Julia Pate-Burris was born in Amite County, Miss., Nov. 14, 1862. She died Oct. 6, 1941, and was buried in the Mars Hill Cemetery, Smithdale, Miss.

1. JULIUS ALVA BURRIS.—Born in Smithdale, Miss., Oct. 1, 1885. Married Ethel Wilkinson, daughter of Jeff and Ada V. (Sharp) Wilkinson, Dec. 25, 1915. Children: Floy Delle, and Lillian Camille.

Ethel Wilkinson-Burris was born Sept. 7, 1896.

a. FLOY DELLE BURRIS.—Born in Smithdale, Miss., Aug. 30, 1917. Married, first, E. L. Wages Feb. 21, 1940. No children. E. L. Wages died Sept. 1946. Floy Delle Burris-Wages married, second, Ralph O. Rodenor Dec. 31, 1948. No children.

They live in New Orleans, La.

b. LILLIAN CAMILLE BURRIS.—Born in Smithdale, Miss., Jan. 21, 1921. Married, first, W. Bruce French Feb. 18, 1943. No children. W. Bruce French died June 26, 1943. Lilliam Camille Burris-French married, second, Herschel H. Davis July 3, 1948. No children.

W. Bruce French was a pilot in the U. S. Navy during World War II. He was killed in action.

2. RAIFORD BURRIS.—Born in Smithdale, Miss., Jan. 25, 1888. Died Dec. 28, 1892, and was buried in the Burris Cemetery, Smithdale, Miss.

3. ROSS MILLER BURRIS.—Born in Smithdale, Miss., Mar. 31, 1891. Died Dec. 24, 1892, and was buried in the Burris Cemetery, Smithdale, Miss.

4. LESSIE LILLIAN BURRIS.—Born in Smithdale, Miss., Feb. 28, 1892. Married Lucius Branch June 16, 1940. No children.

5. LAWRENCE HOMER BURRIS.—Born in Smithdale, Miss., July 24, 1898. Married Ruby Butler, daughter of Billy and Ada Butler, Mar. 5, 1924. Children: Leslie Everett (born May 1, 1927), and Alice Ruth (adopted; born Jan. 4, 1931; married Dr. Benton Hewitt in 1951).

They live near Smithdale, Miss.

6. THOMAS ROY BURRIS.—Born in Smithdale, Miss., Dec. 30, 1903. Married Mavis Burkhalter Mar. 4, 1932. Children: Julie Lu (born June 11, 1940).

I. ENOS PINKNEY BURRIS.—Born in Smithdale, Miss., Jan. 12, 1862. Married Lulu Alma Weathersby, daughter of Walter M. and Lettie Weathersby, Dec. 16, 1886. Children: Walter Hampton, Mamie Lettie, Nolan Pinkney, Bernard Hatten, Leon Louis, and William Culpepper.

Lulu Alma Weathersby-Burris was born Jan. 20, 1862. She lives with her daughter, Mamie Lettie Burris-Simmons, near Magnolia, Miss.

Enos Pinkney Burris died Oct. 23, 1930, and was buried in the Mars Hill Cemetery.

1. WALTER HAMPTON BURRIS.—Born in Smithdale, Miss., Sept. 20, 1887. Married Ida Hilbun, daughter of Fletcher and Hettie T. Hilbun, Dec. 1906. Children: Alma Evelyn, Ruby Ava, William James, Ida Murel, and Walter Hampton, Jr.

Ida Hilburn-Burris died Mar. 1928, and was buried in Kentwood, La.

Walter Hampton Burris engaged first in railroad work, for the I. C. Railway Co. He left this work to work in the Kentwood, La., Bank. He left the bank and went back to work for the I. C. Railway Co. At the time of his death, Feb. 1949, he was employed by the Fernwood Industries, Fernwood, Miss. He was buried in Kentwood, La.

a. ALMA EVELYN BURRIS.—Born in Kentwood, La., Jan. 4, 1907. Married Ted E. Varnado, son of Bob and Bertha Varnado, Mar. 5, 1929. Children: Ted E., Jr. (born Apr. 2, 1930).

Ted E. Varnado, Jr., is a student in Southeastern Louisiana College, Hammond, La.

b. RUBY AVA BURRIS.—Born in Kentwood, La., Nov. 11, 1911. Married Charlie Wall Apr. 18, 1928. Children: Donald (born Apr. 16, 1940), Walter Elwin (born Feb. 19, 1944), and Freddie (born 1951).

They live in Baton Rouge, La.

c. WILLIAM JAMES BURRIS.—Born in Kentwood, La., Sept. 27, 1915. Married Beulah Williams June 13, 1937. Children: Carol Ann (born in New Orleans, La., Sept. 15, 1942), and William James, Jr. (born in Kentwood, La., July 20, 1946).

William James Burris is a veteran of World War II. He is now employed by the Louisiana Light and Power Co., and lives in Ferriday, La.

d. IDA MUREL BURRIS.—Born in Kentwood, La., Nov. 18, 1918. Married William H. Davis May 20, 1938. Children: William H., Jr. (Billy) (born Dec. 17, 1941), and Cris (born July 12, 1944).

e. WALTER HAMPTON BURRIS, JR.—Born in Kentwood, La., Sept. 9, 1922. Married Anna Fay Davis Apr. 27, 1945, in Baton Rouge, La. Children: Walter Hampton III (born in Baton Rouge, La., Mar. 9, 1946), and Bonnie Louise (born in Baton Rouge, La., Feb. 27, 1947).

Walter Hampton Burris, Jr. served with the Merchant Marine for several months during World War II. He was given a leave of absence for some time because of having asthma. He is employed now by the Gulf Utilities Co. of Lake Charles, La.

2. MAMIE LETTIE BURRIS.—Born in Smithdale, Miss., Mar. 2, 1889. Married John Arnold Simmons, son of W. F. and Julia B. Simmons, Mar. 8, 1917. Children: John Lynn.

John Arnold Simmons was born in Magnolia, Miss., Jan. 28, 1894. He died May 23, 1943, and was buried in the Union Cemetery in Magnolia, Miss.

Mamie Lettie Burris-Simmons is one of the outstanding members of the Burris Family. She is one of the co-authors of this history. She lives near Magnolia, Miss.

a. JOHN LYNN SIMMONS.—Born near Magnolia, Miss., Nov. 23, 1924. Married Ruby Pigott, daughter of Boyd and Mamie D. Pigott, Apr. 1941. Children: John Wayne (born near Magnolia, Miss., Jan. 24, 1943; attending St. Mary's of the Pines School, Chatawa, Miss.), and Mamie Lynette (born near Magnolia, Miss., Jan. 1949; died the same day).

John Lynn Simmons is a veteran of World War II. He lives near his mother, near Magnolia, Miss., and is a farmer and merchant.

3. NOLAN PINKNEY BURRIS.—Born near Smithdale, Miss., May 23, 1891. Married, first, Murel Willis Oct. 10, 1916, in Amite, La. No children.

Murel Willis-Burris was born Feb. 5, 1894. She died Mar. 28, 1918, and was buried in Kentwood, La.

Nolan Pinkney Burris married, second, Pearl Forshag Oct. 21, 1920, in Amite, La. Children: Nolan Pinkney, Jr., John Forshag, and Beverly Ann.

Nolan Pinkney Burris died May 11, 1952, and was buried in Kentwood, La.

His family lives in New Orleans, La.

a. NOLAN PINKNEY BURRIS, JR.—Born in Natalbany, La., May 1, 1924. Married Zoe Habisreitinger Oct. 1948, in New Orleans, La. No children.

Nolan Pinkney Burris, Jr., lives in New Orleans, and does clerical work.

b. JOHN FORSHAG BURRIS.—Born in Natalbany, La., July 22, 1926. Married Anne Darwin Mar. 25, 1951, in Baton Rouge, La.

Children: Carolyn Elise (born Dec. 27, 1951). John Forshag Burris is a veteran of World War II. They live in Baton Rouge, La.

c. BEVERLY ANN BURRIS.—Born May 24, 1928. Married Carlos Christina June 14, 1952, in New Orleans, La.

Before marrying Beverly Ann Burris attended L. S. U., and for her outstanding record there, she was entered in the Who's Who for 1950-51.

They live in New Orleans, La.

4. BERNARD HATTEN BURRIS.—Born near Smithdale, Miss., June 24, 1893. Married Matha Wilson,* daughter of Will and Myrtis C. Wilson, Oct. 7, 1917, in East Fork, Miss. Children: Osburn, Donald, and Harold L.

Bernard Hatten Burris is a veteran of World War I.

a. OSBURN BURRIS.—Born in Liberty, Miss., Mar. 4, 1920. Married Nelda Montgomery, daughter of Henry Montgomery, May 23, 1943, in Ponchatoula, La. No children.

Osburn Burris is a veteran of World War II.

b. DONALD BURRIS.—Born in Liberty, Miss., Sept. 25, 1921. Married Mildred Roussel Apr. 21, 1943. Children: Judy Ann (born July 19, 1946), and Donna Susan (born May 21, 1951).

Donald Burris is a veteran of World War II. He lives in Ponchatoula, La.

c. HAROLD L. BURRIS.—Born in Liberty, Miss., June 27, 1923. Married Mary Lou Pearson Aug. 1951, in Ponchatoula, La. Lives in Brookhaven, Miss., and works for the I. C. Railway Co.

5. LEON LOUIS BURRIS.—Born in Smithdale, Miss., Apr. 15, 1895. Married Clara Burns, daughter of Wesley and Laura Burns, Feb. 24, 19.., in Liberty, Miss. Children: Laura Lavada, Lewis Enos, Mary Etta, Paul Ester, and Carolyn.

Leon Louis Burris is a veteran of World War I.

a. LAURA LAVADA BURRIS.—Born in Kentwood, La., Aug. 16, 1920. Married John Smith Allen, son of Joe and Allie R. Allen, Nov. 11, 1939. Children: Robert Earl (born in Magnolia, Miss., Apr. 15, 1942), Dora Dean and Dorothy Ann (twins; born in Magnolia, Miss., July 24, 1944), and Eva Louise (born in Magnolia, Miss., July 15, 1947).

---

*An interfamily marriage.

b. LEWIS ENOS BURRIS.—Born in Smithdale, Miss., Dec. 24, 1923. Married Catherine Smith Dec. 25, 1941, in Magnolia, Miss. No children.

Lewis Enos Burris is a veteran of World War II.

c. MARY ETTA BURRIS.—Born in Smithdale, Miss., Jan. 10, 1928. Married Burnell Morris Nov. 8, 1947. Children: Brenda Dianne (born in Magnolia, Miss., Oct. 9, 1948); Mickey Vernon (born in Magnolia, Miss., Jan. 15, 1950), and Loretta Gale (born in Magnolia, Miss., Jan. 27, 1951).

d. PAUL ESTER BURRIS.—Born in Smithdale, Miss., Apr. 13, 1930. Married Mayma Inez Hodge Oct. 9, 1948, in Virginia. No children.

Paul Ester Burris is in the American occupation forces in Japan.

e. CAROLYN BURRIS.—Born in Picayune, Miss., Nov. 12, 1937.

6. WILLIAM CULPEPPER BURRIS.—Born in Smithdale, Miss., Mar. 5, 1897. Married, first, Lenora Gillelan in 1918, in Ruth, Miss. Children: William Cullen (Billy) (born in Smithdale, Miss., in 1922), and Leo Gillelan (Sonny) (born in Smithdale, Miss., in 1925; married Virginia Alford and has one child, Michael Leo; veteran of World War II).

William Culpepper Burris is a veteran of World War I.

William Culpepper Burris married, second, Josephine Thornton. No children. He lives in Leesville, La.

J. GEORGE ERNEST BURRIS.—Born in Smithdale, Miss., Oct. 5, 1870. Married, first, Cora Prestridge in 1897. Children: Bryan and Maida Lee. Married, second, Mary Alice Butler May, 1906, after Cora Prestridge-Burris's death. Children: Mary Elizabeth, and Lawrence Miller.

George Ernest Burris was the youngest son of Hampton and Mary-Turner Burris. He was a prosperous farmer and lived in the old Hampton Burris house. He died June 10, 1946, and was buried in the Mars Hill Cemetery.

1. BRYAN BURRIS.—Born in Smithdale, Miss., Oct. 4, 1897. Married, first, Tiche Arnold and they divorced. No children. Married, second, Irene May Reddicks. Children: Donald Bryan (born Apr. 23, 1938; died Jan. 1, 1939), and Cora May Burris (born Nov. 28, 1939).

2. MAIDA LEE BURRIS.—Born in Smithdale, Miss., Dec. 3, 1899. Married Marvin Schilling. Children: Faril Marvin, Ruby Laverne, Bobby, and Hilton J. They live near Osyka, Miss.

a. FARIL MARVIN SCHILLING.—Born in Pike County, Miss., Sept. 21, 1923. Married Elnora Miller Mar. 4 1944. Children: Robert Harry (killed in Hammond, La., May 17, 1952, by an automobile; buried in Silver Springs Church Cemetery, Miss.).

Faril Marvin Schilling is a dairyman and farmer. He enlisted in the armed forces Oct. 13, 1944, during World War II, and served sixteen months in the European Area. He was discharged Aug. 8, 1946.

b. RUBY LAVERNE SCHILLING.—Born in Pike County, Miss., May 15, 1925. Married J. B. Lane Sept. 8, 1945. Children: Sylvia Laverne (born Nov. 2, 1946).

c. BOBBY SCHILLING.—Born in Pike County, Miss., Jan. 15, 1931. Married Nedri Mae Morris Dec. 1947. No children.

Bobby Schilling is a dairyman and farmer.

d. HILTON SCHILLING.—Born in Pike County, Miss., Aug. 13, 1932. Unmarried. Is a dairyman and farmer.

3. MARY ELIZABETH BURRIS.—Born in Smithdale, Miss., Oct. 21, 1911. Married Hubert H. Wright June 13, 1944. Children: Rebecca Burris (born May 23, 1945; died June 2, 1945); Hubert H., Jr. (born Sept. 26, 1946), and Ronald Glen (born Mar. 24, 1948).

4. LAWRENCE MILLER BURRIS.—Born in Smithdale, Miss., Sept. 4, 1918. Married Linda Forrest. Children: Patsy Lynn (born Mar. 1949).

Lawrence Miller Burris served in the armed forces during World War II. He is now employed by the I. C. Railway Co.

K. MAGGIE ELIZABETH BURRIS.—Born in Smithdale, Miss., June 12, 1872. Never married. Died Jan. 8, 1949, and was buried in the Mars Hill Cemetery.

HAMPTON BURRIS APPOINTED ELECTION MANAGER
(From The Liberty Advocate of Jan. 9, 1840)

Gov. A. G. McNutt ordered the sheriff of Amite County to appoint managers for a special election for judge of the High Court of Errors and Appeal, to fill the vacancy caused by the death of Hon. P. Rutilius R. Pray of the second district. Hampton Burris, Wm. C. Butler, and Thos. J. Spurlock were appointed for Spurlock Precinct.

XI. ADDISON BURRIS.

Addison Burris was the son of Samuel and Mary (Myers) Burris. It is thought that he was the youngest child. He was born in Amite County, Miss., in 1811. He married, first, Sarah Alice Flowers, daughter of Henry and Nancy (Adams) Flowers, Dec. 25, 1836, at the Flowers' home in Smithdale, Miss. They established a home in the Smithdale community, but fourteen months later, in Feb. 1839, Sarah Alice Flowers-Burris died, and left a little girl, who was given her mother's name, Sarah Alice Flowers-Burris.* Addison Burris married, second, Mrs. Becky Williams, and there was one child by this marriage, a son named James D. In 1844 Addison Burris married Rebecca Irion Ogden, his third wife. By this marriage there were the following children: Duncan H., Annie Ogden, Isabel Ogden, Lucy Mary, Marcy Ann (Mattie), Enos Hampton, Dr. William Addison (Billy), George Samuel, Nora Rebecca, and Hattie Henderson.

Addison Burris's original homestead seems to have been a part of his mother's old homestead, which he owned jointly with his brother, Hampton, and which they sold to their brother, William, Aug. 16, 1838, for $1000. Addison Burris bought later the east half of the northwest quarter of section 9, township 4, range 6 east, containing 80 acres, from E. G. Wicker for $76.00. This land is located about one and one-half miles north of Mars Hill on the Mars Hill-Auburn road.

Sometime after his first wife's death, Addison Burris moved to the delta section of Mississippi, near Yazoo City. His sister, Ann, who married Judge Edmund Smith, had settled in this section and doubtless this had something to do with Addison's moving there. After living in the delta several years, he moved, in the 1850's, to East Baton Rouge Parish, La., on the Baton Rouge-Denham Springs Highway, near the city of Baton Rouge, La. He lived there until his death in 1893. He was buried in Baton Rouge, La.

Addison Burris was a farmer most, if not all, of his life.

A. SARAH ALICE FLOWERS BURRIS.*—Born near Smithdale, Miss., Feb. 20, 1839. Married Dr. Joel Watley Williams Mar. 1, 1855. Children: Cecil, Marshall Eugene, Alice, Dewitt, Andrew W. (Dick), Martin E., and Sallie.

Sarah Alice Flowers Burris-Williams's mother died when she was a little girl, and she was reared by her grandmother, Nancy Flowers.

---

*Copied from "Flowers Kith and Kin" by Mary Louise Flowers-Hendrix.

Shortly after their marriage, they moved to Gillsburg, Miss., to live. Dr. Williams was a practicing physician in Gillsburg.

Sarah Alice Flowers Burris-Williams died May 9, 1879.

1. CECIL WILLIAMS.—Born Dec. 7, 1855. Married Harriet Lambert in 1874. Children: Nonnie, Oma, Sammie, Betrus, Maggie, Lottie, Horace C., Realus J., ... (infant), and Alex Wattley.

Harriet Lambert-Williams was born June 8, 1847, and died Jan. 20, 1925.

Cecil Williams died Aug. 18, 1935.

a. NONNIE WILLIAMS.—Born Sept. 25, 1875.

b. OMA WILLIAMS.—Born May 29, 1880. Married Robert Webb May 22, 1901. Children: Maurice, Dewitt, Glen, Elzy Dees, Margie, Percell, Argie, Pete, Hollis, Dewey, Percy, T. C., and Ray Cecil.

Robert Webb was born Mar. 16, 1876, and died Jan. 2, 1936.

(1). MAURICE WEBB.—Born Aug. 27, 1902. Married Bertha Raborn Apr. 7, 1923. Children: Myrtis (born Mar. 11, 1925), Willie Mac (born June 18, 1927), Natalea (born Dec. 18, 1931), Robert Maurice (born Apr. 19, 1933), Elaine (born June 2, 1937), Eva Lois (born Oct. 10, 1938), Jo Ann (born June 7, 1941), and Dianne (born June 7, 1941—twin of Jo Ann).

(2). DEWITT WEBB.—Born Jan. 24, 1904. Married Annie Rohner. Children: Charlie Glen (born June 18, 1931).

(3). GLEN WEBB.—Born Nov. 10, 1906.

(4). ELZY DEES WEBB.—Born Sept. 5, 1905. Died Mar. 9, 1909.

(5). MARGIE WEBB.—Born Feb. 5, 1908. Married Mike Drensky Aug. 11, 1930. Children: Mike Lamar (born Sept. 1, 1931).

(6). PERCELL WEBB.—Born Mar. 20, 1910.

(7). ARGIE WEBB.—Born Dec. 28, 1911. Married Carolton Kemp Aug. 9, 1931. Children: Bobbye Joyce (born July 7, 1941), and Johnnie Lois (born July 7, 1941; died Dec. 12, 1941). Carolton Kemp was born Feb. 12, 1907.

(8). PETE WEBB.—Born June 8, 1913. Married Olivia

Robinson May 4, 1937. Children: Syvilia (born Dec. 18, 1938), Patsy (born Nov. 6, 1939), and Robert Wayne (born June 4, 1941).

    (9). HOLLIS WEBB.—Born Jan. 29, 1915.

    (10). DEWEY WEBB.—Born May 1, 1916.

    (11). PERCY WEBB.—Born Sept. 15, 1919.

    (12). T. C. WEBB.—Born Sept. 16, 1920.

    (13). RAY CECIL WEBB.—Born Aug. 10, 1925.

    c. SAMMIE WILLIAMS.—Born Dec. 20, 1879. Died Dec. 1, 1882.

    d. BETRUS WILLIAMS.—Born June 9, 1882. Died Dec. 5, 1882.

    e. MAGGIE WILLIAMS.—Born Jan. 22, 1883. Married Amile Bert Nov. 11, 1911. No children. Amile Bert was born Nov. 28, 1893.

    f. LOTTIE WILLIAMS.—Born June 22, 1884. Married Joseph K. Holmes Dec. 28, 1901. Children: Beulah Lee, Odell, Johnnie Cecil, Zella, Edson C., and Gladys Amile.

Joseph K. Holmes was born Jan. 5, 1877.

    (1). BEULAH LEE HOLMES.—Born Sept. 4, 1903. Married A. P. Ramsay Mar. 24, 1923. No children.

A. P. Ramsay was born Mar. 15, 1903.

    (2). ODELL HOLMES.—Born May 28, 1908.

    (3). JOHNNIE CECIL HOLMES.—Born Dec. 25, 1910.

    (4). ZELLA HOLMES.—Born Sept. 2, 1913. Married Wilton B. Oliphant Sept. 15, 1932. No children.

Wilton B. Oliphant was born Feb. 15, 1911.

    (5). EDSON C. HOLMES.—Born May 27, 1918.

    (6). GLADYS AMILE HOLMES.—Born Sept. 21, 1921.

    g. HORACE C. WILLIAMS.—Born Apr. 9, 1886. Married Betty Bennett June 15, 1913. Children: Luther H. (born July 26, 1920).

Betty Bennett-Williams was born Nov. 17, 1891.

    h. REALUS J. WILLIAMS.—Born Apr. 9, 1886. Married Addie Bennett Apr. 13, 1913. Children: Fred (born Nov. 5, 1914; died Mar. 7, 1937), Halzie Lea (born Apr. 6, 1919; died Apr. 11,

1919), Morris (born Oct. 6, 1921), Elcee (born Sept. 18, 1925), and Realus, Jr. (born Nov. 11, 1930).

Realus J. Williams is a twin brother of Horace C. Williams.

Addie Bennett-Williams was born July 5, 1894.

      i. .... (unnamed).—Born Mar. 8, 1888. Died Mar. 8, 1888.

      j. ALEX WATTLEY WILLIAMS.—Born Apr. 18, 1877. Married Elizabeth Jane Strickland* May 26, 1897. Children: Myrtis Dean, Lillian Mildred, Dewitt Ottis, Janie Elizabeth, Johnnie Leuna, James Eward, Donnis, and Alta Dale.

Elizabeth Jane Strickland-Williams was born Feb. 2, 1883.

      (1). MYRTIS DEAN WILLIAMS. — Born Jan. 14, 1901. Died Mar. 4, 1924.

      (2). LILLIAN MILDRED WILLIAMS.—Born Aug. 3, 1905. Married Peter Callia Jan. 1924. Children: Peter, Jr. (born Aug. 7, 1925), Ellen Mae (born Feb. 25, 1927), and Roger James (born Dec. 16, 1931).

      (3). DEWITT OTTIS WILLIAMS.—Born Mar. 11, 1907. Married Louise Loretta Gitz in 1928. Children: Kenneth Blaun (born Feb. 24, 1930), Betty Jean (born June 18, 1931), and Mildred Evonne (born Aug. 4, 1935).

      (4). JANIE ELIZABETH WILLIAMS.—Born Apr. 27, 1908. Married Claude Messersmith in 1937. No children.

      (5). JOHNNIE LEUNA WILLIAMS.—Born Aug. 3, 1911. Married Timothy Di Domenica in 1932. Children: Arnold Ray (born Jan. 4, 1935).

      (6). JAMES EWARD WILLIAMS.—Born Jan. 23, 1920.

      (7). DONNIS WILLIAMS.—Born July 9, 1922. Married Tracy Brown Apr. 1939. Children: Sigrid Ann Elizabeth (born Aug. 23, 1940).

      (8). ALTA DALE WILLIAMS.—Born Mar. 6, 1924.

    2. MARSHALL EUGENE WILLIAMS.—Born Sept. 12, 1857. Married Missouri Ellen Wall. Children: Addie, Leon Wolf, Leonard Eugene, Eunyce, Burnyce, Vernon, Virgil Reed, and Daisy May.

———

*Thought to be the great granddaughter of Elizabeth Burris, which would make her and her husband fifth cousins, and this an interfamily marriage.

Missouri Ellen Wall-Williams was born Mar. 25, 1883. She died Jan. 10, 1928.

Marshall Eugene Williams died Feb. 28, 1942.

a. ADDIE WILLIAMS.—Married Joel Bridges. Children: Mynne, Clytee, Odessa, R. D., Dalton, Barney, Loray, Dale, Russell, and Kenneth.

b. LEON WOLF WILLIAMS.—Born Sept. 21, 1890. Married Dollie Griffin. Children: Evelyn (born Nov. 9, 1916; married Peter Grimes).

Leon Wolf Williams died Oct. 14, 1918.

c. LEONARD EUGENE WILLIAMS.—Born Aug. 26, 1893. Married Lois Stewart. Children: Stewart (born Dec. 12, 1927), and Dorothy (born Dec. 8, 1929).

d. EUNYCE WILLIAMS.—Born May 10, 1896. Married Floyd Harrell. Children: James Fabat, and Eula May.

(1). JAMES FABAT HARRELL.—Born Oct. 5, 1917. Married Velma Lawson. Children: Harlene (born Aug. 31, 1939), and James Wendell (born Sept. 15, 1942).

(2). EULA MAY HARRELL.—Born Jan. 1, 1926.

e. BURNYCE WILLIAMS.—Born May 10, 1896. Died Nov. 19, 1918. Never married. Burnyce and Eunyce Williams were twin sisters.

f. VERNON WILLIAMS.—Born Feb. 16, 1901.

g. VIRGIL REED WILLIAMS.—Born Sept. 5, 1905.

h. DAISY MAY WILLIAMS.—Married Burkett Wall. Children: Hugh V., and Burkett Burnyce.

(1). HUGH V. WALL.—Married Evie Easley. Hugh V. Wall is in the armed forces.

(2). BURKETT BURNYCE WALL.—Married, first, Leslie Wall. Children: Janice Kent. Married, second, Ray Hughes. Children: (Listed under husband, as this is an interfamily marriage).

3. ALICE WILLIAMS.—Born Jan. 26, 1863. Married Jake Miller Carter. Children: McKinnis, James, Mamie, Joel Watt, Samantha, Bettie, and Itaska.

Alice Williams-Carter died July 1, 1916. Her husband died Apr. 16, 1937.

a. MCKINNIS CARTER.—Born in 1896. Died in 1918.

b. JAMES CARTER.—Born Jan. 14, 1900. Married Pearl Anders. Children: Elaine (born Oct. 19, 1925; married Byron Schilling), Charles Ray (born Dec. 11, 1922), and Kenneth Eugene (born June 5, 1930).

c. MAMIE CARTER.—Married Nathan Allen. Children: J. T.

d. JOEL WATT CARTER.—Born Jan. 31, 1905. Married Dora Kirkland. Children: Audrey Mae (born Dec. 13, 1927), Joel Watt, Jr. (born Jan. 6, 1934), and Vernon Lee (born July 10, 1936).

e. SAMANTHA CARTER.—Married Clarence Lilly. Children: Alice (married William T. Bridges), Olivia (born May 9, 1922; married Arthur Hilbun), and McKinnis (born Jan. 7, 1926; serving in the armed forces of the U. S.).

f. BETTIE CARTER.—Unmarried.

g. ITASKA CARTER.—Married Herman Frazier. Children: Herman, Jr., and Melba.

4. DEWITT WILLIAMS.—Born July 4, 1870. Married Bessie Stewart Jan. 1894. Children: Allie, Felix Dreyfus, Dewitt Colliband, Leopold Elliott, and Bessie Bell.

Bessie Stewart-Williams was born in 1876.

Dewitt Williams died Feb. 4, 1909.

a. ALLIE WILLIAMS.—Born Nov. 14, 1895. Married Leon Dudley Williams Oct. 15, 1916. Children: Leon Dudley, Jr. (born Oct. 3, 1917), Reginald Roy (born Dec. 15, 1919; present sheriff of Amite County, Miss.) ; Noraleen (born May 15, 1921), Donald Beverly (born Dec. 15, 1923), and Billie Stewart (born Nov. 27, 1925).

b. FELIX DREYFUS WILLIAMS.—Born in 1897. Married Claudie Dunn in 1917. Children: Felix Dreyfus, Jr. (born Dec. 21, 1922).

Claudie Dunn-Williams was born in 1902.

Felix Dreyfus Williams died Sept. 15, 1942.

c. DEWITT COLLIBAND WILLIAMS.—Born Aug. 5, 1900. Died Aug. 1909.

d. LEOPOLD ELLIOTT WILLIAMS.—Born Nov. 29, 1903. Married, first, Jessye Addison June 29, 1929. Children: Pauline Dare (born Oct. 25, 1931), Lee Joyce (born Nov. 15, 1932), and Jessie Jacqueline (born May 12, 1935).

Jessye Addison-Williams died May 12, 1935.

Leopold Elliott Williams married, second, Norma DeCoux Nov. 27, 1939. Children: James Elliott Williams (born June 16, 1941).

e. BESSIE BELL WILLIAMS.—Born Nov. 9, 1907. Married Lamar Wilson June 26, 1928. Children: Wilton (born June 24, 1929), Princeton (born May 25, 1931), Teddy Emile (born Mar. 14, 1933), Jerry Gale (born Apr. 6, 1935), and Claude Lowrey (born Sept. 27, 1937).

Lamar Wilson was born Jan. 5, 1905.

5. ANDREW W. (DICK) WILLIAMS.—Born July 10, 1872. Married Lela Stewart. Children: Effie, Otis, Gladys, Birdie, Louise O., and Andrew Dewitt (A. D.).

Lela Stewart-Williams was born June 27, 1875.

a. EFFIE WILLIAMS.—Born Aug. 6, 1896. Married Thoburn Welch. Children: Thelma (born Oct. 4, 1915), Erma Lee (born Dec. 22, 1920), and Conway (born May 12, 1924).

b. OTIS WILLIAMS.—Born Jan. 30, 1898. Died June 13, 1899.

c. GLADYS WILLIAMS.—Born Jan. 30, 1898. Died July 13, 1900.

Otis and Gladys Williams were twins.

d. BIRDIE WILLIAMS.—Born Nov. 3, 1901. Married Reginald White. Children: Richard (born Feb. 27, 1925), and Reginald, Jr. (born Oct. 8, 1935).

Reginald White, Sr. died in 1935.

e. LOUISE O. WILLIAMS.—Born Jan. 11, 1908. Died Apr. 8, 1909.

f. ANDREW DEWITT (A. D.) WILLIAMS.—Born Nov. 9, 1909. Married Geraldine Dyson. Children: Dianne (born May 12, 1938).

6. MARTIN E. WILLIAMS.—Born Aug. 11, 1875. Married Jessie E. Easley Sept. 20, 1902. Children: Alma Alene (born June 29, 1903; died Aug. 1, 1903), Odie Bernice (born Dec. 2, 1905; married James Marshall Williams Sept. 1922), Myrtle (born Dec. 10, 1908; died Mar. 1909), Edith Vera (born Feb. 26, 1910; married Ansel J. Bean Nov. 1927), Johnnie Ruth (born Mar. 8, 1914; married Thomas Jefferson Rogers Nov. 1930), and Marjorie Dene (born Aug. 4, 1916; married Sam Desmond Sept. 1936).

7. SALLIE WILLIAMS.—Born June 9, 1877. Married Jack Cleveland Jan. 11, 1894. Children: Lorena, Ethel, Jack, Jr., Hilda, and Mae D.

Jack Cleveland, Sr. died Feb. 4, 1932.

a. LORENA CLEVELAND.—Born July 4, 1903. Married Arthur Spears Apr. 22, 1916. Children: Sherra Virginia (born Dec. 14, 1923), and Dudley Kirkland (born Jan. 7, 1941).

b. ETHEL CLEVELAND.—Born Dec. 30, 1896. Married Hollis Wilson May 29, 1918. Children: Mildred (born Jan. 7, 1919; married R. D. Barron Sept. 16, 1939).

c. JACK CLEVELAND, JR.—Born Sept. 3, 1900. Married Bonita Hughey Jan. 15, 1920. Children: Margie (born Sept. 30, 1924; married Marshall Bowlin July 21, 1941), and Luther (born Aug. 8, 1922).

d. HILDA CLEVELAND.—Born Feb. 4, 1902. Married Murray Nunnery Dec. 24, 1919. Children: Reginald (born Feb. 13, 1922; married Justelia Austin Dec. 25, 1942).

e. MAE D. CLEVELAND.—Born Oct. 12, 1908. Married Hubert Campbell Apr. 17, 1934. Children: Peggy Dianne (born Nov. 23, 1942).

B. JAMES D. BURRIS.—It was said by members of Addison Burris's family that James D. Burris died while away attending college.

C. DUNCAN H. BURRIS.—Born in Mississippi in 1853. Never married. Died and was buried in Baton Rouge, La.

D. ANNIE OGDEN BURRIS.—Born in Baton Rouge, La., in 1859. Never married. Died in the 1920's and was buried in Baton Rouge.

Annie Ogden Burris was dietician in the Louisiana State University dining hall for many years before her death.

E. ISABEL OGDEN BURRIS.—Born in Baton Rouge, La., in 1861. Never married. Buried in Baton Rouge.

F. LUCY MARY BURRIS.—Born in Mississippi in 1845. Married, first, ... Knox. No children. Married, second, Everett Gibbens. Children: Everett, Jr., William, and Buffington.

Everett Gibbens, Sr. was born Feb. 1832, and died Feb. 1906.

Lucy Mary Burris-Knox-Gibbens died in 1891, and was buried in Baton Rouge, La.

1. EVERETT GIBBENS, JR.—Born in Baton Rouge, La. Married Irene McGregor of Canton, Miss. No children.

2. WILLIAM GIBBENS.—Born in Baton Rouge, La. Married .... Skelly. No children.

3. BUFFINGTON GIBBENS.—Born in Baton Rouge, La. Married Jessie McNamee. Children: Doris Rae.

G. MARCY ANN (MATTIE) BURRIS.—Born in Mississippi Apr. 28, 1847. Married Henry Clay Phipps Mar. 30, 1870. Children: Mary Rebecca, Maude Elizabeth, Henry Clay, Jr., Addison Burris, Frelenghuysen, Christopher Henderson, and George Herchener.

Henry Clay Phipps, Sr. was born in Lebonen, Tenn., in 1844. He died in 1915, and was buried in Chicago, Ill.

Marcy Ann (Mattie) Burris-Phipps died Aug. 8, 1886, and was buried in Yazoo City, Miss.

1. MARY REBECCA PHIPPS.—Born in Yazoo City, Miss., Mar. 4, 1873. Married, first, Otey H. Phipps Oct. 26, 1893. Children: Thaddeus Freeman. Married, second, James Washington Biard. Children: Maude Elizabeth. Mary Rebecca Phipps-Biard died in 1940.

Otey H. Phipps was born in Sardis, Miss., in 1868. He died Feb. 16, 1903, and was buried in Paris, Tex.

James Washington Biard was born in Paris, Tex., in 1858.

a. THADDEUS FREEMAN PHIPPS.—Born Jan. 31, 1895. Died Mar. 4, 1913, and was buried in Paris, Tex.

b. MAUDE ELIZABETH BIARD.—Born in Paris, Tex., Oct. 29, 1906.

2. MAUDE ELIZABETH PHIPPS.—Born in Yazoo City, Miss., Feb. 17, 1877. Married Charles A. Lightcap Feb. 17, 1911. Children: Elizabeth Phipps (born in Yazoo City, Miss., Sept. 29, 1912).

Charles A. Lightcap was born in Benton, Miss., in 1874.

They live in Washington, D. C.

3. HENRY CLAY PHIPPS, JR.—Born in Yazoo City, Miss., Mar. 4, 1875. Married Nevellene Morton of Madisonville, Ky., Oct. 11, 1911. No children. Died in 1939.

4. ADDISON BURRIS PHIPPS.—Born in Yazoo City, Miss., Dec. 23, 1870. Married Ella Moore of Evanston, Ill., Oct. 1914. No children.

Addison Burris Phipps died Apr. 5, 1923, and was buried in Evanston, Ill.

5. FRELENGHUYSEN PHIPPS.—Born in Yazoo City, Miss., Feb. 15, 1879. Married Bess Story of Minden, La., in 1920. Children: Betty Jean (born in Dallas, Tex.; married; lives in Dallas, Tex.).

6. CHRISTOPHER HENDERSON PHIPPS.—Born in Yazoo City, Miss., Jan. 22, 1882. Married Mirth Jones of St. Cloud, Minn., in St. Cloud, in 1917. Children: Mary Elizabeth, and Barbara Mirth.

Christopher Henderson Phipps died in 1936.

a. MARY ELIZABETH PHIPPS.—Born in St. Cloud, Minn., Apr. 23, 1919. Married Irving A. Walrath in 1943. Children: Barbara Ann (born in 1946), Michael Phipps (born in 1949), and Katherine (born in 1950).

At the time of his marriage, Irving A. Walrath was a lieutenant in the U. S. Army. They live in Eden Valley, Minn.

b. BARBARA MIRTH PHIPPS.—Born in St. Cloud, Minn., Sept. 2, 1920. Married Clarence T. Sebesta in 1945. No children. They are divorced.

At the time of his marriage, Clarence T. Sebesta was a lieutenant in the U. S. Air Force.

Barbara Mirth Phipps-Sebesta lives with her mother in Litchfield, Minn.

7. GEORGE HERCHENER PHIPPS.—Born in Yazoo City, Miss., Nov. 20, 1884. Died Aug. 6, 1885, and was buried in Yazoo City.

H. ENOS HAMPTON BURRIS.—Born in Mississippi in 1848. Married Clara Smizer-Kitchen, a widow. Children: Charles, and Bessie Rebecca.

Enos Hampton Burris died Jan. 5, 1919, and was buried in Baton Rouge, La.

1. CHARLES BURRIS.—Born near Baton Rouge, La. Died in Dexter, Mo., Feb. 1942. Never married.

2. BESSIE REBECCA BURRIS.—Born in Baton Rouge, La. Married B. Hugh Smith, a lawyer. Children: Irene Virginia (married H. S. Wright, and has one child, Sally Rebecca; lives in Cape Girardeau, Mo.), Mary Inez (Cape Girardeau, Mo.), and Anne Ione (married E. C. Dunn; lives in Poplar Bluff, Mo.).

B. Hugh Smith is dead. Mrs. Smith lives in Cape Girardeau, Mo.

I. DR. WILLIAM ADDISON (BILLY) BURRIS.—Born in Mississippi in 1850. Married Anna Knox. Children: Mabel, William Knox, and Ellesly.

Dr. William Addison (Billy) Burris died in 1885, and was buried in Baton Rouge, La. Anna Knox-Burris died in 1901, and was buried in Bristol, Tenn.

1. MABEL BURRIS.—Married Francis Tharin.

2. WILLIAM KNOX BURRIS.—Born in Baton Rouge, La., Dec. 29, 1882. Married Mary Lee Brown. No children. They live in El Paso, Tex.

3. ELLESLY BURRIS.—Born in Baton Rouge, La. Married .... Fox. No children.

J. GEORGE SAMUEL BURRIS.—Born in Mississippi in 1855. Married Clara Stuart. Children: Stuart Pike, William Blake, and Josie Jones.

George Samuel Burris resided in Baton Rouge, La., most, if not all of his life, where he served as city policeman for many years. He died Feb. 13, 1924, and was buried in Baton Rouge, La.

1. STUART PIKE BURRIS.—Born in Baton Rouge, La., in 1889. Died in 1892, and was buried in Baton Rouge, La.

2. WILLIAM BLAKE BURRIS.—Born in Baton Rouge, La., in 1892. Married Vera Hebert Sept. 1918, in Baton Rouge. Children: Rose Merilyn, William Blake, Jr., and Stuart Hebert.

Vera Hebert-Burris was born in Baton Rouge, La., in 1896.

William Blake (Bill) Burris was a veternarian, and was practicing in Shreveport, La., at the time of his death, which occurred in the 1920's. While attending the Louisiana State University, 1912 to 1916, of which institution he was a graduate, he broke the high hurdles record two successive years in S. I. A. A. track meets. He was buried in Baton Rouge.

a. ROSE MERILYN BURRIS.—Born in Baton Rouge, La., Sept. 19, 1919. Married Major Irving Paul MacTaggart, son of Irving John MacTaggart of Maitland, Ontario, Nov. 1, 1941, in Shreveport,

La. Children: Sheila Ann, Timothy Paul, Patrick David, Kelly, and Colleen. They live in Shreveport, La.

Major MacTaggart is a navigator in the U. S. Army Air Corps. He served in the African Campaign in World War II for thirteen months. He is now stationed at Barksdale Field, Shreveport, La.

b. WILLIAM BLAKE BURRIS, JR.—Born in Shreveport, La., Mar. 8, 1921. Married Audrey Shovan, daughter of Dewey Paul Shovan of Louisiana, in Bayon, Texas, Dec. 11, 1943. Children: William Blake III, Norma Kathleen, and Lynda Carol.

c. STUART HEBERT BURRIS.—Born in Shreveport, La., June 5, 1924. Lives in Shreveport, La.

3. JOSIE JONES BURRIS.—Born in Baton Rouge, La., in 1896. Unmarried. Josie Jones Burris graduated from the Louisiana State University in 1917, and was awarded the B. A. Degree. She is a member of the Baton Rouge Senior High School faculty, where she has taught since graduation from the University, a period of 34 years. She assisted in the preparation of this history.

K. NORA REBECCA BURRIS.—Born in Baton Rouge, La., in 1857. Married George S. Sharp of East Baton Rouge Parish, La. Children: Lucy, Mary Serena, Ogden, William Joseph, Annie Burris, Leodocia Clark, Samuel Robertson, Georgie Lenora, and Joseph Jones.

Nora Rebecca Burris-Sharp died Jan. 12, 1925, and was buried in Baton Rouge, La.

1. LUCY SHARP.—Born in Baton Rouge, La., in 1878. Died in 1878, and was buried in Baton Rouge.

2. MARY SERENA SHARP.—Born in Baton Rouge, La., June 14, 1880. Died Dec. 29, 1930.

3. OGDEN SHARP.—Born in Baton Rouge, La., in 1882. Married Edith Kean. No children.

4. WILLIAM JOSEPH SHARP.—Born in Baton Rouge, La., in 1884. Married Ada Trahan in 1908. Children: Robert, Armand, William Joseph, Jr., Cyril Ogden, and George Trahan. Ada Trahan-Sharp was born in 1886. William Joseph Sharp and Annie Burris Sharp are twins.

a. ROBERT SHARP.—Born in Baton Rouge, La., Aug. 14, 1912. Married Hilda Mae Whitehead of Baton Rouge. Children: Lynda Ann, Kenneth Armand, Valiria, and Sharron Lee.

b. ARMAND SHARP.—Born in Baton Rouge, La., July 11, 1915. Married Willie Mae Mixon, daughter of Bonnie Erwin, May 10, 1947, in Covington, La. No children. Lives in Baton Rouge.

c. WILLIAM JOSEPH SHARP, JR.—Born in Baton Rouge, La., Mar. 17, 1919. Married Bertha Jane Hardisty of Sumpter, S. C. Children: Darwin Cyril, and Thomas W.

William Joseph Sharp, Jr., lives in Baton Rouge.

d. CYRIL OGDEN SHARP.—Born in Baton Rouge, La., Dec. 4, 1922. Married Maryland Alanzo of Baton Rouge, June 18, 1949, in Baton Rouge. No children. Lives in Baton Rouge.

e. GEORGE TRAHAN SHARP.—Born in Baton Rouge, La., Sept. 19, 1910. Died June 26, 1912, and was buried in Baton Rouge.

5. ANNIE BURRIS SHARP.—Born in Baton Rouge, La., in 1884. Married R. C. Calloway in 1914. Children: Nora Inez, Ruby Annie, and Francis William.

R. C. Calloway was born in 1884. He is connected with the Louisiana State University, and lives in Baton Rouge.

a. NORA INEZ CALLOWAY.—Born in Minden, La., in 1915. Unmarried. Is a graduate of Louisiana State University, and is now Home Demonstration Agent of Concordia Parish, La. Lives in Vidalia, La.

b. RUBY ANNIE CALLOWAY.—Born in Baton Rouge, La., in 1917. Married Clovis J. Mire, son of Ernest Mire, in Port Allen, La. Children: Clovis Annie (born Aug. 12, 1942), and Janette Faye (born Dec. 18, 1945).

Ruby Annie Calloway-Mire is now Assistant Home Demonstration Agent of East Baton Rouge Parish, La., and lives in Baton Rouge.

c. FRANCIS WILLIAM CALLOWAY.—Born in Baton Rouge, La., in 1919. Married Dorothy Case, daughter of Louis and Lucille (Tidwell) Case, in Monroe, La., Oct. 1941. Children: William Louis (born Jan. 1949).

Francis William Calloway was a lieutenant in the Naval Air Corps during World War II. He served overseas for two years. He lives in Baton Rouge, La.

6. LEODOCIA CLARK SHARP.—Born in Baton Rouge, La., in 1887. Married C. M. Downs, son of Susan Downs, in 1928, in New Orleans, La. No children. They live in Baton Rouge, La.

7. SAMUEL ROBERTSON SHARP.—Born in Baton Rouge, La., in 1890. Married Elaine Cobb in 1928. No children. Died Jan. 1, 1930.

8. GEORGIE LENORA SHARP.—Born in Baton Rouge, La., in 1894. Married Lloyd Triche in 1942 in Baton Rouge. No children. Lloyd Triche died in 1945, and was buried in Baton Rouge.

Georgie Lenora is known as Nora, also as Aunt "Tootsie." She has been working in the Bursar's Office at Louisiana State University for the past thirty years.

9. JOSEPH JONES SHARP.—Born in Baton Rouge, La., in 1898. Married Evelyn Harelson, daughter of Mrs. Minnie Benton Harelson, in 1926, in Baton Rouge. Children: Jane Ellen.

Evelyn Harelson-Sharp was born in Baton Rouge in 1903. They live in Baton Rouge.

L. HATTIE HENDERSON BURRIS.—Born in Baton Rouge, La., in 1863. Married R. M. Hays in 1902. Children: Addison Burris.

Hattie Henderson Burris-Hays was matron in one of the boys' dormitories at Northwestern State College, Natchitoches, La., for many years. She is living in Beaumont, Texas.

1. ADDISON BURRIS HAYS. — Born in Baton Rouge, La., in 1905. Married Frances Stanley in 1926. Children: Frances Ann.

PART III

Origin and Variant Spellings of the Name "Burris"

Like most names, the name *Burris* is doubtless spelled differently now from the original spelling of the name. This, no doubt, has come about in various ways, but very likely through a lack of knowledge of the correct spelling; through poor and unclear writing of the name; and through careless errors in writing the name.

The following are some of the variant spellings, it is thought, of the name: Burroughs, Burrows, Burrus, Burruss, Burress, and Burriss.

Just which of these spellings is the original is not known. Most people seem inclined to think *Burroughs* is the original name, and that it is of English nationality, pertaining to a small town or village. Some contend that the name is Irish, because of so many people with one or more of these names who claim to be Irish.

According to Weekly, in *Surnames*, the suffix "is" is a corruption of "house." He says . . . "often house as a suffix is changed into 'ows', 'ers', or 'as', 'is', 'os', 'us'." Following this statement, he says, "Burrus is 'bower-house', and Burrows may sometime have the same origin." Weekly, Ernest. *Surnames*. Dutton, 1916.

Dellquest gives a somewhat different account of the origin of Burr, the first part of the name. He says, "Burr—from the old English burh, meaning a town, city, fortress, castle. Burr is a variant of burgh; it may sometimes be from burh, a derivative of Beorh (a hill)." Also, he says, "Barrow should not be confused with the name Burrows, which is usually a form of Burrough, meaning a town or village." Dellquest, A. W., *These Names of Ours*. Crowell, 1938.

PART IV

OTHER PEOPLE BY THE SAME OR SIMILAR NAMES NOTED IN THIS SECTION IN THE EARLY 1800'S

Various records reveal the fact that there were other Burrises (or Burrusses or Burrowses) in Amite County, Miss., and the Florida Parishes of Louisiana about the time the Samuel and Mary (Myers) Burris Family migrated to Amite County in 1809.

In the records of Amite County, it was noted that: 1. Ann Burrows married Sterling Gardner Oct. 21, 1819; 2. Cloe Burrows married Abraham Wilson Aug. 19, 1819; 3. Chas. R. A. Burris sold Thos. Batchelor some land June 17, 1829; and, 4, Geo. W. Burris bought some land from John Lane and wife Oct. 6, 1834.

The U. S. Census of 1810 shows an Arthur Burrows in Amite County, whose household consisted of one white male over 21, including the head of the household; two white females under 21; and 10 slaves.

Gabriell Burris has been noted in the records of St. Helena Parish, La., which borders on Amite County to the southeast. On Oct. 14, 1817, he transferred two slaves to Abraham Anderson.

In the files of Spanish papers in the archives of Louisiana State University, it was noted that John Burris (or Burroughs), of the Baton Rouge District, sold six arpents of land to Antonio Gras, Jan. 15, 1802. Also, in these papers, it was noted that there was a William Burris in the Second Division of the District of New Feliciana Parish in 1805.

In the records of the Register of State Lands' Office in Baton Rouge, La., Wm. Burriss's name was noted as a witness to a receipt for $205.50, final payment on a piece of land situated in New Feliciana Parish, La. This was about 1819. Also, in these records, it was noted that Widow Burris, a resident of Feliciana Parish, La., was desirous of acquiring 500 arpents of land from the royal treasury. This document was dated Aug. 28, 1906.

In Rev. William Winans' Diary, published in Casey and Otken's book, "Amite County, Mississippi, 1699-1865", Vol. 2, it is recorded that he saw Augustus Burruss near Midway (presumably in West Feliciana Parish, La.), July 10, 1832; that C. A. Burruss joined the society at one of Rev. Winans' meetings near Woodville, Miss., Oct. 7 1832; and that Rev. Winans went with Bro. Bob Burruss to the meeting house in Laurel Hill, La., Aug. 13, 1842. Also, in this diary it is recorded that, at the annual conference assembled at Washington (Miss.) Dec. 7, 1821, Rev. Winans' acquaintance with John C. Burruss, local minister formerly of Virginia, began.

The relationship, if any, of these people to the Samuel and Mary (Myers) Burris Family could not be determined. Just because their name is spelled differently does not necessarily mean that they are not kin; for, in several instances in the records, members of the Samuel and Mary (Myers) Burris Family have their names spelled in some way other than *Burris*. Doubtless, back in the Carolinas, or in Virginia, where the Burrises or Burrusses or Burrowses took "root", all of these people have a common "trunk".

PART V

CHARACTERISTICS OF THE BURRISES

In stature, the Burrises, as a rule, are low and stout. Their complexion is ruddy. Their hair in most instances is auburn. As for their eyes, brown and grey seem to be the most prevalent colors of them.

The life span of the Burrises is about average. They are very prolific when it comes to offsprings, as witnessed by the numerous descendants of this pioneer family which settled in Amite County, Miss., about 1809.

The number of bachelors and spinsters among them is at least average, if not above.

In personal traits, they are discreetly frank. They are not contentious; in fact, they are usually slow to offend. They are slightly tempermental, but usually have good control of their tempers. They are persistent in their course of action and above the average in mental acumen.

The Burrises are reserved and care very little for the glamorous things of life. Instead, they prefer the even tenor of its ways.

The Burrises are not lazy, on the contrary, they are rather industrious. Their outlook on life is more or less one of cheerfulness and optimism; although, at times, life is serious with them.

Some are inclined to be sedentary, and some are inclined to be of an exploratory nature. None are content to be ne'er-do-wells; they are always alert to improve their stations in life. As a rule, they are ambitious and usually successful.

By their fellowmen, the Burrises are usually highly regarded. They are considered reliable, trustworthy and honest. They are also known for their fair play.

One of the highest tributes the author ever heard paid their character was one from a former district attorney of Amite, Franklin, Wilkinson, and Adams counties, Miss. This district attorney remarked that, whenever he had a case to come before a jury and there were Burris veniremen, he always accepted them without a question.

In their pursuit of a livelihood, most Burrises are engaged in farming. Many of them are following the profession of school-teaching, some are preachers, and some are following the other professions. Many are holding commercial positions. In fact, Burrises may be found in most any of the fields of human endeavor to earn a living.

PART VI

THE ANNUAL REUNIONS OF BURRIS FAMILIES

THE WASHINGTON PARISH, LOUISIANA, REUNIONS

About the year 1920, the late Edmund Andrews (Ed) Burris of Franklinton, La., initiated the annual reunion of the Burris families of Washington Parish, La. At first this reunion consisted of the descendants of the William Addison and Flora (Magee) Burris Family only, but it was expanded and now includes all of the descendants of the William and Maria (Andrews) Burris Family, the original Burris family to settle in Washington Parish. In addition, these reunions are usually attended by Burrises from Mississippi, the descendants of the brothers and sisters of William Burris—all of whom are descendants of Samuel and Mary (Myers) Burris.

These reunions are held at the Peter Pan Camp on Hayes Creek, which is located on the old William Addison Burris Place, about three and one-half miles north of Franklinton.

The occasion consists of a sumptuous dinner, which is supplied by those attending, and a general mingling of the members of the families, during which old acquaintances are renewed and new ones are made. No formal programs are conducted, nor any officers elected.

Shortly before his death, in 1935, Edmund Andrews (Ed) Burris, realizing that he had about held his last reunion, asked his nephew, Hugh P. Burris, who lives on a part of the old William Addison Burris Place, to serve as general manager and to see to it that the reunion would continue to be held. This behest has been carried out excellently by Hugh P. Burris. Except for a few years during World War II, and one or two other years, the reunion has been held every year, usually the first Sunday in June.

THE AMITE COUNTY, MISSISSIPPI, REUNIONS

These reunions started many years ago in the form of fish fries. Members of the Burris families in Amite County would assemble on the banks of the East Prong of Amite River, somewhere in the vicinity of Smithdale, and catch fish and fry them. No programs were conducted, nor any organizations were formed. They were just get-togethers, in which old acquaintances were renewed, and new acquaintances were made. They were occasions also for members of families, who had moved away somewhere else, to return and meet all of their kinfolks at one time.

This fish-fry type of reunion lasted a number of years, but it was finally discontinued.

In 1947 the present type of reunion was initiated. It consists of a sumptuous dinner, which is contributed by those attending. After dinner a formal program is conducted. These programs usually consist of a welcome address by the president of the organization, and a response by some invited guest. After these addresses, reports are made by the various committees, and a very impressive eulogy is rendered by the chairman of the necrology committee, memorializing those members of the families who have passed on since the last reunion. Interspersed amongst these numbers are beautiful and stirring musical numbers. At the conclusion of the program the election of officers for the new year is held. Those members of the family who have held office, the office and term they held are: From 1947-50, Richard Alton Burris, president; Merwin Burris, vice president; and Hugh C. Burris, secretary-treasurer. For 1951, Raiford Earl Burris, president; Merwin Burris, vice president; and Hilburn Burris, secretary-treasurer.

The organization was first called the Amite County Burris Association. In the last few years, due largely to the increasing number of Louisiana Burrises attending these reunions, the organization has been called, the Samuel and Mary (Myers) Burris Family Organization, after the original Burris parents.

These reunions are held in the Smithdale Community, usually the third Sunday in August. During the years 1947-50, they were held at Richard Alton Burris's place. The 1951 reunion was held at the old Ras Burris place, on the banks of the East Prong of Amite River, which is an ideal location for such an occasion.

THE END.

INDEX

316

317

318

321

322

325

329

334

Part VII

Felicitations from Business and Other Friends

OUR

BEST

WISHES

PASTERNACK'S

FERRIDAY, LA.

Hardware . . . Furniture
and Building Materials

Compliments of

BURRIS BROS. LTD.

(Established 1892)

Franklinton, La.

J. M. Burris—President

Mrs. Nina Burris-Weaver—Vice President

Marie Moore—Secretary-Treasurer

W. H. Burris—Assistant Manager

Compliments of

MECHANICS - STATE BANK

McCOMB, MISS.

"Mingle With the Mechanics"

Member of the Federal Deposit Insurance Corporation

CONGRATULATIONS

and

BEST WISHES

General Gas Corporation

FERRIDAY, LA.

Compliments of

R. J. JONES & SONS,

GENERAL CONTRACTORS

ALEXANDRIA, LA.

Compliments of

FERRIDAY LUMBER and SUPPLY COMPANY

Louis N. Snyder, Owner

"From Foundation to Chimney Top"

FERRIDAY, LA.

COMPLIMENTS OF

Harold Heidingsfelder

SCHOOL PRODUCTS COMPANY

New Orleans, La.

Compliments of

J. E. MARTIN

McComb Equipment Company

McCOMB, MISS.

FARMALL TRACTORS ... INTERNATIONAL TRUCKS
REFRIGERATORS ... FREEZERS

Compliments of

CLARENCE J. DUBOS & SONS

NEW ORLEANS, LA.

——School Furniture and Supplies——

Compliments of

MALTER SUPPLY COMPANY

MANUFACTURERS and DISTRIBUTORS

Soaps . . . Waxes . . . Disinfectants . . . Deodorants . . . Insecticides
Sanitary Supplies

New Orleans, La.

Compliments of

Board of Supervisors
of
Amite County, Miss.

LIBERTY

Compliments to the Burris Family

BARRON BROS. GIN

SUMMIT, MISS.

Route 3

Best Wishes From

ELLZEY BOTTLING CO.

Tylertown, Miss.

Compliments of

DALE INSURANCE AGENCY

"Insure in Sure Insurance"

Phone 114

VIDALIA, LA.

Compliments of

LEWIS-DAY MOTORS, INC.

McCOMB, MISS.

Phones 581-582   Night Wrecker Phone 161-J

Best Wishes To

BURRIS FAMILY

C. E. YOUNG

Tax Assessor, Amite County, Miss.

Congratulations to the

Burrises

BENOIST BROS.

Natchez, Miss.

Compliments of

THOS. J. MORAN'S SONS

NEW ORLEANS 13, LA.

Compliments of

Sansing-Ballew Pontiac Co.

McCOMB, MISS.

Compliments of

LIBERTY MOTOR CO.

John H. Prestridge

Liberty, Miss.

FORD SALES and SERVICE

Compliments of

Gerald Refrigeration Sales & Service

116 Third St., McComb, Miss.

Air Conditioning Specialists — Motor Repairs

E. M. Gerald   H. E. Gerald

Compliments of

JACKSON BEVERAGE CO.

New Orleans, La.

Compliments of

MAGNOLIA BANK

Magnolia, Miss.

Began Business July 27, 1895

OSYKA BRANCH OFFICE

Osyka, Miss.

Compliments of

BICKHAM MOTOR CO.

McComb, Miss.

DODGE and PLYMOUTH CARS and DODGE TRUCKS

Compliments of

SHARP'S

Jimmie Sharp, Owner

Liberty, Miss.

GENERAL ELECTRIC APPLIANCES

Compliments of

RAS M. BRANCH

Goodman, Miss.

Compliments of

NETTERVILLE MOTOR CO.

McCOMB, MISS.

Compliments of

T. P. HERNDON

Liberty, Miss.

Compliments of

WINTON WILLIAMS MOTOR CO.

McCOMB, MISS.

Compliments of

ANNIE ANDREWS, Supt. of Schools

AMITE COUNTY, MISS.

LIBERTY

Compliments of

FORD'S NURSERY

Magnolia, Miss.

www.ingramcontent.com/pod-product-compliance
Lightning Source LLC
Chambersburg PA
CBHW020333270326
41926CB00007B/162